ROUTLEDGE LIBRARY EDITIONS: INTERNATIONAL SECURITY STUDIES

Volume 12

MILITARIZATION AND ARMS PRODUCTION

MILITARIZATION AND ARMS PRODUCTION

Edited by
HELENA TUOMI AND RAIMO VÄYRYNEN

LONDON AND NEW YORK

First published in 1983 by Croom Helm Ltd

This edition first published in 2021
by Routledge
2 Park Square, Milton Park, Abingdon, Oxon OX14 4RN

and by Routledge
52 Vanderbilt Avenue, New York, NY 10017

Routledge is an imprint of the Taylor & Francis Group, an informa business

© 1983 Helena Tuomi and Raimo Väyrynen

All rights reserved. No part of this book may be reprinted or reproduced or utilised in any form or by any electronic, mechanical, or other means, now known or hereafter invented, including photocopying and recording, or in any information storage or retrieval system, without permission in writing from the publishers.

Trademark notice: Product or corporate names may be trademarks or registered trademarks, and are used only for identification and explanation without intent to infringe.

British Library Cataloguing in Publication Data
A catalogue record for this book is available from the British Library

ISBN: 978-0-367-68499-0 (Set)
ISBN: 978-1-00-316169-1 (Set) (ebk)
ISBN: 978-0-367-71055-2 (Volume 12) (hbk)
ISBN: 978-0-367-71056-9 (Volume 12) (pbk)
ISBN: 978-1-00-314911-8 (Volume 12) (ebk)

Publisher's Note
The publisher has gone to great lengths to ensure the quality of this reprint but points out that some imperfections in the original copies may be apparent.

Disclaimer
The publisher has made every effort to trace copyright holders and would welcome correspondence from those they have been unable to trace.

Militarization and Arms Production

Edited by Helena Tuomi and Raimo Väyrynen

CROOM HELM
London & Canberra

© 1983 Helena Tuomi and Raimo Väyrynen
Croom Helm Ltd., Provident House, Burrell Row,
Beckenham, Kent BR3 1AT

British Library Cataloguing in Publication Data

Militarization and arms production.
  1. Disarmament
  I. Tuomi, Helena   II. Väyrynen, Raimo
  327.1'74   JX1974
  ISBN 0-7099-2422-4

This book can also be identified as
Tampere Peace Research Institute Research Report No. 24, 1982.

Printed and bound in Great Britain

CONTENTS

Introduction
Preface
    Inga Thorsson

I.   THE STUDY OF ARMAMENT, DISARMAMENT AND DEVELOPMENT   1

    1. Armaments and Development   3
        Ron Huisken
    2. Linking Disarmament and Development: Some Ideas from a United Nations Research Project   26
        Bo Hovstadius and Manne Wängborg
    3. Defence and Development: a Critique of the Benoit Study   39
        Nicole Ball

II.   MILITARIZATION AND ARMS PRODUCTION IN INDUSTRIALIZED COUNTRIES   57

    4. Economic Problems of Arms Production in Western Europe - Diagnoses and Alternatives   59
        Michael Brzoska
    5. Arms Buildup and Disarmament - Effects on Manpower Situations in Countries of Different Social Systems   93
        Klaus Engelhardt
    6. Efforts at Reducing Military Expenditure in the United States, 1960 to 1978   108
        Milton Leitenberg
    7. Opening the Floodgates: the New U.S. Arms Sales Policy   139
        Michael T. Klare
    8. Transnational Military Corporations: the Main Problems   148
        Helena Tuomi

III.	\multicolumn{2}{l}{MILITARIZATION AND ARMAMENT PROCESS IN DEVELOPING COUNTRIES}	161
	9.	Semiperipheral Countries in the Global Economic and Military Order Raimo Väyrynen	163
	10.	The Transfer of Military Technology to Third World Countries Signe Landgren-Bäckström	193
	11.	Brazil's Nuclear Energy Policy: Dilemmas and Options Clóvis Brigagao	205
IV.	\multicolumn{2}{l}{ALTERNATIVE PERSPECTIVES}	223
	12.	The Economic Effects of Conversion: a Case Study of Norway Nils Petter Gleditsch, Olav Bjerkholt, Ådne Cappelen and Knut Moum	225
	13.	Conventional Disarmament - a Legal Framework and Some Perspectives Allan Rosas	259
V.	\multicolumn{2}{l}{DISCUSSION}	287
	14.	Is the Conversion Idea to be Converted? Some Sceptical Comments from a Non-Convert Jan Øberg	289

Annexes   300

About the Authors   309

TABLES AND FIGURES

Tables

1.1	Military Burden and Economic Performance	5
4.1	Arms Production in Western Europe	62
4.2	Statistical Estimation of Arms Production in Western Europe	65
4.3	Employment in Arms Production: France, Britain, FRG, Italy, 1977	68
4.4	Arms Exports as Percentage of Total Exports of Machinery and Transportation Goods, 1978	69
4.5	Arms Production Companies	71
4.6	Concentration in West European Arms Industry	75
4.7	Dependence on Arms Production	75
4.8	Arms Production Companies with Public Ownership	77
4.9	Summary of Intra-National Interests in Co-production of Weapon Systems within NATO	81
4.10	Some Indicators of the Economy and Arms Production within NATO	82
9.1	Semiperipheral Countries in the Global Military Order	171
9.2	Economic and Military Growth of Semiperihperal Countries, 1970-1978	178
9.3	Involvement in Warfare in Semiperipheral and Middle-Income Countries	180
9.4	The Growth of Manufacturing Production in Different Groups of Countries in 1960-70	181
9.5	The Share of Machinery and Transport Equipment in Exports of Semiperipheral Countries in 1968 and 1978	184
10.1	Cost of Producing Aircraft in India	200
11.1	The Share of National Participation in the Equipment of Brazilian Nuclear Plants	215
12.1	Composition of the Norwegian Military Budget, 1978	228
12.2	Disarmament Scenarios for Norway, 1978-90	232
12.3	Disarmament Scenarios for Norway, 1978	233
12.4	Effects on Employment of Pure Conversion, 1978	239

12.5	Effects on GDP of Pure Conversion, 1978	240
12.6	Effects on Imports of Pure Conversion, 1978	240
12.7	Effects on the Balance of Payments of Pure Conversion, 1978	240
12.8	Economic Effects of Various Counter-Measures, 1978	243
12.9	Effects on GDP of Conversion with Counter-Measures, 1978	244
12.10	Effects on Imports of Conversion with Counter-Measures, 1978	244
12.11	Effects on the Balance of Payments of Conversion with Counter-Measures, 1978	245
12.12	Strategies to Decrease the Negative Effects of Conversion	250
	Annexes 1-6: The Largest Arms Producers in Western Europe	300
	Annex 7: Rank Order of the 25 Largest Third World Arms Importers, 1977-80	307
	Annex 8: Rank Order of 12 Largest Third World Major-Weapon Exporters, 1977-80	308

Figures

2.1	Disarmament and Development: Flow Chart	29
2.2	Additional Development Aid in Leontief-Duchin's Disarmament Scenario Compared with OECD Aid Forecast	35
4.1	World Market Share of Trade in Machinery and Transportation Equipment	85
12.1	Absolute Size of the Norwegian Military Establishment, 1945-79	229
12.2	Relative Size of the Norwegian Military Establishment	230
12.3	Norwegian Official Programme for Development Assistance 1956-78	235
14.1	A Generalized Model of Peace and Development	290

INTRODUCTION

The United Nations undertook in 1978-1981 a major study on the relationship between disarmament and development (UN doc. A/36/356, 5 October 1981). The study - carried out by a Group of Experts and chaired by Mme Inga Thorsson from Sweden - analyzed in great depth and clarity the various economic and social costs of the present-day arms race. It also discussed the benefits of disarmament: how resources now used for the arms race could be converted into constructive civilian use and how more resources could be channelled to the developing countries.

The new feature about this UN study was the use of an extensive international research programme, written particularly for this purpose. The Expert Group commissioned 40 studies, and some 100 scholars in twenty countries were involved.

Tampere Peace Research Institute (TAPRI) was one of the institutes participating in the research programme. During that research we became aware of the fact that more and better international contacts between scholars specialized in disarmament-development problems should be established. This was the reason why TAPRI organized an international seminar on 'Arms production and development' in Tampere, Finland, in August 1981.

This book contains contributions presented at that seminar, to which have been added a couple of other papers which we regarded as fruitful. By including papers about the armament processes of _both_ the industrial _and_ the developing countries we want to emphasize the interrelationship between the militarization processes of both groups of countries.

We are very grateful to the staff of TAPRI for their collegial cooperation; to the Academy of Finland, the Finnish Ministry of Education, the Nordic Cooperation Committee for International Politics and Peace Research as well as to the Finnish Ministry for Foreign Affairs for financial support; in particular we are grateful to Inga Thorsson who finds the time to encourage research despite of her numerous and demanding diplomatic duties.

We hope this book helps to sharpen our analytical tools and deepen our understanding of the disarmament/development relationship in various types of countries and encourages us in our search for a more secure, socially just and less militarized world.

Tampere and Helsinki

Helena Tuomi   Raimo Väyrynen

PREFACE

When we were working on the United Nations Study on the Relationship between Disarmament and Development I was struck by the amount of knowledge available on the disruptive, retarding and weakening effects of large-scale military preparations on the economic and social fabric in all societies, regardless of political systems. I was simultaneously struck by the fact that this knowledge had had virtually no political impact. For most countries, military preparations are judged against perceived threats, and are thus considered rational and cost-effective to the extent they "solve" military security problems. The "economic problem of defence" has, consequently, for most nations been how to finance it without too severe or acute economic disruption.

For the world's security, however, the grand total of military preparations has never been rational, has never contributed to an increased sense of security, but has instead disrupted international trade and cooperation, eroded confidence and the opportunity for arms control and disarmament, and in itself has emerged as a factor of insecurity.

It is indeed a new experience, gained during the late 1970s, that the economic and social costs of military preparations, which may have been bearable ten to thirty years ago, are no longer acceptable. The economic web between countries, the imminent scarcity of petrol and other nonrenewable resources, and a more competitive international economic situation no longer permit such large and expanding preparations, without even higher and more painful costs in the form of increased inflation and unemployment, decreased growth of productivity and losses in international competitiveness. The further fortification of the "garrison states" - using an expression by the American scholar Harold Lasswell - hits the developing countries hard, particularly those who, for various reasons (more often than not superpower rivalry in their region) themselves engage in regional arms races, by receiving arms transfers or, even more damaging, by producing arms themselves.

The UN Study stresses the importance of a reliable data base, something which, unfortunately, but for reasons well understood, it failed to establish. Several recommendations underline the right of people to be informed about their governments' military preparations - and, not least, the socio-economic effects they entail - and consequently the duty of governments to supply such information. Today most countries in the world shy away from close public scrutiny of their military activities. This is also true in the case of some major participants in the arms race. In fact, the Study is based predominantly on figures available in Western countries. This relatively uneven and fragmented access to data naturally hampers analysis, comparison and confidence among nations. Governments, and particularly those of the major military powers, are thus recommended to compile and disseminate data on the military use of human and material resources and military transfers more fully and more systematically; to assess the nature and magnitude of the short- and long-term economic and social costs attributable to their military preparations so that their general public be informed of them; and, further, to identify and publicize the benefits that would be derived from the reallocation of military resources in a balanced and verifiable manner, to address economic and social problems at the national level and to contribute towards reducing the gap between the industrial nations and the developing countries, in the process of establishing a new international economic order.

Too little attention has been devoted to possibilities for alternative work. Naturally, conversion will have to await progress in disarmament. Research, preparation and planning for an economic conversion policy cannot, however, be deferred until such time, nor can a wider international exchange of experiences gained in such a preparation process. Hence, the Study recommends Governments to prepare and plan for the conversion of resources to meet economic and social needs, not least in developing countries, and to make findings available from time to time by submitting reports on conversion problems to the General Assembly.

The disarmament-development perspective, encompassing the vital component of international security, should be effectively incorporated into the activities and current work programmes of all organizations within the UN system, and the Study offers a series of proposals to facilitate this task.

The prevailing contradictions between the harsh realities of international political and economic relations and the legitimate aspirations of the peoples of world is recognized by the UN Study which states - with unanimity among the 27 governmental experts coming from West, East and South - that the world can either continue the arms race or move with deliberate speed towards a more sustainable international economic order. It cannot do both. I hope that the present volume will assist in putting this message over - along with its profound meaning and implications: We find ourselves today at the cross-roads.

Inga Thorsson

Chairman of the UN Expert Group
on the Relationship between Disarmament
and Development

I

THE STUDY OF ARMAMENT, DISARMAMENT
AND DEVELOPMENT

Chapter One

ARMAMENTS AND DEVELOPMENT*

Ron Huisken

1.1 INTRODUCTION

Plain common sense informs us that military preparations are an economic burden. The more resources devoted to military preparations the less there will be for other things including investment in education and technological innovation, activities that produce economic growth and the underpinnings of economic and social development in the wider sense. This chapter will examine the theoretical basis and empirical evidence for this proposition with a view to providing a basis for judging how far we can reasonably hope to proceed towards sustainable global growth and development if the arms race is not brought under control and reversed.

It is well known that since World War II military activities have absorbed resources on a scale that has no precedent in modern history. On the average, over the past 30 years approximately 7 per cent of the world's resources have been devoted to armaments, roughly double the fraction so used during the interwar years or during the years immediately before World War I. In 1980 the resources absorbed by the arms race were valued at about $ 520,000 million.

It is also well known that the distribution of the global military effort is very uneven: the Nuclear Weapon States alone, for example, account for about two-thirds of the total. Increasingly, however, the competitive accumulation of armaments has become a global phenomenon and, because the distribution of global productive capacity is also very uneven, it is now the case that the majority of States in the world undertake military preparations on an economically significant scale.

Ideally, an analysis of the relationship between armaments and development should be made on an individual country basis or within carefully selected groups of countries where the similarities greatly outweigh the differences. This is not feasible in the present context so we shall have to be content with separate discussions on the developed industrialized countries and the developing countries.

1.2. ARMAMENTS AND DEVELOPMENT IN THE DEVELOPED COUNTRIES

The developed countries of the world, approximately 30 in number, account for well over 80 per cent of the resources devoted to military activities worldwide. Military expenditures account for 5-6 per cent of their collective gross national products and, collectively, their per capita military expenditure is an order of magnitude higher than in the developing countries taken as a group. Accepting that military preparations in these countries, as indeed in all countries, are fundamentally politically motivated, it has nevertheless long been maintained - explicitly in the market economy countries and at least by implication in the Socialist countries - that military preparations on this scale have no significant impact on long-term economic and social prospects and can therefore be sustained indefinitely. It has also been argued, at least with respect to developed market economy countries, that military activities can have a net positive economic impact through maintaining and stabilizing aggregate demand, reducing unemployment and contributing strongly to a dynamic technological environment.

This latter view has always been difficult to substantiate. Of greater significance, however, is the fact that it has become steadily more apparent as the postwar period has worn on that even the former view - that military activities are relatively benign in economic and social terms in developed countries - is quite fallacious. Table 1.1. provides some data generally suggestive of this fact. This rather belated awareness that the magnitude and character of contemporary military preparations entails significant economic penalties is due in part to neglect - the economic and social consequences of military spending have never been a particularly fashionable topic for research - but mostly because these penalties are paid indirectly and therefore take time clearly to manifest themselves. In other words, in addition to the magnitude and character of the military preparations undertaken by the developed countries, the fact that this effort has now been sustained for 30 years contributes much to its deleterious economic and social consequences.

Over the past decade or so the majority of industrialized countries have accumulated formidable and persistent economic problems. Both market and planned economies have experienced a marked drop in rates of economic growth, declining rates of return on investment and sluggish productivity. For market economies one can add rapid inflation and chronic unemployment. In the West, this combination of maladies is now commonly known as stagflation and although the present situation is nowhere near as grim as the depression of the 1930s it does appear that economic realities have once again outpaced the theory and practice of economic management. In the East there is similarly a deep concern over the medium and long-term economic prospect.

Table 1.1. Military Burden and Economic Performance

	Defence expenditure/ GDP %			Defence R&D/ total R&D %		Defence R&D/ GNP %		Average annual growth rate			
								GNP		Industrial productivity	
	1965	1970	1979	1971	1975	1971	1975	1969-73	1973-78	1969-73	1973-77
USSR	12.8	12.0	9.6[a]	na	na	na	na	5.3	3.6	5.0	1.4[b]
USA	7.6	8.0	5.2	31	30	0.80	0.64	3.5	2.4	2.2	1.3
UK	5.9	4.8	4.9	25	30	0.53	0.62	3.2	1.1	3.9	0.2
FRANCE	5.2	4.2	4.0	19	19	0.33	0.35	5.5	2.8	4.2	2.1
GERMANY, F.R.	4.3	3.3	3.3	10	7	0.16	0.14	4.4	2.0	4.7	3.5
JAPAN	0.9	0.8	0.9[a]	na	0.6	negl.	negl.	9.1	3.7	9.4	5.8

a) 1977
b) 1974-78

Sources:
1. Defence expenditure as a per cent of GDP: World Armaments and Disarmament, SIPRI Yearbook 1980
2. Defence R&D and productivity: Bernard Delaplame, et. al., Science and Technology in the New Socio-Economic Context, OECD 1980 and OECD Economic Surveys. The figures for the Soviet Union are derived from official data on industrial output and employment and the stock of fixed assets in industry.
3. GNP growth rates: World Military Expenditures and Arms Transfers 1969-78, US Arms Control and Disarmament Agency, Washington D.C. December 1980.

It must be said at the outset that there is no evidence that the persistent allocation of a large volume of resources to military activities is a predominant cause of the economic difficulties now widespread in the industrialized world. At the same time, however, relationships identified theoretically, and generally confirmed empirically between military expenditures and investment, growth, employment, productivity and inflation, suggest very strongly that these various relationships collectively make a significant and certainly underappreciated contribution.

For a more detailed evaluation of the evidence on the economic impact of large and sustained military expenditures, the following discussion is focused on four phenomena - growth, employment, inflation and the balance of payments. To a significant extent the general manner in which military activities impact on the economy will be the same in both market and planned industrialized countries although there will have to be occasional digressions from the general discussion to address important differences.

Growth

Recent empirical investigations have shown a negative relationship over the long term between military expenditures and the rate of economic growth in industrialized market economies. Economic growth is a complex function of population increase, investment and productivity. There is no reason to expect any significant relationship between military expenditure and the rate of increase in population and the labour force. Furthermore, in most developed market economy countries the rate of growth of population and the labour force has been slow and declining and therefore the least important in terms of accounting for economic growth. If military expenditure retards growth, it must therefore do so via investment or productivity or both.

A number of recent investigations - both case studies and cross-sectional analyses of a number of countries - have concluded that military expenditures are competitive with investment, that is, a relatively high share of output for military activities tends to be associated with a relatively low share for investment.(1) There are two plausible theoretical explanations of this result. The first is that military procurement expenditures and investment demands are directed at roughly the same set of industries so that heavy military demand, and particularly any expansion of military demand, may cause supply bottlenecks that constrict investment. Since procurement expenditures account for less than one half of total military expenditures this would be, at best, a partial explanation. A more general explanation would recognise that combined private and public consumption typically accounts for more than one half of total output and that, except in situations of national emergency, this share is highly resistant to downward pressures. Accordingly, military expenditures and investment compete for the remainder of the total productive capacity of the economy with the intensity of the competition determined to some degree by the state of the balance of payments and the overall rate of utilization in the economy. Analogous trade-offs have been observed in studies on Soviet economic performance over the postwar period.(2)

Lagging investment, of course, impedes economic growth directly. In addition, however, because the diffusion of new technology is predominantly accomplished through investment in new capital equipment, it also has a very important indirect effect through constraining the rate of growth of productivity. This line of reasoning can therefore account in part for the prevailing disparities in productivity growth recorded in Table 1.1.

A contributing explanation here has to do with the proportion of the total R+D effort that a nation devotes to military R+D and the relevance of the latter for economic performance. There is no question that military R+D yields civilian spin-offs but the observed negative relationship between the relative scale of military expenditure and the rate of economic growth suggests that this influence is outweighed by the displacement of investment. Moreover, it is now generally recognised that the civilian spin-off produced by military R+D has been very considerably exaggerated in the past. With some exceptions, notably electronics, the gap between military and civilian technology is very wide and, some would argue, growing. Accordingly, securing civilian spin-off from military R+D is quite difficult and to the extent that it takes place it does so with a considerable time lag.(3)

If comparisons are made between the major Western industrialized countries in terms of non-military or economically relevant R+D a pattern emerges that corresponds quite closely with the hierarchy in Table 1.1. In terms of expenditure and employment of professional manpower per unit of GNP in the mid-to-late 1960s the intensity of economically relevant R+D was highest in Japan, with the United States lagging significantly behind both this country and the major Western European countries.(4) A relative decline in capital productivity - which is the same as progressive growth in capital requirements per unit of output -will tend to produce shortages of investible funds and drive up interest rates. It also undermines a country's international competitiveness and introduces or aggravates the balance of payments constraint on economic growth. An important complementary observation is that if a relatively large share of the total R+D resources is devoted to military R+D there is a tendency for the total R+D effort to be heavily skewed in favour of the sectors of primary interest to the military - particularly aerospace and electronics - because private sector R+D expenditures also tend to concentrate in the areas where defence funds provide a solid underpinning. As a result, the older basic industries such as steel, automobiles, railroads and machinery and metalworking suffer relatively heavily from technological stagnation, declining productivity and a loss of competitiveness. This is a particularly serious affect as these industries account for the bulk of manufacturing employment in industrialized countries and for a large share of exports. And, in one of those vicious circles that abound in economics, the declining attractiveness of domestic investment leads to the flight of capital overseas, thus aggravating the situation.

Employment

As we have seen there exists a negative relationship between military expenditure and economic growth, particularly when the former is associated with large outlays on military R+D and an extensive military industrial capacity. A plausible explanation of how this relationship comes about is that military expenditures and investment compete for the available non-consumption resources. To the extent that investment is "crowded out" the growth rate falls, both directly and because new investment is the primary vehicle for the dissemination of technological advances that increase factor productivity. If the State in question also commits a disproportionately large share of its R+D resources to the military sector this effect is exacerbated by the relative paucity of economically useful technological developments. Since States differ markedly in the relative scale and intensity of their military efforts, those that assume the heaviest burden will tend to experience a progressive decline in their international competitiveness, the loss of export markets and the displacement of domestic production by imports. In this general fashion a large military establishment can be said to undermine the capacity of the economy to generate new employment over the long term, that is, military activities may be regarded as contributing to structural unemployment.

A second important and quite distinct aspect of the employment question is that military expenditure itself creates employment. Soldiers and civilians are employed directly, military contracts placed with industry lead directly to the hiring of workers by the prime contractors with additional jobs supported indirectly at the subcontractor and lower levels. More generally, the multiplier operates to diffuse military spending throughout the economy, thereby sustaining yet more jobs. To make a very obvious point, however - but one that is still frequently forgotten - this occurs because it is expenditure, not because it is _military_ expenditure. Indeed, it is now well established that military expenditure is among the least efficient types of expenditures from the standpoint of creating employment, that is, per unit of expenditure, most plausible patterns of expenditure for civilian goods and services require more workers than does military expenditure. The primary reason for this is that non-personnel military expenditures are concentrated in the capital and technology-intensive sectors of industry. Only at the stage of final assembly of weapon systems can military industrial activities be said to be labour-intensive. A related point of some importance is that the sustained emphasis within the military sector on technological sophistication has resulted in steadily rising qualifications required of personnel in this sector, from uniformed personnel to the worker in military industry. The primary military demand for labour has become increasingly selective and largely bypasses the general worker and the so-called hardcore unemployed.

It does not really follow from this that military expenditures cause unemployment: this could be said to apply only if it were possible to determine accurately the civilian goods and services that a society gave up or cutback on as a result of the diversion of income to the military. One of the pioneering investigations in this field attempted to do this for the United States and concluded that, over the years 1968-72, when the military budget was of the order of $ 80 billion, the country experienced a net loss of about 840,000 jobs annually.(5) Several other studies have confirmed this general thesis. One of these contrasted the programme to develop and produce the B-1 strategic bomber with a tax cut and a public housing programme of equivalent magnitude.(6) The study employed a large and sophisticated multi-equation model of the US economy and concluded that both of the hypothesized alternatives to the B-1 programme would generate more employment over a 10-year period primarily because the latter used the manufacturing sector much more heavily and employment requirements in this sector are relatively low. Another study conducted in 1975, which also employed a large input-output model of the US economy, assumed that fiscal policy would maintain full employment and then forecasted the national economy to 1980 assuming, on the one hand, a 30 per cent cut in military expenditure offset by increases in education, health, public assistance and environmental programmes and, on the other, a 30 per cent increase in military expenditure offset by reductions in the programmes just mentioned.(7) The results were again unequivocal: relative to the base forecast of a stable military budget the assumed reduction in this budget yielded higher net output and employment while the assumed increase had the opposite effect.

To reiterate, these results can be used somewhat loosely to argue that heavy military expenditures contribute to unemployment, but the more important conclusion to draw from them is that industrialized countries have nothing to fear as far as employment is concerned from disarmament measures and the conversion and redeployment of resources to civilian ends. Although the empirical evidence reviewed above refers only to the United States, the results can be applied generally and particularly to other States that invest heavily in military R+D and maintain comprehensive military industries.

Inflation

The rapid escalation in the general level of prices is widely regarded as one of the most debilitating economic diseases that can afflict market economies. Rapid inflation and even more unpredictable rates of inflation undermine the inherent efficiency of the price system as a mechanism for the allocation of resources, most particularly the allocations for savings and investment as against consumption. Economists generally distinguish between demand or demand-pull inflation and supply-side or cost-push inflation and although it is not possible even approximately to quantify the extent to which military expenditures contribute to inflation there can be no doubt that these expenditures are among the factors at work on both sides of the inflation phenomena.

The basic proposition that suggests a direct relationship between military expenditure and inflation stems directly from the classic definition of the latter: too much money chasing too few goods and services. The factors of production engaged in the military sector receive incomes or purchasing power but contribute nothing in the way of goods and services. Theoretically, of course, military expenditures purchase security, and security is the fundamental underpinning for all economic and social activity. In the strictly economic sense, however, the output of the military sector can neither be consumed nor invested so that military expenditures can be characterized as demand not matched by supply and thus innerently inflationary. The strength of this inflationary effect depends very strongly on the health of the economy and on the manner in which military expenditures are financed. The more dynamic the economy, the more rapid the growth in productive capacity and in factor productivity, the more readily can military expenditures be absorbed without strong inflationary pressures. If, on the other hand, the economy is relatively static with slow overall growth and a low rate of increase in productivity, military expenditures will exert more severe inflationary pressures across a wide front. Even in the former case the concentration of military expenditures in selected areas of the market for skilled labour and specific industrial capacities can, in combination with civil demand, result in severe bottlenecks and sharp price rises which subsequently affect costs and prices further up the manufacturing chain. For these reasons, among others, the rate of inflation within the military sector is frequently more rapid than in the economy as a whole.

The extent to which the inflationary potential inherent in military expenditure is translated into actual upward pressure on prices is also crucially dependent on the manner in which these expenditures are financed. These pressures will be minimal if all central government expenditure, including military expenditure, is financed from taxation revenues. In many, if not most, industrialized countries, however, the central government budget is frequently in deficit: in the United States, for example, the Federal budget has been in surplus in only four of the last 19 years. Budgetary deficits, of course, are financed by means of increasing the public debt either through government borrowing from the private sector or through resort to the central bank and the printing of money. It is intuitively obvious that the latter alternative has the greatest inflationary potential and empirical research in several countries has indeed established that there exists a strong correlation between the rate of growth of the stock of money and, with a time-lag, the rate of increase in the general price level.(8) It is not possible to attribute budgetary deficits to any particular category of government expenditure. It is a fact, however, that military expenditures are often the largest single component of central government expenditure. In 1978 military expenditures accounted, on the average, for 22.5 per cent of central government expenditure in the developed countries, down from an average figure of 34.1 per cent in 1969.(9) It is clear, therefore, that military expenditures bear significant responsibility for whatever budgetary deficits occur. Broadly speaking, the almost universal difficulty that governments in developed countries have in balancing their budgets stems from the rapid and sustained expansion in the cost of maintaining technologically advanced armed forces.

On the cost side of the inflation phenomenon, military activities exert their influence through investment and productivity. To the extent that (a) military expenditures subtract in a broad sense from the resources available for investment; (b) military capital expenditures compete with the private sector for the productive capacity of industries that produce investment goods; and (c) R+D resources are oriented towards military objectives, then economic theory and empirical evidence suggest that overall growth and factor productivity will suffer and the economy will be rendered more vulnerable to inflation because the real costs of domestic production will tend to rise more rapidly: cost increases from outside the economy are more difficult to absorb. Furthermore, the uncertainty generated by an environment of rapid inflation tends to result in a preference for low-risk projects that produce quick results rather than the longer-term investment commitments needed to restore economic vitality.

In at least one respect, the contribution to inflation that military expenditures make on the demand side also aggravates the cost-push pressures. Specifically, if the Government, in its attempt to cover budget deficits, borrows on the capital market on too large a scale it can constrain the availability of financial capital for private investors and drive up its cost. Something like this happened in the United States in fiscal year 1980 when the Federal Government borrowed a staggering $ 75 billion on the capital market.

As discussed so far in this section, inflation is a phenomenon associated principally with market economy countries but some of the arguments advanced linking military expenditures to inflation clearly have equal applicability to the centrally-planned economies. In particular, the line of reasoning that suggests a relationship between military expenditure and cost-push inflation would appear to be just as relevant for centrally-planned economies. In these countries, too, (a) military expenditures compete with investment for the resources not needed to provide for current consumption; (b) new investment is the primary vehicle for the dissemination of productivity-increasing technological advances; and (c) a heavy emphasis on military R+D will tend to retard technical progress in the areas of economic activity not directly relevant to the military effort. On the demand side, however, the picture is quite different. Prices are fixed and planning endeavours to ensure that supply and demand at these prices are approximately in balance. When imbalances do arise - for example, an excess of demand over supply - markets are cleared on a first-come first-served basis until steps can be taken to restore a balance.

International Trade and the Balance of Payments

The international exchange of goods and services based on comparative advantage is a powerful instrument for the promotion of economic growth and the efficient allocation of resources on a global scale. So important has international trade become that economic circumstances which incline states towards protectionism are feared as something to be avoided at all costs. The fact, therefore, that the arms race or, more accurately, the political circumstances that it reflects, has seriously diminished and distorted international exchange is of the utmost significance in the present context.

The politico-military competition between East and West has inevitably spilled over into the economic sphere and driven a wedge between two giant economic blocs that could engage in mutually beneficial exchange on a massive scale. The most explicit barrier has been the effect on trade in so-called strategic commodities, that is, commodities judged to be of significance directly or indirectly for the military effort. Inevitably, these commodities - which may be anything from raw materials to advanced technology - are frequently also of key importance for the civilian economy. More generally, the arms race has created a psychological reluctance on both sides to accept the interdependence that open trade between them would lead to. The rapid growth of East-West trade during the brief period of détente during the early 1970s is a good indication of the extent to which trade is being suppressed by this intangible factor. And behind these lost opportunities for exchange lies the huge waste of resources in terms of the duplication of effort and the inefficient allocation of resources from the global standpoint.

The evidence reviewed above, that large and sustained military expenditures retard economic growth, also means that trade has grown less rapidly than would otherwise have been the case.(10) The link between military expenditures and inflation has similar implications because governments try to combat inflation by restraining the economy. Furthermore, the relative magnitude of military expenditures - and therefore the economic penalties associated with these expenditures - differs markedly within the industrialized countries and thereby contributes to the persistent and occasionally very serious balance of payments problems experienced by some of these countries. The progressive loss of competitiveness in the international market - due in part, as we have argued, to sustaining a large military programme - constitutes an additional constraint on boosting economic growth because of the greater likelihood that balance of payments deficits will occur. These underlying economic factors are aggravated by the fact that the major military powers typically assume or acquire costly foreign military commitments. The outflow of real and financial resources associated with these commitments must be offset by export earnings or foreign governments must be willing to accumulate even larger quantities of one's currency. The status of the U.S. dollar as a reserve currency allowed the U.S. to take the latter course for many years but when confidence in the dollar declined and exchange rates were freed in 1971 these huge dollar holdings - hundreds of billions of dollars in Europe alone - became a source of potentially devastating instability for the international monetary system.

There are small compensations, of course, and one is of particular relevance in the present context. The handful of countries that maintain the most economically ruinous military establishments also control over 90 per cent of the international market for arms and military equipment. The earnings from the export of arms are not inconsequential but most estimates put the share of arms in the total world trade at about 2 per cent, so that a competitive advantage in this area is easily outweighed if it is acquired at the expense of a loss of competitiveness in the major civilian markets.

1.3. ARMAMENTS AND DEVELOPMENT IN THE DEVELOPING COUNTRIES

If, on balance, the economic effect of diverting resources to military uses is overwhelmingly negative in the developed countries one would expect the same to be true of the developing countries. Indeed, since the modern defence establishment is a heavy consumer of skilled technical and managerial manpower, industrial capacity and, for non-arms-producing countries, foreign exchange, one would expect this negative effect to be especially strong in the developing countries where precisely these resources are particularly scarce.

This thesis was strongly challenged in a study by Professor Benoit.(11) Benoit's major finding was that, statistically, the defence burden and economic growth were complementary rather than competitive, that is, the burden of defence - the share of GDP devoted to defence - was positively correlated with the rate of growth of civilian output. This simple correlation between defence and development could be mainly spurious because both are affected in the same direction by third factors, particularly foreign aid and, to a lesser extent, investment. Even in multiple correlations, however, where the influence of each of these factors is isolated, there remained a small positive relationship between the defence burden and the rate of growth. Thus, in addition to the indirect effects of defence in attracting high levels of foreign aid and encouraging investment, defence spending has direct growth-stimulating effects and together these effects outweighed the fact that defence also withdraws resources from potentially productive uses.

Professor Benoit identified three main growth-retarding effects associated with the defence burden; investment and productivity effects and an income shift effect. The investment effect is the loss of investible resources associated with a rise in the defence burden and a corresponding fall in the rate of growth of civilian output. In quantifying this effect, Benoit assumed that the share of defence resources which might otherwise have gone into investment would be twice the share of total national resources devoted to investment. The productivity effect results from the fact that an increase in the defence burden increases the relative size of the Government sector and this sector normally exhibits very slow rates of productivity increase. Finally, the income shift effect refers to the reduction of civilian GDP caused by an increase in the defence burden. Subsequent growth in civilian GDP, therefore, starts from a lower base than would otherwise have been the case. All told, Benoit calculated that a rise in the burden of defence of 1 per cent of GDP would involve a reduction in the rate of growth of civilian GDP of one quarter of 1 per cent.

The growth-stimulating effects of defence spending identified by Benoit were predominantly qualitative and less susceptible to measurement. In the first place, the defence programme provides a measure of physical security against external and internal threats without which there could be no economic progress at all. Secondly, Benoit argued that defence spending stimulated effective demand and encouraged more complete and effective use of the available factors of production, particularly capital. Part of this process is that an increase in the defence programme leads Governments to pursue more liberal or expansionary monetary and fiscal policies. A third argument was the familiar one, that some aspects of a military programme have direct civilian utility; such things as transportation and communication networks, disaster relief and certain scientific and technical activities. Finally, Benoit placed particular stress on the impact of the military as a modernizing force in traditional societies, accelerating what he regarded as the crucial transformation of attitudes and habits towards those that characterize the western industrial states.

While it should be remembered that Professor Benoit was attempting to provide a sensible explanation of a surprising statistical result, his explanation seems unsatisfactory on several counts. For example, growth in developing countries is more often restrained by shortages of supply rather than of demand. Increasing aggregate demand through military spending may simply divert already fully employed factors of production - capital, skilled technical and managerial labour - to the military sector with significant adverse growth effects. Similarly, the argument that some military activities have direct civilian utility is not necessarily self-evident. The military may build roads and bridges where civilians do not want to go; military communication networks may not be available for civilian use; the skills acquired in military service may be too sophisticated for civilian use or may never become available if the owner can make a career in the military.

Similarly, Professor Benoit's strong belief in the positive effects on economic growth of the habits and attitudes in and disseminated from the military sector is no longer a widely held view. In the late 1950s and 1960s, as the involvement of the military in politics became increasingly widespread in developing countries, an influential group of scholars reasoned that this phenomenon would ultimately be of benefit. As a disciplined institution with a vested interest in national unity and political stability and with a strong professional inclination towards advanced technology and modernization, the military was seen as the most effective instrument available for the mobilization of a society to bring about economic and social development. However, as evidence to the contrary accumulated, the concept of the modernizing army fell into disrepute. If anything, developing countries with military regimes have been more prone to disruptive and violent political instability. Similarly, there is no evidence that military regimes are more likely to succeed in maintaining a steady momentum of economic growth and development.(12)

While Benoit's explanations for the results of his statistical investigation are less than persuasive the results themselves remain. It is necessary, therefore, to question these results; that is, to examine the conceptual model employed, the data used and the statistical techniques applied.

In one recent study - involving data from 50 developing countries for the period 1965-73 - the authors attempted to correct the perceived deficiencies in Benoit's analysis.(13) The analysis theorised that military expenditure may affect growth directly through resource mobilization and the "modernization" effect and indirectly through the ratio of savings to total output. The resource-mobilization effect is broadly similar to that discussed above in connection with Benoit's study: military demand may be met by increased employment of labour or utilization of capital; the priority that normally attends military demands may lead to an overall increase in the rate of exploitation of available resource; and military demands may include a supply response from domestic sources with subsequent backward linkage effects. Similarly, the modernization effect refers to the military's role as the conduit for the introduction of modern technology, imparting technical skills and providing some of the infrastructural elements of a modern society. The analysts also took account of the argument that a larger or more urgent military effort may increase the savings potential of a developing country, with consequent positive effects on growth. This might occur through a spirit of austerity, reduced consumption or "forced savings" due to the non-availability of consumer goods. In a similar vein, if military spending contributes to inflation this may also lead to "forced savings" or an increase in profitability, inducing higher investment and higher growth.

When these relationships were tested statistically, the analysts found that military expenditure depressed the ratio of savings to income and therefore tended to retard growth. The effect of military expenditure on modernization or productivity was positive but also extremely weak: the results did not confirm Benoit's finding of a strong positive relationship between these two variables. Taking the effect of all the variables together, the result was a very small positive effect of military expenditure on growth. Significantly, however, the analysts stress the sensitivity of their results to the manner in which the components of the model are specified and to the estimation method employed. For example, in one experiment with the data, they allowed for the fact that while military expenditure and the savings rate influence growth, they are also, in turn, influenced by it. The result here was that the small direct effect of military expenditure on growth was outweighed by the indirect effect of a depressed savings ratio so that the total effect was negative. Another recent study, utilizing data for 54 developing countries, over some or all of the period 1952-79, estimated a regression equation relating the growth rate of output to changes in exports, population, defence burden, capital inflows and capital stock.(14) For the sample as a whole and for separate regional groupings (Latin America, Africa and Asia) increases in the burden of military expenditure had a clear negative impact on the rate of economic growth. In supplementary analysis, it was demonstrated that increases in the defence burden tend to depress the ratio of investment to GDP, suggesting that military expenditure is, on balance, competitive with investment. These results are consistent with the theoretical hypothesis that, particularly in developing countries, investment is more likely to be limited on the supply side - shortages of crucial production inputs such as capital stock, skilled labour and foreign exchange to purchase required intermediate imports - than by inadequate aggregate demand. And as mentioned above, military activities tend to place a dispropotionately heavy demand on available resources in these areas.

Much the same conclusion was reached with quite different analytical techniques in a study focusing on five South American countries - Argentina, Brazil, Chile, Colombia and Peru.(15) Utilizing aggregated input-output tables for these countries it was found that the Keynesian multiplier for final demand deriving from military expenditure was lower than those for investment, exports and non-military government expenditure. In other words, if military expenditures were to be cut back, the resulting reduction in demand and economic activity could be more than compensated for by directing equivalent resources to these other sectors.(16)

Even bearing in mind the unreliability of the data in the military field and the hazards of equating statistical correlations with causal relationships, this new evidence could support the conclusion that large military budgets are associated with slower rates of economic growth in developing countries. In any event, it is at least clear that there is no empirical basis for the conventional wisdom that military activities stimulate growth in these countries.

1.4. MILITARY ACTIVITIES AND DEVELOPMENT

Development involves satisfying the basic needs and providing steady improvements in the standard of living of the entire population. In this sense experience has shown that economic growth is not synonymous with development. It is therefore pertinent to examine the influence of military activities on the prospects for development in developing countries irrespective of whether the relationship with economic growth is positive, negative or indeterminate.

It has always been recognized that industrialization would be central to economic development but the strategies pursued to date have proved quite inadequate. In the traditional strategy of export promotion, industrial investment decisions are influenced by external demand. Under import substitution, the demand is generated internally but predominantly by the upper income groups in urban areas. Rural populations, who make up a majority in most developing countries, have in both cases been bypassed by such industrialization and growth as did take place. The strategy now being advocated is one that anticipates the basic needs of the majority of the population and promotes the building of an industrial production structure geared to the satisfaction of these needs.

The limitations of the development strategies pursued to date are manifested in many ways. Only a few developing countries, all of them relatively advanced, have succeeded in sustaining high rates of economic growth. In the countries with low per capita income - whose populations comprise a majority of the people in developing countries - growth has been slow both in the aggregate and in industry. Further, and again particularly in the low income countries, the distribution of the benefits of growth has been skewed; the distribution of income has worsened in many cases. In consequence, the ranks of the absolute poor have swelled inexorably and other signs of poverty - high rates of infant mortality, illiteracy, landlessness and unemployment - have become increasingly apparent. An important contributing factor to increasing inequality has been the migration to urban areas where industrial investment has been concentrated.

The chosen industrialization strategies have had little impact on unemployment and underemployment in developing countries. The share of both industry and manufacturing in total labour force utilization has actually declined in many cases, the result in large measure of the need to adopt imported processes based on large-scale production and the heavy use of capital. The capacity of the developing countries to develop technology indigenously - technology that would be more suited to national factor endowments - remains very small; in 1973 the developing countries accounted for only 12.6 per cent of the global stock of scientists and engineers engaged in

Research and Development and for just 2.9 per cent of global expenditure on Research and Development.(17)

One of the primary motives for industrialization was the desire to generate domestic surplus for reinvestment and capital accumulation and thereby lessen dependence on the developed countries. The continuous growth in the external indebtedness of developing countries suggests that, if anything, dependence has increased. The mode of industrialization in the developed countries - adopted in the absence of genuine alternatives - has left them increasingly dependent on imports of intermediate and capital goods to sustain the process, faced with large royalty payments on imported technology and processes and with their economic sovereignty undermined by the heavy involvement of transnational corporations in the industrial and mining sectors. Furthermore, the demands of the industrial sector have led to the neglect of agriculture, particularly food production, in many developing countries; the need to import an increasing proportion of essential food requirements has reduced their capacity to finance the imports needed to sustain industrial investment.

To the extent that military activities contribute to this uneven and unsatisfactory pattern of economic growth in developing countries, failure to halt the arms race will clearly impede progress towards a more broadly-based and sustainable development effort.

The first observation to be made is that all developing countries import the bulk of their requirements for modern weapons and military equipment and most of them rely exclusively on imports. According to SIPRI, the estimated value of major weapons imported by developing countries in the first half of the 1970s (1970-74) was some $ 18,700 million (in 1975 prices). In the second half of the 1970s (1975-79) this figure more than doubled to $ 42,000 in million.(18) While even these figures suggest that the foreign exchange committed by developing countries to arms imports is of economically significant proportions, it is important to note that the SIPRI data is acknowledged significantly to understate the true value of the financial flows associated with the trade in arms: other estimates suggest that the annual value of trade in arms with developing countries in the late 1970s was in excess of $ 30,000 million.(19)

It is true that a major portion of these transactions involved the members of OPEC, whose economic problems do not include a lack of foreign exchange. It is also true that the terms of arms supply contracts range from cash in hard currencies to payment in commodities or in local currencies at modest rates of interest. Nevertheless, in recent years, virtually all arms imports by developing countries, regardless of source, involve payment in one form or another. And given the probable magnitude of these payments it is difficult to avoid the conclusion that military imports contribute significantly to the difficulties experienced by developing countries in financing the import of intermediate and capital goods needed to sustain industrial investment.

Another frequently cited constraint on investment in developing countries (or an explanation for the low returns on new investment) is the acute shortage of skilled manpower. There can be little doubt that military requirements exacerbate this situation. The complexity of modern weapons means that they require an inordinate amount of attention in terms of maintenance and repair in order to be kept operational. For example, if a country has an air force with 100 aircraft (25 combat planes and 75 trainers, transports and helicopters) and an Army with 100 armoured vehicles (25 main battle tanks and 75 armoured cars) - a relatively modest arsenal - it is estimated that about 600 more or less highly skilled technicians and mechanics will be needed for repair and maintenance.(20) In this context it should be remembered that in many developing countries the annual output of engineers, technicians and mechanics from national educational institutions is measured in tens or the low hundreds. The considerable international traffic in skilled manpower is indicative of the fact that the simultaneous pursuit of industrialization and militarization in many cases results in an excess of demand over supply of skilled manpower.

It was mentioned above that developing countries have been generally frustrated in their efforts to industrialize. Whether the predominant strategy has been one of export-promotion or import-substitution, circumstances have led developing countries to adopt the production techniques and to replicate the industrial facilities extant in the developed countries. These techniques and processes pursue the economics of large-scale production and require the heavy use of capital while inputs of labour are minimized and tend towards high levels of skill. Accordingly, the growth of the industrial workforce has been constrained by technology and the sophistication of the techniques has resulted in a lingering dependence on imports for intermediate and capital goods, technology and management. Similarly, the infrastructure requirements of large industrial undertakings - for example, energy, road and rail transportation and communication facilities - has led to the concentration of industry in the vicinity of major urban centres. The so-called 'trickle down' effect of industrialization has been negligible. The real incomes of the majority of the population have remained very low so that the potentially massive demand for manufactured goods has remained dormant.

The suggested response, as we have seen, is to break away from the rigidities of emulative industrialization and pursue what has been called a strategy of endogenous industrialization.(21) A strategy of endogenous industrialization "... would anticipate the needs of the population and tailor the industrial production structure to produce goods to fulfil them. By definition, the dynamics of growth would come from within the country, calling for much greater emphasis on self-help or self-reliance. In carrying out this strategy, income would be generated directly in the hands of the rural and urban poor to help them satisfy their minimum needs for food, clothing, shelter, medical care, education and transportation. Projects would stress a low capital/labour ratio, use less energy and encourage greater use of local skills, entrepreneurial resources, materials, capital goods and technology. The role of small and medium-size industry would be expanded. There would be a symbiotic interaction between farms and industry at the rural level, leading to greater equality in the rural-urban terms of trade. A positive economic role would devolve on the government through the creation of enterprises producing industrial and public goods."(22)

Can this ambition be reconciled with the sustained commitment of resources to armaments on the present scale? Probably not. First of all, a significant share of all the modern technology to which developing countries are exposed and therefore influenced by is embodied in weapons and military equipment. The paucity of statistical data precludes a really satisfactory substantiation of this statement; all that can be done is to compare the value of arms imports with the value of imports of the commodities essential for industrialization such as machinery and transportation equipment (essentially category 7 of the Standard International Trade Classification). The results, however, are quite startling. For some countries arms imports occasionally exceed the value of imported engineering products; shares in the range 30-60 per cent are not uncommon.(23)

These comparisons reinforce the earlier observation that arms imports compete directly and often very strongly with imports that could expand the productive capacity of the economy. Beyond this, however, it can be argued that the relative magnitude of arms imports in many if not most developing countries implies strong pressures in the direction of emulative industrialization. The experience with emulative industrialization thus far has been disappointing, in large part due to the fact that available industrial technology is generally inconsistent with factor endowments in developing countries. But modern weapons, as we have seen, can be characterized as these same technologies elaborated to the highest possible degree. And if industrial technologies are relatively inflexible (as regards the type and proportion of factor inputs and the scale of production) this is even more true of military technology. One indication of this inflexibility is that, as the modern weapon system has spread throughout the world, the armed forces of all States, regardless of political and social setting and of the level of development, have tended towards uniformity of structure and organization.(24)

All States aspire to be independent in providing for their security. The modern weapon system, however, has very rigid requirements for operation, maintenance, repair, assembly and production. However far a country endeavours to go down this chain of increasing independence, the weapon system has a dictatorial impact on the industrial and technical capacities required. These capacities tend to be capital and technology-intensive; by civilian standards, military production requires more highly skilled workers, higher quality materials, more refined production techniques and rigid quality control.

Only a handful of developing countries have undertaken to establish defence industries on a major scale but a steadily growing number of these countries are taking the first steps in this direction. Apart from the essentially political motive of greater independence, the two main rationales advanced for the establishment of local defence industries are the potential to save foreign exchange and the expectation that incentives will be generated for the establishment of related industries further down the manufacturing chain - the phenomenon of backward linkage. Unfortunately, the inherent characteristics of modern defence industries militate strongly against the achievement of either objective. Strong backward linkages are unlikely because defence demand tends to be episodic and limited in volume. Similarly, the demanding requirements for quality and precision in defence-related industries make it difficult for these concerns to compete effectively in the commercial market. Consequently, it is rather improbable that private enterprise will find the military market attractive unless the Government is willing to provide capital support and to underwrite the investment. As regards the expectation that local defence industries will reduce the foreign exchange consumed by the military sector, the experience to date has not been encouraging. Even the few developing countries that have invested very heavily in the military sector have remained totally dependent on imports for the more sophisticated - and costly - components of modern weapons, such things as power plants, radar and fire control systems. Further, the import requirements of the defence industries themselves - machine tools, forging equipment, special metals and materials and the like - remain sizeable for an extended period of time. In combination, these two effects often lead to claims on foreign exchange that equal or exceed those associated with the direct import of complete weapon systems.

In sum, the military sector in developing countries tends to impede industrialization by pre-empting needed foreign exchange and skilled manpower. Developing countries have in any case found the industrialization strategies pursued to date inadequate because the available technologies are inconsistent with their factor endowment. The industrial sector, though costly to sustain, remained relatively small - particularly in terms of employment - and insulated from the rest of the economy. However, as we have argued above, attempts by developing countries to acquire the capacity to repair, assemble and produce modern weapons indigenously will impel them in the same direction, that is, towards an industrial structure that has been rejected as a dead-end so far as development is concerned.

Among the more serious consequences of the costly but, on balance, ineffective industrialization efforts in developing countries has been the strain imposed on the agricultural sector. In the majority of developing countries the only available source of resources to invest in manufacturing has been the surplus generated in or extractable from mining and agriculture. It was found in a statistical investigation that an increase in the burden of defence was associated with a shift in economic activity from the agricultural sector to industry. The cutback in the share of agriculture in GDP was not, however, matched by an increase in the share of industry; much of the difference went into an expanded service sector or into higher unemployment and underemployment. One of the consequences of this structural transformation could be the reduction of food production and greater dependence on imports for food.(25)

1.5. CONCLUSIONS

As we have seen, the diversion of real human and material resources to armaments has, on balance, distincly harmful economic and social effects. The economic and social consequences of the arms race extend far beyond the fact that 5-6 per cent of the world's resources are not available to help satisfy human needs because the expenditure of these resources on armaments contributes to the inefficient allocation of the remaining 94-95 per cent, both within and between nations. These consequences stem from three characteristics of the contemporary arms race. First, there is the magnitude of the volume of resources it has absorbed, of the order of 7 per cent of cumulative global output since 1945. Secondly, there is the composition of the expenditure, particularly the stress on R+D and the production of sophisticated weaponry and equipment in highly specialized facilities. And thirdly, there is the fact that this massive effort has now been sustained for over 30 years.

What, then, might be said of the economic and social consequences of a continuing or accelerated arms race? Since the negative effects identified earlier could not, on the whole, be individually quantified, it is impossible to be specific. Nevertheless, given our earlier conclusion that, in view of the diversity of these negative effects and the fact that many of them exert their influence in a cumulative manner, the arms race may have contributed to a significant - and certainly an underappreciated - extent to the prevailing economic and social problems, it follows that individual countries and the world community as a whole will find it difficult if not impossible to overcome these problems if the arms race accelerates or even if it continues in line with the historical trend. That is, it will be more difficult to bring inflation under control without pursuing recessionary policies; socially useful technical innovation and thus productivity will grow more slowly; the resources available for investment will be diminished and the environment of high inflation and low productivity growth will dampen incentives to invest leading to slower overall growth and compounding, among other things, the productivity problem. Slower growth will also mean less international trade quite apart from the distorting effects of politico-military considerations. In these generally circumscribed economic conditions the developed countries will find it more difficult to provide adequate financial, capital and technical assistance to the developing countries and will, to a greater degree, lack the flexibility to cope with intensified competition in manufactured goods from these countries; the military sector's demand for non-renewable raw materials will continue to grow; progress toward a secure energy future for the world is likely to be slower and environmental considerations will be ignored.

The economic affairs of states are now characterized by a pervasive interdependence with other states. The global economic prospect is almost universally acknowledged to be strongly dependent on the extent to which this interdependence can be managed for mutual benefit. One also has to ask, therefore, whether the requisite spirit of cooperation and mutual accommodation is likely to emerge and endure if international relations continue to be dominated by an arms race mentality. The answer, surely, is no.

In sum, it is quite unlikely that the economic and social aspirations - and, indeed, capabilities - of the community of nations can be reconciled with a continuing arms race.

NOTES AND REFERENCES

*This contribution was originally prepared as an expert paper for the Independent Commission on Disarmament and Security Issues under the chairmanship of Olof Palme.

1. For example, R.P. Smith, Military Expenditure and Capitalism, Cambridge Journal of Economics, July 1977, pp. 63-76 and Jacques Fontanel, Formalized Studies and Econometric Analyses of the Relationship between Military Expenditure and Economic Development. Paper prepared for the UN Group of Governmental Experts on the Relationship between Disarmament and Development, 1980.

2. Stanley H. Cohn, Economic Burden of Defence Expenditures in Soviet Economic Prospects for the Seventies, U.S. Congress, Joint Economic Committee, 1973.

3. Gur Ofer, The Relative Efficiency of Military R+D in the Soviet Union: A Systems Approach, R-2522-AF, November 1980 and The Opportunity Costs of the Non-monetary Advantages of the Soviet Military R+D Effort, R-1741-DDRE, August 1975. Both papers published by the Rand Corporation, Santa Monica, California.

4. Michael Boretsky, Trends in U.S. Technology: A Political Economist's View, paper presented to the National Conference on the Administration of Research, Montreal, September 1973.

5. Marion Anderson, The Empty Pork Barrel, Public Interest Research Group in Michigan (PIRGIM), April 1975.

6. Chase Econometrics Associates, Economic Impact of the B-1 Program on the U.S. Economy and Comparative Case Studies, Cynwyd, Pennsylvania: Chase Econometrics Associates, 1975.

7. Roger H. Bezdek, The 1980 Economic Impact - Regional and Occupational - of Compensated Shifts in Defence Spending, Journal of Regional Science, Vol. 15, No. 2, 1975, pp. 183-198.

8. In the United States the decisive departure from a relatively stable general level of prices occurred in 1965-66 and many economists believe that this was primarily due to the deficit financing of the initial build-up of forces in Vietnam.

9. World Military Expenditure and Arms Transfers 1969-1978, United States Arms Control and Disarmament Agency, Washington D.C. 1980, p.33.

10. One of the studies prepared for the United Nations Group on Disarmament and Development employed an input-output model of the world economy to analyse the impact of alternative trends in global military expenditure through the year 2000. Among the many conclusions was that the volume of world trade was inversely related to the rate of growth of military spending. Wassily Leontief and Faye Duchin, Worldwide Economic Implications of a Limitation on Military Spending.*

11. Emile Benoit, Defense and Economic Growth in Developing Countries, Lexington, Massachusetts 1973.

12. For a brief review of the demise of the concept of the modernizing army see Bhabani Sen Gupta, The Modernising Soldier: End of a Myth, Bulletin of Peace Proposals, 1979, No. 3, pp. 269-274. A wider ranging discussion appears in Mary Kaldor, The Military in Development, World Development, Vol. 4, No. 6, 1976, pp. 459-482.

13. See Dan Smith and Ron Smith, Military Expenditure, Resources and Development.*

14. Lance Taylor et.al. Defence Spending, Economic Structure and Growth: Evidence Among Countries and Over Time.*

15. Jose A. Encinas del Pando, Declaration of Ayacucho: Analysis and Quantification of a Possible Agreement on Limitation of Military Expenditure in Latin America.*

16. The one exception was Argentina where the multiplier for military expenditure ranked second behind exports.

17. See Industry 2000: New Perspectives, United Nations Industrial Development Organization (ID/237) October 1979, p. 181.

18. World Armaments and Disarmament, SIPRI Yearbook 1980, London, 1980, p. 96-97.

19. SIPRI Yearbook, op.cit., pp. 57 and 72.

20. Herbert Wulf et. al. Transnational Transfer of Arms Production Technology, pp. 77-81.*

21. UNIDO Industry 2000, op.cit., p. 11.

22. UNIDO Industry 2000, op.cit., p. 11.

23. Wulf op.cit., p. 84.

24. Mary Kaldor, The Role of Military Technology in Industrial Development, p. 58.*

25. Taylor, op.cit., p. 11.

* Paper prepared for the United Nations Group of Governmental Experts on the Relationship between Disarmament and Development.

Chapter Two

LINKING DISARMAMENT AND DEVELOPMENT: SOME IDEAS FROM A UNITED NATIONS RESEARCH PROJECT

Bo Hovstadius - Manne Wängborg

2.1. BACKGROUND

Introduction

World military expenditure is currently thought to exceed $ 500 billion annually. Tens of millions of people around the world are directly or indirectly working in the military sector.

In this situation, what would the economic consequences of global disarmament be? And how could less developed countries become the main beneficiaries of any conceivable savings? These are the key questions in a research programme under the auspices of the United Nations which was initiated by the 1978 General Assembly Special Session on Disarmament and which has recently been completed.

One of the themes of the reseach project is how disarmament may directly enhance economic development by way of increased international economic development assistance. This chapter presents some of the proposals for the practical implementation of such a direct link between disarmament and development.

How large an addition to international economic aid disarmament might yield, depends on how sizeable the military expenditure reduction would be and what proportion of the savings were allocated to economic aid. In some of the project contributions, the addition would be highly marginal, while in other hypothetical scenarios it would grow to the projected size of present aid transfers by the year 2000, if not as early as 1990. The point is that, because world military expenditure is so much larger than economic aid, a rather modest reduction of the former would correspond to a significant increase of the latter.

The Institutional Framework

In December 1977, the General Assembly adopted a resolution calling for a United Nations study of the relationship between disarmament and development. The terms of reference for the study were confirmed by the tenth Special Session of the UN General Assembly in 1978 devoted to disarmament. Originally, the study was proposed by the Nordic countries - Denmark, Finland, Norway and Sweden - in a joint working paper.

The terms of reference outlined three main areas of inquiry:

1. present-day utilization of resources for military purposes;

2. economic and social consequences of a continuing arms race and of the implementation of disarmament measures; and

3. conversion and redeployment of resources released from military purposes through disarmament measures to economic and social development purposes.

Each of these three broad fields of inquiry has been further subdivided into several more specific topics, resulting in a three-part check-list comprising originally 18 points.

Following the Special Session, the Secretary-General appointed a Group of qualified governmental experts to oversee the work. The expert group invited researchers and institutes around the world to submit research proposals within the frame of reference of the study. It then selected 45 out of these proposals as contributions to the project.

Clarifications

Disarmament is primarily a military and political concept, rather than an economic concept. Ongoing negotiations and the treaties concluded are couched in military, technical and geographic terms. However, economic criteria and indicators have long since been a recurrent theme in disarmament discussions. Several specific disarmament proposals before the United Nations have been based on limiting military expenditure. Some have linked this notion to an increase in development aid, that is, they have proposed that a certain fraction of the military budget cut be allocated to development assistance. Disarmament, then, is taken to mean primarily a reduction in military expenditure, without further military, technical or political elaboration. In keeping with this, it is predominantly with the economic aspects of disarmament that this study is concerned.

Perhaps it should be made clear at the outset that it is not the intention of the project to make future economic aid contingent upon disarmament. Making economic assistance subject to the successful implementation of disarmament measures would presently increase the likelihood of achieving neither. An earlier UN report on the very same theme explicitly states that disarmament and development "fundamentally stand separately from one another", and "the pursuit of each objective can proceed without the other, and it should proceed urgently".

Moreover, the project did not seek to demonstrate that increased production to supply the needs of developing countries would be the best way to ease structural crises for military-industrial enterprises. Ordinarily this is probably not the case and it is certainly not what has prompted the project idea. The logic is rather the inverse. The social and economic needs of the less developed countries require no further substantiation. All resources that can be mobilized for the task are needed in order to ameliorate those conditions.

2.2. THE PROJECT

Why Disarmament and Development?

The United Nations designated the 1970s as both the first disarmament decade and the second development decade. Disarmament as well as economic development are high-priority objectives of the UN - but why link the two, as is done in this research project?

As already mentioned, the link is in itself not unique to this project. The same idea had been attempted earlier in the UN context. One reason behind this is that world military expenditure continues to grow in real terms while, for instance, the OECD countries are presently not approaching their development aid goal of 0.7 per cent of GNP. Another reason is high-level diplomatic bargaining: disarmament has been seen as largely an issue for the industrialized world, while developing countries are more interested in raising development aid. The link is an attempt to offer a common denominator for both categories of countries.

Moreover, great expectations are not infrequently involved in this approach: world military expenditure is large enough for even a minor fraction of it to correspond to substantial amounts of goods and services, in relation to urgent social and economic needs in developing countries. The following formulation by Wassily Leontief, in describing one of his own contributions to the project, is typical:

> The more than $ 450 billion per year currently spent on the maintenance of military establishments throughout the world is the largest existing economic reserve that might be utilized to accelerate the growth of the resource-poor less developed regions.

The Issue in a Nut-shell

Figure 2.1. seeks to illustrate some of the major alternatives for reallocating resources from military purposes to economic develop-

Figure 2.1. Disarmament and Development: Flow Chart

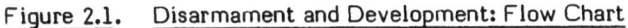

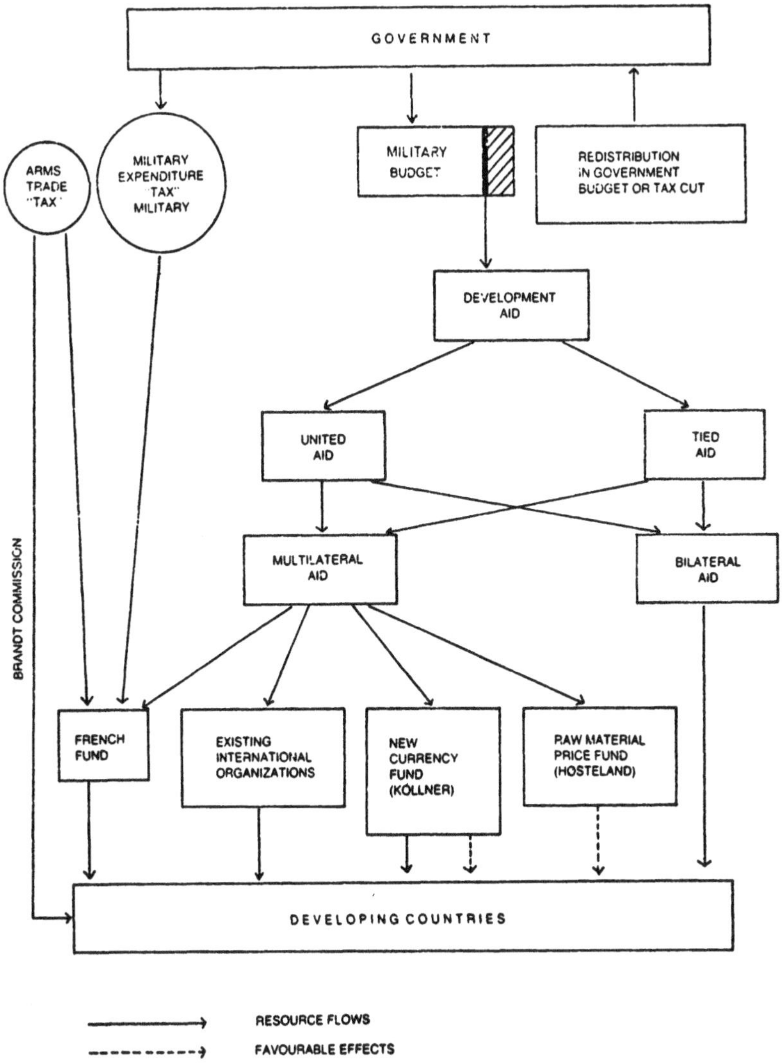

ment aid.

The key part of the chart is the flow market by rectangles, but for the sake of completeness, two "tributaries" are also included - from the two circles at the top left. To begin with the latter - which were drawn differently to indicate that they do not presume any disarmament even in the liberal sense of the word used here - they show, as alternatives to disarmament, two proposals for taxation of military efforts for the purposes of increased development aid: one is taxation of military expenditure, the other a tax on the arms trade. The idea was advanced by France at the UN Special Session in 1978. Briefly, it was intended that the revenue from this international tax would be collected in a special fund - here called the French fund - and from there distributed amongst developing countries. The idea of a tax on the arms trade has more recently been supported by the so-called Brandt Commission.

The major flow illustrates some variations on the main theme. Most of the contributions directly addressing the issue assume that in the event of disarmament only a certain fraction of the reduction of military expenditure would be allocated to development assistance - here illustrated by a "slice" of the defence budget rectangle - while the rest would remain in the disarming country, where it could either be re-distributed within the government budget or used to lower taxes.

The resources earmarked for development aid may be transferred to the recipient countries as either tied or untied aid. In this context, tied aid means resource transfers with certain strings attached, usually a requirement that purchases be made in the donor country. In both cases, the resources may be administered to aid projects either multilaterally or bilaterally. Bilateral assistance is then channelled directly to the receiving country, while multilateral aid may be transferred by way of either the above-mentioned French fund, existing international agencies, or two new funds outlined in individual contributions to the project, here identified by the name of the author(s) in question.

The Contributions

The terms of reference for the project emphasized economic and perhaps bureaucratic as opposed to political or military aspects of and obstacles to disarmament. This tendency is reflected in the contributions to the project.

As can be gathered from the list of titles below, the contributions to the project vary greatly in terms of approach and methodology as well as in terms of substance and scope. Many do not deal precisely with the link between disarmament and development, but rather analyse some aspects of the dynamics of the arms race, such as military use of natural resources, arms trade, military industry in developed or developing countries, the impact of arms spending and military technology on economic growth and so forth.

Among the contributions that specifically address a possible link between disarmament and development, a few focus on the institutional framework and economic mechanisms of hypothetical "disarmament fund" designs. In the following we have chosen to illustrate the analysis of the relationship between disarmament and development with a review of precisely these concrete reform proposals.

Disarmament, Development and the World Economy

Before examining the technical details of these various schemes, however, it might be useful to consider the anticipated economic consequences of conceivable disarmament measures. There are several contributions to the project that deal with this question from one viewpoint or another.

PROJECT CONTRIBUTIONS

A. **Financed by the project fund**

1. A.B. Akinyemi: Disarmament and development: Utilization of resources for military purposes in Black Africa

2. G. Chichilnisky: The role of armaments flows in the international market and in development strategies in a North-South context

3. P. Dabezies: Creation d'un fond international de desarmement pour le development

4. A.E.H. Dessouki: The effects of arms race and defence expenditures on development: A case study of Egypt

5. J.A. Encinas del Pando: Declaration of Ayacucho

6. J. Fontanel: Formalized studies and econometric analyses of the relationship between military expenditure and economic development

7. D. Greenwood: West European defence efforts in the later 1970s and beyond

8. G. Gunatilleke: The armament culture and the diffusion of the values of militarization

9. H. Hveem & R. Malnes: Military use of natural resources: The case for conversion and control

10. M. Kaldor: The role of military technology in industrial development

11. W. Leontief & F. Duchin: Worldwide economic implications of a limitation on military spending

12. S. Melman: Barriers to conversion from military to civilian industry - in market, planned and developing economies

13. I. Nzimiro: Economic and social effects of (military) arms build-up in Nigeria: Implications for national development

14. S. Rana & P.K.S. Namboodiri & R.R. Subramanian: Reallocation of military resources from OECD to primary sectors of LDCs: Mutuality of interests - a Third World perspective

15. K.N. Rao & J.P. Ruina: Disarmament and development: The case of relatively advanced developing countries

16. B.M. Russett & D.J. Sylvan: The effects of arms transfers on developing countries

17. I. Sachs: Reflections on conversion strategies for armament-related arms industries

18. D. Smith & R. Smith: Military expenditure, resources and development

19. F. Sollie & O. Narvesen: Analysis of a proposal to establish an international fund for development

20. M. Thee: The establishment of an international disarmament fund for development

21. P. Wallensteen & O. Frensborg: New wine and old bottles

B. Nationally financed

1. J-T. Bernard & M. Truchon: The impact of disarmament on the Canadian economy

2. O. Bjerkholt & A. Cappelen & N.P. Gleditsch & K. Moum: Disarmament and development: A case study of conversion in Norway

3. M. Brzoska: An assessment of sources and statistics of military expenditure and arms transfer data

4. J. Chmurkowski & J. Misztal & A. Rogucki & B. Tomorowicz & K. Zukrowska: Arms race and global problems of international

economic relations

5. E. Ehrenberg: Political and economic obstacles to disarmament efforts in developing countries: Egypt, Iran and India

6. K. Engelhart & K. Berndt & U. Röhner: Effects of the arms race and disarmament on the labour situation in countries of different social systems

7. J. Hösteland: Stabilizing raw materials prices through redeployment of armament spendings

8. Institute for African Affairs, USSR Academy of Sciences: Comparative analysis of the economic situation of African countries, resource requirements for development, military expenditure and factors affecting the arms race on the continent

9. Institute of Oriental Studies, USSR Academy of Sciences: The arms race and the economic and social problems of the developing countries

10. Institute for United States and Canadian Affairs, USSR Academy of Sciences: Urgent political, social and economic problems of the present stage of the development of mankind, and practical ways of diverting to development needs the resources now absorbed by the arms race

11. Institute of World Economics and International Relations, USSR Academy of sciences: Economic and social effects of a continuing arms race and the implementation of disarmament measures

12. R. Filip-Köhn & R. Krengel & D. Schumacher: Macro-economic effects of disarmament policies on sectoral production and employment in the Federal Republic of Germany, with special emphasis on development policy issues

13. L. Köllner: Financial disarmament, developing aid and the stability of the world monetary system

14. W. Leontief & F. Duchin: Worldwide implications of hypothetical changes in military spending

15. E. Regehr: The utilization of resources for military purposes in Canada and the impact on Canadian industrialization procurement

16. L. Taylor & R. Faini & P. Annez: Defence spending, economic structure and growth: Evidence among countries and over time

17. H. Tuomi & R. Väyrynen: Transnational corporations, arma-

ments and development

18. C. Vlad & M. Nicolaescu & V. Secares & D. Rusu: Disarmament and the new international order

19. H. Wulf: Transnational transfer of arms production technology

One of the contributions, "Worldwide Economic Implications of a Limitation on Military Spending" by Wassily Leontief and Faye Duchin, analyses the influence of hypothetical disarmament scenarios on the world economy. It is based on a global input/output model developed earlier for the United Nations and known as "The World Model". Here the model is used to calculate effects of different disarmament/development aid scenarios on production, consumption, employment, etc.

Leontief and Duchin experiment with differing assumptions concerning the evolution of military spending and development assistance. The most salient conclusion is that even a marginal reduction of military expenditure would permit a quite significant increase of development assistance. Assuming that world military expenditure would grow somewhat more slowly in the coming decades than present trends imply and that the industrialized countries would set aside a smaller portion of the military expenditure "reduction" to development aid, the amount of world development assistance could increase quite considerably as Figure 2.2. shows.

From Military Efforts to Development Assistance

There are thus several contributions to the UN project that discuss institutional measures to accomplish a connection between disarmament and development. Three kinds of disarmament funds are described: an official French proposal, a currency fund introduced by Lutz Köllner and a raw material price stabilization fund advanced by John Hösteland.

The object of all three funds is to channel resources released by disarmament or arms control measures from industrialized to developing countries. In the French proposal the arms race was viewed as a dual threat to mankind, both a threat to world peace and an economic threat, in that armaments consume vast amounts of resources urgently needed for the economic development of the Third World. Worldwide disarmament would alleviate or eliminate these threats. It was hoped, therefore, that the proposed fund would at the same time stimulate disarmament and development assistance.

The contributions by Köllner and Hösteland emphasize the development aid side of the fund schemes. Köllner also discusses the second order consequences of increased aid transfers. Hösteland outlines a scheme to even out the export earnings of less developed countries by

Figure 2.2. Additional Development Aid in Leontief-Duchin's Disarmament Scenario Compared with OECD Aid Forecast

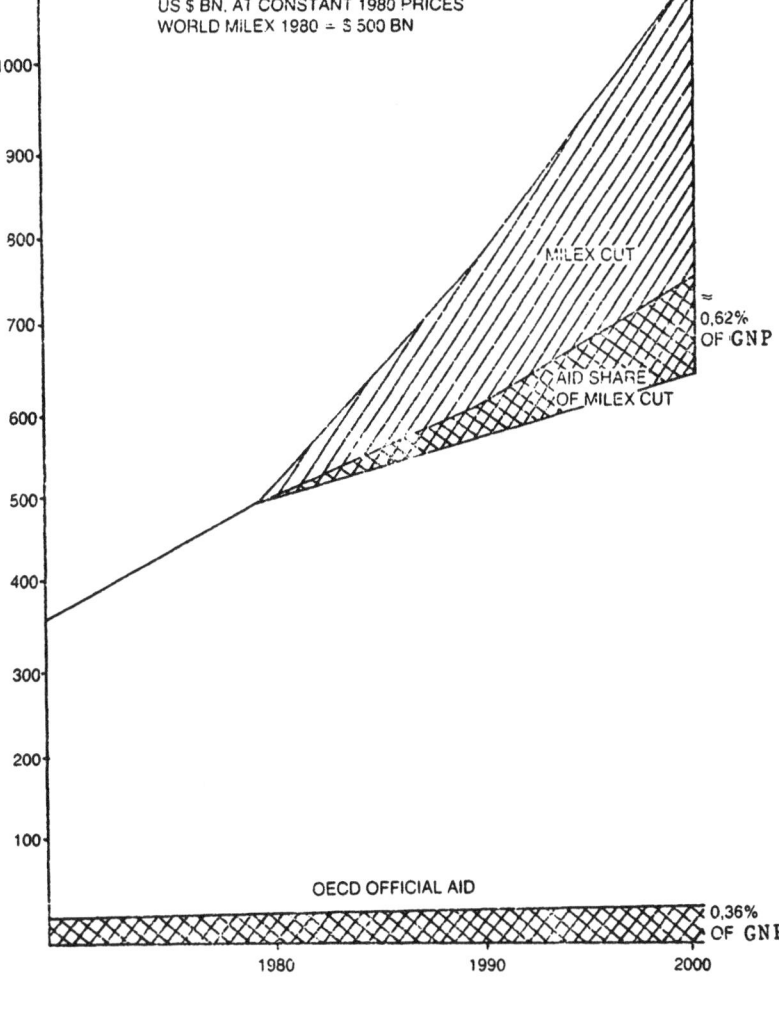

Sources: W. Leontief & F. Duchin, <u>Worldwide Economic implications of a Limitation on Military Spending</u>, Report prepared for the UN Group of Governmental Experts on the Relationship between Disarmament and Development, 1980 and <u>World Development Report 1980</u>, World Bank, Washington D.C. 1980.

counteracting price fluctuations of raw materials.

Problems in the process of disarmament are identified and discussed only in the French fund proposal and a couple of contributions specifically written as comments on the French proposal. Considering that disarmament measures cannot be carried out in conflict with the legitimate requirements for national security of sovereign states, the French proposal envisaged regional coordination of the disarmament process aiming "security at the lowest possible level of armament and military force", a level that was to be determined in negotiations between the states concerned. During an interim period, in anticipation of agreements on optimal regional security levels, the fund was to receive a one-time contribution of one billion dollars from the most heavily armed countries, in other words the great powers. Their individual shares of this contribution were to be proportional to certain objective criteria, such as the number of nuclear weapons and the quantity of certain military equipment.

In their review of the French proposal, Finn Sollie and Ove Narvesen object that an agreed regional level of armaments is not unequivocally tantamount to reduced armaments. An agreed level of arms might instead legitimize armaments up to this level for countries beneath it. Marek Thee, likewise commenting on the French proposal, views disarmament as an urgent issue. He regards the establishment of a fund with global scope as a first priority, but does not consider the concept of regional armaments levels a fruitful way for rapid action. Whether or not the French proposal is realistic, Thee argues that disarmament is a question of political will. The billion dollars of the interim fund, a mere 0.2 per cent of world military expenditure, is mainly symbolic. The problems of the fund are therefore political rather than technical. In line with this, Thee maintains that it is more important that the fund be brought about, than that the contributions be optimally shared by the participants.

Three alternative sources for financing the French fund are suggested of which only the first one presupposes some form of disarmament:

1. Reducing military expenditure
2. Taxing military expenditure
3. Taxing the arms trade

The critics of the French proposal maintain that in order to achieve widespread and immediate support for the fund, controversial forms of financing should be avoided, for instance arms trade taxes or contributions based on "objective" criteria such as numbers of nuclear weapons. Also, it is claimed that contributions to the fund in the form of a tax based on military expenditure would be seen as legitimising continued armaments. Further, the French fund proposal envisaged that all the resources released through disarmament measures would be transferred to developing countries, which might negatively affect the quest for disarmament in the industrialized countries. Sollie and Narvesen suggest that at the most 20 per cent of saved military expenditure should be channelled to development assistance.

Another point of contention is whether contributions to the disarmament fund should be counted against the United Nations official development aid goal of 0.7 per cent of GNP; in other words, should contributions be added to traditional forms of development assistance, as indicated in the French proposal. Thee, Sollie and Narvesen object that this would create opportunities for an undesirable substitution between disarmament fund contributions and traditional development assistance.

While the French proposal dealt primarily with the input side of new transfer mechanisms, Köllner and Hösteland emphasize the output side.

Köllner outlines a fund designed to forestall accelerated international inflation in conjunction with massive transfers of resources from industrialized to developing countries. Hösteland discusses how resources freed through disarmament might be utilized to stabilize export earnings for developing countries.

Köllner thus examines the unwanted side effect on the world economy of disarmament and a concomitant massive increase in development aid, namely drastically increased inflation. To ensure that transferred resources fulfil their purpose, Köllner argues that international inflation must be checked. Köllner proposes a fund channelling disarmament resources from rich to poor countries with the authority and the means to conduct global currency policy in order to stabilize the international currency system.

Hösteland's study of raw material price stabilization is motivated by the importance of this concept for a New International Economic Order. Lack of capital has so far prevented the implementation of this component of a New International Economic Order. Reducing world military expenditure is for Hösteland one way of generating the required amounts of capital to be used for accumulating buffer stocks of raw materials, where purchase and sale of such stock would be coordinated with the objective of stabilizing raw material prices. Somewhat simplified, the principle is to purchase when prices are falling and sell from the stock when prices are going up. Price fluctuations are therefore counteracted and the price level kept more stable.

Hösteland makes the point that it is not raw material prices as much as export earnings from raw materials that should be stabilized. With stable prices but large variations in production - in agriculture for instance - export earnings will fluctuate widely. These variations complicate economic planning, and the resulting uncertainty raises the interest rate and thereby investment costs in developing countries. The objective is rather to even out the fluctuations in export earnings and import expenditure, which would in turn create greater stability in economic planning and lower investment costs, as economic uncertainty diminishes.

Hösteland has constructed an econometric model of the raw material market and distinguishes in his presentation between different kinds of price fluctuations, with on the one hand, long-term changes due to the long-term evolution of supply and demand, and on the other, short-term changes due to speculation and deficient information.

Hösteland recommends that each country build up national raw material stocks with funds released through military expenditure cuts. These stocks could be coordinated under the auspices of a United Nations agency. This would be conducive to greater national security and would at the same time diminish the influence of transnational corporations on the development of raw material prices. A necessary prerequisite would be improved statistics for world trade in raw materials.

2.3. CONCLUSION

While there are certainly economic, technical, political and military problems associated with international disarmament, this summary has demonstrated ways in which at least some of these difficulties could be overcome. Yet in practice, the discussion of technical solutions is still in its infancy and the examples reviewed here are by no means the final word. The important point is that there should be continued discussion, also, of the practical steps along with the political dialogue. In the final analysis, of course, this is inevitably a political issue which can only be resolved in negotiations at the political level. But the practical questions, too, have to be faced.

Chapter Three

DEFENCE AND DEVELOPMENT: A CRITIQUE OF THE BENOIT STUDY*

Nicole Ball

3.1. INTRODUCTION

Although the industrialized-country members of the North Atlantic Treaty Organization (NATO) and the Warsaw Treaty Organization (WTO) remain by far the largest spenders on military-related activities, the share of the Third World in total defence expenditure has risen considerably over the last decades. Particular countries have been raising their defence expenditures at a rapid rate in recent years.(1) According to statistics produced by the United States Arms Control and Disarmament Agency (ACDA), about 30 per cent of the 90 Third World countries for which data were available spent more than 15 per cent of their national budgets for defence purposes in 1977 while approximately half spent over 10 per cent.(2) There are good reasons for suspecting that these figures understate the amount spent for security purposes in some of these countries and that the burden of developing nation military-related expenditures is even higher than these figures suggest.

What, however, is the impact of this burden on the development process? For the industrialized countries, it has been shown that high rates of economic growth, investment and employment are inversely related to high levels of military expenditure.(3) For the developing countries, the evidence is less clear. Resources devoted to one form of expenditure, such as military expenditure, cannot be used in other sectors, such as for investment in productive undertakings or in social services. Nonetheless, the argument is often made that military expenditure may have some net positive developmental effects. The study which is generally cited as supporting this connection is the one conducted by Emile <u>Benoit</u> for ACDA at the end of the 1960s.(4)

The original goal of the Benoit study was to determine what effect military expenditure has on the development process in Third World countries. Benoit, however, narrowed his field of inquiry soon after beginning the project to the effect of military expenditure on economic growth (defined as the expansion of gross domestic product, GDP). This choice was made because comparable data on "qualitative and structural changes (such as the rate of literacy, the share of GDP in manufacturing, or the share of GDP going into health and education programs)" were not available.(5) Benoit analyzed data from 44 countries and did one in-depth case study of India and several shorter ones for Mexico, Argentina, South Korea, Egypt and Israel. Although the Benoit report is frequently cited as showing that military expenditure does not have a negative effect on economic growth for developing countries, Benoit's actual conclusions are somewhat less precise.

> Thus we have been unable to establish whether the net growth effects of defense expenditures have been positive or not. On the basis of all the evidence we suspect that it has been positive, for the countries in our sample, and at past levels of defense burden, but we have not been able to prove this.(6)

There are, however, very good reasons for not accepting even this more cautious conclusion. Benoit's work can be criticized on two levels. First, even if one accepts the notion that regression analysis can reveal something significant about the relation between two processes as complex as armament and economic growth, there are many problems with the way in which Benoit defined the variables he used and the interpretations he placed on the conclusions obtained from his statistical analyses. The most important problems in this respect are related to the definition of foreign aid and the interpretation of its relationship to economic growth and military expenditure. Second, Benoit's suspicion that the net effect of military expenditure on economic growth has been positive did not particularly depend on the results of his regression analyses but on his assessment of non-quantifiable contributions made by military programmes to the civilian economy. On the one hand, the extent to which these unquantified factors are actually "growth-inducing", as Benoit claims, is debatable. On the other hand, even if some of these factors do promote growth, it is unlikely that very many of them were present simultaneously in the countries in Benoit's survey. Finally, as anyone interested in socio-economic development will know, rapid rates of economic growth often bear no relation to the distribution of a society's wealth, social equality or the promotion of self-sustaining economic growth.

Each of these problems will be considered in turn. In addition, the results of three recently concluded statistical analyses of the relationship between military expenditure and economic growth will be contrasted with the results produced by Benoit. In the final section, questions will be raised concerning the value of using macrostatistical analysis to explain the interaction of complex processes.

3.2. THE DEFINITION OF EXTERNAL RESOURCES

The original focus of Benoit's project was to have been on case studies but Benoit concluded shortly after beginning work that the available data were insufficient to produce the kind of detailed analysis necessary for the success of the case-study approach. He thus switched the project's emphasis to a macrostatistical analysis. Benoit obtained what he considered satisfactory data for 36 countries for periods of eleven to sixteen years between 1950 and 1965 and for eight countries for the six years between 1960 and 1965. Two time series were then set up. The first, the "A" series, included all 44 countries and used whatever data were available for them for the entire period 1950-65. The second, called the "B" series, also included all 44 countries but only analysed data for the years 1960-65.

The main variables used by Benoit in his statistical analyses were civilian gross domestic product (gross domestic product minus military expenditure), the defence burden (military expenditure as a percentage of civilian gross domestic product), growth rate (percentage increase in gross domestic product), bilateral (government-to-government) economic aid, and rate of investment (gross capital formation as a percentage of gross domestic product). As a first step, a simple regression analysis was run involving the defence burden and the growth rate. Rather than the anticipated inverse correlation between these two variables, higher defence burdens were found to be positively associated with higher economic growth rates for both the longer and the shorter time periods.

Benoit hypothesized that since there was no evidence of a systematic bias in the data which would account for this unexpected finding, the apparent correlation might be technically "spurious". That is, the defence burden might merely be acting as a proxy for some other variable which was in reality more closely linked with rising growth rates. The variable which Benoit decided to investigate in this respect was the inflow of external resources, specifically bilateral economic aid. It would, however, have been more correct for Benoit to have adopted a more inclusive definition of external resources. By using only bilateral economic aid, Benoit biased the outcome of his statistical analyses of the relation between defence burden, the inflow of external resources and economic growth in favour of the military component.

Benoit divided the foreign financial inflows available to Third World countries into four main categories. First was economic aid which included "official grants and loans whether these be bilateral (government to government) or multilateral (from international agencies) not directly tied to the transfer of military goods or services". Second came long-term private investment which was composed of "direct investment (with reinvested earnings), net portfolio and other long-term private investment, and guaranteed export credits". The third category was military aid (given the American acronym "MAP") which included "the transfer of military equipment or other military supplies or military services (particularly training) at no charge or at concessionary prices or terms of payment". Fourth were military transfer payments, "overseas military expenditures" of foreign governments (primarily the US due to data restrictions) in the country under study.(7)

Using these concepts, Benoit prepared four different estimates of foreign resources inflow. Bilateral economic aid was considered the most satisfactory quantity to use when testing whether or not the defence burden had acted as a proxy for external resource inflow in the simple regression analysis.

> Our analysis was directed toward understanding the extent to which external resources might be enabling recipients to carry heavier than normal defense burdens without correspondingly reducing their civilian investment and hampering their growth.(8)

....

> We later decided that total R (total aid) would be less appropriate to use for this purpose than R2 (bilateral economic aid) since R included private investment and foreign aid from international agencies, neither of which would be, in intention or in fact, related to the level of the recipients' defense programs. It also contained receipts of military assistance (MAP), and balance of payments earnings on military transactions, which though often related to the recipients' defense burdens were only in part a net inflow of economic resources substitutable for those diverted by the recipients into defense.(9)

Benoit appears to have switched purposes in mid-analysis, for surely the point of doing the multiple regression analysis was to discover which variable - the defence burden or the inflow of foreign resources - was more closely associated with <u>economic growth.</u> To ignore foreign private investment, multilateral aid and military assistance was to stack the deck in favour of the defence burden. It was particularly misleading to ignore the inflow of military aid, since for many of the fastest growing countries in Benoit's sample, military assistance accounted for an average of 50 percent of their foreign financial inflows.(10)

Benoit justified the exclusion of military assistance (MAP) in the following way:

> Most of MAP does not provide the recipient with additional <u>economic</u> resources or truly offset indigenous defence expenditures... the gift of military end-items of equipment and training can save the defense programs of LDCs large amounts of physical and financial resources.
>
> On the other hand, a considerable amount of equipment obtained under MAP would simply not be obtainable at all in the

absence of MAP, and the MAP recipients would simply get along with simpler or less equipment, etc., and often be relieved of costly maintenance as well.(11)

In view of the way in which Third World military expenditure has been increasing since the mid-1960s and the arms trade has been flourishing even in the face of cut-backs in the US Military Assistance Program, it seems somewhat divorced from reality to estimate that "a considerable amount of equipment and services obtained under MAP would simply not be obtainable at all in the absence of MAP, and the MAP recipients would simply get along with simpler or less equipment...". This assertion would have to be investigated on a country-by-country basis. In some cases it would turn out to be true. In many cases, it would not.

Benoit argued that multilateral aid and foreign private investment should not be included in the foreign resources variable since, unlike much bilateral economic aid, they were not "in intention or in fact, related to the level of the recipient's defense program". Indeed, Benoit suggested that these two types of inflows were, "if anything, discouraged by too high a defense burden".(12) To substantiate this generalization, he cited only a single case, the "reversal of the IBRD on financing the Aswan Dam in the fifties, which was related more or less explicitly to Egypt's diversion of potential exports to pay for large military imports from Czechoslovakia". Then, in direct contradiction to his own argument, Benoit asserted that "the IBRD was responding to a U.S. government decision not to supply another key segment in the total financing, rather than directly to Egypt's military decision".(13) The decisions of both the US government and the IBRD are most appropriately viewed in terms of East-West politics. The Czech arms deal was concluded only after the Egyptian government had failed to obtain an equally large arms package from the US. The Eisenhower administration had offered to conclude a smaller arms deal, but the size of the arms package proposed by the US government was not related to the belief that the cost of the weapons would interfere with Egypt's development efforts.

The issue here should not be why foreign financial resources are provided to Third World economies, but how much is given and to what extent these resources enable governments to maintain investment ratios favourable to economic growth. The stated reasons for providing foreign financial resources may, in any case, not have much to do with the uses to which those resources are put:

> Linking aid with development makes aid taking and giving respectable, but it is a bit of deception. Actually, in the Third World countries aid helps to sustain a total political and economic structure by lightening the fiscal burden on the rich and powerful and by financing ever-growing non-development expenditure on the bureaucracy, the army and the police and on various types of subsidies, all of which directly and indirectly

benefit the same rich and powerful...(14)

As this assessment suggests, much development assistance is used for non-investment purposes and the inflow of foreign resources cannot, therefore, be automatically equated with an increase in domestic investment rates or with increased economic growth as Benoit appears to have done. Rather, the effect that the inflow of external resources has on economic growth and development must be examined over time on a country-by-country basis.(15)

3.3. INTERPRETATION OF THE ROLE OF FOREIGN AID

Benoit's interpretation of the relationship between the defence burden, economic growth and foreign aid is equally problematic. He ran two multiple regression analyses, one using the longer "A" series data from 1950-65 and the second using the "B" series data from 1960-65, to determine whether bilateral economic aid had acted as a proxy for the defence burden in the initial simple regression analysis. For the "A" series, the defence burden did seem to be acting as a proxy for bilateral economic aid; in the "B" series, it did not.

One possible explanation of this statistical disagreement was that the findings from the "A" series were unreliable since that series did not include data for the same years for all countries. To test for reliability, a multiple regression analysis was carried out on a subset of the "A" series - the 27 countries for which thirteen years of data were available. This subset gave the same results as those from the entire "A" series and Benoit concluded that the results of the longer time series _were_ reliable. The extreme shortness (six years) of the "B" series also argued strongly in favour of using the results of the longer series.

In addition, despite Benoit's insistence that bilateral economic aid was the best measurement of the inflow of external resources, he did run regression analyses using other measurements. His assessment of substituting these values for bilateral economic aid was contradictory. In the introductory section of his study, Benoit asserted that each of the measurements produced more or less the same results.(16) Discussing the multiple regression analysis in depth, however, he stated that when more inclusive measurements of external assistance (such as total economic aid or total aid plus investment) were included in the multiple regression analysis, these resources emerged as even more closely associated with changes in the growth of the civilian economy than just bilateral economic aid. The argument in favour of a correlation between the defence burden and economic growth was thus weakened even more.(17)

Contrary to what one might have expected, however, Benoit did not at this point conclude that the apparent positive correlation between the defence burden and the growth of the civilian GDP was spurious.

Instead, he argued that the process by which multiple regression analysis determined whether or not one variable acts as a proxy of another variable is unsatisfactory for attributing causality. Benoit recognized that the use of regression analysis to attribute causality was an operation which would be considered suspect by many statisticians. Nonetheless, he wanted to "obtain enlightenment about cause and effect relationships" and proposed the following modification to his analysis. In multiple regression analysis, the relationship between two independent variables (in this case, defence burden and economic aid) is determined by the separate relationship that each of them has with the dependent variable (in this case, economic growth). Benoit argued that this "mechanical" procedure gave rise to misleading results and that "the substantive relationship between the independent variables themselves" should be taken into account.(18) The particular relationship that Benoit wanted to introduce here was the fact that countries which carried heavy defence burdens frequently received compensating foreign assistance from their major-power patrons.

When Benoit introduced this "attractive" power of defence burdens, he concluded that, although the defence burden may act as a proxy for bilateral economic aid to some extent, a significant cause and effect relationship between the defence burden and the growth of civilian GDP could not automatically be ruled out. He argued that accepting the apparent results of the multiple regression analysis for the longer and theoretically more reliable time series and saying that the defence burden acted as a proxy for foreign aid to an important degree,

> ... may oversimplify the reality and give a misleading final result if interpreted in a causal sense. For, while the primary causal flow was undoubtedly from R2 (bilateral economic aid) to B (defense burden), it is also likely that the willingness (or need) of certain LDCs to maintain extra large defense programs (which happened to suit the interests of foreign aid donors) was also a cause of their getting an exceptional amount of foreign aid, and these enlarged defense programs may have contributed to their economic growth, not only by attracting these additional external resources, but also in a more direct manner.(19)

Even if a country's willingness to adopt a particular defence posture does guarantee that it receives a much larger inflow of foreign resources than it might have under other circumstances and if these additional resources allow the country to improve its economic growth rate, this can in no way be interpreted as an indication that defence expenditure _per se_ leads to higher rates of economic growth. If foreign aid allows a country to maintain an investment rate sufficient to promote a high level of economic growth, then it is the foreign aid that has been "growth-inducing". To argue otherwise is to substitute arbitrarily one cause for another and to be wilfully misleading.

That Benoit was presenting a rather unrealistic argument is evident when the findings of his case studies are examined. The Indian case study, which was the most detailed one produced by Benoit, was considered particularly important, as it suggested or confirmed many of the hypotheses which Benoit tested in the course of his macro-statistical analyses. Of special interest within the Indian case study was the fact that two years of sharp rises in defence expenditure (1961-63), which resulted from deteriorating relations with China and the Sino-Indian border war, were associated - with a one-year lag - with two years of significant increases in civilian GDP (1962-64). To Benoit, this apparent correlation exemplified the connection which seemed to have been produced in the initial simple regression analysis: higher levels of defence expenditure appeared to be linked to higher rates of economic growth.

In an attempt to explain this apparent correlation, Benoit weighed up the positive and negative effects of military expenditure for economic growth in India. On the negative side were included the income-shift, productivity and investment effects of military expenditure as well as various opportunity costs (manpower, future industrial procurement, foreign exchange and services). Some of the opportunity costs were quite heavy, particularly those for industrial procurement and foreign exchange, and were deemed likely to get heavier should India expand its domestic production of weapons and/or engage in atomic research. Both of these latter activities have, in fact, been Indian policy for many years.

On the positive side, Benoit included increased aggregate demand and other "growth-inducing" inputs to the civilian economy such as the use of the armed forces in the construction of public works and the provision of substitutes for civilian goods and services by the military. Of greatest importance, however, was considered to be the inflow of foreign aid, largely from the Soviet bloc, which began in 1962 as a result of India's border conflict with China. Between 1962 and 1965, the Indian government received as aid about three and one-half times the amount of additional money it expended on the military. On average, this inflow of external resources amounted to $ 1.25 billion per year.

In direct contrast to an Indian analyst who used Benoit's discussion of the opportunity costs of Indian military expenditure to argue that higher military expenditure had had a negative effect on the Indian economy(20), Benoit concluded that the positive effects of Indian military spending outweighed the negative ones.

> The apparent inconsistency between the econometric and structural analysis, on the one hand, and the statistical analysis, on the other, was dispelled by a consideration of certain favorable growth effects of India's military crisis and the enlargement of the defense program it provoked. <u>The chief factor here, undoubtedly, was the vast inflow of foreign aid, which was sufficient to offset not only the full cost of the additional defense expenditures, but also to make a substantial contribu-</u>

tion to India's general economic development.(21)

The importance of external resources was also underlined in Benoit's case study of Mexico. Benoit concluded that a <u>very low</u> level of military expenditure had contributed to Mexican economic growth primarily because the military programme had <u>not</u> siphoned off considerable industrial-type resources and foreign exchange from the civilian economy and because the military had contributed to "maintaining public order... with the minimum use of scarce resources".(22) Benoit then went on to state:

> This does not imply, however, that if the defense program had been larger, it would have been still more favorable to growth. On the contrary, the main reason it appears to have had a net favorable effect is that it has been so small and economical in its use of resources.(23)

Most important, Benoit concluded that should Mexico raise its military spending, it

> ... would probably not receive a large increase in foreign aid to offset the real cost of a rise in defense expenditure, as did India... Thus, Mexico would probably not have the <u>important external resources offset to an enlarged defense expenditure which has been characteristically associated with the combination of high defense burdens and rapid growth rates in other countries.</u>(24)

3.4. THE UNQUANTIFIABLE, GROWTH-INDUCING INPUTS

Benoit hypothesized that high levels of military expenditure increased economic growth in developing countries not only "...by attracting... additional external resources, but also in a more direct manner". He spelled out a number of these "direct" benefits, the most important of which were the aggregate demand effects of military expenditure and the provision of inputs to the civilian economy. As will be discussed below, however, both the degree to which these factors are actually present in individual economies and their beneficial impact on development are debatable.

<u>Aggregate demand</u>: Developing economies frequently suffer from a substantial underutilization of resources. Benoit hypothesized that the decision to spend heavily on defence - generally because of some perceived threat to the state -"may lead a country to tolerate a more expensionary monetary (and/or) fiscal policy and a higher rate of price increase than it would otherwise find acceptable, and this may promote a more intensive utilization of available resources, thereby raising the growth rate".(25)

Benoit argued that prior to the war with China in 1962, India had been following restrictive monetary and fiscal policies and that this was reflected in part in the low level of growth in the Indian economy from 1950-61. The war with China was said to have stimulated the Indian government to expand its money supply, to raise its level of taxation and to carry a larger budgetary deficit. The effect of all this was, in Benoit's view, to cause an increase in the growth rate through the aggregate demand effect.(26)

These conclusions might be contrasted with the findings of Ved Gandhi, an Indian analyst who was also concerned to determine the effect of India's military burden on its development. He agreed that in war periods (1962-64, 1965-66, and 1971-72) the Indian government was able to raise its revenue substantially faster than it was in non-war times.(27) He also pointed out that periods involving wars and rising military expenditure can have some useful short- and long-term fiscal effects. In the Indian case, however, Gandhi believed that no such effects could be documented. The long-term effect occurs when a government which has raised its level of taxation to help finance additional military expenditure maintains taxation rates at the higher level while military spending declines or levels off. "In the Indian context", however, "wars certainly do not seem to have had much ratchet effect because... our revenue effort slackened substantially after every war". The short-run effect is the ability of the government to take some of the extra revenue collected for the military effort and use it for non-military, development purposes. This did not occur in the Indian case either, according to Gandhi. "A very large part of the increased revenue effort during the war years, and surprisingly even in later years, was always absorbed by defence."

What is more, Gandhi demonstrated that the Indian government was progressively less willing to finance development-oriented expenditure during the 1960s. The central government's development outlays fell from 3.28 per cent of gross national product (GNP) in 1961-62 to 2.60 per cent of GNP in 1970-71 while military expenditure was raised from just under 2 per cent of GNP in 1961-62 to 3.07 per cent in 1970-71. Furthermore, development expenditures as a percentage of total (central government and state) expenditures fell from 62.5 per cent in 1961-62 to 55.3 per cent in 1970-71. Even if some development benefits did arise out of increased military expenditure, it is very unlikely that they would have exceeded - or even equalled - the effects of having maintained government expenditure for development at the earlier levels.

<u>Military inputs to the civilian economy</u>. There are two major problems associated with Benoit's second growth-inducing category, the inputs provided by military expenditure to the civilian economy. The first of these relates to the degree to which the civilian economy <u>actually</u> benefits from these inputs and the second relates to the <u>form of</u> development they imply.

One sort of growth-inducing input discussed by Benoit was the provision of substitutes for goods and services that the civilian economy would otherwise have had to provide and the consequent liberation of resources within the civilian economy for the purpose of investment. It seems unlikely that the civilian economy will benefit in this way if the costs of providing the military substitutes are more than that of producing the same goods and services within the civilian economy. That military substitutes are not always cheaper was demonstrated by Benoit's own study of India, where he estimated that the cost to the Indian army (and ultimately to Indian society) of producing its own food on military farms was more than one-third greater than the cost of procuring it from the civilian economy.

Another input cited by Benoit in this category was the educational and vocational training received by military conscripts, which supposedly enables them to make a greater contribution to the civilian economy once they are demobilized than they were able to make prior to their military service. The first question to ask here is whether a country has volunteer or professional armed forces. If the latter, the benefits of training to the civilian economy will be considerably reduced. Benoit made much of the fact that vocational training received in the military gave former conscripts skills that would make them particularly attractive to industrial establishments or which would enable them to become "model" farmers. There are several points which must be considered here.

In countries where the urban unemployment rate is quite high, the benefits of such training are negated if the ex-serviceman is unable to find a job. In countries where inequitable social structures have led to the concentration of wealth and productive resources in the hands of a small rural elite, it is unrealistic to assume that simply because a person has training which should turn him into a "model" farmer that he will therefore have the necessary access to land, water, credits and other agricultural inputs to become one. Furthermore, at the case-study level, reality can and does diverge from theory. For example, Benoit pointed to military training programmes which enabled Indian soldiers to become skilled in printing, bookbinding, blacksmithing, plumbing, the metal trades and so on, but it turned out that these were <u>post-release</u> training programmes rather than skills that the servicemen had been able to acquire in the normal course of their military careers.(28) Similar questions can be posed about a second category of growth-inducing inputs stressed by Benoit - goods and services which the civilian economy is said to be unable to provide for itself, such as the construction of public works or various scientific and technical services.

Finally, there are the truly "unquantifiable" effects of military programmes on the civilian economy proposed by Benoit: the promotion of nation-building, of modernization, and of national security. The notion that militaries, by bringing together people from all corners of culturally, ethnically and religiously diverse countries, teaching them to work together and to speak a common language, are a force for "nation-building" is one that has been popular among proponents of increased military expenditure in the Third World. In fact, militaries frequently work to accentuate cultural, ethnic and religious differences and thus contribute to intra-societal conflict and, upon occasion, to national disintegration.(29)

The notion of the military as a force for modernization raises the question of the sort of development strategy envisaged by Benoit. Benoit's preference of using economic growth as a proxy for development situates him in the mainstream of the 1950s and 1960s development thought. According to the conventional development strategy of that period, the goal of "development" was to increased GNP, primarily through industrialization, and to do so by attracting foreign aid and investment and by adopting an export-oriented industrial policy. The expectation was that the benefits of the GNP growth generated in this way would "trickle down" to the mass of the population from the "modernizing elites" in both the industrial and the agricultural sectors who would be given the responsibility for investing society's resources. The modern industrial sector - which would be created through the import of foreign aid, investment and technology - would increase the demand for agricultural products. The resultant increase in rural incomes would expand the market for industrial goods.

It is now clear that this strategy has failed to promote self-sustaining socio-economic development and has, instead, led to the progressive impoverishment of large numbers of people in the Third World. One reason behind this failure is that the resources concentrated on the "modernizing elites" often did not "trickle down"; rather they were used to enrich the already better-off elites. Furthermore, the emphasis on "modern" industry led to attempts to set up large-scale, capital-intensive industries which employ too few people and often fail to produce the sorts of goods needed to promote self-reliant development. It is also increasingly clear that all too often this inequitable and unsuccessful "development" strategy has been imposed on the populations of Third World countries through the use of organized violence. In other words, military troops, paramilitary groups and increasingly well equipped police forces have been employed by governments to break the opposition of the poor to their continued exploitation rather than to promote development through "nation-building" or security against external threats.

What, then, do Benoit's growth-inducing inputs amount to? Some no doubt do exist at different times in different countries but it seems unlikely that enough of them operate simultaneously in individual countries to produce the growth-inducing effects on the scale predicted by Benoit or to do so consistently. Careful examinations at the individual country level are required before any statements can be made about the contribution of these sorts of inputs to Third World development. Furthermore, to the extent that these inputs do induce economic growth, it is likely only to be growth that hinders, rather than promotes, self-reliant socio-economic development.

3.5. THE TEST OF TIME

Benoit recognized that the relationship which he believed to have identified between the defence burden and economic growth was not immutable and could be subject to change over time. Specifically, Benoit predicted that if countries began to produce their own weapons or to purchase large amounts of sophisticated armaments abroad, their economies would be negatively affected, due to the diversion of foreign exchange and industrial-type resources from civilian investment. It was noted earlier that Third World arms imports have been increasing over the last decade. The domestic production of weapons in Third World countries has also been on the rise.(30) Despite these trends, Benoit published a paper in 1978 in which he reiterated the major findings of his 1971 study.(31)

It seems likely that one reason why Benoit felt able to repeat his earlier findings was that he made no use of newer, post-1965 data. Two recent studies which have explored the link between military expenditure and economic growth using post-1965 data have reached conclusions quite different from Benoit's. One of the studies re-ran Benoit's simple regression analysis between the defence burden and economic growth and found no statistically significant result for a sample of 90 countries for the years 1965-76 when the sample was considered as a whole. Broken into groups of countries, the "OPEC countries plus Oman" showed a significant positive correlation between defence burden and eonomic growth while all other groups failed to show a positive correlation or actually showed a significant negative correlation (notably, the "most seriously affected" countries).(32) The second study, using data from 1965-73 for 50 countries, concluded that "no systematic relation is obvious" between military expenditure and economic growth rates, just the sort of result one would expect from a simple statistical analysis of a large number of economically diverse countries.

> There are two constraints on the growth process - one structural, and the other resource based. The military's social role may contribute to structural changes which stimulate growth, but military expenditure allocates scarce resources away from productive civil investment, fails to mobilise substantial savings by itself and appears to depress the rate of saving. The extent to which the military has a positive structural effect and whether or not this dominates the negative effect on resource allocation are questions best answered by studies of individual countries within an historical perspective.(33)

Equally important is a third recent study which explored the relationship between the defence burden and various economic indicators for 69 countries using data for some or all of the period 1952-70.(34) It thus provided considerable overlap with Benoit's "A" series which ran from 1950-65. Once again, the conclusion reached by the newer study was exactly the opposite of Benoit's: high rates of military expenditure in developing countries were associated with low rates of economic growth.

Also revealing are the results obtained by two of these studies when the relationship between defence burden and economic growth in India was examined. Benoit's entire case study of India was based on the initial discovery of an association between two years of heavy defence expenditure (1961-63) and two years of rapid economic growth (1962-64). It has been argued here that the primary variable identified by Benoit as causing the positive relationship between defence burden and economic growth - the inflow of foreign resources -acted directly on the economy and not "indirectly through" the defence burden as hypothesized by Benoit. For the arguments in Benoit's case study to have any validity whatsoever, it would be necessary for periods of heavy defence expenditure to continue to be associated with periods of rapid economic growth. The study by Brzoska and Wulf, which used data for 1965-76, found no such association. The study by Faini, Arnez and Taylor, which used data for 1951/52-1971/72, found a significant negative correlation between India's defence burden and its rate of growth.(35)

3.6. CONCLUSIONS

The failure of more recent statistical analyses to confirm Benoit's findings is not surprising since, as it was explained above, Benoit's own statistical analyses should have led him to conclude that the level of defence burden did not provide a good explanation of the rate of economic growth for developing countries. At the same time, it must be recognized that the methodology employed by Benoit was a poor way of attempting to assess the relationship between military expenditure and Third World development. This relationship is simply too complex and too varied for a macrostatistical analysis bolstered by a few selected facts from a half dozen cursory case studies to shed much light on the way in which it works. Benoit himself recognized the diversity of the relationship but he drew a rather unexpected conclusion from this information.

> That there is an extraordinary diversity not only in the surrounding circumstances but - as we shall see - in the dynamic interaction between defense and development in LDCs is the chief single conclusion of our country studies. This conclusion tends to support the need for statistical analysis of a wider sample such as we have presented in earlier chapters, since the bewildering variety of situations encountered in individual cases will not readily lead to clear-cut uniform conclusions on the basis of what happened in particular cases.(36)

It is somewhat of a mystery why anyone would think that "bewildering variety" should necessarily produce "clear-cut uniform conclusions". One reason why the conventional development strategy of the 1950s and 1960s failed to promote self-reliant socio-economic development in the Third World is precisely because it ignored economic, ecological and social variety and attempted to impose a "uniform" development strategy on all Third World countries. The same tendency to ignore reality allowed Benoit to draw up his list of "growth-inducing" inputs in which he placed so much faith. Had Benoit concentrated more on case studies and on the reality of each situation and less on regression analyses, he would have found it considerably harder to hypothesize about the beneficial nature of these inputs.(37)

One of the striking things about the Benoit study is that it exists in a socio-political vacuum. East-West politics and competition do not exist. Nor are they presumed to have any effect on conflict patterns or military expenditure levels in the Third World. Inequitable social structures in individual countries are not mentioned. To be fair, Benoit did mention a number of

> ... additional adverse growth effects of defense programs that are not readily quantifiable: shifting governmental attention and emphasis from economic to military problems as defense programs become relatively more important; increased danger of a takeover of political power by the military as the military becomes a relatively larger part of the governmental apparatus...(38)

Yet it is precisely the build-up of the military and the encouragement of the armed forces to become politically and economically active which are the most important aspects of the relationship between the process of armament and the process of development. Not only can statistical analysis not deal with these kinds of issues but Emile Benoit showed himself unwilling to consider them seriously. The only way in which an understanding of how the process of armament affects socio-economic development will ever be reached is if case studies which are founded on the socio-economic, political and ecological realities of individual countries are undertaken.

NOTES AND REFERENCES

* A slightly longer version is to be published in a future issue of <u>Economic Development and Cultural Change</u> in 1983. Reprinted by permission of the University of Chicago Press.

The author would like to thank Milton Leitenberg, Swedish Institute of International Affairs, Michael Brzoska, University of Hamburg, Ron Smith, University of London, Ann Schulz, Clark University, Göran Ohlin, University of Uppsala, and Mario Carranza, University of Mexico for their comments on portions of this paper. The research for this paper was carried out under a grant provided by the Nordiska

Samarbetskommittén för Internationell Politik in Stockholm and is also part of a project on the Role of Military Expenditure in the Development Process, funding by the Swedish Agency for Research Cooperation with Developing Countries (SAREC).

1. Stockholm International Peace Research Institute, World Armaments and Disarmament: SIPRI Yearbook 1980, London 1980, pp. 8-11.

2. Figures derived from United States Arms Control and Disarmament Agency, World Military Expenditures and Arms Transfers, 1968-1977, Publication 100, Washington, D.C. October 1979, pp. 32-69.

3. R.P. Smith, Military Expenditure and Capitalism, Cambridge Journal of Economics, March 1977, pp. 61-76; Kurt W. Rotschild, Military Expenditures, Exports and Growth, Kyklos, Vol. 26, 1973, pp.804-15; Michael Boretsky, Trends in US Technology: A Political Economist's View, American Scientist 63, January-February 1975, pp. 70-82; and Ruth L. Sivard, World Military and Social Expenditure, 1977, Leesburg, Va. 1977, p. 13.

4. First released as Emile Benoit, with Max F. Millikan and Everett E. Hagen, Effects of Defense on Developing Economies, 2. vols, ACDA/E-136, Center for International Studies, MIT, Cambridge, Mass. June 1971. It was subsequently published in book form as Emile Benoit, Defense and Economic Growth in Developing Countries, Lexington, Mass. 1973.

5. Benoit, with Millikan and Hagen, p. 10.

6. Ibid., p.6.

7. Definitions from ibid., pp. 181-82.

8. Ibid., p. 54.

9. Ibid., p. 116.

10. See tables on pages 91 and 190 in ibid. The importance of foreign resource inflow to Benoit's conclusion is also pointed out in Kenneth E. Boulding, Defense Spending: Burden or Boon, War/Peace Report, Vol. 13, No. 1, 1974, pp. 19-21, and Everett E. Hagen, An Observation on the Benoit and Dorfman Analyses, International Development Review No. 1, 1972, pp. 14-15.

11. Benoit, with Millikan and Hagen, p. 188.

12. Ibid., p. 184 (emphasis in original).

13. Ibid., ftn 1 (emphasis added).

14. "Aid: For What?," Economic and Political Weekly 15, 5. July 1980, p. 1114.

15. Some development analysts have argued that foreign aid is beneficial to developing economies even if it is not totally devoted to investment purposes. Others have argued that the evidence indicates that the opposite is true. For examples of the first opinion, see Hollis B. Chenery and N.G. Carter, Foreign Assistance and Development Performance, American Economic Review 63, May 1973, pp. 459-68, and Gustav F. Papanek, The Effect of Aid and Other Resource Transfers on Savings and Growth in Less Developed Countries, Economic Journal 82, September 1972, pp. 934-50. The second viewpoint is set forward in Keith B. Griffin and J.L. Enos, Foreign Assistance: Objectives and Consequences, Economic Development and Cultural Change 18, April 1970, pp. 313-27, and Thomas E. Weisskopf, The Impact of Foreign Capital Inflow on Domestic Savings in Underdeveloped Countries, Journal of International Economics 2, February 1972, pp. 25-38.

16. Benoit, with Millikan and Hagen, p. 56.

17. Ibid., p. 119.

18. Cf. ibid., pp. 111-12.

19. Ibid., p. 112.

20. Ved P. Gandhi, India's Self-Inflicted Defence Burden, Economic and Political Weekly 9, 31. August 1974, p. 1493.

21. Benoit, with Millikan and Hagen, p. 280 (emphasis added).

22. Ibid., pp. 341, 432.

23. Ibid., p. 343.

24. Ibid., p. 344 (emphasis added).

25. Ibid., p. 131.

26. Ibid., p. 243.

27. The following discussion is drawn from Gandhi, pp. 1485-94.

28. Benoit, with Millikan and Hagen, p. 244.

29. On this point, see Cynthia Enloe, Ethnic Soldiers: State Security in a Divided Society, Harmondsworth, UK, 1980, and Police, Military and Ethnicity: Foundations of State Power, New Brunswick, NJ, and London 1980.

30. On this topic, see Peter Lock and Herbert Wulf, Register of Arms Production in Developing Countries, Study Group on Armament and Underdevelopment, University of Hamburg, mimeo, 1977, and World Production of Conventional Armaments, Stockholm International Peace Research Institute, pp. 41-56.

31. Emile Benoit, Growth and Defence in Developing Countries, Economic Development and Cultural Change 26, January 1978, pp. 271-80.

32. Michael Brzoska and Herbert Wulf, Rejoinder to Benoit's 'Growth and Defense in Developing Countries' - Misleading Results and Questionable Methods, Study Group on Armament and Underdevelopment, University of Hamburg, mimeo, c. 1979.

33. Dan Smith and Ron Smith, Military Expenditure, Resources and Development, Department of Economics, Birkbeck College, University of London, April 1980, mimeo, pp. 17-18. This study was one of those commissioned by the UN Expert Group on Disarmament and Development as part of the research exercise initiated by the UN Special Session on Disarmament in 1978.

34. Riccardo Faini, Patricia Arnez and Lance Taylor, Defence Spending, Economic Structure & Growth: Evidence Among Countries & Over Time, MIT, Cambridge, Mass. October 1980, mimeo. This study was commissioned by the UN Expert Group on Disarmament and Development.

35. Brzoska and Wulf, pp. 5-6; and Faini, Arnez and Taylor, p. 14.

36. Benoit, with Millikan and Hagen, p. 329. It has already been pointed out that the authors of one of the more recent statistical studies reached precisely the opposite conclusion: the role of the military in the allocation of resources is best illuminated "by studies of individual countries within an historical perspective". Smith and Smith, p. 18.

37. On the uses of and problems associated with macrostatistical analysis, see Smith and Smith, pp. 42-48, and Dan Smith and Ron Smith, Reader Feedback: Letters to the Editor - Reflections on Neuman, Orbis 23, Summer 1979, pp. 471-77. In their Orbis article, Smith and Smith point out that macrostatistical analysis, if properly used, can help to identify similarities among a large group of countries which can then be further examined through case studies (on both an individual country and a regional level). While this is ostensibly the approach employed by Benoit, it has been demonstrated that he failed to accept the results of his statistical analyses where they contradicted the theory that defence burdens produce greater economic growth and failed to substantiate his theorizing, despite the inclusion of a half dozen case studies of the final report.

38. Benoit, with Millikan and Hagen, p. 24.

II

MILITARIZATION AND ARMS PRODUCTION
IN INDUSTRIALIZED COUNTRIES

Chapter Four

ECONOMIC PROBLEMS OF ARMS PRODUCTION IN WESTERN EUROPE - DIAGNOSES AND ALTERNATIVES

Michael Brzoska*

4.1. ARMS PRODUCTION WITHIN NATO - COMPETITION BETWEEN MONOPSONISTS

Arms production in Western Europe is - from a strictly military point of view - no longer indispensable. NATO planners regularly envisage "Blitzkrieg" scenarios of war in Central Europe, including large-scale destruction of industrial capacity.(1) In the event of war, arms production will therefore not be possible. Only prepositioned equipment would be useful - and it could have been purchased anywhere.

Nevertheless, discussions on arms production in Western Europe hardly ever involve the arms industry - instead the issues discussed are standardization, co-production, technological dependence on the US, etc.(2) If the basic agreement on the necessity of arms production in Western Europe or in one of NATO's European member countries is challenged, the existence of arms production capacity is usually justified along the following lines:

> "The existence of our arms production industry remains essential for the national economy and the social balance of our countries and for the maintenance of our position in the world and to secure our independence."(3)

Arms production is thus viewed as an instrument to achieve a variety of aims. It is part of a large array of policy issues: military policy, employment policy, foreign trade policy, technology policy, foreign policy, social policy.(4) In other words: strictly military considerations represent but one factor in the ensemble of apprehensions supporting both directly and indirectly the accumulation of arms.

As policies in Western Europe continue to be legitimized in the national "theatres" - despite the EC, despite NATO - this multi-functionality of arms production is operated within the nation states.

Unemployment in West Germany, so decision-makers suggest, can only be reduced if arms production in West Germany is expanded; the French balance of payments will improve, so it is argued, only if arms are exported from France, etc.

On the other hand, arms production is technologically and financially outgrowing national possibilities. The Tornado programme costs will be about US $ 40 billion in total,(5) and the Leopard II programme costs are about US $ 4 billion.(6) All in all, the "third generation" of weapon systems for the "Bundeswehr" will absorb US $ 50 billion, more than the FRG can pay if the current allocation of resources is maintained.(7)

At present, arms producers in the larger European countries - Britain, France, the FRG and Italy - are competing with US arms-producing companies in almost all market segments: aircraft, helicopters, ships, electronics, etc.(8) But this is an extremely limited form of competition, a competition of monopsonists in the capitalistic North with an export outlet towards the South. It is monopsonistic because in Western Europe we generally find a single company in any one country manufacturing one product as a supplier and the state on the demand side. Intrastate competition is limited to research and design.(9) Interstate competition is limited to some export markets.

Therefore, it comes as no surprise that standardization/co-production etc. within NATO is proposed as a solution to the economic problems of arms production in Western Europe. We will try to show that the standardization/co-production discussion is not a solution, but rather a placebo.

But first we will explore the parameters of arms production in the four large West European countries, also presenting an estimation of the current and future levels of production overcapacity in Western Europe. This excess capacity is at the core of the economic problems that mark the situation of arms manufacture in Western Europe and is an extremely important push-factor for arms exports to the Third World.

In conclusion we shall take a look at some alternatives for the future of arms production in Western Europe, which finally leads us to consider a joint conversion fund for Western Europe as an urgent priority.

4.2. ARMS PRODUCTION OVERCAPACITY IN WESTERN EUROPE

The Demand for Arms in Western Europe(10)

The demand for arms in Western Europe can be estimated starting from budget figures. To arrive at the national effective demand, the import of armaments is subtracted from that part of the budget spent on procurement.

It is rather difficult to supply the data for this relatively simple definition. The two sets of data that could primarily be used here are:

1. data on procurement from the national budget and imports figures from ACDA(11);
2. data on "equipment expenditures" from NATO(12) and weighted import data from ACDA or SIPRI.(13)

The first set of data is of little practical use as procurement is very differently defined in the various relevant countries. NATO does not publish figures concerning procurement expenditures. NATO figures are only available for the much more limited category of "equipment expenditures". Figures for the years 1970, 1973, 1976 and 1978 from this source are presented in Table 4.1., columns 1 and 2. The import figures are from ACDA, weighted subjectively by estimating the part of "equipment" in imports. The table reveals that while equipment expenditures grew steadily in almost all cases, imports did not. The share of "equipment expenditures" procured in the countries is generally rising. France and increasingly Great Britain and Italy are almost independent of arms imports.

The evidence gathered from Table 4.1. is supported by information contained in Table 4.2., columns 1, 2 and 3. Military expenditures increased on an average of 3 % per annum throughout the 1970s in Western Europe. The "equipment expenditures" as a part of military expenditures also rose, again with an average of 3 % yearly. These two growth rates add up to a remarkable annual increase in real "equipment expenditures" of about 6 % throughout the 1970s. Arms imports remained almost constant throughout this period.

Extrapolation of these trends shows military expenditures to be growing at the agreed NATO rate of 3 % per year.(14) There are, however, indications that a number of NATO members in Western Europe will not increase their military expenditures this much.(15) Another factor may be much more limiting, though: the share of military expenditures earmarked for "equipment expenditures" can probably not be raised to a level above the current 18 %. A projection of the current growth rate of 3 % in the "equipment expenditure" level would result in a ratio that is not compatible with current financial needs to maintain and operate armed forces in Western Europe. Thus, a 6 % increase in "equipment expenditures", as in the past, seems unlikely in the 1980s.

Even if the NATO governments increased their military expenditures by 3 %, the growth rates for "equipment expenditures" will not grow at a rate as high as in the 1970s.

Data on military procurement programmes also suggest a slower increase in the demand for heavy armaments in the 1980s. French

Table 4.1. Arms Production in Western Europe

Production of "equipment", price bases: 1975

Country	1 "Equipment expenditures" in mio US $	2 Import of "equipment" in mio US $	3 National demand for "equipment" in mio US $	4 Export of "equipment" in mio US $	5 Production 1-2+4 in mio US $	6 5:1 in %
Belgium						
1970	167	67	100	4	104	62
1973	141	35	106	41	147	104
1976	220	55	165	77	198	90
1978	324	35	289	70	359	111
Denmark						
1970	103	12	81	0	92	89
1973	131	8	123	4	127	97
1976	176	36	140	0	140	80
1978	164	35	129	2	131	80
France						
1970	2,320	8	2,312	355	2,667	115
1973	2,500	11	2,489	665	3,154	126
1976	2,720	25	2,695	797	3,492	128
1978	3,000	20	2,980	1,010	3,990	133
FRG						
1970	2,060	174	1,886	156	2,042	99
1973	1,815	451	1,374	100	1,474	81
1976	2,020	265	1,765	376	2,131	105
1978	2,170	145	2,025	473	2,498	115
Italy						
1970	534	42	492	22	514	91
1973	765	101	664	100	764	100
1976	621	85	536	158	694	112
1978	773	65	708	324	1,032	134
Netherlands						
1970	353	81	272	5	227	78
1973	250	15	235	56	291	116
1976	460	49	411	39	450	98
1978	573	75	498	35	533	93

Table 4.1. Continued

Country	1 "Equipment expenditures" in mio US $	2 Import of "equipment" in mio US $	3 National demand for "equipment" in mio US $	4 Export of "equipment" in mio US $	5 Production 1-2+4 in mio US $	6 5:1 in %
Norway						
1970	136	30	106	0	106	78
1973	98	40	58	18	76	78
1976	108	29	79	18	77	71
1978	203	35	168	5	173	85
United Kingdom						
1970	1,590	252	1,238	495	1,733	109
1973	2,181	251	1,980	664	2,594	119
1976	2,472	204	2,268	680	2,948	119
1978	2,496	75	2,421	924	3,345	134
Total Nato-Western Europe						
1970	7,263	666	6,597	1,091	7,534	104
1973	7,881	912	6,969	1,653	8,582	109
1976	8,797	748	8,049	2,795	10,130	115
1978	9,703	485	9,218		12,061	124

Methods and Sources: "equipment expenditures": NATO Review 1/1978 and 1/1981; ACDA, World Military Expenditures and Arms Transfers 1969 - 1978, Washington. D.C. 1980

France: estimate;
arms transfers: ACDA data multiplied by 6 to represent equipment;
transfer data for France: Jacques Isnard, La France marchand d'arms. Le Monde, Dimanche, 4.11.1979;
United Kingdom: Lawrence Friedman. The Future of the British Armaments Industry. London 1979, Statistical Index, table 22

arms equipment, though older on average than that of its NATO partners, will not be replaced before the early 1990s. In Britain, the procurement of an additional main battle-tank is hampered by cost-problems. In the FRG, orders to procure the third generation weapon systems have almost ceased. The naval industry enjoyed a boom in the late 1970s with procurements of new and large surface-ships, such as the through-deck cruiser in the United Kingdom, frigates in Belgium, the Netherlands and the FRG. The British naval industry will profit from TRIDENT submarine production, while the situation for the navies in the other countries is dubious at the moment. In the past few years, the aerospace industries in Germany, Italy and the U.K. have been occupied in the TORNADO programme, the Dutch, Belgian and Norwegian industries in the F- 16. From 1984 onwards the aerospace industry will probably have difficulties in selling new aircraft to West European governments. The French airforce will continue to purchase new aircraft, probably including a new fighter aircraft, Mirage 2000.

Growth rates will be much smaller in the 1980s - even though the renewed "alarmism" in the West has led to an increase in military expenditure planning in the early 1980s. But in many countries the financial limits are becoming clearly visible.

The "Safety Valve": Arms Exports

While arms procurement expanded rather rapidly in the 1970s - expecially in the second half of the 1970s - the increase in arms exports was even faster. According to ACDA, which underestimates arms exports in general,(16) arms exports of West European NATO members increased by 19 % per annum in real terms. Excluding 1971 and 1972, when arms exports were extremely low, the growth rate between 1973 and 1978 was 8 %.(17) SIPRI data reveals a similar real increase: 12 % yearly.(18)

With aggressive advertising campaigns, new arms promotion media, government support and special financial arrangements, European arms producers were able to seize a large part of the world armament market, especially in the Third World.

Defining arms production exceeding national demands as over-capacity, we can see from table 4.1. that there has been over capacity in French and British arms industries throughout the 1970s with an upward trend. Italy and the FRG moved from a situation of reliance on imports to one of overcapacity in the 1970s. The arms industries in the smaller countries produced less than those countries procured. But in NATO-Western Europe (including France) there is a large and increasing volume of overproduction. In 1978 it amounted to at least one fifth of total production.(19)

It is doubtful whether we can extrapolate the trend in arms exports of the second half of the 1970s. In many parts of the Third World,

Table 4.2. Statistical Estimation of Arms Production in Western Europe

	Military expenditures NATO-Europe and France in 1000 Mio 1977 US $	"Equipment expenditures"[1] %	Arms imports in 1000 Mio 1975 US $	Arms exports in 1000 Mio 1975 US $
1970	51.0	n.a.	1.6	0.8
1971	53.4	13.3	1.8	0.8
1972	56.3	14.9	2.0	2.5
1973	57.2	14.7	1.4	2.6
1974	59.5	14.1	1.5	2.2
1975	60.2	14.8	1.7	2.3
1976	61.5	15.5	2.3	3.3
1977	62.7	16.5	1.8	3.7
1978	64.1	17.3	1.4	3.9
1979	70.7	17.6	n.a.	n.a.
trend estimates:				
1985	81.6	20.8	1.7	5.9
1990	94.9	23.2	1.7	8.8

1) Weighted according to the following key: Belgium, FRG (7x), Italy (2x), Netherlands, United Kingdom (6x); corresponding to weights of military expenditures

Sources: NATO Review, 1/1977, 1/1978, 1/1979, 1/1981;
ACDA, World Military Expenditures and Arms Transfers 1968-1977, Washington, D.C. 1980

indebtedness has reached very critical levels. The World Bank, which probably does not include armament debts in its data,(20) estimates that the debt ratio might reach 11.3 % in poor and 28.6 % in middle-income oil-importing Third World countries by 1985.(21) This is viewed as very critical in general, and will spell disaster for some countries. Oil-producing and other resource-abundant countries will probably still be able to purchase weapon systems on a large scale. But many of these even now have weapon arsenals that they cannot operate on their own.

In the future there might be a tendency in the Third World to buy cheap and instant(22) weapons. The export success of Israeli and Brazilian "simple" weapon systems supports such assumptions. It remains to be seen whether Third World arms exporters will replace European suppliers in some markets. West European arms manufacturers are not likely to be able to increase their exports in the 1980s as they have done until now. This trend could only be reversed if an already discernible pattern becomes common practice: arms exports financed by the exporter itself. West German companies in particular seem to have won contracts by providing the customer with prefential loans guaranteed by the West German government.(23)

In addition, West European armament firms have few opportunities to increase exports to the United States. The "two-way-street" of exports across the Atlantic within NATO still equals a road with heavy traffic in one direction (towards Europe) and a few pedestrians in the other (towards the US). Although the "Buy American Act" can be waived in favour of standardization and interoperability by the US authorities, in reality it rules US procurement decisions.(24)

Summarizing, it seems that "safety valve" arms exports operate in an increasingly dense atmosphere. The valve will ony function if West European governments push exports even harder than they have done in the past.

Arms Production Capacity

The measurement of production capacity is extremely difficult. There are various concepts of production capacity (economic and technical) and several ways to measure capacity empirically, e.g. questioning of firms, estimation of labour force or embodied capital. No such data on the armament industry is available. Here we must rely on sketchy information supplied by armament producers. This information hints strongly at large unutilized capacities unevenly spread over the various branches of the arms industries and time.

This should be no surprise, as arms procurement is cyclical. Once a weapon system is completely delivered, there is no national demand for several years. The typical replacement cycles are around 15 years for aircraft, over 20 years for tanks and over 20 years for warships.

Arms producing firms usually face problems in filling these procurement gaps. Conversion towards non-military work involves technical, economic and financial problems.(25)

Thus, there is strong evidence that there has been unused capacity in arms production in Western Europe in the 1970s in addition to overproduction (defined above as production exceeding national demand). It is difficult to estimate accurately the volume of this idle capacity, but our guesstimate is that the overproduction capacity of approximately 25 % in 1978 was at least doubled by idle capacities. Before the increase in arms production in the latter half of the 1970s, idle capacities were probably much larger.

When set against probable demand in the 1980s, this leads to the conclusion that the economic problems of arms production in Western Europe will increase markedly. There will be no growth comparable to the rates of the 1970s, which was already marked by unused capacity and overproduction. On the other hand the growth factors inherent in arms production(26) exacerbated by the political factors that govern arms production in Western Europe will force all countries into a deliberate policy for arms production in Western Europe in the 1980s. All suggested policies will have to deal with a number of problems, the most important economic ones being employment in arms production, arms exports as a contribution to balance of payment difficulties and arms producing firms. The following data covers these three problem areas:(27)

a) Employment
There are differing employment estimates from various sources for each of the countries in Western Europe.(28) The estimate presented here is our own, based on comparable data. We start out from the procurement budget(29), subtract arms imports and add arms exports. These figures are related to value added in manufacturing. Under the restriction that capital intensity in arms production is similar to capital intensity in manufacturing(30), we can estimate the employment effect by multiplying the total number of employees in manufacturing with the calculated ratio of arms production in total manufacturing. The underlying assumption is that value added per employee is the same in arms manufacturing and general manufacturing.

The figures given in Table 4.3. cover the four largest countries in Western Europe and represent the 1977 level.

Our estimate of the total number of employees engaged in arms production in 1977 in Britain, France, Italy and the FRG adds up to 1.5 million. Because of lower productivity, Britain is estimated to have the largest number of employees (630,000), followed by France (436,000), the FRG (436,000) and Italy (161,000). These figures have probably not changed much since

Table 4.3. Employment in Arms Production: France, Britain, FRG, Italy, 1977

Country	(1) National procurement in 1000 mio	(2) National procurement as percentage of total manufacturing output	(3) Estimated employment generated by national procurement expenditures, 1000	(4) Arms exports in 1000 mio
FR Germany	DM 9.7	2.20	199	DM 1.9
France	FF 26.5	5.15	285	FF 14.0
United Kingdom	£ 2.2	6.24	462	£ 0.8
Italy	L 900	1.50	85	L 800

Country	(5) Arms exports as percentage of total manufacturing output	(6) Estimated employment generated by arms exports, 1000	(7) Total estimated employment in arms production, 1000
FR Germany	0.43	39	283
France	2.72	151	436
United Kingdom	2.26	168	630
Italy	1.33	76	161
			1.465

Sources: column 1: national budgets
columns 2 and 5: Statistische Jahrbücher der Bundesrepublik Deutschland, various years
column 4: see Table 4.1.
column 3 and 6: ILO, Yearbook of Labour Statistics 1978, Geneva 1979.

1977. If productivity increases in arms production are similar to the general trend in manufacturing, employment grew at a rate of 2 % per year in the late 1970s.(31)

b) Arms exports
Especially for France and Italy, arms exports are a most important balance of payment factor. Table 4.4. shows that although arms production does not amount to more than 3 % of total exports anywhere, arms exports are of importance. This shows the ratio of arms exports to engineering products exports (Standard International Trade Classification Group 7) of 7.2 % for France, 3.3 % for Italy and 6.8 % for Great Britain.(32)

c) Arms producing companies
An empirical investigation into arms production in Western Europe yielded the result that 93 firms had a turnover of DM 100 million of more in 1977.(33) This represents the top half of arms production in Western Europe (Table 4.5.).

A considerable number of the major West European arms producing firms are also among the largest companies in Western Europe. Thomson-Brandt's arms production turnover alone, for example, would put it among the 125 largest West European companies.

Table 4.4. Arms Exports as Percentage of Total Exports of Machinery and Transportation Goods (SITC 7), 1978

	Arms exports in 1000 mio US $	Arms exports in % of exports	Arms exports in % of exports in SITC class 7
France	2.0	2.5	7.2
United Kingdom	1.8	2.5	6.8
FR Germany	0.9	0.6	1.3
Italy	0.6	1.1	3.3

Sources: column 1: see table 4.1.
column 2: ACDA, World Military Expenditures and Arms Transfers, 1969-1978 (corrected figures)
column 3: UN Economic Commission for Europe, Bulletin on World Trade in Engineering Products, New York, 1980.

Arms production is most concentrated in France, followed by Great Britain and Italy, although the differences are not very large. The six largest companies shared 35 % of all arms production in France, 31 % in Great Britain, 30 % in Italy and 29 % in the FRG in 1977.(34)

A most significant political factor is the share of arms production in total turnover, which indicates the dependence on arms production. It also helps to explain resistance towards conversion strategies. The degree of dependence upon arms production is rather high in Italy, France and Great Britain and slightly lower in the FRG. There are only a few firms that are exclusively arms producers. This label has to be tacked to the French state arsenals (DTCN, GIAT), the British Royal Ordnance factories and some smaller firms. While the dependence on arms production is most significant among the ten largest companies but less so for the smaller ones in Italy, France and Britain, the 10 largest companies in the FRG are less dependent than other smaller companies (See Table 4.7. and the tables in the appendix).

A factor which facilitates conversion, at least for financial considerations, is the integration of arms producing factories into larger business units. 55 % of the French, 50 % of the German, 45 % of the British and 40 % of the Italian companies with a turnover in arms production of over DM 100 million in 1977 were among the 463 largest manufacturing companies in Western Europe (with a turnover of above DM 1,000 million in 1977).

Public ownership in the arms industry may be considered to offer a potential means of controlling arms production. Table 4.8. shows the high degree of public ownership in Italy as well as in the British and French arms industry in 1977. But in these countries public ownership is highly concentrated at the "top" of the arms industry and is much less significant if sub-contractors and smaller arms producers are considered. The large companies in particular are state-owned. The obvious exception is the FRG, where only one of the 10 largest arms producing companies is state-owned (DIAG).

To summarize: the main difference between the large arms producing companies in Western Europe is the high level of state ownership in Britain, Italy and France. With regard to concentration, the existing differences are marginal. In general, the West German arms industry is more integrated into the economy than the respective arms industries in Britain, Italy and France.

In most cases, public ownership was a result of financial difficulties of private arms manufacturers.(35) Only in a few

Table 4.5. Arms Production Companies in Western Europe
Turnover in 1977 above 100 Million DM

	Name of company	Country	Rank among the largest manufacturing companies in Western Europe	Turnover in arms production
1	Thomson	France	55	3,000
2	SNIAS	France	(121)	2,955
3	British Aerospace	United Kingdom	141	2,500
4	Dassault	France	178	2,390
5	DTCN	France	(198)	2,300
6	Siemens	FR Germany	9	2,000
7	Rolls Royce	United Kingdom	172	1,900
8	Örlikon-Bührle	Switzerland	171	1,617
9	GIAT	France	(313)	1,490
10	AEG	FR Germany	28	1,400
11	GEC	United Kingdom	56	1,360
12	MBB	FR Germany	259	1,080
13	VFW	FR Germany	280	1,020
14	Philips	Netherlands	5	1,000
15	SNECMA	France	301	1,000
16	Krauss-Maffei	FR Germany	(46)	705
17	Vickers Ltd	United Kingdom	296	-615
18	Royal Ordnance Factories	United Kingdom		+580
19	Bofors	Sweden	438	580
20	Fincantieri	Italy	(272)	+560
21	MTU	FR Germany	441	550
22	Fabrique Nationale	Belgium		530
23	Rheinmetall	FR Germany		520
24	MAN	FR Germany	74	+500
25	British Leyland	United Kingdom	45	+500
26	Plessey	United Kingdom	197	500

Table 4.5. Continued

Name of company	Country	Rank among the largest manufacturing companies in Western Europe	Turnover in arms production
27 Saab-Scania	Sweden	97	+500
28 Agusta-Gruppe	Italy		-500
29 Rijn/Schelde/Verolme	Netherlands	194	-500
30 Matra	France		+475
31 Snia Viscosa	Italy	167	-470
32 Westland	United Kingdom		467
33 SNPE	France		-452
34 DIAG	FR Germany		-441
35 Diehl	FR Germany	375	430
36 Racal	United Kingdom		422
37 Vosper	United Kingdom		379
38 Dornier	FR Germany		370
39 Fiat	Italy	6	+365
40 EMI	United Kingdom	145	362
41 Thyssen	FR Germany	(110)	+330
42 Turbomeca	France		322
43 FFV	Sweden		+330
44 G3S	France	337	+300
45 ITT	Western Europe		300
46 Steyr	Austria	318	-300
47 Creusot	France	98	-294
48 Oto-Melara	Italy		287
49 Ferranti	United Kingdom		266
50 Decca	United Kingdom		266
51 Panhard	France		-262
52 HDW	FR Germany	378	+250

Table 4.5. Continued

Name of company	Country	Rank among the largest manufacturing companies in Western Europe	Turnover in arms production
53 Eidgenössische Militärwerkstätten	Swizerland		250
54 Blohm & Voss	FR Germany		250
55 Dynamit Nobel	FR Germany		+235
56 IWKA	FR Germany		235
57 Renault	France		225
58 Aeritalia	Italy		+221
59 CIT - Alcatel	France	196	-210
60 Swan Hunter	United Kingdom		+200
61 KHD	FR Germany	118	200
62 Volvo	Sweden	64	-200
63 SEP	France		-196
64 Dowty	United Kingdom		195
65 Manurhin	France		-188
66 Selenia	Italy		-182
67 Hunting	United Kingdom		180
68 Lucas Industries	United Kingdom	135	171
69 Wegmann	FR Germany		-165
70 Cable & Wireless	United Kingdom		157
71 IMI	United Kingdom	(258)	-155
72 SABCA	Belgium		-152
73 Perkin-Elmer	Western Europe		150
74 PRB	Belgium	43	150
75 LM Ericsson	Sweden	129	-150
76 ZF	FR Germany	240	150
77 MaK Maschinenbau GmbH	FR Germany		150

Table 4.5. Continued

Name of company	Country	Rank among the largest manufacturing companies in Western Europe	Turnover in arms production
78 Luther Werke	FR Germany		145
79 Sperry Rand	United Kingdom		140
80 Smiths Industries	United Kingdom		130
81 IABG	FR Germany		130
82 Aermacchi	Italy		-126
83 Yarrow	United Kingdom		124
84 Rohde & Schwarz	FR Germany		120
85 DAF - Van Doorne	Netherlands		+110
86 Crouzet	France		108
87 Dunlop Holdings	United Kingdom	(93)	104
88 Heckler & Koch	FR Germany		100
89 Kongsberg Våpenfabrikk	Norway		+100
90 Lürssen-Werft	FR Germany		+100
91 Alfa Romeo	Italy	(184)	+100
92 Daimler-Benz AG	FR Germany	8	100
93 FEG	FR Germany		100

Source: Appendix

Table 4.6. Concentration in West European Arms Industry

Largest companies	FR Germany % of total arms production turnover	France % of total arms production turnover	Italy % of total arms production turnover	United Kingdom % of total arms production turnover
1	8.5	7.9	6.2	10.4
3	19.1	22.0	17.3	24.0
6	28.9	34.6	29.8	31.0
10	36.9	38.6	36.8	38.4

Source: Appendix

Table 4.7. Dependence on Arms Production

Arms production as % of total company turnover	FR Germany number of companies	France number of companies	Italy number of companies	United Kingdom number of companies
+75-100 %	7	6	4	6
+50-75 %	7	2	6	4
+25-50 %	5	6	1	6
+10-25 %	2	1	1	3
under 10 %	9	3	2	5
total number of companies	30	18	10	24

cases has a specific public policy to nationalize arms production led to public ownership. The nationalization of the largest private military companies in France by the Mitterand Government is an exception in this respect.

Policy Alternatives for the 1980s

To summarize our presentation so far it can be noted that:
- mainly because of intra-industrial factors, but also due to the large increases in arms exports, production capacity has exceeded the national demand for arms;
- neither arms exports nor national procurement will sustain the 1970s growth rate of arms production in Western Europe throughout the present decade;
- if arms production grew by about 3 - 4 % because of productivity increases in the range of 4 - 5 % yearly, employment in arms production in Western Europe would drop by up to 30,000 employees per year;
- the highly concentrated and partially highly dependent arms industry in Britain, France and Italy must - despite a high degree of public ownership - be viewed as a decisive factor against all efforts towards conversion due to its concentration, its generally low degree of diversification and the resulting dependence on arms production.

There are several ways that the problem of overcapacity in arms production in Western Europe can be handled. Among them are:

a) a "free market" policy towards procurement, resulting in large-scale redundancies in arms production in Western Europe;
b) an increase in procurement, despite strong financial constraints;
c) an increase in arms exports, despite market saturation;
d) standardization/co-production;
e) conversion programme to decrease arms production capacities.

Alternative a) is not compatible with an employment-oriented regional and structural policy. The number of redundancies would be high. Such a policy would also be strongly objected to by the military and arms producing companies.

Policy b) prevails at the moment, but it is doubtful whether it can be sustained through the economic and financial crises pending in the early 1980s. This policy runs counter to detente policy. Procurement because of industrial pressure clearly indicates that internal, not external, factors govern the armaments process.

The same economic problems apply to policy c). Those countries that are most dependent on arms production do not have the financial means to expand exports substantially through subsidy (France, Britain, Italy). The one country capable of doing this, West Germany,

Table 4.8. Arms Production Companies with Public Ownership (Majority of Stock, Votes etc.)

	FR Germany		France		Italy		United Kingdom	
	N	Arms production turnover of companies with public ownership in % to arms production turnover in same group of companies	N	Arms production turnover of companies with public ownership in % to arms production turnover in same group of companies	N	Arms production turnover of companies with public ownership in % to arms production turnover in same group of companies	N	Arms production turnover of companies with public ownership in % to arms production turnover in same group of companies
among the 10 largest companies	1	5.1	5	55.8	8	81.1	4	54.5
among companies with arms production turnover above 100 mio DM	4 of 30	8.0	7 of 18	52.8	8 of 10	81.1	6 of 24	45.6

is not equally dependent on arms production and arms exports.

Thus, it seems that policies a) to c) are neither acceptable nor feasible. Points d) and e) will be reviewed in greater detail in the following chapters of this paper.

4.3. THE ISSUE OF STANDARDIZATION/CO-PRODUCTION(36)

Placebo Standardization/Co-production

The competition of monopsonists has led to a situation of large overcapacities and highly subsidized prices for weapon systems.(37) Permament cost overruns have - ever since the establishment of NATO - given rise to discussions on standardization, inter-operability and co-production within NATO. The discussions have come in waves, reaching their peak in the latter half of the 1970s.(38) At the beginning of the 1980s, the issue has been obscured by Western "alarmism" over the Soviet military build-up and in the light of co-production "failures" such as the MRCA Tornado.(39) But the issue will certainly re-emerge when the cost problems re-surface.

It is also seen as a way to deal with the overproduction capacities. It has to be realised that co-production procurement has been the exception in the past. Although standardization is claimed to be on the increase, de-standardization is what has actually taken place. When standardization occured, it happened because of specific rationalities, most of them connected with technology policies,(40) financial problems(41) or intra-alliance policy.(42) But co-production offers no solution. While this insight seems to have guided the actual procurement profile within NATO, official rhetoric continues as before. In view of observable reality, the continuing support to co-production has to be judged as a placebo for the perceived problems.(43)

For the analysis of why co-production will remain the exception within NATO, at least two levels of analysis have to be distinguished:

- interest groups within nation states
- interstate competition

Problems within Nations

On the first level, the following actors should be considered:

1. The military
    The military is chiefly interested in a swift and continuous supply of modern weapon systems suiting their doctrine. Standardized weapons and standardized doctrines would, according to most military arguments, foster the military strength of the NATO alliance. The military also hopes to

receive more weapon systems when costs are cut through co-production. But the military in the respective NATO states have observable doctrinal differences(44), e.g. different mobilization systems, differences in training and available manpower skill, in-compatible procurement cycles, etc.(45) The military's position towards co-production is thus open.

2. Government and legislature

    These actors should show serious interest in cost saving through standardi-zation or the acquisition of weapon systems off the shelf. On the other hand, the multi-functionality of arms production is recognized at this decision-making level: workers and local communities are worried about jobs, the Central Bank is concerned with the balance of payments, and interest groups stress the "spillover" effects of military technology in several industries. All three of these "side-effects" are dubious, but for policy-makers they are usually presented as clear-cut. Finally, co-production can be used for example to offset political difficulties. This was the case with the British/French arms production accords in the early 1960s.

3. Arms industry(46)

    The spin-offs of arms production are heavily underlined by firms in arms production. This can only be done convincingly, however, when the firm produces in a given country, employs in that country and also retains technology gains for that country. For this reason, multi-national companies encounter problems in entering the armament market in Western Europe, unless they work with clearly distinguishable national subsidiaries. Therefore, the trend, once envisaged by many, towards European multinational armament firms has not been the overriding one. Instead, concentration has proceeded mainly within the various countries. Cooperation across borders - at least those of the three major producing countries, Great Britain, France, FRG - still lies mostly on a project basis. Capital links are the exception.(47)

    The arms industry will be in favour of projects if the alternative is no project at all; it is clearly against them, however, if they cause a decrease of regular production.

Thus we find no clear-cut trend towards greater co-operation in West European arms production. All actors have interests in co-production as well as interests working against it, these being summarized in Table 4.9. Here, we can note that co-production hinges mainly on political and economic (including technology) issues. As there is a direct trade-off between cost saving and employment problems, co-production agreements seem much more likely in times of financial difficulties or when a serious, large-scale military threat is perceived. Co-production seems most unlikely in situations of high unemployment and technological competition. As shortages of government funds and

high unemployment co-exist today, the aggregation of interests as regards co-production can be summarized as follows:
Co-production is less likely when it is more necessary; when it is easier to achieve, it is not as necessary.

The Inter-State Level

More information is introduced by adding the second level of inter-state confrontation and cooperation. The technological capacities of arms production vary rather noticeably in the various West European countries. The British arms industry produces weapons along almost the entire spectrum of systems. But the competitiveness of British products is - with a few exceptions - low. The British arms industry, 30 years ago on an almost equal footing with the American,(48) is still capable of technological break-throughs,(49) but it lacks the financial strength to take advantage of its possibilities. Both at the industrial and governmental level, the cost-saving argument is thus overriding, leading to a willingness to cooperate if funds are offered.

France, where the arms industry was rebuilt in the 1950s with considerable US assistance, began to strengthen its arms industry on a national level after de Gaulle came to power. This led to an arms industry with substantial technological inefficiencies, but high international competitiveness in some lucrative market segments.(50) Although sceptical of co-production, French officials are ready to agree on co-production schemes offering technology gains.(51)

The West German arms industry was launched with the help of co-production and license schemes especially from the US. Although dependence on technology is high in certain areas(52), German arms producers were quick to learn, and developed highly competitive products of their own. Because of a rather restrictive export control practice, the industry could not exploit all of the advantages of its competitiveness on the world market. The disadvantage is often overcome through co-production, as co-produced weapon systems are not subject to German laws. Unlike French officials, German officials are usually very much in favour of co-production, but have withdrawn a number of times because of employment and technology considerations.(53)

The Italian arms industry is heavily dependent on foreign technology, especially US technology. This applies not to aircraft production, but also to tanks and ordnance. The Italian arms industry has been most successful in export markets by combining technology from various sources, often on a somewhat lower level than usual for NATO purposes.

Arms production in the smaller West European states is much more limited and is competitive only in small market segments.(54)

Table 4.9. Summary of Intra-National Interests in Co-production of Weapon Systems within NATO

		Technology	Alliance-Politics	Arms Production Output/Employment	Government Finance
Military		(Want the most modern weapon systems when they have the need)	Want weapons suiting their special doctrines; want intra-alliance cooperation	(Want close contact with arms industry)	Are interested in large production runs of modern systems
Governments		Are interested in technology gains; do not want to lose technology monopolies	Want national production base; want to keep NATO together politically	Interested in more national production/ employment	Want to save money for other purposes
Arms industry		Want technology gains; are afraid of losses of technological advances	(Want to stay independent; are interested in multinationalising)	Interested in increased orders	(Multinational projects are more difficult to control by national governments)
Co-production	likely	If technology can be gained	If NATO has to be strengthened	(If there will be no production without co-production)	If co-production will result in lower costs
	unlikely	If technological advance will be at stake	If national base or intra-NATO-alliances have to be strengthened	If co-production will result in less output	direct trade-off
Forms of co-production		technological	political		financial

Table 4.10. Some Indicators of the Economy and Arms Production within NATO

1	2 GNP (1977)	3 Military expenditures (1978)	4 Output of arms industry (1976)	5 Personnel working in R&D (1975)
		in % of total		
USA	53	59	69	55
FRG	14	12	6	15
France	11	11	11	13
UK	7	8	9	9
Italy	6	3	2	3
Netherlands	3	2	1	3
Belgium	2	3	.6	1
Denmark	1	1	.4	.3
Norway	1	1	.2	.3
other European NATO	2	1	..	.1

Sources:
(2) OECD, National Account Statistics
(3) Bundesminister der Verteidigung, Weissbuch 1979, s. 271; Nato-Brief 1/79, s. 31; France estimated
(4) Basically, this is calculated by adding up expenditures on heavy equipment and the arms trade balance for heavy equipment: source for expenditures: Nato- Brief 1/79, for arms trade balance: US Arms Control and Disarmament Agency, Military Expenditures and Arms Transfers, 1967-1976, Washington 1978, Afrique Defense 9/78, Hansard 24.1.1977, all trade figures multiplied by .6 to estimate heavy equipment
(5) OECD, Committee for Scientific and Technological Policy, Trends in Industrial R&D in Selected OECD Member Countries 1967-1975, Table I. 1., Annex 1, mimeo, Paris 1978.

This brief description of arms production in West European states can be supplemented with the data gathered in Table 4.10. Here, the overriding importance of the US arms industry within NATO is highlighted. The US share in NATO arms production is much higher than the US share in GNP or military expenditure. The same holds good for the US share in stock of technology, measured by personnel working in research and development. The US dominance is due to the very low level of US arms imports and its high level of exports.(55) Western Germany in particular, with its large arms imports and comparatively small exports, "lags behind" when compared with the US. The French and British share in arms production output is approximately equivalent to their shares in GNP, military expenditures and R & D. The smaller member states of NATO, again, have arms production shares that are "too small".

Results of the Standardization "Game"

It seems that rivalry, especially between Britain, France and the FRG has hindered co-production in the past and will do so even more in the future. The larger general economic and financial potential of the FRG now balances with the larger potential in arms production in Britain and France. In this situation co-production becomes less predictable than it has been in the past. Co-production will continue to exist, but only when one of these states is financially incapable of funding a national programme.(56) The small states buy what seems to be most cost-effective and connected with the most offset work. French, British and German policies are directed towards the maintenance of technological and industrial capacities. Co-production will be only the last resort.

There is, to illustrate the point, only one major project in which French, British and German firms cooperate.(57) The other standard showcases for co-production are bilateral or multi-lateral with a number of junior partners. The Dutch "Defensieraat" constructed a "co-production index" and concluded:

> "Nevertheless, the cooperative coefficient within NATO is rather low. The number of countries participating in NATO multi-national projects average 3.6. There have to be at least two countries to realise cooperation and the alliance counts 15 members, which proves that from an empirical point of view the cooperative coefficient is indeed rather low."(58)

Cooperation, in summary, will only occur if necessary, not if possible. The necessity can be political, but it will mainly be financial or spurred by the desire to overcome technological backwardness.

In a very crude manner we can tabulate the two last criteria for the four countries under consideration:

Capabilities	France	GB	FRG	Italy
Financial	-	-	+	-
General technology	+	+	+	-
Arms technology	+	+	-/+	-

A minus sign indicates that, in general, cooperation with another partner (this can of course be a US company) is necessary to carry out a project. More minus signs might be expected in the future, as projects become more and more expensive and financial means are unlikely to expand proportionally.

An increasing US dominance in certain fields (electronics, components) has to be added. But these pressures towards more co-production will probably be offset by a factor which will considerably qualify the tabulation above: the economic crises of the 1980s throughout the Western capitalist economies.

Thus, we do not see how "placebo" standardization could become a valuable prescription for the future.

4.4. THE PROPOSAL FOR A JOINT CONVERSION FUND IN WESTERN EUROPE

Of the policy choises mentioned above e) remains to be reviewed. Conversion programmes involve economic problems. In the short run, employment relocation into other occupations will be unavoidable and costly. But financial savings are possible through reduction in military expenditure. Here we encounter a very important role for state demand management. Even more difficult to remedy would be the problems linked with the balance of payments. Here, there is no economic agent that could balance incomes from arms exports. A converted industry would probably have difficulties in competing with established exporters of machinery, transportation equipment or other goods envisaged as a result of conversion. We are left with the impression that conversion will encounter strong opposition in those very countries where it is most desirable, because it is here that the largest overcapacities exist.

This conclusion is, however, solely based on short-run economic considerations. In the long run, as has been shown in numerous studies, arms production hampers economic development and growth.(59) In Western Europe, it is precisely those countries with large arms industries, i.e. Britain, France and Italy, that have severe economic problems. A more penetrating analysis would be required, though, to establish a causal relationship here.

In Great Britain and Italy, employees earn a noticeably lower Gross National Product per head than their colleagues in Western Germany

Figure 4.1.　　　World Market Shares of Trade in Machinery and Transportation Equipment (SITC Class 7)

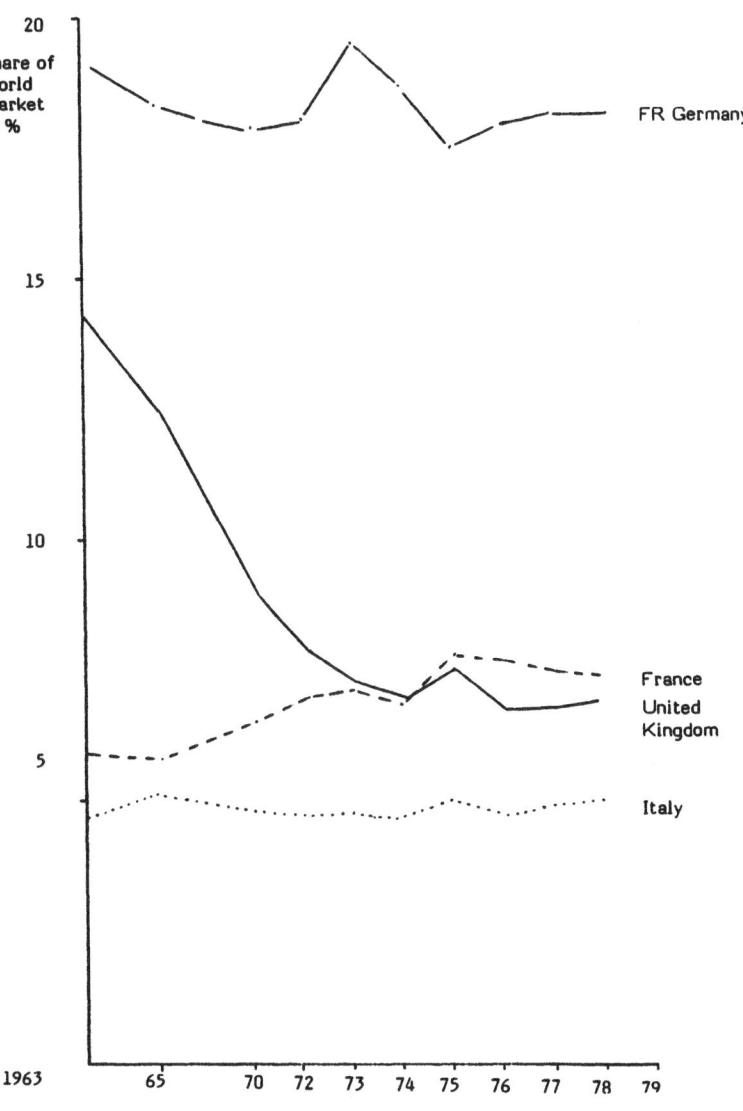

Source:　UN European Economic Commission, Bulletin of World Trade in Engineering Products, New York, 1980

and France.(60) This emphasizes the lower productivity per worker in Britain and Italy. The problem in France is not the lack of productivity and, thus, competitiveness on the world market, but the size of the manufacturing sector. The share of manufacturing in the French economy is smaller than the corresponding ratios in the FRG, Britain and Italy. The French industrial sector seems competitive from the productivity point of view, but vulnerable to conversion because of its lack in size.

These two factors, in addition to several others not mentioned here, express themselves in international competitiveness, easily measured in world market shares in SITC Class 7 (machinery and transport equipment). These commodities probably cover most items envisaged for conversion. We can easily detect from Figure 4.1. that France, Britain and Italy are far less competitive in this vital sector of the world market than the FRG. It is impossible for us to assess in detail here to what degree arms production has contributed to this situation. But we can conclude that conversion in Western Europe is particularly desirable (because of long-term economic considerations) where it is most difficult to achieve (because of short-term economic problems) and less necessary where it would be easier to accomplish (the FRG).

This analysis leads us to recommend a joint conversion fund on a West European scale.(61)

This fund should be financed primarily by the savings achieved by reduced military expenditures and conversion in the FRG. A part of these savings should be used for overcoming the larger conversion problems in France, Britain and Italy. The short-run burden would be shared among the West European partners. Political and economic opposition in France, Britain and Italy could be weakened. The long run benefits of conversion in all West European countries should then be distributed: the flow of funds could be directed towards the Third World by using the available increase in productive capacities for civil means to help fight poverty in underdeveloped countries in the Third World.

While the basic mechanics of such a conversion fund are quite obvious from our analysis, namely a shift of resources from the FRG to the other countries in the short run and the establishment of a development aid fund by all countries in the long run, we are not in a position to outline further details here. These details would have to be based on a more thorough study on the particular difficulties to be encountered in overcoming resistance to conversion in the individual countries. Still, we think that, for instance, the UN Expert Committee on Disarmament and Development should be aware of the political and economic impetus such a joint conversion fund could have. Within the EC, the idea of a joint conversion fund should also be considered. There are already policies for agriculture and backward regions within the EC. As has been shown, arms production will most probably become a common trouble-maker in the future, so why not have a joint conversion policy?

NOTES AND REFERENCES

* The resesarch for the data that went into this was financed by the German Foundation for Peace and Conflict Research (DGFK) with a grant to Peter Lock, Dan Smith and Herbert Wulf. The data was gathered by Michael Brzoska, Peter Lock and Herbert Wulf.
This paper thus presents joint work, put together by one member of the Arbeitsgruppe with the help of the other two.

1. Consider e.g. the following citation: "But in the nuclear age, and especially in relation to European security, the ability to build up production in time of war is now irrelevant to security." Roger Facer, The Alliance and Europe: Part III, Weapons Procurement in Europe - Capabilities and Choices, Adelphi Papers, No. 108, International Institute for Strategic Studies, London 1975, p. 13.

2. See for instance the various reports prepared for NATO, the West European Union and the European Parliament in Strasbourg. Standardization and co-production are also nationally discussed; see for instance: Government of the Federal Republic of Germany, White Paper on Defence 1979, Bonn 1979.

3. This is a quotation from: Assembly of Western European Union, A European Armament Policy Symposium, March 3/4, 1977, page 17, by the President of the WEU, Nessler.

4. The multi-functionality approach is to be found for instance in: Peter Schlotter, Rüstungspolitik in der BRD, Beispiele Starfighter und Pahntom, Frankfurt 1976.

5. Wehrdienst, 793/81- 23.3.81, gives a figure of 22,203 million DM, as of 3.12.1979 for the FRG alone.

6. Wehrdienst, 793/81- 23.3.81, gives a figure of 7,600 million DM, as of 31.12.1979.

7. Wehrdienst, 793/81- 31.12.81 (60 DM billion for major weapon systems). The financial problems of the Bundeswehr were intensively discussed in Western Germany and in NATO in 1981. Constant coverage is given in 'Aviation Week and Space Technology'.

8. Exceptions are nuclear weapons, except for France, electronics in Italy and the FRG or aircraft engine technology in Italy and the FRG. But there are also market segments not covered by

US companies: small submarines, small frigates, etc. Also some arms production in Western Europe depends very heavily on US technology e.g. for electronics or even capital, as in the case of Italy.

9. For a very forceful presentation of the limitation of competitiveness within West German procurement, see the thesis of Bruno Köppel. A very short account of his views is to be found in: International Defense Revue 1, 1980.

10. Arms production in this context is limited to procurement of weapon systems and their parts, maintenance, repair and research and development. Infrastructure investments, fuels etc. are not included.

11. US Arms Control and Disarmament Agency, World Military Expenditure and Arms Transfers, Washington, the edition for 1968 -1978, Washington, 1980.

12. This information can be found in the January/February edition annually in the NATO Review.

13. Stockholm International Peace Research Institute, World Armaments and Disarmament, SIPRI Yearbook, London, last edition: SIPRI Yearbook 1981, London, 1981.

    SIPRI started to gather information on the arms trade between industrialized countries only a few years ago.

14. This was agreed in the NATO long-term development plan early in 1977.

15. See Aviation Week, 9.3.81 and 18.5.81, as examples. The election of Francois Mitterand as President of France will probably change the French armament expenditures somewhat.

16. See IFSH Arbeitsgruppe Rüstung und Unterentwicklung, An Assessment of Sources and Statistics of Military Expenditure and Arms Transfer Data, mimeo, Hamburg 1980.

17. See note 11.

18. See note 13.

19. All this data probably represents a very low estimate, since there are extensive exports of components etc.

20. Estimates put them at one fourth or one fifth of the total Third World debt: see e.g. Hans Bernd Schäfer, Gefährdete Weltfinanzen, Bonn 1980.

21. This is repayment and interest over export; World Bank, World Development Report 1980, table 2.7.

22. "Instant weapons" are weapons not requiring maintenance and stored somewhere for a one-time use only, e.g. anti-tank missiles.

23. Examples are the submarine deals with Indonesia and Argentina.

24. The Wehrdienst, an information paper by and for the West German arms industry, often complains about the US arms imports policy, e.g. Wehrdienst 715/79, 724/79. Here, information can be found on the difficulties of the American subsidiary of Siemens to get orders in the US. The best-known example of difficulties in cooperation across the Atlantic is the Leopard II/XM I tank competition.

25. For an overview of problems of conversion see: Ulrich Albrecht, Rüstungskonversionsforschung, Baden Baden 1979; a condensed version can be found in: Peter Wallensteen, Experiences in Disarmament, Uppsala University, Dept. of Peace and Conflict Research, Report No. 19, June 1978.

26. The arguments for inherent growth of arms production capacity are most ably presented in: Mary Kaldor, European Defence Industry, ISIO monograph, Sussex 1972.

27. The following data was collected in a project financed by the German Foundation for Peace and Conflict Research (DGFK), by Michael Brzoska, Peter Lock and Herbert Wulf.

28. For overviews see: Helena Tuomi & Raimo Väyrynen, Transnational Corporations, Armaments and Development, Tampere Peace Research Institute, Research Report No. 22, Tampere 1980 and the studies in Wallensteen, op.cit., note 25.

29. The data used here differs from the data used above.

30. This assumption is obviously very problematic. The arms industry is somewhat more capital-intensive than other forms of production. See Albrecht, op.cit., note 25.

31. According to an estimate by the UN European Economic Commission for Europe, labour productivity (output per employment hour) in Western Europe grew 4.6 % yearly in the 1970s. In a mid-term projection for 1985, an increase of labour productivity of about 4 to 5 % is estimated. ECE Bulletin for Europe, Labor Force and Employment in Western Europe, The Prospects to 1985 by Major Sectors, 2/1979, pp. 37.

32. Again, this information has to be treated carefully, as there are

large data problems with arms transfer data.

33. Exchange rate for 1977; 1 DM = 0.43 US $.

34. The methods for this estimate and more data presented in: Michael Brzoska, Peter Lock, Herbert Wulf, Rüstungsproduktion in West-europa, <u>IFSH-Forschungsberichte, Heft 15</u>, Hamburg 1979, pp. 44.

35. Examples are DIAG in the FRG, Rolls Royce in Great Britain or Fincantieri in Italy.

36. Standardization is defined as the assimilation of weapon systems <u>ex ante</u>, while interoperability refers to the assimilation of weapon systems <u>ex post</u>. Co-production is a form of standardization in which standardization is guaranteed by joint production in various countries.

37. See e.g. the so-called Kelpsch-Report, <u>European Community, European Parliament, Document 83/78</u>, p. 17: "The main problem which confronts governments in procurement decisions is the recurrent problem of choice between an American system and a comparable European system where because of economies of scale and a large national market the American system will be much cheaper." Many examples can be cited, e.g. the F 16: "If the Europeans had preferred procurement of the F 16 in the US the price per system would have been 4.2 million US $ instead of 5.3 million US $ in European production." (<u>Interavia</u> 11/1979, p. 1091)

38. The intense discussion was stimulated by a report by Thomas A. Callaghan, <u>Economic Cooperation in Military and Civil Technology</u>, rev. ed., Georgetown University, Washington Sept. 1975. In this report, Callaghan hinted at cost reduction by standardization in the range of several billion US $.

39. A number of cost problems are discussed as resulting from co-production. At least in the FRG - because of problems of financial control - the government is by now rather critical of co-production agreements. See also: <u>SIPRI Yearbook 1981</u>.

40. The German aircraft industry was e.g. very eager to gain technology throughout the '60s and '70s.

41. This problem must not be connected with very large absolute sums; for a less important weapon system, a smaller total project cost might exceed national possibilities.

42. Examples are the British/French aircraft deal of the early 1960s after the "Nassau-deal" and the French partial departure from NATO and the "Kampfpanzer 90", a joint German/French

project for which, as Defence Minister Apel stated, there are only political reasons.

43. The constant reverbaration of co-production as one important element of the NATO strategy has also led some critical analysts of military policies into the wrong direction. Some have viewed these co-production discussions as more real than they actually are.

44. This is most visible in the differences in the British, French and German tank doctrine. While the German army prefers a fast-moving tank with fast-moving infantry, the British tank doctrine stresses survivability. The French doctrine is built around smaller tanks than are the main force in Britain and the FRG.

45. See WEU-Symposion, Note 3., p. 23. Also J.L. Delpech, La standardization des armements, in Défence Nationale, May 1976, p. 19-36. Delpech, Délégué ministérielle pour la l'armement, is very critical of standardization. See also Elliot R. Goodman, France and Arms for the Atlantic Alliance: the Standardization/Inter-operability Problem, in Orbis, Fall 1980.

46. Arms industry does not refer to a distinguishable sector of the economy. Arms industry, in our concept, is the sum of those companies producing products that are procured for armed forces or are used in arms production (see also note 10).

47. See the appendix for the largest arms producing companies. Further information gathered by the authors of this paper seems to point in the same direction. Tables on capital links are available from us.

48. Three prototypes were developed, for instance, for the first British strategic bomber after the Second World War.

49. Examples are the Chobham/Armour, aircraft electronics or Rolls Royce aircraft engines.

50. Problem areas are: large battle tanks, electronics, aircraft engines and until recently ship-building. Strengths are air-frame manufacture, small tanks and missiles.

51. On this see, Goodman, op.cit., note 45.

52. This refers especially to electronics, aircraft engines and airframe design.

53. Cases in point are the frigate programme or the discussion on the Kampfpanzer 90 in the FRG.

54. To name a few: Philips (electronics), RSV (warship building) in the Netherlands; Fabrique Nationale (small arms) in Belgium; Kongsberg (missiles) in Norway.

55. The ratio of arms imports to arms exports for the US in the period from 1974 to 1978 according to ACDA (note 12): 1 to 50; for the Third World alone: 1 to 500.

56. Obviously the partners do not have to be Europeans. There is some degree of cooperation with US companies, although competition is fierce. There is also some limited cooperation with Third World countries, e.g. for the Italian-Brasilian AMX aircraft, which will be procured by the Italian air force. There might also be cooperation with Arabian states, e.g. between France and Saudi Arabia for a Mirage fighter aircraft, destined for both air forces.

57. This is the Euro-missile Dynamics company.

58. Report of the Netherland's Advisory Council on Defence Affairs, European Cooperation on Defence Equipment, The Hague, March 1978, p. 80.

59. Authors to be named here are: Seymour Melman, Ron Smith and Kurt Rothschild. See the bibliography by Seymour Melman in the Political Issues Series of the Center for the Studies of Armament and Disarmament, California State University, Los Angeles, 1980.

60. Data taken from Brzoska/Lock/Wulf, op.cit.,note 27., where OECD and EEC statistics are presented. Important background reading for the relative position of industries within the EEC is Frank Blackaby, ed., De-Industrialization, London, 1979.

61. A similar suggestion is condensed out of a discussion of prospects of arms export control by Lawrence Franko, Restraining Arms Exports to the Third World: Will Europe Agree? in Survival, Vol. XXI, No. 1, 1979.

Chapter Five

ARMS BUILDUP AND DISARMAMENT - EFFECTS ON MANPOWER SITUATIONS IN COUNTRIES OF DIFFERENT SOCIAL SYSTEMS

Klaus Engelhardt

Representatives of the military-industrial complex have in recent times repeatedly suggested that at least three advantageous consequences could be expected from the arms buildup: the preservation of jobs, stability of economic growth, and acceleration of techno-scientific progress. Drastic cutbacks in spending on social services in Western countries, caused primarily by priority emphasis on armaments, have, however, clearly demonstrated the contradiction between the wishful thinking of militarist circles and the economic and social reality.

Heated discussion has begun on the political and social consequences of the arms buildup. This has been aggravated in that growing sections of the general public, even in capitalist countries, are beginning to understand that with rapid progress in arms technology, a continued arms race is likely to bring mankind to the brink of a nuclear disaster. Furthermore, chronic and continuously spreading mass unemployment and economic crisis in many countries have compelled trade unionists, scholars and politicians to scrutinise more thoroughly the correlations between armament and social progress and to search for alternatives. An analysis of the effects of arms buildup upon unemployment is directly associated with one of the basic human rights, i.e. the right to a safeguarded material livelihood.

5.1. EXPERIENCE FROM IMMEDIATE POST-WAR PERIOD

Any empirical analysis of the relationships between disarmament and employment is somewhat difficult, as practical experience regarding large-scale reduction of troops and arms is largely restricted to data originating from the period immediately following the Second World War. Ever since, worldwide arms spending has increased dramatically to unprecedented levels over a period of roughly three decades, except for the world wars and preparations for them.

Short-term stagnation or even reduction of arms buildup in certain countries is not comparable with the conditions of effective international disarmament measures. Such internationally agreed effective disarmament measures would provide opportunities for all countries to re-allocate budgets, personnel, and hardware from armament to peaceful purposes, to bring about conversion of arms production and to use tax incomes for supporting the re-integration of military personnel with peaceful activities in an effective way.

Practical experience obtained from the post-war period has thus been inadequately evaluated. It is often pointed out that the situation at the end of World War II is not comparable with the present: civilian demands had by that time accumulated, and arms technology was far less developed. The current disarmament problems are said to be quite different. It should not be forgotten, however, that the vast economic and organisational conversion problems were actually resolved then in the countries most strongly affected. The dimensions of that conversion, in terms of people involved in armies and arms sectors, were even more extensive than what would have to be achieved by total disarmament today.

The Soviet Union alone demobilised 8.5 million soldiers by early 1948, for whom retraining and upgrading courses were held throughout the country. Planning and other preparations for conversion had been initiated by the authorities in the USSR even before the end of the war. The following assessment was published by R. Faramasyan, a Soviet scholar: "There were problems, indeed, when it came to transformation of the national economy. Yet, measures taken by the Communist Party of the Soviet Union helped to overcome those problems with good success. The volume of industrial production grew rapidly, and the pre-war level was exceeded as early as in 1948."(1)

Conversion of single enterprises of the defence industry, planning and preparation of conversion of the national economy at large, choice of and technological preparation for alternative civilian production as well as the involvement of workers and public organisations in this process are subjects which have been analysed in several publications of topical importance today.(2)

Conversion on a similar scale took place in the USA: the strength of the Armed Forces was reduced from 11.6 million men in 1945 to 1.5 million in 1948. Arms spending decreased from US $ 81.2 billion to US $ 11.8 billion over the same period . All anxiety originally expressed to the effect that US unemployment might increase to the level of eight million proved to be entirely unfounded. Unemployment throughout the early post-war years remained below the pre-war figures, despite extensive re-integration of military and armament personnel within the civilian sector. Very similar developments are observable in the post-war situation in the United Kingdom.

The following points were made by U. Albrecht with regard to planning and control of conversion of arms production in the USA: "Several acts were passed by Congress on re-integration of labour and conversion of arms industries, all for the purpose of maintaining war prosperity and keeping unemployment low... Generously financed education programmes helped to absorb manpower."(3)

So, after the Second World War, countries with different social systems, using their own inherent tools of planning, management and regulation, succeeded in getting to grips with the conversion of their war economies. No-one underestimates the problems of conversion then facing those countries. Nevertheless, they were resolved to the advantage of the civilian sectors and to the benefit of the people.

In the context of post-war experience, two conclusions of general validity should be noted: first, the successful conversion of war economies would not have been possible had it not been for a strong, world-wide anti-war and peace movement, which had created the political conditions for disarmament and arms conversion. Secondly armament budgets, no longer required for war, were applied to solving economic and social problems, a process actively supported by governments and other social forces, although by clearly different methods in the various countries.

5.2. CHARACTERISTICS OF PRESENT-DAY ARMAMENT AND ECONOMIC CONSEQUENCES

The economic and social benefits of disarmament are found to depend directly on the quantity and even more the quality and the specific nature of the military and armament resources to be released.

Due to certain characteristics of present-day armaments and to specific aspects relating to the revolution in arms technology, the qualitative factors of the arms buildup and their impact on the national economy are of growing importance. In this context, reference should be made to the following new aspects:

- Science and technology have made enormous advances, much of which has been used for military purposes. The USA has always been the first to develop new mass destruction weapons and to invent strategic offensive weapons and has thus accelerated the arms race. Roughly 35 per cent of all research and development resources are applied to technologies of destruction in the USA. One quarter of all electronic products manufactured in the USA are intended for military use. The average amount of research and development funds used on armament production is between six and ten times higher than that available for civilian production in the leading NATO countries. Yet, since science and technology are of crucial importance in relation to economic effectiveness and growth, any arms buildup is likely to draw intolerable amounts of research and development potential from the civilian areas of the national economy. This is why arms production and in particular the enforced arms buildup today has a very specific negative impact on the conditions of economic reproduction and on the job situation at all civilian levels of national economy.

- Arms production and all manufacturing activities relating to army equipment have become highly capital-intensive and less labour-intensive. While US $ 9,000 was spent on average on one soldier in 1949, the corresponding figure in the fiscal year 1982 will be US $ 115,000. These figures reflect, first of all, extremely high spending on highly advanced arms technology. This trend has been confirmed in a study conducted at the US Center of Defense Information. According to the centre, about 110,000 military and armament jobs were created by US $ one billion in 1964, but only 45,800 jobs could be provided by an investment of the same amount in 1977.(4)

- Armament products and, consequently, the machines with which they are manufactured, are highly susceptible to obsolescence, due to NATO's aggressive political and military strategies, which aim at gaining military superiority over the socialist countries. Major weapon systems are being renewed at an average interval of ten years, with each new generation exhibiting new tactical and technological parameters. These, together with extremely high armament profits, have doubled the prices for each new generation. Before World War II, destruction technology developed rapidly only during direct war preparations and when wars were fought with fire-arms. After World War II, there was no typical post-war stagnation: extremely rapid development of military technology has become a permanent phenomenon of our time.

Today, any armament sector in whatever country is found to be absorbing multiple amounts of civilian economic resources as compared to the past, mainly due to three primary factors, i.e. extremely high R&D input into arms production, disproportionate growth of capital investment, and grave obsolescence. Military expenditure curtails especially the material and financial resources needed to secure and increase employment in civilian areas. Unemployment has become an overriding social problem in the majority of capitalist countries. In the OECD countries, the annual unemployment average has risen from 16.5 million in 1979 to 19 million in 1980, and the 24 million mark was reached in mid 1981.

The direct impact of arms buildup on unemployment has been analysed in a study by <u>Marion Anderson</u>. Here are some of her conclusions: "Contrary to a long-adhered popular opinion, no advantage to economy can be derived from arms spending. Unemployment rather than employment is the outcome. Any increase in military spending by one billion US-Dollar entailed a loss of 11,600 jobs in the USA throughout the years covered by this study. The net job loss amounted to 907,000, between 1970 and 1974, when the average military budget went up to 78 billion US-Dollar."(5) For 1979, when the military budget reached

US $ 124 billion she calculated a net job loss of 1.44 million for the entire US economy.(6) A loss of about two million jobs can be estimated by the same method for the fiscal year 1982.

This analysis confirms the author's own assessment that the manifestations of crisis in capitalist countries and in particular of social insecurity are being aggravated by the arms buildup. With the characteristics of modern arms production, this assessment is now more valid than ever before. The economic and social effects of the arms race are additionally reinforced, in the 1980s, by the simultaneous intensification in the arms buildup and a further deepening of long-lasting processes of cyclic and structural crisis in the capitalist countries. Stagnation or declining economic growth rates, rapidly increasing unemployment, rising rates of inflation as well as stagnant or dropping levels of real income are characteristic phenomena in the capitalist countries.

5.3. STEPS TOWARDS DISARMAMENT AND EMPLOYMENT

The very fact that labour is required for arms production is presented by the military-industrial complex as an argument to support the claim that additional jobs are created by arms programmes. The arms buildup is therefore said to be advantageous to the economy, since it maintains and creates jobs. Such arguments conceal the detrimental economic and social consequences of armament, not to mention the dangerous political and military implications. Nevertheless, such propositions are dangerously misleading.

The following questions should be asked and answered with regard to the economic and social aspects: What economic input is necessary to create or maintain jobs in armament and military sectors? What are the dimensions of the economic and social advantages or disadvantages to the national economy that such a positive approach to the arms buildup is likely to create? What advantages or disadvantages, in terms of manpower, may emanate from alternative uses of armament resources for civilian purposes?

A number of studies on the effects of arms buildup or disarmament upon employment have been conducted by scholars in several countries in the 1970s. While some of their methods have differed strongly, their findings have been largely congruent.

5.4. REDISTRIBUTION OF PUBLIC FUNDS

Congressman <u>Les Aspin</u> undertook a comparative study to find out how many jobs could be provided with a government investment of US $ one billion in the military and civilian sectors respectively. His conclusions were as follows:

Sector	Number of jobs
Defence	35,000
Housing construction	66,455
Public services	87,500
Labour deployment programmes	151,000

(Source: Economic Notes, New York, Febr. 1975, p. 6)

Aspin's findings show that roughly twice as many jobs can be created in the civilian sectors than in the arms sector. There are certain areas of civilian activity in which the number of obtainable jobs would be even four times higher than that in the arms sector. It should be borne in mind, however, that capital intensity and income levels in certain civilian areas are higher than in others, and that in these the number of obtainable jobs would be lower than that feasible in, say, public services. Yet, in the capitalist industrial countries, only about 40 per cent of the gross national product comes from industrial production. Re-deployment of man-power should somehow correspond to the structure of the given national economy. It should be emphasised that in Aspin's analysis, attention has been paid to areas which are of primary social importance.

Another study, based on the same methodology and conducted in 1977, has been presented by the Center of Defense Information, Washington, D.C. According to the Center's findings, an investment of US $ one billion would give the following employment yield:(7)

Sector	Number of jobs
Arms production and military activities	45,800
Civilian production	53,000
Federal or State campaigns against recession	71,000
Public services	98,000

The aspect of youth unemployment has been studied at the GDR Institute of International Politics and Economics.(8) Young people between 16 and 24 years of age account for 22 per cent of the OECD countries' total population, but they represent 40 per cent of the unemployed. The amount of money required for the establishment of training places is much smaller than, on the other hand, investment needed to create jobs for skilled workers. Vocational training for the occupations listed below would have required the following sums in the FRG in 1974:

Moulder	DM	15,765,-
Process control mechanic	DM	11,435,-
Toolmaker	DM	10,605,-
Electrician	DM	9,925,-
Chemical worker	DM	8,180,-
Bricklayer	DM	6,660,-
Painter and varnisher	DM	4,640,-

In all, 100,000 young people could thus have been given vocational training for a total sum of DM one billion, this estimate being based on 1974 cost levels. The reduction in youth unemployment follows general social services as an urgent priority for the use of funds obtained from reduced armament spending. With effective disarmament policies, the problem of employing young people on completion of vocational training would no longer be relevant. A transitional period, roughly identical in length with vocational training, would be sufficient for evidence to emerge of additional employment effects in the national economy resulting in growing demand for labour.

5.5. RESULTS OF CORRELATIVE ANALYSES

Leontief, in an input-output study in the 1960s, found that a 20 per cent reduction in arms spending would cause a loss of 300,000 jobs in arms industries; this, however, would be offset by the possible creation of 697,000 additional jobs in civilian industries.(9) These results, too, confirm that the arms sector is the least suitable for resolving employment problems. Reference to another notable analysis has been made by the American scholar David Gold: "Roger Bezdek, then an economist with the US Department of Commerce, published a study in 1975 that traced the effects of five years of three different levels of military spending. One was a normal increase in the defense budget assuming a high employment economy. The second was a 30 per cent increase along with a tax rise of equal amount. The third was a 30 per cent cut in military spending and an accompanying tax reduction. Employment and net output was 2.1 per cent higher with the defense budget cut than with normal growth. Employment and net output were 1.3 per cent lower with the highest military budget than with normal growth. The highest level of defense spending resulted in the lowest level of employment and output."(10)

Expenditure on the planned B-1 bomber programme was compared in another economic study with the alternative use of the same funds on tax cuts or public housing construction. The number of jobs obtainable from tax cuts would have been 30,000 more than what would have been achievable from arms programmes over five years, and the positive difference obtainable from housing construction would have been as much as 70,000 as compared to arms production during the same period (11).

The Bureau of Labor Statistics has produced evidence in an analysis that if US $ one billion of armament money were made available for individual consumption through tax cuts, this would create 112,000 additional jobs.(12)

5.6. JOBS BY RE-INVESTMENT

Creating jobs through re-investment is another methodological approach to the problem. Real disarmament will probably be accompanied by combined use of this and other methods. This will be even more the case as redistribution of armament funds will have to go hand in hand with due consideration of the cost structures for wages and fixed assets in the military and arms industries.

Re-investment can be of particular importance in terms of new civilian products and new markets. The argument mentioned earlier, that the immediate pos-war period is not comparable with the present because of the then considerable accumulation of public demand caused by the war and its aftermath, is of only limited validity. Arms spending has been a heavy burden for more than three decades. Hence, important sectors of the national economy have suffered global neglect. The problems linked with energy, raw materials and environmental protection as well as the economic and social problems of the developing countries are challenges of the 1980s that are certainly no smaller in magnitude than those facing the world in the '40s and the '50s. New technological approaches have to be taken at all levels. New problems are waiting to be tackled. New markets and jobs will be the result.

The alternative use of part of armament money should be based on a comparison between fixed assets in arms and military industries and those in civilian industries. The relevant figures concerning the arms and military sector are not, however, available, and in any case their comparability would be very poor due to factors of obsolescence and many other characteristics.

On the other hand, savings on armament funds for a period of one year could not usefully be compared with the investment capital needed for one civilian job, as a civilian job, once created, will usually be available for ten years on average. Annual savings on armament funds and funds set aside for arms re-investment should therefore only be compared with one tenth of the investment capital (assets for one worker) required for one job. Or, with a job survival of ten years, all investment capital required for one job should be compared with ten years' arms funds. The 1977 defence budget of the FRG was DM 33.5

billion, including DM 18.2 billion for procurement, operational expenses and equipment maintenance. Assuming that the same sum of money would not be used on armaments during the ensuing decade but on civilian production, the same sum every year, the savings over ten years would amount to a total of DM 182 billion.

Sector	Gross value of fixed assets (DM) per worker, 1977
All industries	78,000
Basic and capital equipment industries	135,000
Consumer goods industries	53,000
Food and beverage industries	144,000
Investment products industries	54,000

Hence, 2.33 million jobs (DM 182 billion divided by 78,000) could be provided by re-investment in the course of ten years throughout all industries. However, the approx. 400,000 jobs which would have resulted directly or indirectly from arms orders, would have to be substituted by others. Attention must also be paid to the fact that job creation costs will continue to rise over the coming ten years. Despite all these restrictions, arms savings over one decade would be sufficient to create four to five times as many civilian jobs, than what would be possible in the arms sector, provided that all other conditions remain constant.

How would it be possible then to finance the demand for the products thus created? People engaged in civilian industries differ from those in the military sector in that they earn their wages through product sales, thus creating national income, while those in the military sector simply consume national income which has been redistributed through the national budget. It was assumed that only part of the redistributed armament funds and resources was earmarked for re-investment. Other parts, therefore, could be allocated to areas for direct stimulation of demand. Such an investment boom, resulting from the redistribution of armament funds, might also be conducive to the production of civilian goods which could immediately be used for reproduction; the outcome of this would stimulate the national economy as a whole. Nationally financed investments rising to a magnitude of redistributed arms spending would swiftly exceed the dimensions of any boom programme so far known in history.

Such a hypothetical calculation is intended to demonstrate the contrast between the long-term armaments burden and the potential long-term benefit. Such an approach to the calculation of present conditions must, of course, be regarded as no more than a snapshot, and cannot be applied to longer periods of time in the future. It is, nevertheless, an indication of the magnitude of the wastage of resources in the arms race.

All potential benefits and drawbacks of all the methods cannot be described within the limits of this paper.(13) All methods, including input-output tables, have one drawback in common: they do not reproduce dynamic processes. Yet, this drawback is likely to scale down the potential benefit, rather than to exaggerate it. First, there will be cumulative effects in the long run that are continuously reinforced by lasting disarmament, just as there are cumulative detrimental effects as the arms race continues. Secondly, due consideration is given in the various models to qualitative factors likely to result particularly from re-allocation of formerly military research and development resources.

Differentiated, as all these methods may be, they have yielded similar results. The number of jobs obtainable in the civilian sector is about twice as high as that feasible in the military and armament areas. The effect will be even higher, when it comes to the challenge of reducing youth unemployment.

5.7. SOCIALIST COUNTRIES AND JOBS

There is neither structural nor cyclical unemployment in the CMEA countries; even essential defence spending has not led to unemployment.

Absence of unemployment in the CMEA countries, including the GDR, by no means suggests the absence of negative effects caused by the burdens of military and defence spending. It is rather a reflection of the basically different political and social objectives and of the different socio-economic and political foundations of these states. Production, work and the distribution of the results of work are all planned in socialist countries. Hence, additional economic burdens can be planned as well, and they are planned to rest on the shoulders of society as a whole rather than on those of the underprivileged groups, as is the case in capitalist countries. In socialist countries it is, after all, quite impossible for the arms buildup to become a source of wealth for certain groups. Disarmament, on the other hand, does not bring any disadvantage to any group.

The right to employment is laid down in the Constitution of the GDR, as in the other socialist countries. Paragraph 24 of the GDR Constitution reads as follows: "Every citizen of the German Democratic Republic has the right to employment. He or she is entitled to a job and its free choice in line with the requirements of society and individual skills. Every citizen is entitled to payment by quality and quantity of work."(14)

Although unemployment does not exist in socialist countries, the general economic repercussions of defence spending are considerable.

These countries are similarly exposed to the negative effects of the lasting arms race, as enforced by NATO. They are also exposed to damage emanating from high-quality resources being absorbed by defence. True, long-term economic growth rates in the socialist countries are higher than those in the capitalist countries, but more rapid economic and social progress is prevented by defence spending. The burden of defence decelerates economic growth and thus narrows the physical framework for comprehensive satisfaction of the needs and requirements of the general public. It is an obstacle to full-scale international cooperation and limits more effective support to developing countries. Labour urgently required for economic development is blocked.

The GDR, as other socialist countries, is in need of more manpower. Hence, some of those now involved in the defence industry and in the National People's Army could easily be transferred to existing civilian jobs, in the event of internationally agreed disarmament, without any need for additional job-creating investments. A sizeable economic effect might be generated by such restructuring with reduction of the military sector, in which national income is consumed rather than produced. The national income of the GDR could be increased by 500 million marks to every 20,000 employees who are transferred from military to civilian sectors, a sum equivalent to 0.3 per cent of the country's entire national income.

Since no additional demand would have to be stimulated in the GDR, the redistributed funds would be fully available for more comprehensive satisfaction of the existing material, social, intellectual and cultural needs.

The socio-economic structure together with the political and social objectives of the GDR guarantee that the benefit of disarmament will be a benefit to society at large. A "social-policy programme" is the core of the GDR's Five-Year Plans and the very basis of those plans, their goals and their implementation.

For armament conversion, advantage should be taken not only of the experience gained after the Second World War, but also of the results achieved from restructuring within civilian sectors. The GDR itself offers a number of examples, such as the conversion of textile industries to electrical engineering or metal processing and from pit coal mining to mechanical engineering, automotive engineering and construction.

Pit coal mining in the GDR had to be converted under difficult circumstances which were somewhat similar to those prevailing in armament industries. The installations to be carried out required highly-developed specialisation, and the application of the equipment to other technological processes was extremely difficult. The workers, too, were highly specialised, higly skilled and highly paid.

The government ministries in charge of the production concerned under the economic system of the GDR, trade unions, the executive bodies of the Socialist Unity Party of Germany (SED), factory managements and local government bodies were called in to participate in the preparations for decision-making. Their representatives set up a joint working party to identify all problems which called for solutions, including the technological basis, stocks, the effectiveness of production, fixed assets and their composition, the working and living conditions of the labour involved, the structure of age and skills, positions of the miners' homes, and specific vocational traditions.

The next phase was devoted to studying the possible variants of different economic structures in the regions concerned. In this context, emphasis was laid on the existing infrastructure, home-to-job transport, energy and water supplies, and other regional characteristics.

The third phase was initiated to study the possibilities for establishing replacement industries, with due consideration of social and regional aspects. The types, volumes and effectiveness of alternative production were also investigated.

It was only after these preparations that the Presidential Committee of the GDR Council of Ministers took positive decisions, the first on 21 December 1967, and the second on 6 June 1974. These decisions provided orientation and policy rules for tackling the major issues, such as redeployment of manpower, vocational retraining, social services for the miners involved, financial treatment of transferred assets and the responsibilities of the authorities involved. These decisions and the measures to be taken for their realization were discussed at countless meetings and at various levels with the pit coal miners and other employees concerned as well as in the housing areas with the general public.

In the face of a high demand for labour power throughout the GDR, it would have been possible to let the re-integration of miners happen spontaneously. Yet, such practice would have been incompatible with the economic and social policies of the country. Therefore, two major objectives were formulated for conversion:

(a) The pit coal mining management shall secure a job for every worker in harmony with his or her skills and availability.
(b) Replacement production, on the basis of preceding investigations, shall be selected with specific attention paid to ensuring high economic effectiveness.

Pit coal production in the Martin Hoop mine of Zwickau was then replaced primarily by the following production areas:

A. A new factory for the manufacture of labour-saving aids to

        rationalise soft coal mining;
B.   A new plant for prefabrication of concrete slabs for housing construction;
C.   A certain number of miners were incorporated in a nearby motorcar factory.

The new factories were constructed on sites in immediate proximity to the former pit coal mine, certain sections of them right on the former mining site. This offered several advantages: it was unnecessary to change the existing housing structure or to rehouse the miners elsewhere. Most of the original home-to-job transport network could be used without modification. The new factories were also able to use most of the other elements of the existing infrastructure, including energy and water supplies, sewerage systems, roads, heating, telephone and social services, such as canteens and the medical outpatient department. This saved a significant amount of investment capital.

The following relations were characteristic of the amount of necessary retraining:

(a)   One third of the workers decided to accept employment in other industrial branches than those for which they were trained, all such decisions being made by free choice.
(b)   One third could be employed immediately in the replacement factories, because their primary or secondary crafts and skills matched with the requirements of the new production.
(c)   One third had to be retrained for new crafts, for which an average training period of five months was required. Retraining periods differed noticeably by crafts, and ranged from several weeks to one year or, in some exceptional cases, up to two years. All the workers participating in retraining schemes were paid their former average wages. Additional compensations were paid to those who suffered temporary losses.

A number of complex economic, social and human problems had to be tackled in the course of this conversion process. Some of the planned measures were modified in the wake of discussions with the people concerned. Yet, as a whole, conversion was carried out to the benefit of the workers concerned as well as of the localities involved and the national economy as a whole.

All of the workers retained their qualification levels, and some were even able to improve them.

Conditions could hardly be any more difficult in a number of highly specialised armament companies. This conversion process as a whole has been carried out with preferential consideration of all workers' social needs as well as of the preservation or even improvement of the workers' occupational skills and qualification standards and to the benefit of the national economy at large.

Arms production has negative economic and social consequences for all peoples. This applies even more strongly to the current new round in the arms race, accelerated by the USA and the leading circles of NATO.

However, in the context of the social consequences of armament, there is a basic difference between countries with different social systems. In the capitalist countries, the working classes have to bear the burden of the arms buildup, while monopolistic companies acquire opportunities for expansion and generate extremely high profits. In capitalist countries, arms buildup generates additional unemployment.

In socialist countries, the burden of necessary defence spending is borne by all areas of the national economy and by the entire population. There are no social groups to which defence might be a source of wealth. As to the employment situation, the generally prevalent shortage of manpower is further aggravated by the defence effort.

Alternative use of armament funds, in all countries, would improve the conditions, personal and material, for greater economic growth and a higher standard of living. Unemployment in capitalist countries could be drastically reduced. Calculations undertaken in and for capitalist countries have shown that the average funds needed for one job in the military and armament sectors would be sufficient to create two civilian jobs. In socialist countries, the labour shortage could be reduced, which again would provide and open up additional resources for faster economic, social, intellectual and cultural growth. These are the economic and social reasons underlining the urgent need for an immediate halt to the arms race and for agreed disarmament.

Conversion of armament and re-integration of military and armament employees with the civilian sectors of national economies are practicable in all countries by using the means available in their given social systems. Of decisive importance is to create the political prerequisites for disarmament and arms conversion. Cooperation between national and local government, trade unions and industrial management is a common practice for conversion in the socialist countries. In the Western countries, the demand for cooperation of this sort has so far been the preserve of some unions and peace researchers. Foreign, economic and social policies of the socialist countries have guaranteed supreme priority positions for peace and disarmament efforts. They ensure that all the economic and social advantages achieved through disarmament will go fully to the benefit of the general public.

NOTES AND REFERENCES

1. R. Faramasyan, Economic and Social Problems in Conversion from War to Peace Productions, in J. Huffschmid & E. Burhop,

From War to Peace Production, Cologne 1980, p. 46.

2. Soviet Peace Committee, Socio-Economic Problems of Disarmament, Vienna 1979.

3. U. Albrecht, Rüstungskonversion - eine Literaturstudie mit Forschungsempfehlungen, Baden-Baden 1979, p. 78.

4. The Defense Monitor, Washington, Sept.-Oct. 1977, p. 3.

5. Marion Anderson, The Empty Pork Barrel, Unemployment and the Pentagon Budget, Lansing, Michigan, USA, 1978, p. 1.

6. Marion Anderson, The Impact of Military Spending on the Machinists Union, Washington, January 1979, p. 2.

7. The Defense Monitor, Washington, Sept.-Oct. 1977, No. 7, p. 3.

8. P. Klein & K. Engelhardt, Weltproblem Abrüstung, Berlin 1979, p. 168.

9. Quoted from U. Albrecht, op.cit., 1979, p. 47.

10. Roger H. Bezdek, The 1980 Impact - Regional and Occupational - of Compensated Shifts in Defense Spending, Journal of Regional Science, 15.2.1975, pp. 183 - 198; quoted in D. Gold, Testimony before the Group of Governmental Experts on the Relationship between Disarmament and Development, UN, New York, September 1979.

11. Chase Econometrics Associates, Economic Impact of the B-1 Programme on the US Economy and Comparative Studies, Cynoyd, Pennsylvania, 1975; quoted in D. Gold, cf. 10.

12. United States Department of Labor, Bureau of Labor Statistics, The Structure of the US Economy in 1980 and 1985, 1976.

13. U. Albrecht, op.cit.

14. Constitution of the GDR, October 7th, 1974.

Chapter Six

EFFORTS AT REDUCING MILITARY EXPENDITURE IN THE UNITED STATES, 1960 TO 1978

Milton Leitenberg

6.1. INTRODUCTION

In 1977-78, the Nordic proposal to the United Nations' Special Session on Disarmament proposed a UN study on Disarmament and Development with the eventual hope of reducing international military expenditure and effecting some transfer of the resources to development aid.(1) Other initiatives in the UN concerning reduction of military expenditure and the related efforts to devise uniform international accounting methods for the reporting of military expenditure have produced no result and have been deadlocked since 1973 and 1975 respectively. In contrast, military expenditure has been rising nearly universally in recent years, and in many cases quite sharply.(2)

Western sources claim that military expenditures of the USSR and of the Warsaw Treaty Organization have been rising continuously with a small but steady rate of annual increase for some fifteen years. The military expenditure of the USSR is probably between three and four times its publicly announced figure, and is approximately equal to that of the United States.(3) In the West, the United States and its NATO allies committed themselves in 1977 to a 3 per cent annual increase in military expenditure, which was to have lasted through 1985. This effort did not succeed uniformly and was more or less suspended in the spring of 1981. In the United States itself, military expenditure dropped in the 1970s in real terms (in constant dollars), falling below the levels of the pre-Vietnam base years of 1964-65, both by coming down from the high levels of the Vietnam War years and by not keeping pace with the annual rate of inflation.(4) However, that trend has now been sharply reversed, both for domestic political reasons and in the face of apparent continuous rising USSR military expenditure. In the last year of the Carter administration, increases in military expenditure of 5 per cent per year were projected through 1985. With the entry of the Reagan administration, these annual increases and the projections were dramatically increased. By 1984, US defence expenditures are projected to reach $ 250 billion and $ 300 billion by 1985.(5) Though they may not attain such levels, the increase will be dramatic enough.

The reduction of military expenditure is often suggested as a mechanism for arms control, particularly because of the difficulties associated with and the meager results obtained from negotiations on specific weapon systems or force balances. This paper highlights some of the frustrations involved in achieving reductions in defence expenditure within an organized framework of some sort.

In order to understand the political circumstances in which one of the major powers might consider reductions in military expenditure, the experience of the United States in the 1960s and 1970s, when the government faced such potential decisions on several occasions, is examined. The first occasion involved bilateral and multilateral international discussion - if not negotiation of the more prolonged variety. This was the 1963-65 US-USSR "mutual-example" exercise in the reduction of military expenditure. The second series of events was almost entirely dependent on domestic political considerations and pressures. They involved events which occured between 1960 and 1970 in which US administrations, both Democrat and Republican, anticipated reductions in military expenditure. The framework in which policies were discussed in these contexts was defence industry conversion. In addition to an examination of executive actions and the outcome of political interactions in those cases, one can also examine the political history of specific defence-industry conversion legislation that reached the US Congress, and of the proposals for alternative military expenditure budgets in those same years. The paper brings together these two subjects, the short 1963-65 US-USSR military expenditure reduction exercise, and defence industry conversion, because both affect military expenditure and they were at least loosely connected during the Kennedy administration.

6.2. THE EARLY 1960S AND THE MUTUAL REDUCTION EXERCISE

There were two periods during the 1960s when US administrations anticipated a reduction in military expenditure. The first period spanned the years 1960-65 and culminated in the 1963-65 US-USSR "mutual reduction" exercise. The second period came at the end of the decade when it became clear that the US involvement in Vietnam would be reduced and there was talk of a "fiscal dividend" which was expected to result from a reduced US role in Southeast Asia. In the first period, considerable governmental attention was given to the question of defence industry and military base conversion. In the second period, however, the administration showed no interest in the conversion issue.

The Impetus Behind Defence Conversion Plans

There was a conjunction of several major influences in the 1960-65 period which led to US governmental consideration of the possible economic impact of disarmament. Some of these influences were quite abstract; others were quite pragmatic and real.

Probably the major influence in this respect was the anticipation that there would be a more or less continuous termination of a series of US weapons programmes over a period of a half dozen years. In 1962, it was decided to curtail a series of major air defence, bomber and missile programmes. At the least, this promised to produce significant shifts within the weapons production sector. Similarly, as early as March 1961 Secretary of Defence McNamara had embarked on the first of a series of military base closures as a Department of Defence (DoD) economy measure. These base closures would have the same result as the curtailment of the various procurement programmes, that of shifting the pattern of allocations within the defence sector. In order to help local communities adjust economically to these closures, the Office of Economic Adjustment had been set up in the DoD.

Even more important, by 1963 several senior administrators in the DoD had reason to anticipate that there might soon be substantial cuts in the total defence budget, not necessarily in the next year, but perhaps in three or four years, by 1965 or 1966. By then, the major US missile procurement programmes, Minuteman and Polaris, would be approaching completion. In addition, by 1962-63, these DoD officials knew that US intelligence had shown that the USSR had not embarked on the rapid production of the same kinds of weapons, as had been predicted in the 1958-60 "missile-gap" period. The mid-1960s would see the US with an enormous superiority in these weapons and it was anticipated that it would be impossible to justify procuring any more of them.

In October 1963, Deputy Defence Secretary Roswell Gilpatric estimated that annual US military expenditures would fall from $ 55 to $ 50 billion in the next five years, i.e. a reduction of roughly 5 per cent over a period of five years. In fiscal year 1963, the DoD budget accounted for over one half of the total Federal government budget of $ 98 billion. There were also estimates of somewhat larger reductions within the Department's management. Nevertheless, the administration's position, voiced by Deputy Secretary Gilpatric, was that special aerospace industry production accounted for only 20 per cent of the Defense Department's annual budget, and that the economic impact of changes in defence programmes - either from changes in spending or from changing patterns of procurement within a relatively steady total budget - could be handled by the nation without overall economic disruption. The Secretary of Defense appointed a special assistant, Deputy Assistant Secretary of Defense for Arms Control, Dr. Arthur Barber, whose responsibilities included defence industry conversion considerations. The Department of Defense funded numerous studies concerning defence industry conversion, to be carried out by various corporate members of the industry itself, and between 1962 and 1972 the US Arms Control and Disarmament Agency funded some 29 major studies under four categories:

1. implications for the national economy,
2. implications for industries,
3. implications for regions and communities and,
4. implications for individual warheads.(6)

The second major factor influencing US governmental thinking about military conversion was that in the period after the signing of the 1963 Limited Test Ban Treaty, the USSR was seeking agreements with the US on the limitation of military expenditure. This effort began with summit-level discussions on "mutual example reductions of military expenditure" in August-September 1963. This exercise, which was shrouded in secrecy until recently, will be discussed in detail below. It should just be noted here that this process helped to formalize internal US government interest in the topic of military conversion. On 10 July 1963, <u>Walter Heller</u>, Chairman of the President's Council of Economic Advisors, had organized an informal committee to review and coordinate the work of US government agencies relating to the economic impact of defence and disarmament. On 21 December 1963, within weeks of the unilateral cuts in military expenditure announced by both the US and the USSR governments as a result of the August-September summit meetings, a Presidential Committee was established on the Economic Impact of Defense and Disarmament.(7) This group subsequently became known as the "Ackley Committee", after its chairman, <u>Gardner Ackley</u>. Even without explicit agreements with the USSR, it was anticipated that the initiation of a period of "détente" following the signing of the Test Ban Treaty would slow down strategic weapon procurement.

Less important than these first two factors was a survey undertaken by the Disarmament Subcommittee of the Committee on Foreign Relations of the US Senate in early 1961. Some 439 companies engaged in defence contracting to various degrees, including the approximately 150 major defence contractors, were sent a questionnaire which asked their opinion on the economic impact of arms control agreements, conversion possibilities and so on. Eighty per cent of the companies replied, and a short summary of the study appeared in the <u>Congressional Record</u> in October 1962.(8) One response from the aerospace industry media came quite early. It suggested federal funding for five "compensating" projects, which were all barely disguised weapons programmes under DoD or NASA auspices - i.e., more of the same.(9) The first Congressional Hearings and reports relevant to the subject began to appear, and these were often quite comprehensive and useful.(10) In some of these, at least, some industry spokesmen indicated their scepticism that defence expenditure would actually decrease, in which they were to be proven correct.(11) Even so, there were indications that defence contractors were seeing their Senators and expressing their willingness to convert defence production facilities. At the same time, they made it clear that they hoped to see some direction from the government in terms of establishing priorities for civilian programmes and, to this end, they asked their Senators to devise programmes of alternative Federal spending. The first of

Senator McGovern's proposals for legislation along these lines also appeared at this time. It suggested the formation of a National Economic Conversion Commission for the purpose of study and planning.(12)

Finally, the fourth and most abstract of the factors encouraging US government officials to think seriously about military conversion concerned the activities that accompanied the discussion of General and Complete Disarmament (GCD) which had been going on in the United Nations for half a dozen years. The first UN report related to the GCD discussions, The Economic and Social Consequences of Disarmament, was completed on 16 February 1962.(13) Its preparation during 1961 had provided the impetus for a similar US report since the UN has asked Member Governments to provide information relevant to the topic. Shortly after its inauguration in 1961, the Kennedy Administration began to set up the Arms Control and Disarmament Agency (ACDA) which was mandated, among other things, to conduct research and to develop studies regarding "the economic ... consequences of arms control and disarmament, including the problems of readjustments arising in industry and the reallocation of natural resources." Even before ACDA was established, however, John J. McCloy, Adviser to the President on Disarmament, formed an expert panel to provide a report on the economic impacts of disarmament. This report, The Economic Impacts of Disarmament, which was released to the public in January 1962, sought

> ... to summarize the various sources of concern within the country as to possible economic difficulties arising from general and complete disarmament, to project the net reductions in defense expenditure (after various offsets), and to appraise the likely economic impact under various assumptions with respect to adjustment policies.(14)

The 1963-65 "Mutual-Example" Reduction in Military Expenditure

While the primary reason for US administration interest in military conversion programmes in the early to mid-1960s was undoubtedly the purely domestic decision to reduce the outlays on a number of major military programmes, it is worth examining in some detail the "mutual-example" military expenditure reduction exercise carried out by the United States and the Soviet Union between 1963 and 1965. This is one of the most interesting episodes in post-WW II US-USSR arms control history and until very recently, the events surrounding it were classified. Indeed, some of the information concerning these events remains classified to this day.

The exercise involved four separate sets of discussions over a period of four years. They began between President Kennedy, US Secretary of State Rusk, USSR Foreign Minister Gromyko, Ambassador Dobrynin and British Foreign Secretary Douglas-Home in 1963. There then followed the Rusk-Gromyko and Foster-Tsarapkin talks of November-December 1964 and the Rusk-Gromyko talks of September-October 1965. The subject was again introduced, from a somewhat different focus, in the Johnson-Kosygin Glassboro Summit in July 1967. Until 1976 and 1977, these events had been referred to in only a few short and scattered references of a few lines, and in some cases, these short allusions were quite misleading.(15) The initiatives were in effect part of three kinds of "mutual-example" reductions that occurred within the years 1963-65: military expenditure reductions, troop withdrawals form Central Europe, and reductions in the production of fissionable material.

Some years earlier, in a speech on 16 April 1953, President Eisenhower had stated that "This government is ready to ask its people to join with all nations in devoting a substantial percentage of the savings achieved by disarmament to a fund for world aid and reconstruction. The purpose of this great work would be to help other people to develop the under-developed areas of the world...". Not long after, at the Geneva Summit Talks of July 1955, French Premier Faure put forward a plan for a percentage reduction of military expenditure in which a part of the saving would be devoted to the developing countries. The plan required an international secretariat to determine a common definition of military expenditures, to collect the reductions, and to oversee their use by developing countries. To bypass the problem of verification, a form of automatic sanction was suggested by which each party would provide an agreed amount of the reduction from the military budget it had announced. The US and the UK were sceptical of the proposal and did not support it. In the following months, the French government submitted the proposal in the form of a draft agreement to the Disarmament Subcommittee of the United Nations Disarmament Commission.

In the succeeding years the USSR raised the question of military budgets in the UN several times, in 1957, 1958 and 1961. However, the "mutual-example" exercise which was to follow actually began in reverse. In March 1961, President Kennedy increased US defence appropriations as part of the new administration's defence plans. Premier Khrushchev explicitly stated that he was responding to the US increase when he announced an increase in the Soviet defence budget in early July. This in turn contributed to a second US military expenditure increase in late July related to the Berlin crisis. This second US move was given by Premier Khrushchev as the justification for a second Soviet move, the prolongation of military service. There were thus two parallel moves on each side, and in both cases the USSR explicitly stated that its action was a response to the prior US action. According to Arthur Schlesinger, Jr., by the autumn of 1961, this sequence had produced the notion in the minds of some of President Kennedy's advisers that if increases on the two sides could parallel each other in the upward direction, the same process might work for reductions as well.(16)

In the early summer of 1963, at the time of the Limited Test Ban Treaty negotiations in Moscow, Premier Khrushchev indicated Soviet interest in a European disengagement. On 19 July 1963, during the talks, he also publicly stated Soviet interest in a freeze or reduction of foreign troops in the territory of the German Democratic Republic and the Federal Republic of Germany.(17) The question was apparently first dealt with privately in Moscow, on 6 August 1963, at the Tripartite talks. It was then discussed again in New York on 28 September 1963, 3 October 1963, and 10 October 1963.

The discussions had begun in the context of reductions of foreign troops in the two Germanies. The USSR proposed a formal agreement, which involved verification by observation posts and military missions. "The United States was not prepared to consider a formal agreement. At the same time, however, both sides agreed on 'mutual-example' reductions of military expenditures." A summary of the 10 October 1963 discussions reads as follows:

> Secretary Rusk again noted the difficulties inherent in a formal agreement on the subject and said that since both sides appeared interested in limiting military expenditure perhaps there could be reciprocal actions in this field so that each side could draw its conclusions from the actions of the other side.(18)

The documents stress that the US decision to reduce its own defence budget was made before discussions on the subject were held with the USSR, and they assume that Soviet decisions to reduce their military expenditure were similarly taken prior to these discussions.

Following these talks, Secretary of Defense McNamara intimated in an 18 November 1963 address that the US defence budget would be reduced. On December 7, the Defense Department announced that it was planning a series of steps to save $ 1.5 billion in the current fiscal year 1964, and $ 4 billion by fiscal year 1967. On 13 December, Premier Khrushchev announced that the USSR would make some reductions in its military appropriations for 1964, and by the end of the month, the USSR had announced that the reduction would amount to 600 million rubles.(19) On 21 December, President Johnson announced the formation of a US government committee on the Economic Impact of Defense and Disarmament. Both Premier Khrushchev and Polish First Secretary Gomulka called on other nations to make further cuts. It was claimed that "other...Socialist countries followed the example of the Soviet Union and also cut down their military budgets".(20) On 8 January 1964, President Johnson announced that the forthcoming defence budget would be reduced for fiscal year 1964.

On 28 January 1964, the USSR proposed in the Eighteen Nation Disarmament Committee (ENDC) that an "agreement be reached to reduce military budgets of States by 10 to 15 per cent".(21) The USSR had apparently made other private suggestions to Washington in earlier years, proposing 30 per cent and 15 per cent reductions in US and USSR defence budgets. In February 1964, the USSR again indicated that "some other countries" besides the US and the USSR had also taken steps to reduce military budgets, left them unnamed, but asked additional countries to do the same. On 20 April, President Johnson and Premier Khrushchev also made parallel announcements of reductions in fissionable material production for weapons purposes. In response to Soviet requests for more sizeable cuts in military expenditure, however, the reply by the US spokesmen at the ENDC in April was a rather merciless dissection of all that was not known about the Soviet military budget. It began with the point that the Soviet proposal spoke of "budgets" rather than of "expenditures". It pointed out that the sole information made public by the USSR concerning its military budget was a single number, and that the USSR claimed that its military budget had declined from 1955 to 1961, at the same time as it was testing and deploying new strategic weapons and that this did not seem very plausible.(22)

The problem with all of the USSR's suggestions for more serious cuts in US and USSR military expenditure, such as those of 10, 15 or 30 per cent, directly concerns the words "budgets" and "expenditures" and their content. The USSR does, of course, release the single annual figure which it designates as its defence budget. It is widely understood, however, that this figure omits several large budgetary components that are included under military expenditure in other nations. The official Soviet figure is not considered credible by any source outside the USSR, including sources in Eastern Europe.

It is known that a detailed "estimate" (smeta) of expenditures on items for military use is compiled each year. The Soviets have not made this "estimate" public, but they have indicated that it is not defined in the same manner as the published "Defence" budget. The level and trend of the published "Defence" budget in the past two decades have not matched the observed changes in Soviet military manpower, operations, and weapons procurement.

The view that the announced Soviet military budget differs in coverage and is not comparable to most other budgets is expressed in the 1978 UN report, Economic and Social Consequences of the Arms Race and of Military Expenditure. Through buried in a footnote, the statement appeared in a consensus report of a group which included a Soviet expert, and therefore it carries an official connotation:

> Owing to differences in coverage and difficulties with currency conversion rates, these (official military budget figures for the Soviet Union from 1968 to 1977) figures are not directly comparable to military budget figures elsewhere in this report.(23)

The fact that the announced figure does not represent the complete military expenditure of the USSR has apparently even been admitted in recent years by Soviet representatives meeting with ministerial counterparts in Western Europe.

Holloway also quotes the following Soviet remark from 1968:

> "(a pricing system) of goods for military use ought to express fully the costs of live and concealed labor in their production... (only thus) is it possible to know the real outlays of society on the defense of the country and to compare them with other indices of economic development".(24)

An equally significant remark was apparently made by a USSR Gosplan specialist in 1970:

> Our national income is only 65 percent that of the United States. Yet it is obvious that we cannot spend less than the US does on National Defense... This means that the burden of our country is much greater than that of the United States.(25)

The categories of Soviet military expenditure which are presumed to be omitted from the USSR's announced figure are, among others, those for:

- military research and development,
- construction and maintenance expenditures for military facilities,
- the operational costs of military training establishments,
- the cost of stockpiling strategic defence materials,
- the financing of the defence industry,
- and possibly, the costs of civil defence programmes, as well as yet other small components.

These are, of course, sizeable categories and taken together their omission produces a situation in which the announced USSR defence "budget" bears only a marginal and indeterminate relation to actual USSR military expenditure. When the reductions were small, this was acceptable. In a formal agreement, and with far more sizeable cuts, it would not be. The announced USSR reduction of 600 million rubles amounted to 4 per cent of the official USSR defence appropriation for 1963. At the same time, the official 1963 USSR defence budget had risen by 10 per cent over that for 1962. Such an increase, taken together with the other unidentified portions of Soviet military expenditure, would easily compensate for any announced decrease. In addition, all the cuts made between 1963 and 1965 only amounted to 0.7 and 2.4 per cent of their base figures, depending on the method of calculation.(26)

The second round of US-USSR talks took place in November-December 1964 between Secretary Rusk and Foreign Minister Gromyko and

Ambassadors Tsarapkin and Foster. The context was once again the discussion of mutual force reductions in Europe. In late 1964, both sides had made small reductions. Rusk and Foster informed the Soviet representatives that the US military budget would be at least $ 1.25 billion lower in fiscal year 1966 than it had been in fiscal year 1964. This had been publicly announced by Secretary of Defense McNamara on 10 November 1964. The US did not want a formal agreement, since that would limit its freedom of action. There would be strong domestic political opposition to such an agreement, as well as opposition from particular NATO allies. However, the US now asked the USSR to agree to talks about the content of the respective US and USSR military budgets and how a limitation agreement could be verified. The US offered to send a high-level delegation to Moscow for secret negotiations for this purpose. The Soviet Draft Treaty on General and Complete Disarmament of 22 September 1962 had contained provisions in Articles 13, 26 and 35 (corresponding to the Soviet first, second and third stage proposals) granting inspectors from an "International Disarmament Organization ... unimpeded access to the records of central financial institutions..."(27)

The US request for discussion on the differences in the US and USSR military budgets was clearly a request for a good deal less. Nevertheless, the USSR did not accept the proposal for technical talks on the composition of military budgets or on verification problems. Instead, the USSR indicated that it would reduce its military budget for calender year 1965.(28) It further stated that the military budget would be reduced by 0.5 million rubles. "This amount", it was argued, "represented a proportion comparable to the reductions planned by the United States" - clearly indicating that the USSR was at least carrying out some sort of explicit calculation of amounts on its own. The public Soviet announcement came on 9 December 1964, in a speech by Premier Kosygin, in which he stated that US representatives had informed the USSR that there would also be US military expenditure cuts in fiscal year 1965 and fiscal year 1966. On the day of Premier Kosygin's statement, the White House Press Secretary was questioned about it and replied, "There is no agreement between the two countries on budget cutting, nor any effort whatsoever at mutuality in this matter". The US had simply transmitted the same information that Mr. McNamara had stated publicly on 10 November. A statement by Secretary Rusk also claimed that the reduction of military budgets on both sides "did not represent an agreement of any kind". Later Soviet statements made clear that the USSR believed it had an unwritten agreement to reduce military budgets on the basis of mutual example.

Washington's decisions in 1965 regarding the Vietnam War put an end to the exercise. In May 1965, the administration asked for a supplemental defence appropriation. Additional supplemental requests were also made in August 1965 and January 1966. By July 1965, Premier Kosygin announced that the USSR could not "economize on defence" because of the changed international situation. But Soviet spokesmen pointed out that the Soviet increase from 1965 to 1966 of 0.5 billion rubles was much lower than the US increase. No information at all has been made public about the content of the Rusk-Gromyko talks in September-October 1965, so it is impossible to know whether discussion of this subject again took place at that time and, if so, what its nature was. During the Glassboro talks of June 1967, President Johnson informed Premier Kosygin that he wanted to engage in negotiations on limiting military expenditures, and that he was holding back on authorization of the full development of a US ABM system until the possibility of budgetary limitations could be explored with the USSR. The nature of the Soviet reply is not known. In this case - with the Vietnam War continuing -Soviet interest in the subject was apparently not indicated again until a March 1971 statement by Party Secretary Brezhnev. At the end of 1973, the USSR again announced a reduction in its military expenditure, the first in ten years, for 1974.(29) However, since the announcement and the supposed reduction came in the midst of a major Soviet build-up of its strategic weapons, naval forces and tactical aircraft, it was not taken very seriously by Western nations.

It is interesting that the 1963-65 episode coincided with a period in which independent analysts identify a slowdown in the rise of USSR defence expenditure. Lee claims that the most rapid growth in Soviet military expenditure took place in the years 1959-63 and 1966-70, a period split exactly by the mutual expenditure reduction exercise.(30) If this is correct, it would indicate that Soviet political decision-makers did intervene to some unknown but perhaps small degree in what would ostensibly otherwise have been a somewhat different pattern of Soviet defence decision-making in those years, with perhaps some temporary implications for weapons acquisition processes. Limited as they were, the 1963-65 events are nevertheless a significant and atypical episode in the post-WW II US-USSR military competition.

Conversion Legislation and the Ackley Report

At the same time as discussions were being held with Soviet officials concerning mutual US-USSR military expenditure reductions and US officials were planning to end various weapon procurement programmes, legislation relating to the conversion of military industries began to be introduced into the two houses of the US Congress. For example, in October 1963, fifteen Senators introduced a bill to provide for a National Economic Conversion Commission (Senator McGovern and fourteen others, S-2274). Two other bills were put forward at roughly the same time, proposing a Commission on the Application to Community and Human Needs (Senator Hart and two others, S-2298) and a Commission on Automation, Technology and Employment (Senator Humphrey and five others, S-2427). Somewhat later, in January 1965, 30 Senators introduced a bill to provide for a National Economic Conversion and Diversification Commission (Senator

McGovern and 29 others, S-30). Companion legislation in the House of Representatives was proposed by fifteen Congressmen. The Johnson administration opposed this legislation.

In fact, despite governmental interest in the economic effects of disarmament, conversion legislation fared poorly. The only exception was legislation relating to the Office of Economic Adjustment in the Department of Defense. The OEA had been set up in March 1961 and, as noted above, it was solely concerned with military base closures. As such, it was not directly linked to the issue of defence industry conversion.

In the eighteen months between the initiation of the Ackley Committee and the appearance of its report in July 1965, there was a considerable amount of interest in the economic effects of reductions in military expenditure and the need for defence industry conversion.(31) At the same time, it was recognized that military expenditure was not "dropping off steeply as some expected"; rather, it "...probably will remain more or less level during the next four years".(32) In addition, while an entire series of major weapons procurement programmes had been cancelled or cut between 1961 and 1963, the period as a whole was one of increasing defence industry employment. For example, while at least seven major missile and aircraft programmes were cut, defence industrial employment nonetheless increased by 10 per cent over an eighteen month period in 1961-62. The Ackley Committee was clearly directed to be as much concerned with changes within the composition and pattern of defence expenditure as it was to be with the total level of such expenditure.

It is not surprising, therefore, that an unpublished Congressional committee report of August 1964 was even more emphatic in taking the view that,

> These concepts ("defense industry conversion") have little or no relevancy to our present problems. Inasmuch as we anticipate no immediate major reductions in defense spending, the phrase "defense industry conversion" appears misleading and inappropriate. However, defense is not a growth industry and if existing defense industries are to share in our national economic growth, some will have to diversify. Therefore, despite the title of the subcommittee report, we shall use the word "diversification", rather than conversion. It is possible that at some future date a major agreement with the Soviet Union might lead to sudden reductions in defense expenditures and a large "conversion" program. We believe that contingency plans for such an eventuality, however unlikely, should be prepared, but this is not the present problem and therefore will not be considered in this report...
>
> What is the problem? In the years ahead changes in composition of defense spending will result in increased sales for some

companies and decreased sales for others. This will create problems and opportunities not only for industry, but also for communities and individuals. Furthermore, it will provide an opportunity for the reallocation of national resources.(33)

The report of the Ackley Committee was delayed into 1965 for domestic political reasons relating to the 1964 Goldwater-Johnson Presidential election. When the report appeared in July 1965, it stated,

> This report is designed to accomplish four main purposes:
>
> 1. To provide information on the impact of changing defense programmes on the American economy;
>
> 2. To describe existing policies and programs for aiding employees, companies, and communities in adjusting to changes in the pattern of expenditures for defense;
>
> 3. To suggest and analyze additional policies and programs which may be needed;
>
> 4. To help to stimulate thinking about opportunities for the productive use of resources which may be released as needs for defense change.(34)

It did some of these things, particularly discussing existing government programmes and classical fiscal strategy that was applicable to various shifts in government expenditure. However, there were no new suggestions, no new programmes. By July 1965 the Vietnam build-up was in progress, and the government was soon to produce quite the opposite sort of economic problem by a rapid increase in military expenditure.

The expansion of US involvement in Vietnam had brought an end to the US-USSR mutual reduction exercises. Nonetheless, within a few years, some discussions began to take place within government concerning the post-Vietnam period when military expenditure was expected to decline. In early 1967, the Cabinet Coordinating Committee on Economic Planning for the End of Vietnam Hostilities was organized with Gardner Ackley, now chairman of the President's Council of Economic Advisers, as its chairman. The Committee was described as being,

> ... hard at work on the plans for an orderly economic transition when war ends. The Committee is drawing up not only plans to minimize the pain of post-Vietnam dislocations, but also plans to maximize the opportunities created by the end of hostilities.
>
> In his charge to the Committee last January, the President asked it
>
> 1. "to consider possibilities and priorities for tax reduction;

2. to prepare, with the Federal Reserve Board, plans for quick adjustments of monetary and financial policy;

3. to determine which high-priority programs can be quickly expanded;

4. to determine priorities for the longer-range expansion of programs to meet the needs of the American people...

5. to study and evaluate the future direction of federal financial support to our state and local governments;

6. to examine ways in which the transition to peace can be smoothed for the workers, companies and communities now engaged in supplying our defense needs and the men released from our armed forces."

In response to these instructions, the task force has had groups working in nine subject areas: tax policies for peacetime; the nation's peacetime fiscal-monetary needs; spending priorities; federal-state-local relationships; plans for demobilization; regional and industrial problems; manpower problems; the balance-of-payments outlook; and the liquidity problems in individuals, business, and government after the return of peace.

From these assignments, it is apparent that part of the planning job is aimed at minimizing the drop-off of economic activity and speeding its redirection as demobilization progresses. This requires careful programing and early agreement on moves that the Executive Branch can take to speed up certain expenditures, replenish military stockpiles depleted by war, and work with the Federal Reserve System to ease money and lower interest rates. It also involved plans for quick introduction of tax-cut legislation in Congress.(35)

The report of the Committee came in January 1969.(36) It was remarkably thin and, in any case, it could confer no particular obligations on the new Nixon administration about to take office, which might have rather different views on questions of national defence needs (i.e., new weapon systems), economic policy or "the urgent needs of our society".

6.3. THE NIXON-FORD PERIOD

The "fiscal dividend" which was expected to be produced by reduced US activity in Southeast Asia never really materialized, at least not as a coherent entity to which alternative planning and priorities would be applied.(37) Some of it was absorbed by new strategic weapon systems, some by inflationary costs of on-going domestic programmes. Welfare transfers, for example, rose dramatically in the next half dozen years.

Furthermore, the attitudes of the highest echelons of the DoD and the administration were quite different in 1969-70 to those expressed by McNamara and other administration officials in the 1962-63 period. There was no planning for new jobs other than to assume that industry would move into new sectors as needs and opportunities presented themselves. One million new jobs had been created specifically by the war economy between 1965 and 1975 - 38 local areas had experienced increases in defence employment exceeding 5 per cent of their total work force - and these levels were unlikely to be maintained.(38) Yet, without the expressed administration interest and support for defence industry conversion studies that Secretary McNamara's office had shown - at least for the largest and most specialized aerospace corporations in the defence industrial sector - defence firms now expressed reluctance to consider conversion.

There were two ad hoc examinations of the impact of military expenditure on the national economy during the Nixon administration. The first appeared in the statement of Paul McCracken, the new chairman of the President's Council of Economic Advisers, before an extensive set of Hearings on the Military Budget and National Economic Priorities in 1969.(39) The second was in the Economic Report of the President for the year 1970, in which the subject did not, however, appear in any explicit way in a report of nearly 200 pages.(40) In March 1970, President Nixon had formed a "President's Interagency Economic Adjustment Committee", whose role, however, was only to facilitate the work of the already existing Department of Defense's Office of Economic Adjustment in regard to the closing of military bases within the US. This was the only area in which the Nixon-Ford administrations provided readjustment assistance. There was a series of very extensive base closures in 1969, 1970 and 1973, as a means of obtaining more funds for weapons procurement. In 1973, the budget authorization for the OEA was $ 50 million.(41) Nixon's interagency Economic Adjustment Committee was provided with representation from nineteen Federal departments, agencies and offices, to facilitate this effort.

Although defence spending fell in real terms during this period, defence industry conversion was a non-topic. In fact, in a period of high unemployment, the maintenance of employment began to be heard more and more as a "reason" for maintaining military expenditure, aerospace production and overseas arms sales. However, shifts within the segments of military expenditure were again expected to take place. Weapons procurement would again shift, this time from conventional hardware back to missiles and aircraft, exactly reversing the changes that had taken place in 1961-64. Inflation and higher military pay scales would even force a cut in military manpower to pay for increased weapon procurement.(42) In 1974, the administration explicitly increased the defence budget "to provide additional employment", while cutting civilian expenditures that would have had the same effect.

At least for the ten-year period of 1967-77, there was substantial US Congressional suspicion that the budget authorization requests for the US DoD, put forward by the military services, the Department and the Office of the President, were "padded" in advance to compensate for the cuts of 1-5 per cent that Congress often made in particular programmes. In at least one instance, it was clear that the administration had also padded the DoD budget to maintain or increase jobs in the defence sector and to act as a stimulus to the economy.(43) At the very same time, the same administration was impounding Congressionally legislated funds for projects in the sectors of education, housing, water resources and municipal sanitation - all of which would have provided greater numbers of jobs than equivalent expenditure in the defence sector and would implicitly have performed some "conversion" - on the argument that the appropriations for these non-defence purposes were "inflationary". The House of Representatives voted funds to procure two additional B-1 bombers, which had been authorized earlier, though the programme had been cancelled in the interim. The motive was at least in part to maintain 5,500 jobs at the contractor, Rockwell International. However, the expenditure for the two aircraft was $ 462 million, at a cost of $ 84,000 per man employed, for two aircraft that would not be used.(44) Federal public works programmes cost about $ 12,000 per year per person employed. The same sum of $ 462 million could therefore have funded some 20,000 jobs in the civil sector for two years. It is calculations such as these, which are readily available to the Congress, which make it quite difficult to argue that the decisions are made for the sake of "jobs" per se.

In general, the Congress has viewed proposals for the conversion of military industry unsympathetically. Even so, there has been an impressive and surprisingly large amount of specific legislation dealing with either defence industry conversion or the reduction of military expenditure put to both Houses of Congress since 1963. Some of the early attempts at conversion legislation have already been mentioned. It is impossible to review all the details of the conversion legislation proposed during the three administrations preceding the present one. In 1971 alone, for example, some 30 separate conversion-related bills were before Congress.(45) The following, therefore, is an illustrative, rather than exhaustive, listing.

- In March 1969, 35 Senators introduced a bill to provide for a National Economic Conversion Commission (Senator McGovern and 34 others, S-1285). Companion legislation in the House was proposed by 50 Congressmen.

- On 14 August 1970, a bill was introduced proposing a Conversion Research, Education and Assistance Act (Senator Kennedy, S-4241).

- On 2 October 1970, a bill was introduced proposing a National Economic Conversion Act (Senator McGovern, S-

4430).

- On 11 March 1971, thirteen Senators introduced a bill proposing a National Peacetime Transition Act (Senator McGovern and twelve others, S-1191). At the same time, there were three other conversion bills before the Senate, seven before the House, and six other employment aid bills in the House.

- In August 1971, there were more than 30 piece of conversion-related legislation, for the purpose of converting defence industries and retraining defence workers, pending before the US Congress.(46)

- In May 1977, a bill proposing a Conversion Adjustment Assistance Act of 1977 was introduced (Congressman Bingham, H.R.-2002).

- On 2 November 1977, a bill was introduced proposing a Defense Economic Adjustment Act (Senator McGovern and one other, S-2279).

- In 1979 Senators McGovern and Mathias again submitted similar legislation, S-1301, which was reintroduced in 1980.

An important aspect of the funding usually suggested to enable defence industry conversion is support for workers displaced as a result of the closing of defence plants. American labour unions have already made proposals for adjustment assistance to workers displaced as a result of changes in international trade legislation. They have also indicated that they would probably advocate essentially the same kinds of support for workers involved in a conversion programme from military to civilian production.(47) In 1966, a US Congressional study surveyed worker relocation programmes in Belgium, Canada, Denmark, France, Holland, Norway, Sweden, the UK, West Germany and the United States.(48) More recently, several interesting defence industry conversion studies were carried out in England, but these have attracted no attention in Washington.(49)

Not only has defence industry conversion legislation failed to attract the support of many members of Congress, the trend since 1976 has been for rising military expenditure in real terms. While increased allocations to the military have generally been popular in Congress, there was one additional category of legislation designed to reduce military expenditure. These were the "transfer amendments" which began to be offered during the 1976 (FY 1977) US Department of Defense appropriations process. Over many years and through many administrations, there had often been amendments during this process which suggested one or another cut in the DoD appropriations requested by the administration. Reduction amendments were usually rejected, though now and then one or two would pass. Sometimes cuts were made in the Senate-House Conference Committee, which had to resolve differences in the legislation passed by the two Houses of Congress. Amendments for such direct cuts continued in the first years of the Carter administration. However, in addition to them, "transfer amendments" appeared. These proposed specific cuts in the requested DoD appropriation but, in addition, specified in detail the alternative uses to which the cut funds were to be applied. For example, in 1976, the Holtzman transfer amendment proposed a reduction of $ 7.5 billion in DoD budget authority and $ 2.5 billion in outlays. The $ 2.5 billion was divided into specific sums to be appropriated to eight civilian programmes. It was calculated that the $ 2.5 billion, if applied to the eight alternative programmes, would have generated 235,000 jobs. The amendment was defeated in the US House of Representatives by 317 to 85 votes (29 April 1976). (An amendment for a straight $ 2 billion cut in budget authority, and $ 0.3 billion in outlays, with no transfer involved, was defeated by fewer votes, 255 to 145; 28 April 1976). In general, "transfer amendments" have been as unsuccessful as conversion legislation.

Groups of Senators and Representatives have also attempted to affect the budgetary process by presenting alternative budgets for military expenditure. Alternative budgets for military expenditure were put forward in the early and mid-1970s by the Members of Congress for Peace Through Law, a loose affiliation of some 31 US Senators and over 100 members of the House of Representatives. The proposals of this group are routinely backed up by detailed and substantial analysis and critique.(50) A second Congressional group that has carried out similar studies is the Democratic Study Group.(51)

The reductions suggested were usually arrived at by specifying particular weapon systems which it was felt should not be purchased at all, or should be purchased only in reduced quantities. The analyses simultaneously provided to support these alternative defence appropriation recommendations have at times been quite detailed. The sums which it has been suggested could be cut have ranged from $ 5-10 billion to $ 30 billion (at times, from 5-30 per cent of the total defence budget). In addition, it has quite often been argued that the resultant defence budget and force structure would increase US national security and improve US defence, rather than detract from them, despite the expenditure cuts. It was further argued that the cuts were either of "fat" - procurements that were excessive to real military requirements - or were counterproductive to US military security.

Yet none of these broad, alternative defence budget proposals, which offered plans for coherent and reduced US military expenditure, have ever had the slightest political impact, neither on the Office of the Executive to accept them, nor on the Congres to enact them. None has ever been put before the US Congress in the form of legislation. The sizeable reduction of US defence expenditure was an important aspect of Senator George McGovern's unsuccessful presidential election campaign of 1972.(52) In 1976, President Carter advocated a somewhat smaller reduction in US defence expenditure as part of his election campaign, but the opposite took place almost immediately after his administration took office. Other, non-governmental groups also made proposals for reductions in or realignments of defence expenditure during the 1970s, but these also had no political impact.(53)

6.4. CONCLUSIONS

In the early 1960s when Secretary of Defence McNamara and his closest deputies anticipated a reduction in US defence expenditure in the coming years, the Kennedy administration initiated studies on the question of defence industry conversion. Coincidentally, following the easing of US-USSR relations in the wake of the October 1962 Cuban missile crisis and the subsequent signing of the Limited Test Ban Treaty, the United States and the Soviet Union initiated several informal mutual-example reduction exercises. These were extremely interesting episodes, anomalous in post-WW II US-USSR relations, and they have been studied very little. One of these exercises concerned military expenditure reduction and lasted from 1963 to early 1965. For a short period these two concerns, military expenditure reduction and defence industry conversion, interacted and simultaneously obtained at least marginal attention from the administration.

Though the mutual reduction episode was short, and in many respects remains ambiguous due to the absence of complete information, what is known seems nevertheless to provide some strikingly explicit lessons.

"Mutual-example" interactions had certainly worked - both for increases and for decreases. In the 1963-65 cases, the US seemed to find the Soviet statements of its decreases acceptable without any verification, perhaps because they were quite limited and perhaps for other reasons concerning US estimates of USSR military expenditure at the time as well. When pressed for further decreases, formal agreements, and for troop reductions, the US made clear that "the prospect of further US action was not promising". There were limits beyond which the US government was not prepared to go. The constraints were its NATO allies and domestic political considerations.

The USSR was not interested in negotiations to identify the content of its military expenditures. It is fair to presume that such identification would be the only basis for continuous and really sizeable - and formal -agreements to reduce military expenditure. The Soviet position on this question in these private negotiations, and again since their own more recent proposals concerning military expenditure reduction in 1973, is at least in some contradiction with the sections of their GCD proposals of 1962 which dealt with the verification of military budgets. When decreases took place, the US was at pains to indicate that they were not made by agreement, but were at its own initiative.

Though formal agreements were not involved, clearly the exercise would not have run through more than one or two phases on the part of either participant without a parallel act from the other. The USSR, on the other hand, particularly identified US collaboration in the reduction process in their public statements. Further, when the process ended, Soviet spokesman privately complained to important US visitors that an agreement or understanding had been broken.

The consideration of defence industry conversion in the early 1960s was primarily prompted by the concern of the DoD itself. It meant studies for the nation's major defence contractors in diversification or alternative production, and it was as much concerned with transitions within the mix of defence procurement as it was with changes that might follow the absolute reduction of the Department's budget. The issue was made obsolete by an entirely irrelevant event, the decision to escalate US military involvement in Vietnam. But at no time, and even less during the subsequent Republican administrations and the post-Vietnam period of actual real decline in US defence expenditure, did any of the administrations show the slightest sympathy for planning defence industry convercion. They opposed all Congressional legislation over a fifteen-year period designed to facilitate such planning.

This paper has been primarily an examination of United States policy and politics, focusing on official considerations to reduce US military expenditure within some sort of explicit arms control framework. This did not succeed in any substantial sense. Nevertheless, as already indicated (see p. 108 above and ref 4) real US military expenditure did drop substantially in the early and mid-1970s during the Nixon and Ford administrations, albeit for other domestic reasons. The USSR therefore had another chance, for a period of a half dozen years during the height of the "détente" period, to repeat the mutual-example pattern of parallel reductions that were carried out in the 1963-65 period, either with or without prior discussions with the US. By all indications, the USSR did not do so. The question that is of most relevance to recent and present events is therefore why the USSR did not do so, and what light this sheds on expectations for the near term.

It is impossible to know if there were any high level discussions again during the 1970s regarding resumption of a mutual reduction of military expenditure, initiated either by the US or the USSR. The US record for this period remains classified,(54) and there are no indications in any of the volumes describing the SALT negotiations or in already published memoirs by diplomats of the period that would suggest that reduction of military expenditure was being discussed.

The USSR did two things during the time that US military expenditure was falling in real terms during the period of the 1970s. The first of these was to make its proposal in the UN in 1973 for a 10 % reduction in military expenditure. The second was to announce a series of small reductions in its own "Defence Budget", starting with a drop of 300 million rubles form 1973-74, a second drop of the same amount for 1974-75, 100 million each in 1976-77 and 1979-80, and finally 50 million in 1980-81.(55) Superficially these two moves might lead some analysts to think that the USSR was making some kind of gesture. However, as the supposed reduction came during a period of major build-up in Soviet weapon systems and in view of the more detailed analysis below, the announcement was not considered very credible.

The USSR's defence sector is mostly, if not entirely, funded through its National Budget, with the published "Defence Budget" as only one of the accounts funding defence. The Science account funds some of the military R&D, and the National Economy account includes some, if not all, of the procurement outlays. The USSR's National Budget since 1965 has grown at over 7 per cent year, and other defence-related accounts, representing nearly 40 per cent of the National Budget, have grown at about 10 per cent per year over the same time span.(56) Nevertheless, from 1970 through 1977 and on through 1981 the USSR reported a constant, or declining, "Defence Budget".

Even more astonishing, the <u>announced</u> East European defence budgets, which <u>do</u> represent most of the major defence outlays of these nations, continued to rise in the same 1970 to 1977 period with average growth rates, apparently including that due to inflation, for the DDR of 7.3 per cent, Poland of 6.2 per cent, Hungary of 5.8 per cent and Czechoslovakia of 4.7 per cent.(57) It is preposterous to imagine that these states have been increasing their military expenditure during this period while that of the USSR, with its entire new generation of ICBMs, SLBMs, naval vessels, and tactical aircraft has been decreasing.

Estimated Soviet defence spending in rubels reflects the costs of military activities within the Soviet economy and is meant to replicate, in a general sense, the resource allocation choices confronting the Soviet leadership. Ruble defence spending is defined in two ways. A lower range of spending estimates is based on the definition of defence used in the US. The definition of spending is broadened in the upper range to include additional military-related activities which the Soviets may view as part of their defence effort. These include civilian space activities (operated in the United States by the NASA, construction, railroad, and MVD internal security troops, foreign military assistance, military stockpiling, and some civil defence activities. Estimated USSR ruble defence spending in 1980 totaled between 61 and 66 billion rubles for the narrow definition of defence, and as much as 72 billion rubles for the broad definition.(58) In contrast, the official Soviet "Defence" budget for 1980 was 17.124 billion rubles, only one-quarter (27 %) the estimate of real Soviet military expenditure. Since 1978, Soviet military spending has continued to increase at roughly its long-term historical rate of four per cent (in constant prices) while economic growth has slowed sharply. Estimates indicate that the share of economic output absorbed by the Soviet military has risen to the range of 12 to 14 per cent as a result. While these estimates use the Western concepts of constant prices and gross national product in making these judgments, it is likely that similar trends would appear when Soviet officials made their calculations using current prices and net material product (roughly equivalent to gross national product minus depreciation and services such as education and health).

It is possible to hazard a guess that the differing Soviet responses in the two periods - 1963-65, and post-1970 - have something to do with the different relationships of Khrushchev and of the Brezhnev leadership to the Soviet military. In addition the USSR's political situation in the mid-1970's also differs critically, in clear and pronounced ways, from that in the 1960s:

- The European political situation had been stabilized dramatically through the various treaties between the USSR and its WTO allies and the Federal Republic of Germany

- the USSR finally achieved parity in strategic nuclear weapons with the United States, a situation that was publicly recognized by the SALT process

- The USSR began to develop - and to utilize - military projection forces for engagement in geographic areas far from its borders in various third world areas.

Another analyst has formulated this situation in a slightly more indirect way. Finley suggests that a failure of the USSR leadership to change the status quo of its ongoing weapons procurement decisions in the light of an altered context is equivalent to a new policy goal:

> The evolution of the Soviet and WTO margin of conventional superiority is traceable less to acceleratd Soviet increases in various categories of forces than to US and NATO decreases during the early 1970s. This fact sustains credibility for the hypothesis that Soviet superiority proceeds in part from the momentum of Soviet R&D and procurement programs, rather than completely from a deliberate decision to seeks superiority. The highly visible downturn of U.S. defense budgets in real terms, throughout the first half of the 1970s (which cannot be attributed to post-Vietnam reductions alone), manifests a policy change that has not been met by any response in kind from the USSR. Acceptance of parity would have produced decisions to contradict growth sustained by inertia. With each passing year, the hypothesis of momentum has become less credible. By the mid-1970s, an observer could only conclude that superiority of conventional forces in Europe was a priority for which the Soviet leadership was willing to sacrifice important alternative allocations of resources.(59)

Irrespective of what the causes may have been, the point of overriding significance is that during the 1970s the USSR, by all apparent indications, did not follow suit and reduce military expenditure when the opportunity was clearly present to do so in parallel with US reductions that were taking place. The implications of this for those seeking such reductions at the present time and in the near future is thus crucial. It would appear that USSR military expenditure will continue to rise in the coming years for several reasons:

- Data on planned growth in machine building and metalworking (the key military production sector), capital investment, and consumer durables in the latest Soviet five year plan indicate that substantial room has been left for significant increases in military procurement.

- There has been no significant reduction to date in the rate of expansion of Soviet military production facilities.

- The number of weapon systems in development and testing has remained virtually constant for the past decade. Both of these trends point to ongoing increases in military production and procurement.(60)

- Soviet comments on planned increases in US defence spending have made it clear that there will be a strong response from the USSR. The Soviet military has stressed Brezhnev's statement regarding Soviet actions to counteract increased US capabilities.

Several other recent studies agree with this assessment that USSR military expenditure will continue to increase in the coming years.(61)

It is important for those who suggest international arms control initiatives to understand the political realities they are attempting to modify. The political climate and state of affairs that were faced by the 1977-79 suggestions for reduction of military expenditure prompted by United Nations activities were entirely different from those during the 1963-65 period. This was so even before the sharp rise in military expenditure that was set in train by the incoming Reagan administration and that is almost certain to provoke a USSR response. And even in that earlier period, the subject matter of this paper demonstrates the very limited and fragile nature of the agreements that were possible. What kinds of policy recommendations could be made on the basis of the analysis presented above is another and more difficult question, but there will be no success for proposals based on fanciful premises. The promise for a continued severe military environment for the coming years is clear and obvious.

NOTES AND REFERENCES

* An earlier version of this paper appeared in Public Policy, Vol. 29, No 4, Fall 1981, pp. 437-471. The studies which resulted in this paper were originally done as part of a project commissioned by the Swedish Ministry of Foreign Affairs and were carried out at the Peace Studies Program, Center for International Studies, Cornell University. The author would like to thank Nicole Ball for extensive help in editing the final version of the paper.

As an Appendix to this chapter the author prepared a detailed list of sources regarding military expenditure and defence industrial structure in the USSR. Due to the lack of space the list - consisting of 231 references - cannot be published here. A shorter version was published in the Journal of Peace Research, Vol. 16, No. 3, 1979, pp. 263-277.

1. Nicole Ball and Milton Leitenberg, Disarmament and Development: Their Interrelationship, Bulletin of Peace Proposals, Vol. 10, No. 3, 1979, pp. 247-259.

2. See the sections on "World Military Expenditure" in Stockholm International Peace Research Institute, World Armaments and Disarmament. SIPRI Yearbook 1979, London 1979, as well as the analagous sections in the volumes for 1977, 1978, and 1980.

3. For an extensive compilation of sources pertaining to estimates of USSR military expenditure see, Milton Leitenberg, The Counterpart of Defense Industry Conversion in the United States: The USSR Economy, Defense Industry and Military Expenditure. An Introduction and Guide to the Sources, Journal of Peace Research, Vol. 16, No. 3, 1979, pp. 263-277.

4. Department of Defense, Annual Report Fiscal Year 1981, Harold Brown, Secretary of Defense, pp. 292-295.

5. Office of Management and Budget. Figures cited in W. Williams, Military Spending: Fight on Rise Grows, New York Times, March 19, 1981.

6. US Senate, Committee on Labor and Public Welfare, Testimony of Deputy Secretary R. Gilpatric, in Nation's Manpower Revolution. Part 7, 88th Cong. 1st Sess., Washington, DC: US Govt. Printing Office, 6 November 1963, pp. 2405-2423, and Defense Impact on Jobs Studied, Gilpatric Discounts Effect in Senate Testimony, New York Times, 6 November 1963. The studies funded by the ACDA are listed and summarized in The Economic Impact of Reductions in Defence Spending, ACDA Publication 64, July 1972, 31 pp.

7. J. Raymond, President Orders Survey on Disarmament Outlook, New York Times, 22 December 1963.

8. Economic Impact of Arms Control Agreements - Study by Senate Subcommittee on Disarmament, Congressional Record 108:182 (5 October 1962): S-21391 to S-21395.

9. Will Arms Control Bankrupt the Aerospace Industry, Space/Aeronautics 35, April 1961, pp. 42-43.

10. US Senate, Select Committee on Small Business, Hearings and Report: Impact of Defense Spending on Labor-Surplus Areas, 88th Cong., 1st Sess., Washington, DC: US Govt. Printing Office, 19 August 1963; US Senate, Committee on Labor and Public Welfare, Subcommittee on Employment and Manpower, Hearings: Nation's Manpower Revolution, Parts 7, 8, 9, 88th Cong., 1st Sess., Washington, DC: US Govt. Printing Office, October, November, December 1963; and US Congress, Joint Economic Committee, Economic Policies and Practices, Paper No. 8, Programs for Relocating Workers Used by Governments of Selected Countries, 89th Cong., 2nd Sess., Washington, DC: US Govt. Printing Office, 1966.

11. US Senate, Nation's Manpower Revolution, Part 8, op. cit., pp. 2725-2726.

12. National Economic Conversion Commission, Congressional Record (Senate) 109:175 (31 October 1963): S-19723 to S-19741.

13. United Nations, Department of Economic and Social Affairs, Economic and Social Consequences of Disarmament, E/3593/Rev. 1, New York 1962.

14. US Arms Control and Disarmament Agency, Economic Impact of Disarmament, Washington, DC: January 1962. In Britain, a private foundation, the United World Trust, commissioned a study by the Economist Intelligence Unit which was published as, Economist Intelligence Unit, The Economic Effects of Disarmament, London 1963.

15. Much of the narrative in this section of the paper is based on two recently declassified documents: a) "Summit Talks on Military Expenditure Limitations, 1955-1967", Arms Control and Disarmament Agency paper, declassified and released in 1976 to David Linebaugh, and b) "American-Soviet Bilateral Talks on 'Mutual-Example' Force Reductions in Europe, 1963-1964", declassified in September 1976.

In addition, the records of the Kennedy Library provide the dates and topics of meetings between US and USSR cabinet-level officials during this period.

The record of most of the public statements regarding military expenditure reductions that accompanied the 1963-1964 diplomatic discussions appear in the volumes of Documents on Disarmament for the years 1963 and 1964, published by the US Arms Control and Disarmament Agency. Individual page references appear in the references below. These volumes, however, give no indication that US-USSR discussions were taking place.

A parallel rendition to that appearing here, with slightly different emphasis, appears as "Appendix B. The US-USSR 'Mutual-Example' Episodes, 1963-1964", pp. 117-121, in Abraham S. Becker, Military Expenditure Limitation for Arms Control: Problems and Prospects, Cambridge, Mass. 1977.

16. A.J. Schlesinger, A Thousand Days: John F. Kennedy in the White House, Boston 1965, pp. 499, 503.

17. Premier Khrushchev, 19 July 1963, Documents on Disarmament, 1963, US Arms Control and Disarmament Agency, Washington, D.C. 1964, pp. 247-248.

18. These quotations come from the recently declassified material cited in reference 17.

19. Documents on Disarmament, 1963, op. cit., pp. 593, 638-639, 643, 651-653.

20. ENDC/PV. 168, Documents on Disarmament, 1964, Washington D.C., US Arms Control and Disarmament Agency, 1965, pp. 49-53. See also, I. Glagolev, Reducing Military Expenses, A Soviet View, Disarmament No. 12, December 1966, pp. 1-4, 15.

21. ENDC/123, 28 January 1964, Documents on Disarmament, 1964, op. cit., pp. 12-15.

22. Statement of US Ambassador Adrian Fisher, ENDC/PV. 182, 19 April 1964, p. 38. Also in Documents on Disarmament, 1964, op. cit., pp. 152-157.

23. Economic and Social Consequences of the Arms Race and of Military Expenditure, New York: United Nations, 1978, footnote 63, pp. 33, 36.

24. B.V. Sokolov, ed., Military Economic Questions in the Political Economy Course, Moscow: Voenizdat, 1968, p. 227, cited in David Holloway, Technology and Political Decisions of Soviet Armaments Policy, Journal of Peace Research, Vol. 11, No. 4, 1974, p. 268.

25. US Congress, Joint Economic Committee, Hearings: Allocation of Resources in the Soviet Union and China - 1978, Part 4: Soviet Union, 95th Cong., Washington D.C., US Govt. Printing Office, June, July 1978, p. 198.

26. Becker, op. cit., pp. 118, 120.

27. Documents on Disarmament, 1962, Washington D.C., US Arms

Control and Disarmament Agency, 1963, pp. 913, 922, 928-929, 932.

28. The USSR has consistently opposed any detailed examination of its military expenditure, both in these private 1963-1965 US-USSR discussions, and in the framework of the post-1973 CCD-Geneva discussions and their related series of UN studies on military expenditure reduction and the establishment of uniform accounting methods for the reporting of military expenditure.

29. M. Parker, Soviet Union to Reduce Military Budget in '74, Baltimore Sun, 13 December 1973.

30. W.T. Lee, Soviet Defense Expenditure in an Era of SALT, USSI Report No. 79-1, United States Strategic Institute, Washington D.C. 1979, p. 30. Lee also shows a drop in USSR military expenditure in the years 1955-1956. If this is so, and if it then was simply a coincidence or whether it was any sort of Soviet "signal" at the time that the 1955 French proposal was being considered is not known.

31. Defense Industry Lacks Plans for Civilian Production, New York Times, 16 August 1963; What Can Industry Do As Pentagon Cuts Back, Newsweek, 7 October 1963, pp. 87-90; The Urgent Need for Conversion Planning (Senator George McGovern), Congressional Record (Senate), 23 April 1964, pp. S-8649 to S-8655; Aerospace Industries of America, Survey Forecasts a Further 3.4 % Decline in Aerospace Employment by Fall 1964, Economic Data Service, Washington D.C.; Recent and Pending Layoffs in 14 Major Defense Firms, 24 March 1964; Defense Cuts Bring a New Kind of Job Crisis, U.S. News & World Report, 18 March 1964, pp. 80-83; Impact of Defense Spending Shifts and Curtailments on Small Business, Notice of Hearings (Senator Sparkman), Congressional Record (Senate), 4 June 1964, pp. S-12235 to S-12237; D. Oberdorfer, Where to Cutback Cuts Deep, Saturday Evening Post, 12 September 1964, pp. 17-20; D. Allison, Defense Cutbacks, International Science & Technology, October 1964, pp. 19-31.

32. R.F. Janssen, Spending for Peace, Plan Sought to shift Defense Brainpower to Big Public Projects, Wall Street Journal, 7 October 1964.

33. Report of the Subcommittee, on Possibilities and Policies for Industrial Conversion, Washington D.C., August 1964, unpublished.

34. Report of the Committee on the Economic Impact of Defense and Disarmament, US Govt. Printing Office, Washington D.C., July 1965.

35. W. Heller, Getting Ready for Peace, Harpers Magazine, April 1968, pp. 57-62.

36. Report to the President from the Cabinet Coordinating Committee on Economic Planning for the End of Vietnam Hostilities, pp. 181-211, in Economic Report of the President, Washington D.C., January 1969.

37. C.L. Schultze, The Fiscal Dividend After Vietnam: Military Versus Civilian Spending, pp. 45-86, in Hearings: The Military Budget and National Economic Priorities, Part I, US Congress, Joint Economic Committee, 91st Cong., 1st Sess., US Govt. Printing Office, Washington D.C. 1969; C.L. Schultze et al., Vietnam and the Peace Dividend, pp. 102-107, in Setting National Priorities, The 1972 Budget, The Brookings Institution, Washington D.C. 1971.

38. Million Jobs Created by Intensification of War, New York Times, 14 January 1967.

39. P.W. McCracken, Statement, pp. 648-664, in The Military Budget and National Economic Priorities, Part II, US Congress, Joint Economic Committee, op. cit.

40. Economic Report of the President, Washington D.C., January 1971.

41. S. Rich, U.S. Senate Approves Funds for Cities Hit by Military Cuts, International Herald Tribune, 26 September 1973 (and Washington Post, 25 September 1973).

42. B.D. Nossiter, Arms Firms See Postwar Spurt, Washington Post, 8 December 1968; B.D. Nossiter, Defense Firms Leery of Civilian Work, 'No-Risk' Contracts Heighten Appeal of Arms Business, Washington Post, 9 December 1968; N. Sheehan, U.S. Study Denies War's End Will Aid Domestic Programs, New York Times, 26 August 1969; E.L. Dale, 'Normal' Increases Seen Using $ 45-Billion of 'Peace Dividend', New York Times, 11 September 1969; W. Beecher, Laird Says Defense Cuts Will Cost 1,250,000 Jobs, New York Times, 16 January 1970; Aerospace Tries to Pick up the Pieces, Business Week, 12 December 1970; W. McAllister, Aerospace Crisis Defense Firms Find it Isn't Easy to Switch to Peacetime Work, Wall Street Journal, 25 February 1971; and J.W. Finney, Civilian Defense Jobs Cut to Aid Combat Strength, New York Times, 23 November 1974.

43. M. Getler, Military Said to Add to Budget to Aid Economy, Washington Post, 27 February 1974; J.W. Finney, Military Budget Spurs Economy, Schlesinger Says Increase was Intended as Stimulus to Some Lagging Areas, New York Times, 27 February 1974; J. McCartney, Schlesinger Admits New Defense Budget Props U.S. Economy, Philadelphia Inquirer, 27 February 1974; G. Sherman, Budget Cushion Revealed, Washington Star News, 27 February 1974; 'Congressman Says Nixon Inflated Arms Requests',

Baltimore Sun, 27 February 1974.

The same administration even sought to use military purchases as a microeconomic - or political - mechanism in another instance in the same year. When there was a monetary lull in beef cattle sales in 1974, the Department of Defense sought to increase beef purchases as a stimulus to the cattle industry: Defense Department Seeks Aid for Cattle Industry, New York Times, 6 April 1974.

44. Aspin Blasts Vote for More B-1 Bombers, 8 December 1977, mimeographed.

45. Statement by Senator Alan Cranston, Transcript of Hearings on Diversification of Defense and Aerospace Corporations, US Senate, Committee on Banking, Housing and Urban Affairs, 10 August 1971, unpublished.

Detailed descriptions of eighteen of these proposed pieces of legislation can be found in J. Bergsman, Economic Adjustments to New National Priorities, The Urban Institute, Washington D.C., July 1971, pp. 37-39.

46. Cranston, ibid.

47. Woodcock Urges Congress to Reject Nixon Trade Bill, News From UAW, 15 May 1973, mimeographed.

48. US Congress, Joint Economic Committee, Economic Policies and Practices, op. cit.

49. Dave Elliott, Mary Kaldor, Dan Smith, and Ron Smith, Military Spending and Arms Cuts: Economic and Industrial Implications: Alternative Work for Military Industries, Richardson Institute, London 1977; Lucas Aerospace Combine Shop Stewards' Committee, Corporate Plan, January 1976; Alternatives to Military Production and to Unemployment, Development Dialogue (SIDA), No. 1, April 1977, pp. 31-33; Labour Party Study Group, Aspects of Conversion of Arms Industries, January 1976; Labour Party Study Group, Tornado -Cancellation, Conversion and Diversification in the Aerospace Industry, November 1976; Philip Gummett and Michael Gibbons, Redeployment and Diversification at Harwell, June 1977, mimeographed. Based on Redeployment in British Government Research Establishment, submitted to the Science Council of Canada, August 1975.

50. For example, Military Spending Report of Members of Congress for Peace Through Law, Congressional Record (Senate), 31 July 1970, pp. S-12556 to S-12574; MCPL Defense Posture Statement, Congressional Record, May 19, 1976, pp. S-7508 to 7533.

51. Democratic Study Group Fact Book - Fiscal Year 1970 Defense Budget, Congressional Record (Extension), 26 September 1969, pp. E-7876 to E-7888. See also, ADA (Americans for Democratic Action) Looks at the Defense Budget, Congressional Record (Extention), 5 March 1973, pp. E-1275 to E-1276; On Defense Spending Cuts - Defense Budget Cuts of $ 10.8 Billion Seen Feasible, Congressional Quarterly, 28 June 1968, reprinted in Congressional Record (Senate), 15 July 1968, pp. S-8628 to S-8633.

52. Toward a More Secure America, An Alternative National Defense Posture, US Senator George McGovern, 56 pages, mimeographed, nd.

53. These groups have nearly always had a reasonable knowledge of defense and security matters, and often close connections to official Washington, either with various executive agencies or with Congress. For example, the Brookings Institution, a Washington, DC research institute, has also provided alternative military expenditure recommendations and analyses since 1970. In that year, it began publishing the first of an annual series of volumes, Setting National Priorities, which looked at each year's national budget, including that for the US Department of Defense. Yet another Washington-based group, the Federation of American Scientists, has also supplied critiques of the annual DoD budget, recommending specific reductions. Most recently, in December 1977, a report was issued by two former high US defense officials (Dr. Herbert Scoville and Townsend Hoopes), under the auspices of six national organizations (the United States Conference of Mayors, the United Auto Workers, the National Urban League, the National Education Association, the International Association of Machinists and the American Federation of State, County and Municipal Employees). The report recommended cuts in specific weapon systems totalling $ 10.5 billion for the fiscal year 1979 DoD budget, and cuts of $ 10.8, $ 9.8 and $ 11.1 billion respectively for fiscal years 1980, 1981 and 1982; Townsend Hoopes and Herbert Scoville, Military Policy and Budget Priorities, Fiscal Years 1979-82, Council on National Priorities and Resources, 1977, 28 p. (Townsend Hoopes was Under Secretary of the Air Force (1967-1969), principal Deputy Assistant Secretary of Defense for International Security Affairs (1965-1967), Assistant to the Secretary of Defense (1949-1952). Dr. Herbert Scoville was Assistant Director, Arms Control and Disarmament Agency (1963-1969), Deputy Director and Assitant Director, Central Intelligence Agency (1955-1963), Technical Director, Armed Forces Special Weapons Project, Department of Defense (1948-1955).) Such plans have also appeared in several volumes by Dr. Seymor Melman, the author of a series of books on defence industry conversion since 1962.

54. The documents that have been declassified by the US government

(see ref. 17 above) clearly contained sections for some unidentified years after 1965 and even after 1968, as discussed in the text. However, these sections were not declassified.

55. Svyatoslav Kozlov, Military Expenditure Highlights Foreign Policy, <u>Soviet Weekly</u>, May 30, 1981. In detail, the budget reductions announced by the USSR were as follows:

    - between 1973 and 1974, from 17.9 billion rubles to 17.6
    -    "   1974 and 1975, " 17.6   -"-   17.3
    -    "   1976 and 1977, " 17.3   -"-   17.2
    -    "   1979 and 1980, " 17.2   -"-   17.1
    -    "   1980 and 1981, " 17.1   -"-   17.054

    Kozlov incorrectly repeatedly refers to USSR military "expenditure": the USSR announces only a figure for its "budget" (see ref. 29 above). Interestingly, the last two alleged reductions came during a period when the United States was already increasing military expenditure in real terms.

56. US Congress, Joint Economic Committee, Subcommittee on Priorities and Economy in Government, Hearings: <u>Allocation of Resources in the Soviet Union and China - 1978. Part 4-Soviet Union</u>, 95th Cong., 2nd Sess., June 26 and July 14, 1978, Washington D.C.: US Govt Printing Office, 1978, pp. 194-195.

57. Ibid.

58. Allocation of Resources in the Soviet Union and China - 1981, Defence Intelligence Agency, to the Joint Economic Committee, US Congress, July 8, 1981, pp. 89-90.

59. David D. Finley, Conventional Arms in Soviet Foreign Policy, <u>World Politics</u>, 33, 1, Oct. 1980, pp. 1-35.

60. See ref. 58, above.

61. Defence Spending and the Economy, Part II, <u>Challenges for US National Security</u>, A Preliminary Report, Carnegie Endowment for International Peace, 1981, p. 50; Michael Howard, Return to the Cold War, <u>Foreign Affairs</u>, Vol. 59, No. 3, 1980/81, pp. 459-473.

Chapter Seven

OPENING THE FLOODGATES: THE NEW U.S. ARMS SALES POLICY

Michael T. Klare

7.1. INTRODUCTION

Arguing that military sales can serve as "a vital and constructive instrument of American foreign policy," Under Secretary of State for Security Assistance James L. Buckley annouced a new U.S. arms transfer policy on May 21, 1981. In an address to the Aerospace Industries Association in Williamsburg, Virginia, he denounced the "arms restraint" policy adopted by President Carter in 1977, and declared that the Reagan Administration was determined to enhance the self-defence capabilities of U.S. friends and allies - including those cited for persistent human rights violations - by loosening the reins on U.S. arms exports. Rejecting the notion that such sales are "morally reprehensible", Buckley affirmed that arms transfers are a valid adjunct to America's own military programmes because they enable other countries to share more of the burden in defending the free world against aggression. The Administration will, he vowed, substitute "a healty sense of self-preservation" for the "theology" of the Carter administration.(1)

Buckley's announcement was followed six weeks later by a formal White House statement on conventional arms transfers. The Reagan declaration, released on July 8, rescinded Carter's policy statement of May 19, 1977, and established new guidelines for the conduct of U.S. arms programmes. These guidelines, which proclaim a greater willingness to supply favoured allies with sophisticated arms, are expected to produce a new boom in military sales. According to The Wall Street Journal, total U.S. arms exports will rise from $ 15 billion in fiscal year 1981 to an estimated $ 20 billion in 1982, and expand by similar amounts in the years thereafter. Most of the added deliveries will go to established markets in the Middle East and Western Pacific, but the Administration is also expected to increase sales to other, less developed markets in Latin America, Africa, and South Asia.(2) This sales effort is certain to provoke more intensive marketing by America's competitors in the arms business - especially France, Great Britain, and the Soviet Union -and thus will provoke a further intensification of local arms races in the conflict-prone areas of the

Third World.

Clearly, the adoption of a new arms transfer policy by the Reagan Administration has many implications for U.S. foreign policy and for the world at large. In order to calculate these effects, it is first necessary to examine the Reagan policy itself; and to better understand what is <u>different</u> about this policy, it is useful to begin with a brief look at the Carter policy it is meant to replace.

7.2. THE CARTER POLICY

During the 1976 campaign, Jimmy Carter denounced the arms trade as an "unsavoury business", and pledged to "reduce the commerce in weapons" if elected president. Then, upon entering the White House, he ordered the State Department to conduct a review of U.S. arms export programmes and to propose new measures for their control. Following several months of internal debate, the Department produced a series of recommendations which, after final modification by the National Security Council, were adopted into policy on May 13, 1977 with the signing of Presidential Directive Number 13 (PD-13)(3). PD-13 was presented to the public in an official White House statement on May 19, and thence governed U.S. arms sales programmes until Mr. Reagan announced his own guidelines four years later.

As denoted in a preface, the Carter directive was based on two fundamental assumptions: first, that unrestrained spread of conventional (i.e., non-nuclear) weaponry "threatens stability in every region of the world", and second, that, as the world's leading arms seller, the United States bears "special responsibilities" to take the lead in restraining its weapons sales. Carter acknowledged that U.S. restraint would not succeed in curbing world arms sales unless other suppliers adopted restraints of their own, but he argued that, " because we dominate the world market to such a degree", America should "take the first step" in controlling this trade.(4)

On this basis, Carter enunciated a new principle to govern U.S. arms export decision-making: instead of viewing military sales as a normal instrument of U.S. policy, "the United States will henceforth view arms transfers as an <u>exceptional foreign implement</u>, to be used <u>only</u> in instances where it can be clearly demonstrated that the transfer contributes to our national security interests". (Emphasis added.) The United States will continue to satisfy legitimate requests for arms on the part of its allies, he affirmed, but when deciding on such requests "the burden of persuasion will be on those who favor a particular arms sale, rather than on those who oppose it".

To implement this "policy of arms restraint", as he called it, Carter imposed several specific controls. But while the principles enunciated in the preface theoretically applied to all arms transfers, the controls were not so universal in their application: they did not, for instance, apply to countries with which the United States had "major defence treaties", namely Australia, Japan, New Zealand, and the NATO countries; and they could be suspended if in conflict with America's "historic responsibilities to assure the defense of Israel". They did not, moreover, apply to military services (training, technical assistance, construction work), which comprised about 30 per cent of total U.S. military sales. And finally, they could be waived by the President because of "extraordinary circumstances" or because "I determine that countries friendly to the United States must depend on advanced weaponry to offset qualitative and other disadvantages in order to maintain a regional balance". Having established all these exceptions, Carter listed his specific controls:

(1) Ceiling: The total dollar value (in constant 1976 dollars) of U.S. arms transfers to the non-exempt countries in fiscal year 1978 and thereafter would not exceed the $ 9.3 billion reached in fiscal year 1977.

(2) Sophistication: The United States would not be the first supplier to introduce into an area "newly-developed, advanced weapons systems which could create a new or significantly higher combat capability".

(3) Modification: The development or "significant modification" of advanced combat systems "solely for export" was prohibited.

(4) Co-production: The United States would not enter any new co-production projects that would allow other countries to export U.S.-designed weapons produced under licence or in collaboration with U.S. firms.

(5) Promotion: U.S. Government personnel assigned to embassies and military missions abroad would no longer be permitted to help representatives of U.S. arms firms to market their products to foreign governments. (This prohibition was subsequently contained in the so-called "leprosy letter" of August 31, 1977, sent to all U.S. embassies and military missions abroad.)

(6) Human Rights: In deciding on proposed arms transfers, the United States would attempt " to promote and advance respect for human rights in recipient countries".

When first announced in May 1977, these guidelines were the subject of considerable criticism, both from representatives of the arms industry, who thought they were too restrictive, and from arms control and disarmament experts, who thought they were too weak. The industrialists and their allies in Congress and the military argued that the guidelines unfairly penalized U.S. companies by permitting firms in other major supplying countries - none of which adopted similar restrictions of their own - to pursue sales that would otherwise have gone to American producers. The arms controllers argued that while the guidelines might have been useful if universally applied, they were relatively meaningless given all the exceptions and presidential waivers.(5) At first, both sides could claim that their arguments were justified: on one hand, some U.S. firms did lose sales to foreign competitors in areas where the guidelines were rigorously enforced (mainly Latin America), while on the other Carter did employ the exceptions to permit major sales of advanced hardware to such favoured allies as Iran (under the Shah) and Saudi Arabia. As time went on, however, the Administration became more and more concerned about Soviet military activities in the Third World and thus found itself less inclined to resist the powerful corporate and bureaucratic forces which coalesced behind each major arms transaction. As a result, U.S. arms exports continued to rise during the Carter Administration - reaching a near-record level of $ 15.3 billion in fiscal year 1980 - and the specific guidelines fell increasingly into disuse.(6)

7.3. THE REAGAN REPLACEMENT

Given Mr. Reagan's political beliefs, there was never any doubt as to his intention to rescind the Carter restrictions. As one White House insider explained in early 1981, "arms sales will no longer be regarded essentially as something evil that has to be curbed".(7) Consistent with this outlook, the Administration moved quickly to consummate transactions that had been held up by the previous Administration because of their conflict with Carter's guidelines. These sales included: two squadrons of supersonic F-16 fighters to South Korea; several hundred advanced AIM-9L Sidewinder air-to-air missiles and five Boeing E-3A "AWACS" radar surveillance planes to Saudi Arabia; and a squadron of F-16's to Venezueal. At the same time, Reagan ordered Buckley, the former Conservative Party Senator from New York State, to draft a new arms transfer policy to replace the now-defunct Carter policy.

The Reagan policy, first unveiled in Buckley's Williamsburg speech of May 21 and later released as a presidential statement on July 8, begins by repealing PD-13 (the original Carter directive). In its place, Buckley restored the general operating principles which were in effect during the Nixon and Ford Administrations, when U.S. arms sales rose from an average of $ 1 billion per year to approximately $ 15 billion per year. But the Reagan policy represents far more than a return to the status quo ante: as we shall see, it introduces new features which will actually make it easier for U.S. arms firms to market their products abroad, and especially in the cash-starved countries of the Third World.

Like the Carter directive, the Reagan policy is based on a number of fundamental propositions: first, that the greatest threat to world stability is the growing military assertiveness of the Soviet Union, and second, that the United States cannot defend the free world against this threat by itself, but must "be prepared to help its friends and allies strengthen their (defences) through the transfer of conventional arms".(8) From this perspective, arms sales are not seen as an independent foreign policy concern, but rather as a vital adjunct to America's own military modernization effort. As Buckley explained on May 21, "We are faced not only with the need to rebuild and modernize our own military forces, but to help other nations in the free world rebuild theirs".

Consistent with this outlook, Buckley enunciated a new governing principle: instead of viewing arms transfers as an "exceptional foreign policy implement", they are to be considered as "a vital and constructive instrument of American foreign policy". The Administration will continue to weigh the merits and hazards of pending transactions on a case-by-case basis, but favourable consideration will normally be given to transfers which help enhance "the state of preparedness of our friends and allies".

Turning now to the six specific controls originally imposed by President Carter, the Reagan policy substitutes the following:

(1) Ceiling: Pending arms transactions will be judged on their own merits, irrespective of their effect on the total dollar values of such exports. Total U.S. sales in Fiscal 1982 are expected to set a new record of $ 20 billion.

(2) Sophistication: The United States will take care not to overburden the defence capabilities of less-developed nations, but sale of high-technology arms will be governed more by "their net contribution to enhanced deterrence and defence" than by fears of a local arms race.

(3) Modification: In place of the ban on such activities, the new Administration will actively "encourage" U.S. firms to "produce equipment which, in terms of cost, complexity, and sophistication, is more appropriate to the needs of non-industrialized nations". It should be noted that the Carter Administration had already reversed itself by approving the development of a low-cost fighter for foreign sales known as the F-X.)

(4) Co-production: No new guidelines have been announced, save that the Administration will consider such arrangements on a case-by-case basis, taking into account the economic interests of U.S. suppliers and the need to protect "sensitive technology" against dissemination to hostile parties.

(5) Promotion: The "leprosy letter" of August, 1977 was rescinded on April 2, 1981, and Reagan mandated U.S. officials overseas "to provide the same courtesies and assistance" to firms selling arms as to other U.S. companies seeking business abroad.

(6) <u>Human Rights</u>: The United States will no longer withhold essential security support from friendly nations because of a poor record on human rights. As Reagan explained shortly after his election, "I don't think that you can turn away from some country because here and there they do not agree with our concept of human rights".(9) This outlook is reflected in the Administration's decision to ask Congress to repeal the embargo on arms transfers to Argentina, and to step up the delivery of high-technology arms to South Korea.

All these alterations suggest that, at the very least, the Reagan policy represents a complete break with the restrictive approach of the Carter Administration. But Reagan goes beyond this, to introduce new elements into the arms programme which will reinforce the shift towards a relatively unrestrained, export-oriented policy. These elements include:

(a) <u>The politicization of the arms trade</u>: U.S. arms exports, like those of other countries, have always reflected fundamental political realities: one normally sells arms only to friends and allies, or to neutral countries which pose no threat to one's own interests. But President Carter viewed the arms trade as a problem in its own right -as a phenomenon which "threatens stability in every region of the world" - and he therefore made its control an <u>independent objective</u> of U.S. foreign policy (just as the prevention of nuclear proliferation was made an independent objective of U.S. policy). President Reagan, however, has erased this distinction: arms transfers are now to be considered as an inseparable instrument of military policy, and the equivalent, in international terms, of the arms buildup now underway in the United States. To a large extent, of course, this merely represents a return to the priorities which governed U.S. arms sales during the Cold War epoch. But in restoring these priorities, Reagan seeks to employ arms transfers as an active, even aggressive instrument of a policy designed to put the Russians and their allies on the defensive. In the most spectacular demonstration of this approach, Reagan has approved the sale of sophisticated military hardware to China - a step which is certain to cause great anxiety in Moscow, and to produce a generalized intensification of the arms race in East Asia. In the same vein, Washington has agreed to provide Pakistan with $ 2 billion worth of advanced arms - a move supposedly intended to offset the Soviet presence in Afghanistan, but which will end up producing a new arms race with India - and to accelerate deliveries to Egypt, the Sudan, and other countries supposedly threatened by Libya. These initiatives will undoubtedly provoke comparable moves by the Soviet Union and the other major suppliers, leading to a fresh round of arms-buying in many Third World areas and thus, inevitably, to an increased risk of war.

(b) **Liberalized credit programs:** As part of his effort to curb the trade in armaments, President Carter sought to discourage U.S. firms from entering foreign markets by banning the development of weapons exclusively for export and by limiting the amount and types of credit available to foreign buyers for U.S. arms. The Reagan policy, on the other hand, calls not only for the repeal of the Carter restrictions, but also for the taking of new initiatives designed to increase export sales of U.S. armaments and to facilitate the purchase of such hardware by cash-starved Third World nations. These initiatives include some form of governmental "encouragement" for the development of export-oriented weaponry as noted above, and the provision of arms credits at "concessional" rates (i.e., at a lower percentage rate than the U.S. Government must itself pay to borrow money). Noting that "in today's economic climate a number of nations cannot afford to purchase equipment on commercial terms", Mr. Buckley proposed that Washington provide them with loans to buy arms at interest rates of as low as three percent. Such measures, which constitute a form of indirect subsidy by the U.S. taxpayer (since the Treasury will have to borrow the money at much higher rates of interest), will obviously make it easier for over-extended Third World nations to buy arms that they otherwise couldn't afford. (Among the nations which will be eligible for such concessional credits in fiscal year 1982, if Congress approves, are: Egypt, Turkey, Thailand, Kenya, Somalia, Sudan, El Salvador, and Honduras.(10))

(c) **The penetration of new markets:** In line with these initiatives and the loosening of restraints on the sale of high-technolgoy gear, the Administration clearly seeks to boost U.S. military sales to Third World areas which have not recently been major market for U.S. arms. A particular target of this drive is Latin America, which in recent years has obtained much of its front-line equipment from Europe (where credit terms are softer and political requirements less stringent). In order to win back this market, Reagan will eliminate all human rights restrictions and begin selling new, high-technology weapons - such as the F-16's offered to Venezuela - which could not be sold to Latin America under the Carter guidelines. Washington also seeks to boost U.S. sales to South Asia, where India and Pakistan appear headed towards a stepped-up arms race, to Africa (especially Tunisia, Morocco, Kenya, and the Sudan), and to Southeast Asia (especially Thailand, Indonesia, Malaysia, and the Philippines). These efforts are certain to stimulate increased marketing activities in these areas by other major suppliers, particularly the French and British, and thus will produce a long-term increase in high-technology arms sales to the Third World.

These initiatives, and the repeal of the Carter restrictions, will obviously have profound and lasting consequences for U.S. foreign policy and for the politico-military situation in the world at large. To begin with, of course, it will result in a marked increase in U.S. military exports to the Third World, and thus exacerbate all the problems which have become associated with such sales: intensified local arms races in conflict-prone areas, leading to increased instability and a greater risk of regional conflicts; the growing proliferation of high-technology arms, leading to ever-increasing levels of violence in whatever conflicts do occur; the further diversion of scarce economic resources to military purposes, thereby perpetuating the underdevelopment and indebtedness of many Third World countries; and the empowerment of Third World military forces, resulting in a continuing dissolution of democratic institutions in favour of military rule.(11) These problems did not originate with the Reagan Administration - indeed, even under the Carter guidelines, most of them continued to proliferate (although perhaps at a slower rate than before). But while the previous Administration at least acknowledged their existence, the current one is behaving as if these problems did not exist at all. This means that it will be much harder for concerned policymakers, both inside and outside the Administration, to argue for restraint in the case of provocative or risky arms transactions. It also means that the voices of restraint in other countries will be drowned out by those calling for stepped-up marketing in order to counter the aggressive U.S. sales effort. And the net effect, of course, will be an accelerated flow of arms at a time of growing world instability.

Furthermore, there are some aspects of the Reagan programme which will further heighten the instabilities produced by uncontrolled arm transfers. By employing arms transfers as an instrument of Cold War competition, Reagan is certain to aggravate regional rivalries which have become entangled in the superpower conflict - such as those in the Horn of Africa and the Middle East -with unforeseeable and possibly perilous consequences. This tactic, and the decision to sell advanced arms to China, will also aggravate relations between the superpowers themselves, again with unforeseen consequences. It may be that Mr. Reagan hopes thereby to put Moscow on the defensive, and thus to score gains for U.S. policy in contested areas; but it is just as likely that this will produce a reaction in kind, and thus expose the whole world to an increased risk of war.

Clearly, Mr. Reagan's plan to open the floodgates on U.S. arms exports could wind up endangering Western security far more than it would safeguard it. Yet, at this point, there appears to be little opposition in Congress to the Administration's policy (save, of course, for those supporters of Israel who opposed the proposed AWACS sale to Saudi Arabia). In Europe, where opposition to nuclear weapons is growing, relatively little attention has been paid to the problem of conventional arms transfers. But if American and European policymakers are truly concerned about growing world instability, they must begin to accord the same degree of urgency to controlling conventional arms exports as they have long accorded to the control of nuclear exports.

NOTES AND REFERENCES

1. James L. Buckley, Address before the Board of Governors of the Aerospace Industries Association, Williamsburg, Va., May 21, 1981 (U.S. Department of State transcript). All subsequent references to the Buckley talk are taken from this text.

2. Gerald F. Seib, Reagan's New Policy is Likely to Spur U.S. Exports of Arms, The Wall Street Journal, June 4, 1981. See also: U.S. Does an About Face on Selling Arms, U.S. News and World Report, March 16, 1981, p. 35.

3. For background on the evolution of Carter's policy, see: Michael T. Klare, How We Practice Arms Restraint, The Nation, September 24, 1977, pp. 268-73.

4. Presidential statement on arms transfer policy, Washington, D.C., May 19, 1977 (White House press release). All subsequent references to the Carter policy are taken from this text.

5. For discussion, see Herbert Y. Schandler, et. al., Implications of President Carter's Conventional Arms Trade Policy, Washington: Library of Congress, Congressional Research Service, 1977.

6. For discussion, see Michael R. Gordon, Competition with the Soviet Union Drives Reagan's Arms Sales Policy, National Journal, May 16, 1981, pp. 869-73.

7. Quoted in U.S. News and World Report, March 16, 1981, p. 35.

8. Presidential statement on arms transfer policy, Washington, D.C., July 8, 1981 (White House press release, July 9, 1981). All subsequent references to the Reagan policy are taken from this text unless otherwise noted.

9. Quoted in Newsweek, December 15, 1980, p. 53.

10. U.S. Department of Defense, Congressional Budget Presentation: Security Assistance Programs, Fiscal Year 1982, Washington: author, 1981, pp. 14-15. See also David R. Griffiths, Reagan Administration Pushes Arms Transfers, Aviation Week and Space Technology, June 8, 1981, pp. 1976-81.

11. For discussion, see Stockholm International Peace Research Institute, The Arms Trade with the Third World, Stockholm, 1971. See also Wolfgang Mallmann, Arms Transfers to the Third World: Trends and Changing Patterns in the 1970s, Bulletin of Peace Proposals, Vol. 10, No. 3, 1979, pp. 301-7.

Chapter Eight

TRANSNATIONAL MILITARY CORPORATIONS: THE MAIN PROBLEMS*

Helena Tuomi

8.1. INTRODUCTION

The concept of transnational military industry should not be taken as given or self-evident. Because military production is first of all aimed at national defence and because many secrecy rules and security considerations have to be taken into account, it is not possible for the arms industry to go international or transnational in the same way as civilian industry does. Also, the large public funds in all phases of arms production (R&D, production lines, army procurements and finally government control of exports and credits for exports) make the industry a special kind of activity. It is no free enterprise(1) - even if privately owned - but a scrupulously protected and carefully supervised activity which enjoys considerable public funding and political control. We should therefore realize that if the concept of transnational military industry is used, it is not the same type of transnational industry we speak of in the civilian sector. The military industry is nowadays transnational, but it has its own special characteristics.(2) The concept should therefore preferably be used only in empirical contexts, bearing in mind that the expansion or internationalization of military industry has various political, security and other constraints.

The main reasons why military production has nowadays become transnational can be summarized as follows:

- The military industry is dependent on foreign sources of <u>raw materials</u>, special alloys, steels etc.(3) In some cases, arms producers have invested in raw material ventures abroad - which has resulted in the expansion of their own international organization - while in other cases they rely on transnational corporations (TNCs) specialized in raw material production.

- The <u>complex nature of modern military technology</u>, the need for highly skilled research personnel, technicians and workers, large and complex production lines etc. are factors which tend to concentrate the production of modern arms into the largest corporations. Small enterprises simply do not have enough human or material resources to make heavy arms or weapon systems. Instead, they may function as subcontractors for the large arms producers. Thus, the more complex the weapon in question, the more probable it is that production can take place only in the largest corporations. These, then, are often transnational even on the basis of the civilian divisions of the same corporations - the production of military electronics being a good example of how civilian and military activities are mixed in transnational operations.

- Arms production has become very expensive: the R&D phase is expensive, the raw material costs have risen, there is a need for very special raw materials, the production lines are expensive, the highly skilled personnel is expensive etc. It is fully justified to characterize the current situation as <u>the cost crisis of arms production</u>, and this problem is notable both in the West and in the East. The cost crisis calls for various strategies of rationalization. Thus, mergers of different producers into bigger units, coproduction with foreign partners, export expansion, subcontracting to find cheap components or labour, and finally a move into foreign production have taken place within the military industry. The cost crisis is perhaps the strongest single factor urging the arms industry to go transnational.

- Because arms production is carried out to back national defence, many states maintain these companies even if it is not economically reasonable. The possibility of a military crisis or even war keeps arms production lines running, despite the enormous expense. It is evident that arms are produced in excess of world demand: there are too many companies, there is too large an output and a production capacity. It is difficult to pinpoint when the <u>overcapacity crisis</u> began or to give accurate data on its dimensions. There are also problems concerning empirical measurement: some scholars measure overcapacity on the basis of exports - arms which exceed the country's own needs - while others also take idle production capacity into account.(4) The existence of serious overcapacity problems is indirectly proven by the very intensive competition between arms producers over new sales. All possible methods - including illegal ones such as bribery - are used to secure new sales. The fierce competition, again, urges the companies into transnational operations: sales of licences, subcontracting agreements, offset deals etc. are used if the purchaser so wishes. The arms supplier who is ready to transfer technology is often preferred by the buyer, and <u>technology agreements</u> are thus one of the main forms of competition. The result is growing transnationalization of military production. This competition can be observed in connection with almost every arms deal - be it small weapons or heavy arms.

- The problems of state finance have also enhanced the role of the largest industries. Those countries which previously used to give military aid have increasingly moved into commercial deals. Arms sales, education, maintenance and service have increasingly been delegated to specialized industries. <u>The commercial basis</u>, again, emphasizes the role of the large industries and in fact strengthens the transnational organization of the companies.

8.2. TRANSNATIONAL ARMS CORPORATION VERSUS STATE

Arms decisions are made by a trio of social institutions: the government, the army and the military industry. Inside this group there can be subgroups which further their own particular interests: e.g. the air force can ally itself with the aircraft industry to beat the demands of the navy, the infantry etc. On a general level, the common interest is national defence and foreign obligations or influence, but in concrete decisions and in the struggle for the scarce funds, subgroups are formed. There is no agreement among scholars as to whether it is the government, the army or industry that is the dominant party. All parties have their own power tools: the government has the money, the military is responsible for the defence, while industry in many cases has the technological initiative and the best skills in this respect. The actual situation varies from one country to another.

<u>If</u> the situation is such that industry, indeed, holds the monopoly on modern arms technology, this particular feature can give it a strong position vis-à-vis the others. <u>If</u> the industry is financially strong enough to invent new military technologies without being totally dependent on state funding, it may also be able to promote its initiatives actively. The transnationals involved in military production can acquire this financial strength. On the other hand if the army or defence department are well equipped as far as technological skills are concerned, they are able to judge which new weapon developments they want. In general, there is much <u>faith in new military technologies.</u> This gives ample power to those who command it, be they in the defence department, in the army or in corporations.

The long development phase of each new weapon - five to ten years is not unusual - and its consequent high costs are also factors strengthening the position of the armament firms. After all, it is the normal practice that the company carries out <u>both</u> the R&D <u>and</u> production. The companies often use a kind of <u>creeping method</u> to be able to acquire a new R&D contract, i.e. they start out with a modest proposal and a modest sum, but when the programme is well under way they increase their demands and add new costs. After the company has completed the long and costly R&D phase, it is most probable that it will also start production. If not, the R&D costs would have been wasted and there would be no use for the experience and skills developed by the firm. It is the role of the corporation in R&D and the link between R&D and production which further strengthen the role of the large firms in the armament process in general and with regard to the state authorities in particular.(5)

What is evident, however, is that the trio of the defence department, industry and the army is a very strong social coalition and very difficult to control politically. It may not be very fruitful to ask which one of the three is the strongest - they usually act together anyhow.(6) But it should also be noted that industry is in any case much more active now than it has traditionally been. The capability to develop and produce new military technologies can also have an impact on the military doctrines: thus the expansion of the electronic and communication industry has been followed by the predominance of the military C3 systems and electronic warfare. Perhaps the rise of the chemical industry will be reflected in a new interest in chemical weapons? These examples may suffice to show that the relationship between industry, technology and the military is a complex one and cannot easily be evaluated.

A particular problem in transnational military production is the very fact that transnationality gives the company more autonomy vis-à-vis the state. If the government blocks a plan in country A, the company can start it in country B. If country A blocks the exports of arms, or spares from country A, the company can export them from country B.(7) If the government A prohibits the company to do business with country X, the transnational firm can operate from country B, which wants to have good relations with country X. A transnational firm can declare that it exports parts or spares to its subsidiary or test area in country B, but it can then re-export the cargo to destination C or via C to D.(8) There are many concrete examples of these various cases.(9)

The transnational organization of the firm makes these cases possible: the firm can escape government regulations and increase its autonomy vis-à-vis the state.

Many transnational producers are diversified companies, in which one or two divisions are engaged in the military programmes while the others manufacture civilian products. The company can now use the civilian organization to mask its military operations abroad. E.g. in the transnational electronics industry it is almost impossible to identify the military transfers among all operations. The problem becomes even more difficult in cases where the same product can be used for both civilian and military purposes (cf. the nuclear industry). Thus the dual technology and the diversified nature of the company together with the transnational organization make the identification of military transfers almost impossible in present circumstances.

Another factor which facilitates the growing autonomy of the companies is their resistance to give information on their accounts, turnover composition, industrial organization and network of subsidiaries and partners. A good example is the transnational electronic firm Philips, whose annual report or normal business handbooks do not give any information whatsoever of the military aspect of the company. After time-consuming and laborious investigations, an analyst is able to discover, however, that the company has a large number of military subsidiaries in various countries and the turnover of these firms must be sizeable - otherwise the company would hardly tolerate these subsidiaries. The fact that the companies hide information further enhances their autonomy. For this reason it is also impossible to tell exactly how deeply a given firm is involved in the military programmes of various countries.

The factors mentioned above point to the growing autonomy of transnational military industries and difficulties of political control. On the other hand the relationship between the state and the TNC is one of both conflict and cooperation. The TNCs must cooperate with the home and host governments because they need a lot of public funding for research, development and production contracts. In fact, they would hardly be interested in military programmes at all if these public funds were not available. The financial support of course gives the state - at least in principle - one very efficient means to control the military programmes of a given firm. It is not, however, always easy for the accountants to discover how, exactly, the company uses the funds supplied by the state, because it is difficult to isolate the reasonable price of each phase of the arms programme - the companies are known to use maximum pricing methods. Because of the uncertainty of markets, the companies also make heavy claims: the state should guarantee all costs and a good profit. There have been cases in which the firms have acquired or demanded too high profits - e.g. the U.S. Congress has for this reason discussed what a reasonable profit should be in arms programmes.(10)

On the other hand, military programmes are not necessarily profitable as such. Actually, rather few companies would stay in military programmes in the event that state funding ceased. But the companies can use the military programmes tactically to press for money for their difficulties: thus e.g. AEG-Telefunken, Chrysler, Lockheed and Rolls Royce have been saved from bankruptcy because of their military programmes. It is the large public funding, particularly for new R&D, which keeps most TNCs in military production. In addition to the funding, the states encourage the firms to export arms; this way the unit prices of weapons decrease and the pressure on the military budget is somewhat decreased.

One important aspect is that many TNCs are involved in military production in a number of ways, which means that they can exert pressure on the state from many directions. Also, their impact on the global militarization can multiply. Firm A is engaged in nuclear reactor production, and aeroengines; firm B is making sophisticated radars and nuclear energy products; firm C is making various types of military electronics and is engaged in nuclear technology; firm D makes not just cars but also has connections to aeroengines, aircraft, nuclear energy etc.(11) Thus the total influence of these firms on the armament programmes can be massive, but this is not so easily noticed, because they do it step by step or in various directions and perhaps via different state authorities.

8.3. FORMS OF TRANSNATIONAL MILITARY PRODUCTION

All leading Western military producers are transnational to some degree - transnational being defined as having operations in at least three countries. This process has been intensive during the last 10-15 years, mainly due to the fact that since the end of the 1960s the European companies have become more competitive with regard to the U.S. companies. The transnationalization process started in Western Europe, then moved to Southern Europe and Japan, and is now reaching the Third World.

The socialist arms industries are also transnational in the sense that they have large exports, and licences and technology are sold to foreign countries. The transfer of technology normally takes place between the Soviet Union and its allies (with the exception of India and Peru),(12) but export takes place on a global scale.

Arms transfers, as noted previously, are a consequence of arms economics in the leading armament centres. The political and military motives are not discussed here, as they do not explain the transnationalization process.

Internationalization usually starts with arms exports. Although readymade weapons are exported, the organization can become transnational even in this phase. The fierce competition calls for sales offices and a network of efficient sales agents (either of own nationality or local agents). The service and maintenance network as well as education programmes connected with the arms sales can also speed up transnationalization. These networks can also develop into component production, assembly etc. The superactive sales promotion methods of the largest arms producers as well as some extreme forms of marketing (particularly bribery) can be noted in this context. Although the export normally takes place under state control (both buyer and supplier), there are also signs of <u>independent marketing by the TNCs</u>.(13) Certain places, such as Singapore, have developed into real market places for various weapons.

The transnational organization enables <u>intra-firm arms transfers</u>, but it is not known how common this is in the arms trade. In certain cases the firms have founded "foreign test areas" in places from where it is easy to export arms to third countries.

International subcontracting increases military transfers in two directions: the TNC can import components from countries where the labour costs are low (or raw materials are easily available), but the TNC can itself be a subcontractor of complex components into foreign weapon systems (e.g. engines, electronics, more sophisticated weaponry). Usually, the TNC makes capital and research intensive parts at home and labour intensive parts in low-wage countries.

The sales of licences, foreign assembly and finally coproduction of arms with foreign partners are further forms of transnational arms production. In licence production, there is usually one TNC which controls the cooperation, while in coproduction the partners are in principle more equal - perhaps several TNCs. A comparison of the MRCA and F-16 programmes in Europe is illustrative in this respect.

The ownership patterns of arms industry are a combination of nationalist concerns and internationalization. Minority shares of the US companies in European industries became common as early as in the 1950's and 1960's; later on, the European industries started to buy themselves into foreign arms industries, too. Usually, the TNC purchases foreign shares or forms a foreign joint venture (with the TNC in the minority) to secure markets and future cooperation. For the foreign partner, this is a measure to acquire technology and to tie the TNC to the economic success of the company. The problem with these ownerships is that the basically and originally national military-industrial complex may develop into an international one with possible negative consequences. A category of its own is formed by companies like Euromissile or Panavia, which are founded to administer coproduction.

The TNCs usually use their organization in a manner which has been accepted in both the sender and the recipient country. There are, however, also examples of operations which are not legitimate in one or the other end of the path. The TNCs have sometimes founded cover partners abroad to mask their illegal financial transfers. A famous bribery case was connected with Widows' and Orphans' Fund in Singapore, but others have used less extreme methods of concealment. Also, the illegal use of civilian transport technology can be noted: e.g. artillery shells have been smuggled to South Africa with falsified shipping documents and destinations. Often the TNCs use small private airlift or shipping firms and various stops en route when they mask the transfers. It is also very common to put incorrect producer names or countries on weapons to mask the original producer.(14)

The largest military TNCs are in the United States, and their absolute military transfers are the most extensive. On the other hand the West European companies are relatively speaking (and on an average) more dependent on military production and military exports.

8.4. SOME EFFECTS OF TNC-CONTROLLED ARMAMENT PROGRAMMES IN THE LDCs

We will here examine those negative consequences that are directly related to the transnational character of the leading arms suppliers, that is, we will not discuss the negative aspects of military programmes in general.

The TNCs basically want to increase their markets in the LDCs and they are flexible in forming various cooperation programmes to secure the markets. The TNCs can act together with their home governments, but they may also act "on their own".

The TNCs are obliged to keep the newest military secrets in their home countries and only export those arms or weapon systems which have an export licence. In the military sense the "best" technology is therefore not exported - only the "second best" is sold abroad. The equipment for electronic warfare capability, for example, is a prime example of the difference at the moment between the export model and the 'domestic' model. It is probable that exported radars or radar systems also differ from those for home use.

The buyer who is technologically less informed does not usually know whether his imports are obsolete by some secret standards or not. Nor does he know in what way his imports are out-of-date, because these matters are connected with military secrecy rules. The extent of this problem is not known, but it evidently causes irrationality in arms transfers. The technology you have bought may be the "newest" according to the military adviser (often from the supplying country) and according to sales agents or advertisements - and two years later you find out that some new innovations make your purchases obsolete. Any electronic equipment will, in any case, become obsolete rather quickly. Thus the buyer is faced with a permanent dilemma here, but all he can do is rely on the information given by the TNC.

Another problem is the pricing policy of the TNCs. They naturally use lower prices for ready-made arms than for parts and technology transfers. This makes the import of ready arms often half as cheap as would be the case in licensed production of the same weapon.(15) For countries wanting to start their own military production, technology agreements with the TNCs can thus be very expensive.

In general, the TNC comes from the developed world and represents an industrial concept of warfare. What it produces may require a whole military-industrial complex. Thus cooperation with the TNCs can have an intensive impact not only on military affairs and production, but also on the whole culture, as new values and habits are introduced. This process was clearly visible in Iran during the rule of the Shah, and a comparable process is now under way in Saudi Arabia. The consequences of this sort of transformation can be very radical and unpredictable.

The LDC starting cooperation with a military TNC usually wants more security and, with indigenous arms production, also more military independence. The more complex the technology desired, the more contradictory are the goals of independence and the technological dependence on the TNC. As noted before, particularly military electronics, radar networks, C3 systems, military engines for airplanes, ships and tanks as well as more sophisticated weaponry have proved to be bottlenecks in the LDC arms industry. If arms are imported, the dependence on TNC technicians, service, maintenance and know-how may continue for a very long time.

The technology agreements also usually prevent the LDC partner from becoming an independent producer. The TNC does not want competitors.

Together with the technological dependence - which is a security risk - totally new forms of security risk have arisen. Certain TNCs with global markets advertise that "they have huge data banks to be able to serve their customers well". Here, the security risk is evident: a huge data bank on the defence systems of customer countries - probably also on potential enemies of future customers. How would this information be used in the event of a crisis?(16) Strong dependence on foreign personnel, spares and service is also a security risk, because supplies and cooperation on the side of the TNC is not guaranteed. The defence of Iran since it has been at war with Iraq is an example in this respect - on the other hand it seems that Iran has to some extent recently been able to use the transnational organization of certain military firms by importing spares and equipment from Southern Europe and Israel while these imports from the United States were forbidden.

8.5. TOWARDS CONTROL?

In general, the TNCs have too many secrets, but this is particularly notable in connection with the military TNCs. In fact, it is impossible to present any detailed empirical analysis of the extent of transnational military production.(17) It is up to the home governments to get the information. It is important to note that it is in the interest of the home states to have this information because the home states do not benefit from the growing autonomy of the TNCs. Why deny arms exports to some areas if the TNCs can easily circumvent the regulations? Why work for a peaceful settlement of some political conflict if the TNCs push in arms through the back door? Why work for the nonproliferation of nuclear weapons if the TNCs at the same time can export sensitive technologies by means of their international organization? Why give large public funds to a firm which suffers from financial problems at home but can afford extensive bribes abroad? Why secure the rights of small private shareholders and investors and demand reliable corporate information when the companies transfer money abroad and do illegal or otherwise secret business abroad? As can be noted, there are several reasons for calling for a more thorough control on military industries, particularly TNCs. The primary level of control is national, in our view, as far as the total transparency of operations is demanded.

For research purposes certain minimum requirements regarding information should be agreed on. At present, conducting a comprehensive analysis and especially finding the crucial information is most laborious.

Certain military transfers have also disclosed the need for the home countries of the military TNCs to <u>register the staff</u> working in these companies. Although civilians, these people, above all technicians, planners and researchers, can have a significant impact on military developments. We can only point to the role of key planners in certain countries which are future nuclear weapon candidates.(18) For the same reason there should be some <u>evaluation of foreign student programmes</u>, perhaps even sanctions in case of a misuse of information. Above all, the responsibility of those who work with sensitive technologies, be it conventional or nuclear, should be a matter of <u>education</u>. So far, the labour market for experts in military technology has been free. The control in this respect cannot take place at the international level, but certain national measures should be conceivable.

Despite their interest in technological innovations, the companies are very often rather conservative in their planning. If some firm is used to producing export fighters, it tends to continue along the same lines, even though government policy would discourage fighter exports.(19) This conservative attitude in production planning is one factor which keeps military production going. The companies should be encouraged to start <u>alternative planning</u> and in this way facilitate a diversification into peaceful activities. Sooner or later military production will become so expensive that this kind of change will be inevitable - it would be easier for the companies if they had prepared themselves for it. <u>Workers' organizations and trade unions</u> should also be encouraged to participate in conversion planning.

The new arms programmes are often started with deficient information as to the industrial impact of the programme as well as the real costs. The UN member countries should be encouraged to carry out such analyses in case they start new arms programmes. The information should also be available in an accessible form so that taxpayers know how much they pay for the arms race. At present, many countries do not reveal much information in this respect. Since the TNCs absorb a great deal of public funding, they should disclose more information on how they use those funds.

Arms trade is an area where national control is no longer efficient, because of the transnational forms of military production. Therefore, only multilateral talks between all main producing states can bring about results in this respect. Particularly <u>the rules of behaviour</u> in the Third World - political, military, economic and cultural - should be agreed on. Otherwise the militarization will only intensify.

Most arms trade is dangerous and increases military tensions. There is no reason why special attention should be paid only to the TNCs involved in arms trade. The national firms can be just as harmful. What makes the TNCs crucial, however, is their enormous flexibility and ability to escape controls and partial agreements as well as their efficiency in production and marketing. Unless an international control of arms transfers succeeds, the national firms will undoubtedly follow the models shown by the present TNCs.

NOTES AND REFERENCES

*The first version of this paper was presented at the SIPRI-TAPRI seminar in Stockholm on October 13, 1981. I wish to thank the participants of the seminar as well as Prof. Raimo Väyrynen for their valuable comments.

1. As far as the U.S. military industry is concerned, the same point is frequently made by Jacques S. Gansler, <u>The Defense Industry</u>, Cambridge, Mass. and London 1981 (third printing), passim.

2. For some documentation see Helena Tuomi & Raimo Väyrynen, <u>Transnational Corporations, Armaments and Development</u>, Aldershot (GB), 1982.

3. Cf. Helge Hveem, Militarization of Nature: Conflict and Control over Strategic Resources and Some Implications for Peace Policies, <u>Journal of Peace Research</u>, Vol. 16, No. 1, 1979, pp. 1-26.

4. On the problems of overproduction and overcapacity see Gansler, <u>op.cit.</u> 1981 and Michael Brzoska, Economic Problems of Arms Production in Western Europe - Diagnoses and Alternatives, in this book.

5. On the so-called "buy-in" methods of the military firms when introducing new R&D programmes see Gansler <u>op.cit.</u> 1981. It seems that the link between R&D and production creates automatism in the armament process. For this reason it has been suggested that R&D and production be separated from each other.

6. An indication of the close cooperation between the industry and the Department of Defence is the transfer of personnel between the two. Individuals with valuable experience in R&D intensive firms are particularly welcome to join the DOD. See Gordon Adams, <u>The Iron Triangle. The Politics of Defense Contracting</u>, Council on Economic Priorities, New York 1981.

7. The ability of Iran to acquire spare parts for her American

weapons in the war with Iraq despite the U.S. embargo is an outcome of a transnational network.

8. The arms exports of the Canadian Space Research Corporation to South Africa are a good example of this. The case was carefully documented by the BBC in a TV programme in 1978. See also Michael T. Klare, South Africa's U.S. Weapons Connections, The Nation, July 28 - August 4, 1979, pp. 75-78.

9. Cf. Tuomi & Väyrynen, op.cit. 1982 for more detailed information.

10. The problem of profits is discussed in detail by Gansler, op.cit. 1981.

11. The production profiles of many military corporations are discussed in Tuomi & Väyrynen, op.cit. 1982.

12. Cf. Herbert Wulf et al., Transnational Transfers of Arms Production Technology, Institute für Friedensforschung und Sicherheitspolitik an der Universität Hamburg, Hamburg 1980.

13. During the 1973 arms boom in Iran a Pentagon memo said that "the Shah was unhappy about the independent agents running around his country on commission even though the aircraft are being purchased through the U.S. government". International Herald Tribune, January 26-27, 1980.

14. Cf. Tuomi & Väyrynen, op.cit. 1982, p. 133 and the references used there.

15. Cf. The Arms Trade with the Third World, SIPRI, Uppsala 1971, pp. 738-739 and Tuomi & Väyrynen, op.cit. 1982, pp. 204-205.

16. When being asked how it was possible for the foreign aircraft to land on the Iranian territory without permission (when the United States made her unsuccessful attempt to rescue the American hostages), President Bani-Sadr replied: "They know so well the holes in our radar network".

17. For some attempts, however, see Peter Lock & Herbert Wulf, Register of Arms Production in Developing Countries, Arbeitsgruppe Rüstung und Unterentwicklung, Universität Hamburg, Hamburg 1977 (mimeo), Wulf et al., op.cit. 1980 and Tuomi & Väyrynen, op.cit. 1982.

18. The history of the Pakistani nuclear programme is illustrative in this respect.

19. The arms restraint policy of President Carter prohibited the design of weapons solely for exports, but Northrop managed to

proceed with the plan for a new export fighter FX. Cf. Aviation Week and Space Technology, January 14, 1980. Northrop specializes in export fighters.

III

MILITARIZATION AND ARMAMENT PROCESS IN DEVELOPING COUNTRIES

Chapter Nine

SEMIPERIPHERAL COUNTRIES IN THE GLOBAL ECONOMIC AND MILITARY ORDER

Raimo Väyrynen

9.1. INTRODUCTION

The international system is not only divided into a core and a periphery, but also into a semiperiphery; this trichotomy has existed since at least 1640. Semiperiphery, as well as core and periphery, are, in a world system perspective, structural states 'which continually emerge and reemerge over long historical eras, encompassing and reencompasing, integrating and disintegrating, defining and redefining the roles and positions of diverse actors in a world system'.(1) Thus, the semiperiphery has consisted in different periods of different countries and groups of them. In this sense semiperiphery has never been a stable category of states, although its international function may have remained pretty much the same.

Semiperipheral countries have, by definition, an intermediate position in the world economy; they are both exploiters and exploited. The same point is essentially made by characterizing these countries as subimperialist. An important function of the semiperiphery in the international system is to enhance its economic and political stability. Politically, an international system without a middle stratum would be far less stable, for 'it would be a polarized world-system. The existence of a third category means precisely that the upper stratum is not faced with the unified opposition of all others'.(2) This conclusion is based on the premise that in some important respects, the interests of a semiperiphery differ from those of a periphery and they would hence not form any united front. A further premise is that a core state has, to varying degrees, influence over the behaviour of semiperipheral states through economic and other forms of dependence. Therefore a unified alliance of semiperipheral states is hardly conceivable. This is also shown by the relatively modest success of the potential '<u>pariah international</u>' (pariah states being a particular type of semiperipheral entity).(3)

The international position of semiperipheral states is modified by the dynamics of the world system itself. This does not, of course, mean that internal preconditions of development within these states are unimportant, but that they should rather be seen in conjunction with international changes. These changes are characterized by economic and possibly also by political cycles. They are constitutive to the entire world economy but also have bearing on the external relations of individual states. According to the world-system analysis, a long cycle consists of an expansionist stage which is connected with the accumulation of capital and the revival of economic activity as well as contraction.

It is often concluded that the expansion of the economic world system results, together with the concentration of power to one core state, in the multilateralization and liberalization of international trade. These developments enable the dominant state to penetrate into the periphery and thereby strengthen its hegemony. Gradually the dominant position of the leading core state in the accumulation pattern starts to weaken and is further undermined by the rise of new core countries, partly from the ranks of semiperipheral countries. This leads to increasing protectionism and bilateralization of trade between core countries and peripheral states. A consequence of this is the formation of spheres of interest for each of the core states. These tendencies coincide with the contraction or stagnation of the world economy which correlate, in turn, with the increasing rivalry between core states. Their expansion into the periphery of the international system also becomes less pronounced.(4)

This means, among other things, that the stagnation of the world economy tends to improve the position of semiperipheral countries in the international hierarchy:

> In moments of world economic downturn, semiperipheral countries can usually expand control of their home market at the expense of core producers, and expand their access to neighbouring peripheral markets, again at the expense of core producers.(5)

Semiperipheral countries are thus able to utilize the relative weakening of core countries by increasing their economic autonomy in the domestic market and by establishing their own regional spheres of interest. The rise of semiperipheral countries is no doubt selective, both in terms of individual countries as well as in terms of industries. In some industries, especially in technologically advanced industries, the dependence on core states tends to remain strong even during a world recession.

In Wallerstein's analysis the group of semiperipheral countries includes a great variety of nations ranging from semi-industrialized countries of the First World, through certain socialist countries of the Second World to more advanced and stronger nations of the Third World. His examples include such countries as Brazil, Venezuela, Cuba, Portugal, Greece, Saudi Arabia, Algeria, Nigeria, Turkey, Israel, Canada, South Africa, Finland and Norway. All of these semiperipheral powers are not, however, equally favoured by the economic stagnation. Wallerstein also claims that in fact only few of them are able to advance at the expense of the core and other semiperipheral states.(6) Semiperipheral countries are thus part and parcel of <u>uneven development</u> in the international system.(7)

The rise of a semiperipheral state in the international economic hierarchy normally coincides with the growth of nationalism and the strengthening of the state machinery. In peripheral countries, the expansion of state power is largely stimulated and sustained by external forces, which include both individual political and economic actors as well as the world political culture based on the nation-state system. This means that in peripheral countries the state machinery and society are not usually very firmly linked to each other. The relative separation of the state from society tends to create problems of legitimation and other types of conflict.

As a given nation state climbs upwards in the economic hierarchy, forces emerge to nationalize the state machinery and to extend its control over society, partly for reasons of economic strategy. The aggregation of political and economic power, which no doubt continues to depend on external forces in all the countries, enhances the ability of semiperipheral powers to steer its internal development and to pursue a policy of autonomy vis-à-vis core nations. It is, however, interesting to observe that the expansion of state power in (semi)peripheral nations does not normally lead to increased stability of the regime or to its legitimization, but rather to new conflicts and turbulence. Semiperipheral states are thus ridden by conflicts and are in the long term an unstable category of nations.(8)

This instability (and inclination to conflicts) is partly related to the fact that economic and political nationalism tends to become stronger in periods of economic depression in the world system. This concerns not only core countries but also semiperipheral nations, which during economic downturn have the opportunity to improve their international standing. As the economic contraction comes to an end and the period of expansion begins, international preconditions for strong state machineries partly disappear and conflicts within semiperipheral nations, and in other nations for that matter, tend to become more pronounced.

The world economy has been in a downturn since the beginning of the 1970s. During this period at least some semiperipheral countries have been able to improve their international position. This has, in turn, coincided with the growth of authoritarian tendencies, in particular in the Third World. Richard A. <u>Falk</u> has made a distinction between three forms of authoritarianism, viz. Brazilianization, Leninization and Praetorianism. <u>Brazilianization</u> takes place in capitalist developing states which normally possess a measure of economic strength, while <u>Leninization</u> refers to newlyborn socialist states, primarily in Africa and Asia. These two types of authoritarianism appear to be the most common manifestations of a strong state in emerging semiperipheral countries of the Third World. Praetorian regimes, whether left-wing or right-wing, are more common in genuine peripheral countries in which

> autocratic rule is a reflection of 'political underdevelopment', that is, a lack of procedures and institutions capable of legitimating governmental authority in a sustainable manner without reliance on force. In such a society, arbitrary force at the disposal of the rulers is the basic political premise, and the military or paramilitary political system is needed to secure the compliance of the population.

<u>Praetorianism</u> is thus not in the same way connected with the centrally-directed economic strategy as in the two other types of authoritarian states.(9)

A central problem in a world-system analysis of political and economic processes is the selection of a unit of analysis. The original Wallersteinian approach stresses very heavily the impact of the world-wide division of labour and economic exchange to which political processes are subordinated. The international society is seen as an integrated world economy which is, however, divided into politically heterogeneous nation states. Wallerstein describes this as <u>world economy</u>, while the international society with a single economic division of labour and with common political and cultural systems is correspondingly called <u>world empire</u>. The present system is without any doubt a world economy in which nation states have primarily a rule-making function. The key issues in state policy are thus:

> a) the rules governing the social relations of production, which critically affect the allocation of surplus-value; and
> b) the rules governing the flow within and across frontiers of the factors of production - capital, commodities and labour -which critically affect the price structures of markets... It is the states that make these rules, and it is primarily the states that intervene in the process of other (weaker) states when the latter attempt to make the rules as they prefer them.(10)

The dynamics of the world economy are, however, shaped by economic forces and processes which dictate the making of political rules.

Some authors prefer to see the relationship between economic and political factors as complementary to each other:

> The capitalist world economy cannot be understood only as a historic and geographic concretization of the capital-relation. The capital-relation constitutes together with the nation-state-relation a totality, the capitalist world economy, which can and must be studied on different levels of abstraction.(11)

The economic system is characterized by at least three significant tendencies which operate within the framework of uneven accumulation of economic and other benefits. Concentration is thus both in the national and international systems a central tendency which is shaped by the transnationalization of political and economic activities. In the economic sphere, transnationalization and the ensuing growth in the power of transnational corporations is manifested in the integration of markets and even more so in the worldwide integration of production and its financing. Transnationalization tends to intensify the trend towards concentration as well as to give new dimensions to it. The third tendency is the prominence of technology which is monopolized to the hands of relatively few corporations and nation states. Control over technology is an instrument to accumulate economic and political power and to steer transnational relations. Technological power is an important factor in determining the nature of the international hierarchy.

Nation states and their politico-bureaucratic machineries operate in the international economic environment guided by these factors. Political activities are in many ways based on existing economic capacity, but no deterministic relationship can be discerned; the wealthiest nations are not always the most powerful, nor vice versa. Military capacity is probably more closely shaped by economic prerequisities, as military production requires considerable amounts of economic and technological input.

9.2. TYPES OF SEMIPERIPHERAL STATES

The dividing lines between the core and the semiperiphery on one hand and between the periphery and the semiperiphery on the other are at best arbitrary. We shall not attempt to give any precise definitions or empirical categories here; the starting point used will be a rather abstract concept of the semiperiphery. Suffice it to point out that semiperipheral states can be defined either by capacity factors such as economic, technological or military strength or by relational variables which describe the nature of economic and other forms of exchange by semiperipheral actors with their environment. Although capacity measures would be more simple to apply, the relational approach is theoretically more justified, because the semiperiphery is essentially defined by its relations with more powerful and weaker states. Although some general criteria can and should be used in the definition of semiperipheral states, the final decision has to be made in casu because of the heterogeneous nature of the intermediate category of states between core and periphery.

In this paper the semiperiphery is divided into four separate categories of nations. A common characteristic of them is that their economic, and in most cases also their political and military role has been expanding in the international society; in other words, their relative power has expanded. This means that we do not deal with such countries that are declining from the core to the semiperiphery (England might be a relevant example). This kind of analysis would, however, be interesting, as the economic and political role of these types of semiperipheral powers may differ in some important respects from that of ascending states. A common feature might be the observation that, at these turning points, both ascending and declining states appear to be more prone to offensive external behaviour than countries which have a stable international position.(12)

During the last ten years or so, new regional power centres have forcefully emerged in the world economy and polity. These centers are truly semiperipheral powers in-between the core states and the periphery. In this sense they are both exploiters and exploited, whose domestic system is characterized by the cleavage between the elite and the masses, in a word by polarized accumulation. A part of their home market, especially high-profit and high-technology sectors, has been captured by dominant transnational corporations on which the regional power centre has become dependent. Yet at the same time strong state machineries and economic forces are expanding from these centres to the surrounding areas, thus establishing their own spheres of influence. This partly but only partly happens at the expense of core states which may indirectly participate, via their economic and political dominance, in these activities.(13) Brazil and South Africa are often mentioned as examples of regional power centres described above.(14)

The oil-exporting nations partly overlap with regional power centres, because the wealth of oil exporters has enabled them to expand their political and economic activities to surrounding regions at the expense of oil consumers. Saudi Arabia, Libya, Nigeria and Venezuela are examples of oil producers which have given extensive aid or have otherwise expanded to neighbouring countries. Their importance in the international currency system has also grown. The main difference with other semiperipheral countries is the lack of industrial and other forms of infrastructure in oil-exporting nations. For this reason they are almost completely dependent on the imports of processed and semiprocessed goods as well as technology from core countries. This considerably reduces their economic autonomy, though at the same time it intensifies their search for domestic industrial and technological capacity.

Another type of semiperipheral actors are newly-industrialising countries (NIC). They are gradually capturing an increasing share of the world market, in particular in light industries. NICs, including such countries as the Republic of Korea, Taiwan, the Philippines and Turkey, are more often than not governed by repressive regimes protecting the interests of domestic and transnational economic forces. Though the economic significance of these countries has been on the increase, they have remained largely dependent on core nations. According to an OECD study, exports of manufactures from this area to the NICs have risen much more than imports from them. Furthermore, this surplus has been increasing, from $ 4 billion in 1963 to $ 18 billion in 1977.(15)

In semi-industrialized countries, the rapid growth rates of the economy are related to the decision to give up import substitution and to concentrate, partly because of the limited size of the domestic market, on the promotion of exports. This has in many instances taken place with the aid of transnational corporations and has led to heavy debt burdens, which have increased economic instabilities at home. A thorough commercialization of the society has biased the development against the production for basic needs. Consequently, large-scale rural poverty as well as the marginalization of parts of the urban population have remained essential features of this type of semiperipheral economy. Polarized accumulation means, in other words, that well-being created by the export-led growth coincides with the persistence of mass poverty.(16)

The three categories of semiperipheral countries analyzed above are all predominantly based on economic considerations: each of them has a specific, though to some degree overlapping position in the international division of labour. Pariah states are somewhat different in this respect, as their defining characteristics are more political. Pariah states are normally rather small but industrially fairly developed nations surrounded by hostile and either potentially or actually stronger countries. They thus face the external threat of being overwhelmed by their neighbours. This is closely connected with the fact that the legitimacy of the national existence of pariah states or, at minimum, their ruling elite is questioned. They are more or less visibly outlawed by the international community, which gives their adversaries freer hands to oppose them.

The security dilemma of pariah states is reinforced by the uncertainty of their relations with mentor countries. Their alliance with a core country is precarious and the commitment to them is thus open to different interpretations. This is connected with the uncertain supply of conventional weapons from core states to pariah states. This gives them an incentive to build up domestic capacity to produce weapons and arms technology, often including nuclear-weapon technology. Pariah states are sensitive points in the chain of nuclear proliferation. By applying these criteria it has been concluded that genuine pariahs of the international community are Israel, South Africa and Taiwan, and to a lesser degree, South Korea and perhaps even Chile and Pakistan.(17)

9.3. MILITARIZATION OF SEMIPERIPHERAL STATES

A basic point of departure in this analysis is that an increase in a nation's economic power almost invariably correlates with its military capacity. Baran and Sweezy with great clarity make the point that military capacity is needed to maintain or to improve a nation's economic position in the exploitative hierarchy. This concerns primarily leading nations, the core of the world economy, which are also drawn into intra-core competition and the show of force.(18) On the other hand, a viable economic base is needed to sustain a strong military apparatus. This is why it is not surprising that a close statistical association exists between a nation's economic and military standing. In addition, the entrance of a country into a phase of rapid economic growth usually means the entrance into a phase of rapid military growth as well. Economic stagnation tends to have the opposite effect.(19)

In the light of these arguments it is apparent that the improvement of the economic position of a semiperipheral country in the international hierarchy normally leads to its militarization, too. This coincides with the merger of nationalism and a strong state machinery, which may use military instruments to enhance both its domestic and external control. Military force is thus consciously developed as a coercive instrument of power. This presupposes, in turn, endeavours to build up domestic military industry in order to reduce the dependence on arms imports. The pattern of polarized accumulation, the relative lack of industrial infrastructure and the intermediate position of semiperipheral countries in the world economy mean, however, that they must remain dependent on the importation of sophisticated foreign technology, both military and civilian. The overall economic and technological dependence of semiperipheral countries also reproduces itself in the military field.(20)

The small size of the domestic market makes the production of arms, to the extent that it has been initiated for political or other reasons, a nonviable proposition in economic terms. To compensate for the smallness of the domestic market, to cut down production costs per unit and to wield some political influence, semiperipheral countries may become exporters of arms, as the cases of Brazil, Israel, India, South Africa and South Korea indicate.(21) Technological dependence on core powers means, however, that the exports of arms can be complicated or even prevented by these powers because of political considerations or of fears that markets will be lost to emerging semiperipheral entities. A relevant example is the U.S. decision to hamper the export of Israel's Kfir fighters to several destinations for the ostensible reason that they are powered by General Electric engines.(22)

These reflections deal with the militarization of semiperipheral countries only at a very general level. Obviously there are differences in this respect between various kinds of semiperipheral countries. These differences are approximated in the following table by the aid of some relevant variables:

Table 9.1.   Semiperipheral Countries in the Global Military Order

	Regional powers	NICs	Oil exporters	Pariahs
Motive of militarization	Regional control Domestic instability	Domestic repression	Domestic instability, control of territory	Security dilemma, domestic repression
Arms industry	Strong, technologically dependent	Modest, but emerging	Modest or nonexistent	Strong, partly dependent, partly autonomous
Arms imports	Extensive, imports of military technology	Average, repression technology	Extensive, high-technology weapons	Extensive, but declining/imports of military technology
Arms exports	Growing rapidly	Non-existing, emerging in some cases	Non-existing	Growing
Nuclear weapons	Potentially, medium probability	Potentially, low probability	No	Yes
Examples	Brazil, India	South Korea, the Philippines, Singapore	Saudi Arabia, Iraq, Libya	South Africa, Israel, Taiwan

It was pointed out earlier that some of the categories of semiperipheral countries may overlap and an individual nation may belong to two separate categories. This is, of course, a problem in constructing a typology. The significance of this problem is reduced, however, by the fact that by combining the characteristics of both categories, an apt description of the role of a nation in the global process of militarization may be reached. Let us take the example of Nigeria, which is both an oil exporter and a regional power centre in West Africa. Without going into details, we can say that Nigeria in fact differs from typical oil exporters such as Saudi Arabia, Kuwait or even Libya in the sense that it has started to build its military industry gradually, it is importing fewer arms than most other oil exporters and it is using the predominant military power to assure its neighbours of its superiority. On the other hand, the country has not shown any plans for acquiring nuclear weapons or sensitive nuclear technologies.

The pattern emerging from the table above is one in which the strength of the domestic economy, its transnational linkages, development alternatives and political ambitions are the central factors in the militarization of semiperipheral countries. In regional power centres, there is a relatively strong domestic ruling elite which is composed of a coalition between the economic elite, the military establishment and techno-bureaucrats. This coalition tries to maintain domestic stability, by military force if needed, and attempts to expand outwards, primarily by economic means. Military strength creates an umbrella by which the credibility of expansionist policy can be enhanced. The build-up of military industry is a logical extension of the domestic programmes for civilian industrialization. In both fields, dependence on transnational capital and technology cannot be avoided, however. Arms exports are initiated partly for political reasons, but they may also be used to obtain foreign currency and to lengthen the production series.(23)

Regional power centres may be examples of dependent capitalist development, though they constantly strive to move away from this position towards a higher degree of autonomy. Newly-industrialized countries are in fact a better example of this model of development. In these countries, there is a triangular power base consisting of the local bourgeoisie, bureaucrats and foreign capital. Domestic stability is maintained by internal repression which is implemented by imported weapons and technology. Domestic capacity to procure arms is small, but may be emerging together with the progress of dependent industrialization. In reality, the military production remains, however, subordinated to external economic and political forces for a long time, and hence arms exports develop only slowly. In dependent capitalist countries

> the political stability required to attract foreign capital and cement its alliance with the state and the local bourgeoisie is guaranteed by organized force. The military is professionalized, being trained with the assistance of Western arms suppliers to

> perform internal security as well as conventional defence functions... Dependent development is fraught with contradictions. Accumulation tends to become blocked by balance of payments difficulties due to rising imports, profit and interest transfers and payments for military equipment which development itself increases.(24)

Oil exporters are even more dependent on foreign arms and military technology, as they have only minimal capacity to produce these themselves. The lack of industrial capacity is, however, compensated by abundant capital resources. In the oil-exporting countries, the purchase of arms is in fact just another form of luxury consumption, if seen from the economic perspective. From the political point of view, the military force so accumulated is, however, needed to preserve the existing class arrangements. Saudi Arabia is here a case in point, and it may also serve as an example in another context. Oil-exporting countries may be accumulating arms also for the defence of their resource-rich territories, as core nations start making claims on the availability of oil, by military force if necessary. Oil wealth may also be used for external expansion as the Shah of Iran did and as Libya and Iraq have recently attempted.

Pariah states may in fact belong to any of the three categories above. In reality, they appear to be closest to regional power centres (the case of South Africa) and to newly-industrialized countries (the case of Taiwan). The relevant economic category in effect determines to a large extent the type of militarization that the pariah is following. The pariah states have, however, some special traits. They include heavy emphasis on the domestic capacity to produce weapons and their acquisition over and above the existing economic capacity. These tendencies can be explained by deeply-felt security dilemmas but they cannot, however, remedy economic problems produced by this over-consumption on military equipment and their maintenance.

The final problem to be dealt with in this context is the <u>proliferation of nuclear weapons</u> among semiperipheral countries. In Table 9.1. we concluded that the propensity towards proliferation is greatest among the pariah nations. Their situation can be illustrated by the following comment:

> While pariah states have the most compelling security reasons to proliferate, the extant nuclear powers are most reluctant to alleviate these concerns through direct measures such as security treaties, precisely because of the very real possibility that their fears may come to pass... Although the pariah states are the strongest candidates for proliferation, the international community as a whole has the least leverage in discouraging them from making the final transition to become nuclear powers. By virtue of their pariah status, they are already suffering the consequences of adverse publicity, economic sanction and political isolation... Thirdly, from the perspective of

the actual or tacit sponsors of the pariah states, efforts to discourage their nuclearization may clash with the pursuit of other major policy objectives.(25)

Pariah states are developing their nuclear capability to acquire a deterrence posture, however modest at first, in order to convince their regional adversaries of their ability to retaliate and, as happens often in reality, to blackmail them politically.

According to our analysis, oil-exporting countries are least prone to acquire nuclear weapons of their own, which can also be said to apply to the NICs, unless their international status includes traits of a pariah state (e.g. Taiwan) or those of a regional power centre. We are maintaining that regional power centres are another category of semiperipheral countries which feels the temptations of nuclear capability. These observations are supported by an empirical study which concluded that the proneness to acquire nuclear explosives is highest in relatively great and militarily strong countries, while the membership in a military alliance, for instance, does not have any appreciable impact. Furthermore, domestic instability, high-level ambitions among the political leadership as well as a conflict-ridden environment and threat perceptions prompted the decision to start acquiring nuclear weapons.(26) These factors are most visible in pariah states and to a somewhat lesser extent in regional power centres.

The proliferation of nuclear weapons is intimately connected with the emergence of new, relatively autonomous decision-making centres in the Third World; that is, semiperipheral countries also start making independent decisions nuclear weapons. Their security policies are shaped largely by regional concerns and ambitions. As a consequence of this, regional systems are gradually <u>decoupled</u> from the central strategic relationship between the Great Powers. This development is, of course, gradual, and the dominant military and technological powers doubtless have means at their disposal to decelerate it, though not to eliminate it.

Nuclear weapons are sought for reasons both of prestige and of security; it is thought, often erroneously, that nuclear weapons will yield political influence and prop up the security position of a country against its regional adversaries. The net outcome is often, instead, an increase in <u>uncertainty</u> and <u>insecurity</u> for the states involved. Would-be nuclear powers may use <u>calculated ambiguity</u> as a political means by 'concealing the fact but promoting the fear' that they have assembled deliverable nuclear weapons.(27) This is precisely what Israel and South Africa are doing by following a 'bomb-in-the-basement' option.

9.4. AN EMPIRICAL ANALYSIS OF THE SEMIPERIPHERY

In the preceding analysis, we have treated semiperipheral countries as a rather loose category of nations. We have relied more on the overall notion of semiperiphery as a tool of analysis in international politics and economics than on any detailed categorization of countries belonging to it. A typology of semiperipheral countries was developed, however, and some individual nations were mentioned as relevant examples. This typology shows that we are not interested only in economic parameters of semiperipheral countries, but that we also want to take political and military characteristics such as the state structure and the process of militarization into account. As the purpose of this chapter is to delineate in an empirical fashion the category of semiperipheral countries, we have to look for a <u>differentia specifica</u> by which this endeavour can be carried through.

It is close to self-evident that whatever criterion of semiperipherality one is using, the ultimate result is a heterogeneous group of countries. Semiperiphery is, in other words, no uniform category of nations. After some painstaking considerations we have come to the conclusion that economic criteria must be central, though not the sole attributes in any effort to define the semiperiphery. In this respect there are two principal options: either we focus on the relational position of nations in the international hierarchy or select for further scrutiny countries at a certain intermediate level of capability and development.

This would mean that the production structure of a nation is at the heart of scrutiny. It is in fact assumed that the production structure is transformed in the upward mobility in the international hierarchy and that this transformation will also influence the character and composition of external exchange. The focus on the production structure is justified for the reason that according to certain investigations, the dynamics of industrial production, including both its quantitative and qualitative dimensions, are the most sensitive indicator of a nation's upward or downward movement in the international hierarchy.(28) Sometimes the relational position of nations is analyzed, however, by mere transaction data without paying any attention to the production structure. One such analysis produced an intermediate group of 32 countries and showed that there is a reasonably high positive correlation between the rate of economic growth and the position in the international hierarchy; the higher up in the hierarchy, the more rapid the growth rate.(29)

This analysis, however, also included socialist countries of Europe as well as some other countries which are normally considered developed. The analysis is therefore less useful for our purposes. This conclusion is reinforced by the fact that the analysis does not take into account various capability factors and domestic political and economic structures which, in our understanding, are necessary to complement the relational approach in the investigation of the international hierarchy. In addition, it would be important to look at the development of <u>internal markets</u>, as the increase in domestic purchasing power, while preventing excessive dependence on exports, is an important factor in fostering industrialization and economic development.

The procedure adopted in this investigation focuses on a given income and capacity group of nations which can roughly be characterized as semiperipheral. We decided to proceed on the basis of the World Bank category of <u>middle-income countries</u>, to which we added three capital surplus oil exporters. The GNP per capita in the middle-income countries varied between $ 390 (Egypt and Ghana) and $ 3500 (Israel). Most of these countries have, however, a per capita income varying in the range of $ 500 - $ 2000, in which range maximum growth rates and most profound structural changes in the economy also take place. Industrial development in middle-income countries also leads to an increase in the technology content of external trade.(30)

This evidence supports the proposition that the level of economic development, measured by GNP per capita, can be used as a rough indicator of the development of <u>productive forces</u>, which is a central characteristic of semiperipheral countries. The size of the internal market can, in turn, be indicated by the GNP, which at the same time measures national capability. The GNP of $ 12 billion, in 1975 prices, was used as a dividing line to denote the <u>economic size</u> of a country and to separate small powers from middle-sized countries. By defining semiperipheral countries as those which belong to the middle-income bracket and which have an economic capacity of $ 12 billion or more, we arrived at the following list of 25 countries (listed below in order of GNP):(31)

1. Brazil	11. Nigeria	21. Colombia
2. Spain	12. Greece	22. Iraq
3. Mexico	13. South Korea	23. Israel
4. Iran	14. Portugal	24. Libya
5. Argentina	15. Philippines	25. <u>Egypt</u>
6. Turkey	16. Kuwait	26. India
7. Yugoslavia	17. Thailand	27. Indonesia
8. South Africa	18. Algeria	28. Malaysia
9. Saudi Arabia	19. Taiwan	29. Zaire
10. Venezuela	20. Peru	

There are 29 countries in all in the semiperipheral group. The next task would be to check the <u>validity</u> of this extensional definition of semiperipherality. A benchmark which can be used in the evaluation of validity is the OECD classification of developing countries 'with good industrial prospects'. These countries were defined by the aid of four criteria: GNP per capita has to be above $ 500, the share of industrial production of GNP has to exceed 20 per cent, natural resources must be sufficiently rich and the past economic performance has to be above average. The countries in question, altogether 23, were divided into three groups on the basis of the extent to which they met these criteria. If we exclude the countries of Southern Europe - which were not considered by the OECD - we find that of those countries included in our list, Colombia, Egypt, Kuwait and Peru were not regarded as industrially promising. On the other hand OECD listed Chile, Costa

Rica, Ghana, Hong Kong, India, Indonesia, Malaysia, Panama, Singapore, Tunisia and Zaire in the category of industrially promising countries.(32)

The validity can further be checked by comparing the list of semiperipheral countries with those 38 nations which were considered 'rising' developing countries by the Swiss economic research institute Prognos. This list is similar to the OECD category in that only genuine developing countries are taken into account; all European countries plus Israel and South Africa are excluded. All the countries on our list of semiperipheral countries are also on the Prognos list, while additional candidates for the semiperipheral category are Angola, Bolivia, Chile, Ecuador, Hong Kong, India, Indonesia, Ivory Coast, Kenya, Malaysia, Morocco, Mozambique, Pakistan, Paraguay, Senegal, Singapore, Zaire, Zambia and Zimbabwe.(33)

Our list of semiperipheral countries is based on objective, albeit somewhat incomplete criteria, while the two other lists are subjective in the sense that they are defined by economic interests shown in them by industrialized countries. In general, the validity of our list appears to be relatively good and at least acceptable. There are, however, some countries which consistently appear on both subjective lists, viz. India, Indonesia, Hong Kong, Malaysia and Zaire. Hong Kong might be excluded from the category because of its small size and special political status, while the four others are more serious candidates. Compared with our criteria, Malaysia is a bit too small in economic size, while in India, Indonesia and Zaire the income per capita is so low - in Indonesia only marginally, however - that they do not qualify as middle-income countries. On the other hand, a low per capita income may be compensated by sheer size in terms of economy, population and area. Therefore we have decided to stretch the original criteria somewhat and add India, Indonesia, Malaysia and Zaire to the list.

Semiperipheral countries are in an in-between position between the centre and the periphery. As the international system is inherently dynamic, so these countries, unless their international position is exceptionally stable, are either ascending or descending in the international hierarchy. To explore the upward and downward dynamics of the international system, we examined the growth rates of the economies and military budgets of the semiperipheral countries between 1970 and 1978.(34) On the basis of this information it is possible to construct a fourfold typology indicating the rise and decline of semiperipheral countries on economic and military dimensions:

Table 9.2. Economic and Military Growth of Semiperipheral Countries, 1970-1978

		Growth rate of GNP	
		High	Low
Growth rate of military expenditures	High	(A) Egypt, Iran, Iraq, Indonesia, the Philippines, Saudi Arabia, South Africa, South Korea, Turkey, Venezuela	(B) Algeria, Greece, Kuwait, Libya, Mexico
	Low	(C) Brazil, Colombia, Malaysia, Nigeria, Taiwan, Thailand, Yugoslavia	(D) Argentina, India, Israel, Peru, Portugal, Spain, Zaire

All four groups of semiperipheral countries specified above are fairly heterogeneous, including regional power centres, oil producers and newly-industrialized countries. The only common characteristic that the bulk of the countries listed above appears to share is the authoritarian political rule to which there are only few exceptions. In fact, democratic tendencies seem to be stronger in those semiperipheral countries which are declining in the military and/or political hierarchy. Ascending semiperipheral powers favour more authoritarian state ideologies by which the population can be mobilized or coerced to work for the upward mobility of the country. Nationalism and authoritarianism are important ingredients in fostering economic and military expansion.

The uneven rise and fall of semiperipheral countries support the conclusion drawn by Immanuel Wallerstein that this type of an actor 'rises to core status, not merely at the expense of some or all core powers, but also at the expense of other semiperipheral powers'.(35) Naturally, one should not draw too drastic conclusions from Table 9.2. on the rise and fall of individual nations, as it covers only a relatively short span of time, i.e. eight years.

It was presumed earlier in this paper that rapid economic growth enhances national economic and technological capacity and creates more resources for investment, hence leading to the expansion of the military establishment. This contention is, however, only slightly supported by data; 17 out of 29 countries are concordant in terms of their simultaneous upward or downward mobility on economic and military dimensions. A problem in this analysis is that it neglects the size dimension. To take this dimension into account, the size of a nation was measured by its population. The analysis conducted on this basis yielded some interesting results.

In the semiperiphery, the countries with the largest populations are, statistically speaking, either growing rapidly on both economic and military dimensions or are stagnating on both dimensions. The top club of bigger, rapidly growing countries included Egypt, Iran, Indonesia, the Philippines, South Africa, South Korea and Turkey, while Argentina, India, Spain and Zaire were stagnating.

These examples show that even big, rapidly growing semiperipheral countries are unstable both economically and politically. Contradictions between the government and opposition are strong, resulting in some cases in takeovers by the opposition (Iran) or in efforts to seize control (Egypt). In many of them, authoritarian or outright military solutions (Turkey and South Korea) have been adopted to pacify the opposition. To put it crudely: the growth of the military establishment is advocated to cope with the instabilities which rapid economic growth is creating, for example in the form of polarized accumulation, in a semiperipheral country.

In addition to authoritarian rule, a common denominator of the semiperipheral countries appears to be political instability, created by the special mode of accumulation prevailing in these countries. Semiperipherality reinforces inequality and social polarization as well as an unwelcome dependence on external influences. There are also grounds for assuming that semiperipheral countries are more prone to involvement in war than other countries. Involvement in conflicts may be a means of acquiring weapons and other military equipment, either through domestic production or arms imports, and recruiting men to arms. Weapons acquisition may, in turn, provide an instrument by which the political and military elites of semiperipheral countries are able to extend their power or to maintain their position in the regional environment or within society.

The assumption above was tested by calculating how many of the countries under review have actually been involved in either civil or international wars.(36) An important finding is that semiperipheral countries are extremely prone to aggressive behaviour: 18 out of 29, i.e. 62 per cent, waged one or another sort of war between 1970-77. In the entire group of middle-income countries, the corresponding share is somewhat lower, 44 per cent (N=55), but still higher than in industrialized countries, of which only few have been waging wars during the 1970's. This finding is corroborated by Istvan Kende, who concludes that interventions by third parties from the Third World in external or internal wars waged in the region have increased during the 1970's. The leading countries in the Third World, i.e. semiperipheral nations are most often behind these interventions.(37)

To deepen our understanding of the relationship between involvement in warfare and various manifestations of semiperipherality, we calculated the share of nations having waged war in 1970-77 of the total number of semiperipheral and middle-income countries, respectively. The first column in the table below gives the relevant percentage for semiperipheral and the second column for the entire group of middle-income countries:

Table 9.3. Involvement in Warfare in Semiperipheral and Middle-Income Countries, per cent

		Growth rate of GNP		
		High	Low	Total
Growth rate of military expenditures	High	70/53 (A)	80/77 (B)	80/61
	Low	14/9 (C)	86/38 (D)	50/26
	Total	47/36	83/52	62/44

Table 9.3. leads, without hesitation, to the conclusion that nations with rapid economic growth combined with a below average increase in military capability have been more peaceful than others. The only exception to this rule has been Thailand. Conversely, countries experiencing rapid growth of military expenditure and slow growth of the economy (B) have been, all in all, most inclined to become involved in wars. Among the group of semiperipheral countries, those which are either consistently ascending or declining in economic and military terms have been more inclined to resort to weapons than the corresponding group of all middle-income countries. This indicates that the conclusion on the proneness to aggression in the upward and downward slope of relative national capability has special relevance among semiperipheral countries.(38) In addition to dissolving opposition within the country, they have to fight to move upwards in the international hierarchy as well as to prevent the downward slide in this very same hierarchy.

A more general conclusion emanating from this material is that the involvement in wars correlates more strongly with the growth of military spending than with economic growth. This suggests that economic development, if not combined with the process of militarization, is conducive to peace (or equally well that peace is conducive to economic development). On the other hand, slow growth of the economy, irrespective of the rate of the militarization process, is connected with frequent outbreaks of military conflicts. Among semiperipheral countries: a systematic downward movement in international hierarchy seems to be specially conducive to conflict behaviour. The difference that exists between semiperipheral and all middle-income countries in that respect can be perhaps explained simply that semiperipheral countries have more to lose as a consequence of the decline. Resort to aggressive behaviour is an effort to stop the decline.

9.5. IS THE THEORY VALID?

In the beginning of this paper we presented a brief summary of an approach usually termed the world-system analysis. This theory hypothesizes that in the conditions of stagnated world economy, semiperipheral countries are able to expand both their domestic market and their share of the world market in spite of the protectionist tendencies in industrialized countries. In particular it is supposed that they are able to strengthen their manufacturing production and its export trade. The participation of the public sector in the promotion of manufacturing creates the backbone for an industrial strategy, which is usually geared to international markets in order to capture a bigger share of them.

To test the viability of these assumptions in the group of semiperipheral countries, as defined above, we decided to focus on the growth of their manufacturing production and exports in 1960-70 and 1970-79. During the former period, the world economy continued to grow, while the period of stagnation started in the latter period. Hence, 1970 offers a convenient cut-off point for analysis and makes the comparison between the two periods meaningful. The growth of manufacturing production in semiperipheral countries was slightly higher in the 1970s than in the 1960s, viz. 8.6 per cent and 8.2 per cent respectively. These figures have to be compared, however, with the growth performance of the other categories of countries.(39)

Table 9.4. The Growth of Manufacturing Production in Different Groups of Countries in 1960-1970; annual averages, per cent

	1970-79	1960-70	Difference
Semiperipheral countries	8.6	8.2	0.4
Non-semiperipheral middle-income countries	5.3	7.4	- 2.1
Low-income countries	3.7	6.5	- 2.8
Industrial market-economy countries	3.0	6.2	- 3.2

The table shows that the growth of manufacturing production of semiperipheral countries was higher than in other countries even during the 1960s. The differences were, however, quite small. During the 1970s the situation changed and the semiperiphery alone could increase the growth rate of manufacturing production, which correspondingly declined in other countries, most notably in industrial market economies. This means that other countries, especially those belonging to the semiperiphery, were able to improve their relative position in the world production structure. This finding is concordant with the hypotheses derived from the world-system analysis.

An interesting feature in the growth performance of individual countries in the semiperiphery is that those which were declining in the international hierarchy in general economic and military terms also experienced <u>relative deindustrialization</u>. Their average growth rate in the manufacturing sector decreased from 5.2 per cent in 1960-70 to 3.4 per cent in 1970-79. By that figure these countries - of which Argentina, Peru, Portugal and Zaire are good examples - approached the average growth performance of industrial market economies during the 1970s. In fact, more attention should be paid to those semiperipheral countries that are moving downwards in the international system of stratification.

The build-up of the technological base for manufacturing industries in semiperipheral countries does not, however, take place without sacrifices. A detailed analysis of the industrialization strategies of Algeria, Brazil, Mexico and South Korea, which all belong to the semiperiphery, showed with great clarity how their public external debt has escalated during the 1970s. From 1971 to 1978 public external debt increased in Mexico by 542 per cent, in Brazil by 404 per cent, in Algeria by 753 per cent and in South Korea by 715 per cent, while the corresponding growth figure for all the developing countries was 308 per cent. The same pattern is revealed in the distribution of export credits for purchase of capital goods, i.e. technological inputs for production. The main recipients of export credits were Brazil, Peru, Argentina and Mexico in Latin America; South Korea, the Philippines, Thailand and Taiwan in Asia; Egypt, the Ivory Coast and Morocco in Africa; Algeria, Iran, Libya, Saudi Arabia and Indonesia within OPEC and Turkey, Yugoslavia, Portugal, Spain and Greece in Europe. Practically all these countries are also on our list of semiperipheral nations.

In the light of this information, it is possible to speak of <u>indebted industrialization</u> in the semiperiphery. A new characteristic in this strategy of industrialization is that external debts originate increasingly in private commercial banks and are allocated to corporations in the public sector. A relation of interdependence develops between the private financial sector of the capitalist world economy and the public sector in semiperipheral nations. It is well known that in many semiperipheral countries the arms industry is a strategic sector to which external debt is also directed. Although the relative importance of transnational corporations in leading semiperipheral countries appears to be declining, the technological and financial dependence of the semiperiphery on the world economy persists and in fact assumes new forms.(40)

An imbalance in the development of the economy, together with technological and financial dependence, leads in the longer run to a deficit in the current account balance. South Korea and Brazil are examples of semiperipheral countries that have during the last few years experienced considerable deficits in their external balance of payments. True, these deficits are partly brought about by the increase in oil prices, but their mode of industrialization has also contributed to this outcome. In general one may say, however, that semi-industrial countries have suffered less from external shocks to their balance of payments in 1974-78 than developing countries on average; their problems are more often domestic in origin than is the case in other countries. The external problems of semiperipheral countries are primarily caused by the increase in import prices, including oil, and by the shortfalls in export volume arising from the recession in the OECD countries in the middle of the 1970s. The adjustment to the external shocks was dispersed rather evenly between structural adjustment, additional external financing and slower economic growth which narrows current account deficits by restricting imports.(41)

Indebted industrialization, external deficits and patterns of dependence are furthermore connected with increasing polarization between the rich and the poor. There is evidence that the rapid industrialization in Brazil has taken place at the expense of a growing gap between rich and poor regions as well as between privileged and underprivileged strata of population. In South Korea, even though its income distribution is by no means the most skewed in the Third World, a similar tendency towards more unequal distribution can easily be discerned.(42) Apparently, this is a reflection of a phenomenon more common in rapidly industrializing countries, namely that, as they move upwards in the international hierarchy, so their domestic inequality increases. The United States faced this experience during the nineteenth century, a period when the country expanded both economically and geographically.(43)

In addition to industrial production and its economic and social preconditions, attention should be paid to the export trade of semiperipheral countries. It is commonly assumed that the machinery and transport equipment share of the total exports is the most sensitive indicator of the emergence of industrial or semi-industrial countries. The shares of these technology-intensive items in the total exports in 1960 and 1978 are given in the table below:(44)

Table 9.5.   The Share of Machinery and Transport Equipment in Exports of Semiperipheral Countries in 1960 and 1978, per cent

	1978	1960	Difference
Semiperipheral countries	7.7	1.5	6.2
Non-semiperipheral middle-income countries	4.2	0.9	3.3
Low-income countries	1.5	1.6	- 0.1
Industrial market-economy countries	38.0	29.0	9.0

The table shows unequivocally that industrial market-economy countries are dominant in the export of technology-intensive goods. They can be matched only by nonmarket, i.e. socialist, industrial countries of which some - such as Bulgaria, Czechoslovakia, the German Democratic Republic, Hungary and Poland - are strongly geared to exports of machinery and transport equipment. Even though the export of these goods has increased from a zero level both in semiperipheral and other middle-income countries, a considerable gap between them and industrial countries still exists. The gap has widened rather than decreased from 1960 towards the end of the 1970s.

This conclusion does not, however, render the conclusions of the world-system analysis invalid. Rather, it shows that those countries defined as semiperipheral in this study vary considerably in the composition of their exports; some of them, for instance, are exporting textiles and clothing or other light manufactures instead of machinery and transport equipment, which require a more sound and broad-based industrial infrastructure. The semiperipheral countries of whose total exports more than 10 per cent consists of machinery are Brazil, Israel, Malaysia, Mexico, Portugal, Republic of Korea, Spain and Yugoslavia. To these countries we have to add Hong Kong and Singapore, which were excluded from our list on the basis of their small size, and Romania, excluded because of its socialist system of economy. On the foreign-trade criterion these countries represent the hard core of the semiperiphery.

Another way to look at the 'hard core' is to explore the viability of the industrialization strategy which a semiperipheral country is pursuing. It is apparent that without a strong state sector, viability cannot be achieved.(45) An illustrative example is provided by the state-controlled aircraft industry, representing the most sophisticated sector of technology, in India (Hindustan Aeronautics), Israel (Israeli Aircraft

Industries), South Africa (Atlas Aircraft Corp.) and Brazil (Embraer). In all of them the aircraft industry is considered a pioneering industry, and it is also intensively supported by the state. In all of these corporations, with the partial exception of the Brazilian one, the share of military production is high, as the commercial versions of aeroplanes are not internationally competitive, and the production has to be directed to the domestic military market. The development of competitiveness is partly hampered by the dependence on foreign technology and other inputs for manufacturing, which may even be withheld deliberately to discourage expansion in the world market. A bottleneck is created by high costs of production, partly due to the dependence on foreign technology as well as to the small size of the domestic market, which have necessitated efforts to create new exports. This has happened in particular in Brazil and Israel.

Taiwan offers another example of bottlenecks which semiperipheral countries are experiencing in their policy of industrialization, including their military production. Taiwan's transformation into a vigorous semiperipheral country has been based on a cheap labour force, cheap and plentiful energy and open foreign markets - not to mention U.S. investments, amounting to $ 600 million during the last 25 years. Roughly during the same period, Taiwan's military expenditures have increased from $ 370 million in 1955 to $ 1880 million in 1978, accounting in the latter year for 7.5 per cent of the GNP. Taiwan's emerging prosperity is, however, currently threatened.

The competitiveness of Taiwanese export products is declining because of a considerable increase in labour costs as well as in the oil bill. In 1980 Taiwan experienced a deficit in its foreign trade for the first time in five years. Although exports are still growing rapidly by international standards, Taiwan's economy, partly because of the heavy military burden, is facing new problems of adjustment. The government has tried to solve the problems by investing heavily in technology-intensive industries, which are less dependent on a cheap labour force and energy, as well as in the development of the infrastructure. The intention is to transform Taiwan into a modern industrial giant, which would also mean the build-up of domestic military industry. The overconsumption of weapons would thus continue.(46)

So far, most of Taiwan's military production, i.e. in the field of aircraft and non-nuclear missiles, is taking place under licence arrangements concluded with the U.S. companies. The major manufacturing programme has been the licensed production of Northrop's F-5E fighters by the Aero Industry Development Center. As the technology-intensive muscle of Taiwan gets stronger, there have been efforts to make the arms industry more indigenous. Delays in the construction of heavy industry are not a major problem, because arms manufacturing is now more dependent on electronics than on the steel industry.(47) It is, however, obvious that the domestic arms industry, which is encouraged by the U.S. hesitation to sell advanced aircraft to

Taiwan, will prove to be prohibitively costly to the country and will produce complications for the industrialization strategy, which is already under stress from other complications.

9.6. SEMIPERIPHERY AND THE TRANSFORMATION OF WORLD ORDER

The international system is undergoing a profound process of fragmentation due to the gradual redistribution of power within it. The redistribution is brought about by the relative decline of the national capabilities of great powers and the consequent rise of some middle-sized industrial powers and semiperipheral countries in the Third World. The rise of the semiperiphery is related to the long-term economic and political dynamics of the world. The period of economic stagnation that began in the early 1970s has reinforced this tendency. The political aspirations of most semiperipheral countries are rooted in the nationalistic revolutions which they went through in one way or another during the twentieth century. Mexico, Turkey, Egypt, Indonesia, India, China and Vietnam are examples of semiperipheral countries which have experienced a nationalistic revolution during their history, though all of them have not been able to sustain their revolution but have returned to an economically and politically less nationalistic road. The interconnection between the nationalistic revolution and semiperipherality has cemented nation states in the Third World against which the capitalist core has adopted a hostile attitude.(48)

The political consciousness created by the national revolutions in semiperipheral countries was an important force in the estbalishment of the Movement of Non-aligned Countries. It is no accident that the founding fathers of this movement included such countries as India, Egypt and Yugoslavia and, to a lesser extent, Indonesia and Ghana. They reacted on political grounds against the core of the international system. Now the political motives of semiperipheral countries have become diluted, and the economic rise of such semiperipheral countries as oil exporters or newly-industrialized countries has gained more weight. It has to be stressed that modes of accumulation vary considerably, however, from one group of semiperipheral countries to another. If we exclude oil-exporting countries the semiperipheral model of production has normally involved import substitution to protect domestic industry and the establishment of a base for exporting of consumer manufactured goods. Both of those production models are, however, vulnerable to penetration of external forces such as the transnational corporations and banks. This penetration is, furthermore, assuming new forms in semiperipheral countries. The government of a semiperipheral country may, for example, assure a transnational car manufacturer a considerable share in the domestic market and to combine it with an agreement to start producing in the country a massive number of components needed in the assembly of cars in the plants of the same corporation in other countries. The result is a new form of industrial division of labour combining the simultaneous production for domestic and foreign market.(49) Spain, Mexico and Brazil are examples of countries in which this method of relocating industry has been implemented.

This new form of division of labour does not concern only the car manufactauring. In fact it is an increasingly common arrangement in the military production as well. A deal may be struck between a semiperipheral government and a transnational aircraft corporation which involves, for example, the production of a fighter aircraft for the domestic needs under licence and the production of certain components for the international market. This type of vertical co-production can be illustrated by the licence production of Northrop's F-5 fighter in Spain.(50) It is to be expected that this form of co-production will increase in the future. These remarks refer to the fact that the character of semiperipherality has changed: its political and nationalistic manifestations have become less important and it has turned more into an economic phenomenon. The international economic division of labour is changing rapidly giving a greater slice to semiperipheral countries but integrating them at the same time more firmly in the transnational network of technological and financial dependences. As a consequence the policies of semiperipheral countries, whose power base is primarily economic, are less politically oriented than those belonging to the 'first generation' of semi-peripheral countries. This does not mean, however, that conflicts between core and semiperiphery have disappeared; they have only changed their nature. While the conflicts, say in the 1950s, contained a confrontation between internationalism of the core and nationalism of the semiperiphery, present disputes concern more market shares of labour-intensive export products and international financial relations. This also means that the problem of legitimacy of the international order has assumed new shades. In the 1950s non-aligned countries questioned the legitimacy of political, military, and to a lesser extent economic imperialism of major industrial countries. In the 1980s the problem of legitimacy is discussed more in terms of the asymmetric nature of rules and norms regulating the operation of international economic mechanisms and the redistribution of the results of the production process.

The international system is fragmenting if looked upon from the perspective of the nation states. In the Third World regionalism is on the rise: new economic groupings, such as ECOWAS and ASEAN, are established and military-political conflicts are also becoming more regionally encapsulated as the examples of the Persian Gulf and Central America indicate. Naturally this regional encapsulation does not mean that great powers are not involved in them; they cannot, however, steer their course any more and hence become more prisoners of these conflicts and less able to solve them.(51) Political forces in the Third World are not, however, strong enough to shape the process of regionalization in their own favour. The primacy of economics over politics is a fact in the present stage of the evolution of the international system. This means that the position of most semiperipheral countries in the Third World is shaped more by the capitalist logic of the international market - creating a new, rather invisible corporate world and network of economic dependencies - than by their political aspirations. The military power of semiperipheral countries, for instance, is not primarily based on the nationalistic political decision to build up arms industry to serve domestic needs. The arms industries of developing countries are shaped rather by the global economic logic which operates roughly in the same way as in the civilian market.

There are, however, good reasons to expect that in a long-term perspective political motives and aspirations will emerge to complement the new, though vulnerable, economic power base which semiperipheral countries have acquired in the process of climbing up the ladder of the international hierarchy. This can only mean greater assertiveness from the part of the Third World to pursue their economic and political claims. Taking into consideration the continuing economic and social crisis in semiperipheral societies, created by a combination of external indebtness and dependence as well as domestic polarization, it is apparent that assertiveness vis-à-vis core countries is likely to also be used to pacify the domestic opposition. Military capability is needed both for external and domestic purposes and it would hence be premature to expect any process of demilitarization to take place in the semiperiphery of the international system. In fact it might be a characteristic of the future that extra-economic political and military means would be increasingly used to regulate the operation of the world economy as well.(52) Semiperipheral nations aim at the primacy of politics to safeguard their position against both external and internal challenges.

NOTES AND REFERENCES

1. W. Ladd Hollist, Conclusion. Anticipating World System Theory Synthesis. International Studies Quarterly, Vol. 25, No. 1, 1981, p. 151.

2. Immanuel Wallerstein, The Capitalist World-Economy. Cambridge 1979, pp. 22-24.

3. This problem is explored by Robert E. Harkavy, Pariah States and Nuclear Proliferation. International Organization, Vol. 35, No. 1, 1981, pp. 155-58.

4. More details on the basic points of departure of the world-system analysis can be obtained, for example, from the following publications: Wallerstein op. cit. 1979, Terence Hopkins & Immanuel Wallerstein (eds.), Processes of the World-System. Beverly Hills 1980 and Folker Fröbel, Jürgen Heinrichs & Otto Kreye (eds.), Krisen in der kapitalistischen Weltökonomie. Reinbek bei Hamburg 1981.

5. Wallerstein op. cit. 1979, p. 99.

6. Ibid., pp. 100-102.

7. Uneven development of the international economy as a persistent historical tendency has been briefly documented by Paul Bairoch, The Main Trends in National Economic Disparities since the Industrial Revolution, in Paul Bairoch & Maurice Lévy-Leboyer (eds.), Disparities in Economic Development since the Industrial Revolution. New York 1981, pp. 3-17.

8. Cf. George M. Thomas & John W. Meyer, Regime Changes and State Power in an Intensifying World-State-System, in Albert Bergesen (ed.), Studies of the Modern World-System. New York 1980, pp. 139-58.

9. For further analysis see Richard A. Falk, A World Order Perspective on Authoritarian Tendencies. World Order Models Project Working Paper No. 10. New York 1980 (the quotation is from p. 29).

10. See Immanuel Wallerstein, The States in the Institutional Vortex of the Capitalist World-Economy. International Social Science Journal, Vol. 32. No. 4, 1980, pp. 743-51 (the quotation is from p. 746).

11. Jan-Otto Andersson, Capital and Nation-State. Meddelanden från ekonomisk-statsvetenskapliga fakulteten vid Åbo Akademi, ser. A:159. Åbo 1981, pp. 2-3.

12. On this point see Charles F. Doran & Wes Parsons, War and the Cycle of Relative Power. American Political Science Review, Vol. 74, No. 4, 1980, pp. 947-65.

13. For a more thorough analysis see Raimo Väyrynen, Economic and Military Position of Regional Power Centers. Journal of Peace Research, Vol. 16, No. 4, 1979, pp. 349-69.

14. An interesting case study on South Africa has been carried out by Ruth Milkman, Contradictions in Semi-Peripheral Development: The South African Case, in Walter L. Goldfrank (ed.), The World-System of Capitalism: Past and Present. Beverly Hills 1979, pp. 261-84. Milkman (op.cit. 1979, p. 279) makes an interesting point that 'there seems to be a striking parallel between South Africa's apartheid system and the social structures, in most cases not racially based, of other semi-peripheral countries at a comparable level of industrialization'. Milkman (p. 264) also criticizes the semi-periphery as 'one of the weakest and most ambiguous components of Wallerstein's framework'.

15. See Stephen Marris, OECD Trade with the Newly Industrializing

Countries. <u>OECD Observer</u>, No. 99, 1979, pp. 28-34.

16. For more details see <u>World Development Report</u>. The World Bank, Washington, D.C. 1979, pp. 87-95.

17. For further details see Harkavy <u>op.cit</u>. 1981, pp. 135-63, Robert Harkavy, The Pariah State Syndrome. <u>Orbis</u>, Vol. 21, No. 3, 1977, pp. 623-49, and Steve Chan, Incentives for Nuclear Proliferation. The Case of International Pariahs. <u>Journal of Strategic Studies</u>, Vol. 3, No. 1, 1980, pp. 26-43.

18. Paul A. Baran & Paul M. Sweezy, <u>Monopoly Capital: An Essay on the American Economic and Social Order</u>. London 1968, pp. 178-214.

19. Gernot Köhler, Toward a General Theory of Armaments. <u>Journal of Peace Research</u>, Vol. 16, No. 2, 1979, pp. 117-35.

20. These points are more extensively documented in Helena Tuomi & Raimo Väyrynen, <u>Transnational Corporations, Armaments and Development. A Study of Transnational Military Production, International Transfer of Military Technology and their Impact on Development</u>. Aldershot 1982.

21. For details on the arms exports by semiperipheral countries see <u>World Armaments and Disarmament. SIPRI Yearbook 1980</u>. London 1980, pp. 85-89.

22. See Ben Kocivar, US Hampers Kfir Exports. <u>Flight International</u>, 24 June 1978, pp. 1908-1909.

23. The case of Brazil is a good example here: see Clóvis Brigagao, The Case of Brazil: Fortress or Paper Curtain? <u>Impact of Science on Society</u>, Vol. 31, No. 1, 1981, pp. 17-32.

24. See Robin Luckman, Armaments, Underdevelopment and Demilitarization in Africa. <u>Alternatives</u>, Vol. 6, No. 2, 1980, pp. 205 and 208-209. South Korea is somewhat of an exception here because of its relatively strong military industry, which has now also begun to try to sell arms, in particular to ASEAN countries; see <u>Business Week</u>, 29 June 1981, p. 62.

25. Chan <u>op. cit</u>. 1980, pp. 26-43 (the quotation is from pp. 27-28). See also Harkavy <u>op. cit</u>. 1981, pp. 158-62.

26. See Charles W. Kegley, Jr., International and Domestic Correlates of Nuclear Proliferation. A Comparative Analysis. <u>Korea and World Affairs</u>, Vol. 4, No. 1, 1980.

27. John W. Weltman, Nuclear Devolution and World Order. <u>World Politics</u>, vol. 32, No. 2, 1980, pp. 169-93, and David C. Compert

et. al., Nuclear Weapons and World Politics. Alternatives for the Future. New York 1977, pp. 221-40.

28. See, e.g., Charles P. Kindleberger, Dominance and Leadership in the International Economy, International Studies Quarterly, Vol. 25, No. 2, 1981, pp. 242-54.

29. See David Snyder & Edward L. Kick, Structural Position in the World System and Economic Growth, 1955-70. A Multiple-Network Analysis of Transnational Interaction. American Journal of Sociology, Vol. 84, No. 5, 1978, pp. 1096-1126. The semiperipheral countries are, according to this study, Venezuela, Peru, Argentina, Uruguay, South Korea, Cuba, Ireland, the German Democratic Republic, Hungary, Cyprus, Bulgaria, Rumania, the USSR, Kenya, Iran, Turkey, Iraq, Lebanon, Jordan, Israel, Finland, Saudi Arabia, Taiwan, India, Pakistan, Burma, Ceylon, Malaysia, and the Philippines.

30. See North/South Technology Transfer. The Adjustment Ahead. OECD, Paris 1981, p. 27.

31. World Development Report... op. cit. 1979, pp. 128-29.

32. North/South Technology Transfer... op. cit. 1981, pp. 28-29.

33. The list by Prognos is published in Helsingin Sanomat, 9 September 1981.

34. This information is extracted from World Development Report 1980. World Bank, Washington, D.C. 1980, pp. 110-11, and World Armaments and Disarmament... op. cit. 1980, pp. 20-24.

35. Wallerstein op. cit. 1979, p. 101.

36. Data on conflict behaviour is obtained from William Eckhardt & Edward E. Azar, Major Military Conflicts and Interventions, 1965-79. Peace Research, Vol 11, No. 4, 1979, pp. 201-207. Only those major international or domestic conflicts that have taken place in 1970-77 have been considered here.

37. See Istvan Kende, Wars of Ten Years (1967-1976). Journal of Peace Research, Vol. 15, No. 3, 1978, pp. 227-41.

38. Cf. Doran and Parson op. cit. 1980, pp. 947-65.

39. The basic material is extracted from World Development Report 1981. The World Bank, Washington, D.C. 1981, pp. 136-37.

40. See North/South Technology Transfer... op. cit. 1981, pp. 47-49, and Jeff Frieden, Third World Indebted Industrialization: International Finance and State Capitalism in Mexico, Brazil, Algeria and

South Korea. <u>International Organization</u>, Vol. 35, No. 3, 1981, pp. 407-31.

41. World Development Report... <u>op. cit.</u> 1981, pp. 65-71.

42. See. e.g., Dieter Senghaas, Quo vadis Südkorea? Ueberlegungen zum Entwicklungsweg Südkoreas, Preface to H.D. Luther, <u>Südkorea. (K)ein Modell für die Dritte Welt</u>? München 1981, pp. 8-27.

43. Jeffrey Williamsson, Inequality Accumulation, and Technological Imbalance: A Growth-Equity Conflict in American History? <u>Economic Development and Cultural Change</u>, Vol. 28, No. 2, 1979, pp. 231-53.

44. World Development Report... <u>op.cit.</u> 1980.

45. This point is stressed, for example, by Frieden <u>op. cit.</u> 1981, pp. 407-31.

46. See Taiwan Gears Up to Go It Alone. <u>Fortune</u>, Vol. 99, No. 3, 1979, pp. 72-77, <u>Far Eastern Economic Review</u>, May 8, 1981, pp. 48-49 and <u>The Economist</u>, September 12, 1981, pp. 73-74 and 76.

47. See, for example, <u>Newsweek</u>, 31 March 1980, pp. 20-23.

48. See Daniel Chirot, <u>Social Change in the Twentieth Century</u>. New York 1977, pp. 144-45 and 202-14.

49. See, e.g., Alain Lipietz, Towards Global Fordism? <u>New Left Review</u>, No. 132, 1982, pp. 33-47.

50. For more details see Ulrich Albrecht, Dieter Ernst, Peter Lock & Herbert Wulf, <u>Rüstung und Unterentwicklung</u>. Reinberk bei Hamburg 1976, pp. 54-58.

51. Cf. Pierre Hassner, New Centers of Weakness: Beyond Power and Interdependence, <u>Social Research</u>, Vol. 48, No. 4, 1981, pp. 677-99.

52. Volker Bornschier, The World Economy in the World-System: Structure, Dependence and Change. <u>International Journal of Social Science</u>, Vol. 34, No. 1, 1982.

Chapter Ten

THE TRANSFER OF MILITARY TECHNOLOGY TO THIRD WORLD COUNTRIES*

Signe Landgren-Bäckström

10.1. INTRODUCTION

The postwar global arms race differs in many respects from what was previously called the "arms race". The main difference is found in the number of participants: while only a few European states, together with their allies (the USA, Canada, Australia and Japan) were involved in the arms build-up in the 1930s, the trend since 1945 has been towards the spread of increasingly more sophisticated weaponry to an increasing number of countries, so that the arms race has become distinctly global. The exceptions are very few - Costa Rica and the demilitarised territory of Finnish Åland.

The classic method of measuring the global arms race is to compare military expenditure statistics. In order to cross-check the official statistics, or in order to obtain an independent means of measuring the arms race, it is possible to use other indicators, such as, for example, the acquisition of weapons as well as the acquisition of a weapon production capacity. SIPRI treats the issue of the transfer of military technology as a part of the international trade and transfer of armaments - the arms trade statistics published each year in the SIPRI Yearbook, for example, include the transfers of production licences. In connection with the problems of disarmament, the transfer of military technology, as compared to the transfer of armaments, takes on a specific importance, since as a rule such transfers are not covered by the existing national arms export controls. (Only a few of the arms exporting countries have placed the export of technology under the same supervision as the export of arms and military equipment, notably the United States, France and FR Germany.) SIPRI's treatment of the issue of military technology transfers as an integral part of the international arms trade is motivated primarily by the disarmament perspective - that is, all of SIPRI's data collections are undertaken for the same reasons, namely: to arrive at an understanding of the scale and scope of the existing arms race and of the mechanisms behind it; and to fill in the missing data required by the disarmament community for the ultimate purpose of enabling that community to present realistic disarmament or arms reduction proposals. This approach should not, however, be taken to imply that the transfer of military technology cannot be treated as a research subject per se, given the far-reaching implications at different levels of the problems of under-development in Third World countries (all countries except Europe, the USA, Canada, the USSR, Japan, Australia and New Zealand), and also the problems which arise from exaggerated investments in military technology in the industrialized world, sometimes described as the permanent war economy (Seymour Melman).

One example of a previously unresearched field is the real scope of resources - monetary as well as manpower - mobilized in connection with the transfer of military technology. For example: what are the precise economic implications of the involvement of approximately 85 European companies in the offset deal for the licence production of the US F-16 fighter aircraft; and should the overall turnover in monetary value be counted in terms of billions or trillions of dollars? This type of question, which deals with the spread effect, becomes even more significant in regard to military technology transfers to the Third World countries, considering the need for resources for social development purposes.

10.2. THE ARMS ACQUISITION METHODS

There are, at the national level, basically only two ways of acquiring weapons - either by importing them or producing them. Those countries which are the leading innovators in the field of military technology are also, obviously, the leading exporters of both weapon systems and military technology (they are, of course, also the leading technology innovators in general), and are easily identified in the relevant literature as the USA, the USSR, France, the UK and some other European countries.

These two methods of acquiring arms are chronologically interrelated. The common pattern is to start with the import of weapons, related support equipment and training etc. The acquisition of a local arms production capacity, or the import of technology or technological know-how, is normally a continuation of direct arms imports, and the military technology is normally taken from the same exporter. Egypt, for example, has during the past few years received relatively large numbers of US weapons and is now proceeding to local production of US F-5 fighter aircraft. This chronological relationship is well illustrated in the existing arms import statistics (in both the Arms Control and Disarmament Agency (ACDA) and SIPRI series) - those Third World countries which today are the leading regional arms producers have all, after 1945, been among the largest weapons importers, that is South Africa, India, Israel, Brazil, Argentina, Taiwan and South Korea. However, the reverse is not true - there are numerous countries which stand out as large weapons importers without proceeding to acquire a local production capacity.

A local production capacity ranges from the mere assembly of imported sub-assemblies to the entire process connected with indigenously researched and developed weapon systems. The sequence when building up a domestic arms industry is, most often, to begin by setting up an overhaul and maintenance plant for weapons already in service with the national armed forces - this stage was being reached in Iran under the Shah's regime, for example, as a first step in a highly ambitious long-term plan. The second step is to import sub-assemblies or "knocked-down" weapons and assemble them at a local plant, followed by the next phase, of assembling imported components locally; next, the components are manufactured locally from imported raw materials, the final goal being to produce most of the raw materials. Except in the case of some less sophisticated weaponry, this last stage is hardly ever reached, even in industrialized countries, for various reasons. The Swedish aerospace industry has found, for example, that it is cheaper to import US aeroengine designs for its modern fighter aircraft than to invest in a local project. The procedure mentioned above is sometimes described in terms of phases of a production programme, aimed at increasing the indigenous contribution either as a percentage of contents or a percentage of value. The investment of resources in a weapons production programme is obviously on a scale entirely different from the import of a finished weapon.

10.3. WEAPONS ACQUISITION: THE ODD EXAMPLE

The "normal" procedure of acquiring technological know-how in the field of armaments production is complemented by three less common methods: the import not only of a production licence, but of an entire production line; the investment in an established producer country in a specific new weapons project, and "reverse engineering". The first two methods are open only to those Third World countries which possess adequate financial resources, and the third method represents an attempt to take a short cut from the conditions of a less developed economy into modern advanced weapons technology.

In 1967 Israel purchased a production line together with full marketing rights for the Jet Commodore business transport aircraft from the Rockwell Corporation. This plane has since been developed into the Westwind 1124 Seascan maritime patrol for the Israeli air force. This method of acquiring know-how takes more than financial resources - it requires the existence of the necessary infrastructure, and is more typical for developed economies than for less developed countries. (Switzerland, for example, expanded its arms production capacity by the acquisition of a production line for the Flamingo trainer of German design in the purchase of the Britten-Norman company in 1979).

South Africa acquired know-how in missile technology through its participation in the Crotale SAM programme in France from 1964. The project was undertaken by Matra and Thomson-CSF according to South African specifications, and 85 % of the development costs were financed by South Africa. This missile system, known in South Africa as Cactus, is now deployed along the border with Mozambique. It is believed to be in production in South Africa, since it has been offered for export.(1)

There are other examples of non-producers investing in new military technology in established producing countries. For example, the Shah's government of Iran purchased a substantial share of Krupp, and also invested in the development of the Shir Iran main battletank by Vickers in Britain; and Saudi Arabia ordered a specific version of the French Crotale, called Shahine. These cases have, however, not involved the acquisition of technology by the importer. The third method, reverse engineering or "copying", has mainly been attempted by China from the time of its break with the Soviet Union in 1960 up to its rapprochment with the West towards the end of the 1970s. The Chinese had by the beginning of the 1960s acquired several production licences from the Soviet Union, and proceeded with further developments of, for example, the MiG-19 fighters and the T-55 tanks even after the licence agreements had been cancelled. During the Vietnam war there were several reports about Chinese interceptions of Soviet shipments of MiG-21 and surface-to-air missiles, in an effort to copy the more modern technology incorporated in these weapons. In this particular case, however, it was evident by the end of the 1970s that "reverse engineering" was less than practical as a method of achieving modern weapons technology - the lack of processed raw materials and certain components made duplication a rather hazardous technique, and China is now concentrating, instead, on purchasing Western military technology. The various local developments and modifications of the MiG-19 fighter are still the main aircraft produced in China, in spite of the various, apparently highly exaggerated reports of a new indigenous fighter that began to appear by 1970 (the so-called Fan-Tan.)

The Chinese example, in addition to illustrating the near impossibility of taking any "shortcut" to the acquisition of modern technology, also illustrates an important aspect from the arms control point of view. Once a production licence has been acquired, that is, once the know-how has been acquired, it is for all practical purposes not possible to withdraw that knowledge by revoking the licence. (There are many other examples of this - for instance the continued South African production of the Uzi machine gun in spite of the cancellation of the licence agreement in 1963.)

There are, in addition to the various methods discussed above, some further means of acquiring technological know-how in the military field. These are best summarized under the heading of industrial espionage, and occur very seldom in the case of the Third World producers. The most publicized example would be the Israeli effort to build its own fighter aircraft, which really began after the French embargo of 1967. In 1969, Israel managed to obtain blueprints for the Mirage-3 and Mirage-5 as well as for the Atar-9 engine via private sources in Switzerland. The end result, after a series of local developments, is the Kfir fighter-bomber, powered by a US engine, now offered on the export market.

Israel ranks among the leading arms exporters in the group of new arms producers, and the Israeli example in turn illustrates yet another aspect related to the arms control debate. Exports take on a vital importance for those arms producers who have invested in a domestic research and development capability, in comparison to those who stop short at the acquisition of foreign production licences. Once the technological problems have been mastered, the financial problems encountered, in the established arms producing countries are huge. These problems are obviously multiplied in the case of new producers, and particularly for new designers. Many projects remain at the blueprint stage, either because of unacceptable performance of the weapon in question, or because of unacceptable costs as compared to the cost of importing the weapon. When a project succeeds, such as the Israeli Kfir or the Brazilian armoured cars from Engesa, the weapon must be able to compete on the international market in order to sustain the domestic research and development establishment. In the arms _trade_ field, the producer has moved his position from that of a large arms importer to an increasingly competitive arms exporter, which in turn means that he may suddenly find himself entangled in a more or less serious international conflict, obliged according to the arms sales contracts to provide spare parts and maintenance equipment for arms sold to one or another belligerent states (such as was the case of Brazil in the Iraq-Iran war).

10.4. THE MOTIVATION FOR SALES AND ACQUISITION OF KNOW-HOW

The reasons why established arms producing countries decide to part with military know-how for the production of armaments are roughly divisible into two main categories - political and economic. Traditionally, both of the superpowers have been reluctant to share their weapons production capacity with countries other than those belonging to NATO or the WTO, a policy different from that of some of the leading West European arms producers, notably France, Italy, FR Germany and Britain. When they do part with their weapons technology to Third World countries, the main reasons are usually to be found among the same political considerations that govern their arms sales or arms transfer policies (in other words, what was called the "hegemonic supply pattern" in the SIPRI study "The Arms Trade with the Third World" in 1971). When India, for example, gained access to Soviet weapons technology with the acquisition of the production licences for the MiG-21 fighter and its Atoll air-to-air missile in 1963, this is more easily understandable in the context of general Soviet politics in South Asia at the time than for any economic reasons. In the case of the United States, the transfer of know-how to countries outside NATO has to be exempted from the normal arms export regulations. Under the so-called Carter policy on arms exports, such transfers were explicitly prohibited: "The United States will not permit co-production agreements with other countries for significant weapons, equipment and major components". Hence, the sales of production licences for the F-5E Tiger-2 fighter to South Korea and Taiwan have to be regarded as exceptions to the rule: they were "political" sales. The repeated Israeli requests for production rights for the F-16 Fighter have so far been turned down. This also illustrates the fact that the leading technological powers do not readily part with the most sophisticated armaments technology indiscriminately - the F-16 may be co-produced in Europe, but not in the Third World.

On another level, that is at the company level, the continuing multinationalization of the arms industries is the most typical trend, taking place for reasons of cost-efficiency - what can be more profitably produced elsewhere is placed in the Third World countries. The Indian aerospace industry has for some time been producing parts and components for the Alouette helicopters and has reexported them to France. The presence of, for example, Lockheed Aircraft Singapore, Vosper Thornycroft Singapore and the Bofors-owned Allied Ordnance Company in Singapore, and the various foreign companies located in South Africa obviously has more to do with the liberal local laws for business enterprises, cheap labour etc. than with any political preferences.

The medium arms exporters - that is France, Italy and similar suppliers - tend to show a much less restrictive attitude towards the sale of military technology than do the superpowers, presumably because of the need to compete on the arms market.

10.5. THE BUYERS ARGUMENTS: POLITICAL AND MILITARY INDEPENDENCE

The demand to set up domestic defence industries is, in the case of the Third World countries, practically always buyer-oriented in contrast with arms imports, which may often take place on the initiative of the seller. The decision to invest in a local production capacity reflects political and military ambitions on a scale different than occurs with the mere import of weapons. National security is the most commonly evoked reason for the build-up of local arms industries, in particular in those Third World countries which during the last 15 years have become the most prominent in the field - Argentina, Brazil, India, Israel and South Africa. The national security argument is in all of these countries coupled with the notion of military independence, that is independence from foreign arms suppliers, and the embargos imposed on all of them have served as an impetus to the investment in local defence industries. The relatively speedy and successful development of the capacity to master military technology for a wide range of weapons can be described as an unforeseen effect of embargo policies. But there are some important additional points to be made. In none of the countries listed above was it necessary to start building defence industries from scratch. Many of the necessary conditions were already present, such as an educated work force including foreign specialists, embryo arms industries of various types (weapons have, for example, been produced in Brazil since 1862), important raw material supplies and foreign capital. Rather than drawing the conclusion that embargos are automatically counterproductive, insofar as they foment the establishment of domestic military industries, it can be said that arms embargos only have a short-term effect on most nations - apart from nations at a most primitive state of development.

Apart from possessing the necessary conditions for industrial development, the new arms producing states also show some common political features: for example, the quest to become leading regional powers, in both a military and an economic sense.

The coupling of national security and military independence is of course not unique for the Third World countries. The neutral countries, Sweden and Switzerland, for example, both emphasize the need for a neutral country to possess adequate armed forces, preferably equipped by local industries. However, while it may be adequate to state that the possession of the means of production in the armaments field ensures or reinforces a nation's claim to being independent of foreign military suppliers, this is only theoretically true in the case of the new producers in the Third World. The bulk of the equipment of the Israeli armed forces still has to be imported from the USA; the Argentinian defence industries produce very little for the country's own forces; the Brazilian armoured cars are mainly produced for export. The relatively large Indian defence industry establishment is one of only two capable of producing its own jet fighter aircraft - the MiG-21 - the second being the South African aerospace industry, which has assembled Mirage F-1 under French licence. Self-sufficiency is a long way off, and is moreover hardly a realistic goal, even in industrialized countries.

10.6. ECONOMIC ADVANTAGES

Economic advantages are often evoked as arguments in favour of establishing domestic defence industries, in addition to the perceived political advantages of becoming more self-sufficient in weapons procurement. It is held, for example, that domestically produced weapons will result in budget savings and savings in foreign exchange. In practice, however, the evidence available contradicts this idea, at least as it applies to modern weapons incorporating the latest technology.

Table 10.1.   Cost of Producing Aircraft in India

US $ thousand; $ 1-Rs 7.5

	A Total production cost	B Cost of importing equivalent aircraft	A/B (%)
HJT-16 Kiran (basic jet trainer)	340	200	170
MiG-21 (supersonic fighter)	1520	830	180
HF-24 Mark I (supersonic fighter)	940	600	160
Alouette (helicopter)	270	170	160
HS-748 (transport)	1490	1000	150
Gnat[a] (fighter)	380	200	190

[a] 1956 price.

Source: SIPRI correspondents in India. See Arms Trade with the Third World, Uppsala, 1971

For a developing country, in particular, the build-up of local defence industries becomes a very costly and complex undertaking.

Even where the technological basis exists, the soaring costs for the development of modern weapons are often deemed prohibitive - Switzerland, for example, is now importing more of its new armaments from foreign countries for cost reasons, and an Austrian study in 1976 came to the conclusion that it would take 12-15 years of sustained effort to achieve even partial independence in weapons production, and that the costs involved would be double those of direct imports.

There are very few Third World illustrations of a local arms project producing a net profit: the Israeli Uzi submachinegun, which became accepted as a standard NATO arm, is an exception rather than the rule. On the contrary, there are many instances of projects where costs have escalated far beyond quoted import prices for an equivalent weapon. The reasons may be technological, but the problem is also a consequence of the changed import structure - it is generally more expensive to purchase certain components than a complete weapon.

In reality, when looking at individual weapons projects in Third World countries - as well as in industrialized countries - what might be termed the "prestige motivation" stands out as one of the main reasons behind many projects which then fail to materialize. The Egyptian missile programme in the 1960's and the Indian effort to construct an indigenous jet fighter over the past 20 years are two standard examples, although, of course, no official spokesman ever admits the existence of any such technological prestige motivation.

The economic argument is better applied here, since it is linked to a particular aspect of economic development, the trade pattern; instead of merely exporting raw materials and importing manufactured goods, the country can develop a manufacturing capability; this applies also to the manufacturing of military hardware as a part of a larger development of the economy. The oil-rich countries in particular have been in the focus of attention since 1973 as "rich and underdeveloped", implying that they possess at least the capital required for whatever investment wanted. Other countries, such as South Africa (which possesses large resources of various minerals), also fit into this group - the past decade has shown a development away from supplying raw materials and towards export capacity of a range of manufactured goods, including certain types of weapons.

South Africa and Brazil are standard examples: during the 1970s there has been a move away from exports of raw materials towards the export of a higher share of manufactured goods, in this case including indigenously produced weapons.

10.7. TECHNOLOGICAL DEPENDENCE

As was stated above, the professed goals of self-sufficiency in weapons production have so far not been achieved by any of the arms producing countries. The armed forces of the Third World are for all practical purposes dependent on supplies from the established arms producers in the industrialized world, at least for the most vital equipment such as jet fighters, engines and electronic components. Indeed, there are very few cases of "self-sufficiency" in the industrialized world expect for the leading technological powers - the USA and the USSR - and they too import certain types of military equipment.

The magnitude of any effort to establish a local defence industry is illustrated by looking at the structure example in the United States. There are some 95 major industries involved in defence production. But, in addition, there may be as many as five tiers of subcontractors involved in one final product, comprised of small firms in the machinery and electronics sectors. The former produce the tools, moulds and dies needed for making weapon parts. The latter manufacture the control elements that make the sophisticated weapons systems work. Small firms in both these sectors make up over 50 per cent of all firms in the sector producing for defence. It is impossible for a developing country to create this entire infrastructure with the resources available, and therefore a wide range of components and equipment still have to be imported.

Further, it is also the case that for the vast majority of the new arms producers, the investment in military technology means the import of foreign expertise at various levels as well as the invitation of foreign companies - the producers are not the nations but individual enterprises such as for example General Electric, Siemens and Bofors.

Finally, the latest weapons technology is by definition a capital-intensive technology which has developed according to the needs of the industrialized world. The present international arms transfer pattern is showing a move away from the direct purchase of arms towards offset deals and licence production deals. This would be the same type of development that the arms producing nations of Western Europe have gone through since 1945, but the consequences for less developed economies of this particular type of "military industrialization" can only be speculated about.

10.8. FACTUAL SURVEY

In 1945 only four countries in the Third World regions possessed any domestic arms industry capable of producing weapons systems other than small arms and ammunition. These were Argentina, Brazil, South Africa and India; and in all of them the Allied Powers' war effort had influenced local arms production. In Argentina, the aircraft industry dated back to 1927, when the FMA (Fàbrica Militar de Aviones) was set up and work started with licence production of US aircraft. In Brazil, aircraft were produced under German licence in the 1930s, and later under US design. The shipbuilding industry was fairly advanced in both countries, and frigates and corvettes of foreign design were produced in the 1940's. Other Latin American countries had previously been engaged in aircraft manufacture. In Mexico, both aircraft and aeroengines were locally designed and produced at a state factory between 1915 and 1929. During World War II this plant produced the US Vought Corsair under licence, but when this production came to an end, no new projects were undertaken. In Peru, an Italian plane was produced under licence from 1937 until 1941, when the factory was changed into an ovehaul and repair factory. In Chile, an indigenous design was tested in May 1947, but after 1962 there is no further information on any aircraft industry.

In South Africa, wartime arms production was stimulated with British aid, and a range of small arms, ammunition and armoured vehicles were produced. Production ceased at the end of World War II and was not revived until the early 1960s.

In India, arms production also took place as a contribution to the British war effort. In 1940, the first aircraft plant was set up at

Bangladore, now the Bangladore unit of the HAL concern, to produce British aircraft under licence. The British preferred, however, that the Indian factory concentrate on repair and overhaul during the war (in particular the maintenance of US planes in RAF service), and thus aircraft manufacture was postponed until 1946. At that time, several British-built shipyards also existed, as did some ordnance factories.

Israel was one of the first new states after 1945 to invest in a domestic arms industry. Only four years after its establishment, in 1953, Israel set up the Bedek Aviation company, the forerunner of the present Israel Aircraft Industries, and commenced a licence production programme. The first indigenous research programme did not start until 1966. In India, the wartime experience gained in repair and overhaul work, together with some preliminary efforts at indigenous research resulted in 1949 in the locally designed HT-2 military trainer.

Currently, the SIPRI arms production register lists 24 new arms producers in the Third World which are engaged in a sustained effort to produce major weapons systems. In 1980, there were 86 ongoing aircraft projects, 60 ship projects, 25 missile projects and 11 armoured vehicle projects. Brazil, India, Israel and Argentina show the largest number of individual projects over time followed by South Korea, Taiwan and Indonesia, which are in the process of expanding their domestic defence production efforts.

Of the various arms categories, small ships and small arms are the most common capacities. Seventeen countries in the Third World have an aircraft industry, but production in general is confined to light transport aircraft. Modern jet fighters are produced only in India (Mig 21 under Soviet licence), South Africa (Mirage F-1 under French licence), Taiwan (F-5 under US licence), and Israel (Kfir fighter-bomber, indigenous). Counter-insurgency aircraft, or jetpowered strike/trainer aircraft are produced in Argentina (IA-58 Pucará, indigenous) India (HJT-16 Kiran MkII, indigenous and the Gnat MkII under British licence), Brazil (AT-26 Xavante under Italian licence), South Africa (Impala MkII under Italian licence).

Missiles are produced under licence in Brazil (Coha ATM under FRG licence), India (SS.11 ATM under French and Atoll AAM under Soviet licence), Pakistan (Cobra ATM despite the licence being cancelled by the FRG in 1965). Indigenous missiles are in production only in Israel (Shafir AAM and Gabriel ShShM). Other missile projects are under development, but have not reached the production stage, for example in Brazil (ASM and ATM), India (ShShM), Israel (SSM and ASM), South Africa (AAM) and Taiwan (SSM).

No heavy ships - corvettes, destroyers, frigates, submarines - have been designed or developed in the Third World. Production of this type of ship is confined to licence agreements: in 1970 Argentina purchased two Type 42 armed destroyers from the UK, one to be built in Argentina with British aid, and in 1975 Argentina purchased eight Type

21 destroyers, of which six will be built in Argentina. Brazil bought six anti-submarine warfare frigates in the UK in 1970, of which two will be built in Brazil under a ten-year programme. Colombia has since 1972 produced two Italian designed mini-submarines, the Midget experimental assault type with a displacement of only 70 tons. Since 1965 India has produced six British Leander class frigates. Peru in 1974 began production of two Italian Super Alpino class missile-armed frigates. In 1973 Venezuela ordered 21 corvettes from Italy, of which some will be built locally.

10.9. CONCLUSION

Briefly, the main problems connected with the transfer of military technology to the Third World countries can be summarized as follows:

1. The transfer of military know-how to a growing number of countries enhaces global militarization.

2. Investment in a domestic arms production capacity creates a vicious circle - in the end, the producing country, in addition to remaining dependent on the import of foreign technology, finds itself dependent also on being able to export arms.

3. The most commonly evoked arguments in favour of "a military industrialization" do not stand up to reality: self-sufficiency in armaments is for all practical purposes unattainable. What is achieved is rather a move away from a direct dependence on the arms suppliers to a technological dependence with a much more profound impact on the civilian sector of the economy, in particular in less developed economies.

4. The local production of major arms is as a rule more expensive than importing the same system, in particular for new producers, and especially in less developed economies.

5. The current trend of the proliferation of armaments points towards an increase in the sales of know-how rather than the sales of weapons.

NOTES AND REFERENCES

* This paper is a part of a forthcoming SIPRI publication, called the Global Arms Trade, where the spread of armaments to the Third World will be presented under the following headings: I. The Transfer of Arms to the Third World. II. The Transfer of Military Technology to the Third World: part 1. Factual survey; part 2. The Economic and Political Impact of the Transfer of Military Know-How from Industrialized Countries to Third World Countries.

1. Defence Minister Botha's List of Arms to Be Exported to Friendly Countries, Armed Forces Journal, February 1972.

Chapter Eleven

BRAZIL'S NUCLEAR ENERGY POLICY: DILEMMAS AND OPTIONS

Clóvis Brigagao

11.1. FIRST STEPS

In theory and practice, nuclear politics in Brazil have pursued a zigzag course, mixing patriotism and folklore and inspiring policies sometimes realistic, sometimes melancholic.

It was after 1951, with the foundation of the National Research Council (CNP), that Brazil's research programme tried to elaborate a more systematic plan. For many years, Brazilian scientists had wanted to create such a Council, the goal of which was to stimulate autonomous scientific research in all fields, especially energy research, while at the same time retaining control over the atomic energy programme in the country.

From 1951 to 1954, under the Getúlio Vargas Government, the CNP tried unsuccessfully to obtain US support for nuclear development. Brazil had for many years secretly exported monazite sand (a mineral rich in thorium) to the United States. Instead of demanding payment in dollars or in wheat, as had previously been the practice, the CNP asked the US Atomic Energy Commission for information on nuclear energy and cooperation in the field of reactor technology. The MacMahon Act in the USA prohibited such cooperation and since it was unrealistic to expect a reversal of this attitude, the CNP then turned to Europe. Authorized by President Vargas, the CNP Director Admiral Alvaro Alberto contacted German scientists in order to gain access to equipment for uranium enrichment, using ultra-centrifuges. Brazil proposed to do what the Allies had prohibited the Germans from doing during the period of occupation: to enrich uranium.

After conversations with the High Commissioner of the Allies and with the President of the US Atomic Energy Commission, the CNP Director planned, with the Physical-Chemical Institute of the University of Bonn, the production of three centrifuges for Brazil.

Plants were ordered from France for the production of natural uranium, although an Allied veto meant that the contracts were not implemented; nevertheless, the first atomic reactor in Brazil went into operation at the University of Sao Paulo.(1)

The contents of these negotiations were made public in 1956 by the former CNP Director, Admiral Alvaro Alberto, who testified before the Brazilian Chamber of Deputies. As a result of the Hearing Commission publication, and influenced by the United Nations Conference on Nuclear Energy (Genebra), all contracts and agreements on the export of uranium and thorium from Brazil to the United States were cancelled.

The new atomic policy was established in 1956, during Kubitschek's Government, which was determined to have a national nuclear energy programme in order to produce nuclear fuel under the control and ownership of the Federal Government. The National Commission of Nuclear Energy (CNEN) was set up with the objective of coordinating all programmes in the area of nuclear energy and of providing Brazil with reactor technology. In addition, with the emergence of industrialization in the 60s, the goal was to develop sectoral programmes - as a spin-off - ranging from mineral prospecting to R&D activities. Also, new institutional channels were created to serve CNEN's goals: the Institute of Atomic Energy (Sao Paulo); the Institute of Technological Research (Sao Paulo); the Institute of Nuclear Engineering (Rio de Janeiro); the Institute of Military Engineering under the Army Ministry (Rio de Janeiro) and the Institute of Radioactive Research (Belo Horizonte, MG).(2)

In 1957, the Brazilian authorities negotiated with the Adenauer Government for the sale of centrifuges. Eventually they were delivered to the Institute of Technological Research (IPT) - the University of Sao Paulo - where they served as experimental equipment for academic education. They were later abandoned without any reasonable explanation. At the end of the 50s, the Government decided to build a uranium enrichment plant (200 MW) in Mambucava (Rio de Janeiro) and in 1961, during the heady days of Janio Quadro's Government, the project was replaced by a new one: a natural uranium reactor, using graphite and gas as in the first French therminal reactors.

The viability study had indicated that the national industry would have an 80 per cent participation in the construction of the plant. Brazilian technicians were sent to France to get acquainted with the functioning of that kind of reactor. French engineers arrived in Brazil by 1961, prepared the infrastructure, and started the programme: by the end of the year the project had collapsed, again with no explanation. The French technicians left Brazil for Argentina, where they assisted in the building of the Atucha reactor.

11.2. SECOND PHASE

After the military coup in 1964, Brazil entered the second phase of its nuclear programme, following the modernization of the country's economy, both in terms of market and of trade. The military Government felt that the country was lagging behind in the field of nuclear technology and that the superpowers were trying to institutionalize the economic, political, military and technological inequalities of international affairs. The superpowers were accused of deliberate indecisiveness on the issue of real and complete disarmament. The Brazilian military and foreign policy-makers therefore claimed that they were justified in pursuing their own independent nuclear programme, on the grounds that Brazil refused to be regarded as a "strategically vulnerable nation".(3) The immediate consequence was Brazil's refusal to sign the Non-Proliferation Treaty, because of its discriminatory character and its intention to legitimize the freezing of the world distribution of power.(4)

Feeling that the Brazilian authorities were willing to advance nuclear capabilities, the United States sent the President of the US Atomic Energy Commission to Brazil to convince the client that the United States wanted to cooperate with the new policy. It was an effort by the Washington administration to maintain its control over the second stage of the Brazilian nuclear development. Also, it was Washington's response to the French-Brazilian agreement in the domain of peaceful nuclear technology. In his communique the President of the Brazilian Atomic Energy Commission pointed out the divergencies between the two countries' approach to production of nuclear power for peaceful uses. The US Atomic Energy Commission estimated that it would be more profitable for Brazil to buy the nuclear fuel it needed directly from the United States, but Brazil insisted on its right to proceed with the peaceful use of nuclear power. During a visit to Washington, the representatives of the Brazilian Foreign Ministry emphasized the satisfactory outcomes on matters of nuclear cooperation and, as a practical measure, Washington promptly announced that the US Embassy in Brazil had opened a special office for nuclear affairs.(5)

In 1968, suggesting that the country was being left behind in the technological race and claiming national security and strategic interests, the Government laid down its nuclear policy: Brazil would seek the necessary support abroad to execute its programme, so that the country would acquire the entire fuel cycle in the next decades. The overall development of nuclear energy would inevitably lead, in a controlled process, to the development of nuclear weapons, said the Ministry of Foreign Affairs. To impede that progress, "... would mean to hinder the development of nuclear energy for peaceful uses".(6) The superpowers were apparently unwilling to believe that other countries - especially the underdeveloped ones - were capable of using the existence of nuclear weapons as a deterrent, "qualifying themselves to own the nuclear weapon, to menace using it and, notwithstanding, keeping it without use".(7)

In 1969, Brazil and West Germany signed the agreement on Cooperation for Scientific and Technological Development providing Brazil with technical assistance that in the medium range will cover the entire fuel cycle. In 1970, India and Brazil signed an agreement to exchange scientists, material, etc. Under the terms of the agreement, Brazil was to be informed of all phases of India's nuclear experiments.(8) In 1971, Brazil and Ecuador exchanged protocols ratifying an earlier bilateral agreement for the peaceful use of nuclear energy. In the same year, another agreement was signed with West Germany on nuclear cooperation and technical assistance. On a bilateral level, the most important contract - and the most restrictive one - came in 1972, with the US Government. Westinghouse International won a 30-year contract to supply Furnas Centrais Elétricas (the first Brazilian holding company on nuclear development) with the first power plant located at Angra dos Reis (RJ). The Export-Import Bank and two US private banks were to provide credits worth 140 million dollars, repayable over 15 years from the date of completion of Angra I. Originally, this was expected to be in 1977, but in fact the plant started to operate in April 1982.

The USA committed itself to sell a limited quantity - not more than 12,300 kg - of uranium for the reactors. According to the terms of the contract, the plutonium produced in the reactors will be rented to Brazil, which will not be allowed to dispose of it freely. Brazil's share of the entire contract was only 8 per cent, and the US authorities refused to make any further agreement on the transfer of enriched uranium. As regards the system of safeguards, the contract gives the US the right to inspect all the reactor equipment and to control everything related to special nuclear materials. The Brazilian Government, in turn, will facilitate the application of the safeguards. The contract does not enable interchange between Brazilian and American personnel, since Brazilian technicians are forbidden to visit the American plants that will enrich Brazilian natural uranium. The dependency on uranium and the energy-directed goal of the Brazilian nuclear policy forces the Government to accept compromises contradictory to stands taken at the multilateral level. Such an asymmetry produces a paradoxical picture as Brazil is trying to guarantee its right to carry out peaceful nuclear explosions when, in reality, it is still at the basic atomic level.(9)

Nonetheless, from 1973 to 1980 Brazilian authorities continued their policies which included the transfer of nuclear technology, cooperation with Europe, and the Middle East (mainly Iraq) and closer cooperation with Latin American countries such as Peru, Chile, Ecuador, Venezuela and Mexico.(10)

The Brazilian-Argentine cooperation is of particular interest. Neither the International Atomic Energy Agency nor the Tlatelolco Treaty could give either regional power assurances that the other is not advancing a programme of nuclear development and nuclear weapons research. Thus, the question of safeguards, inspections and mutual limits is an open one in the context of Argentine-Brazil nuclear cooperation. Each sees the other's moves towards atomic capability as a justification for developing superior strength; thus, nuclear weapons could become the greater equalizer for both countries in attempting to gain regional supremacy. There is an additional regional power element - as well as an international one - in the case of nuclear ties with England, France and West Germany. For example, the nuclear cooperation agreement with England, which will provide technology and asistance to set up a uranium enrichment plant worth several million pounds, involves a wide-ranging defence agreement cooperation, mainly between the two navies. In the case of cooperation with France, there are other implications. In 1976, a contract worth 150 million francs was signed between Nuclebrás and French Societé Technique d'Enterprise Chimiques for a uranium processing plant, which started in 1979, with an initial production of 500 tons to be used for nuclear reactors. In the aftermath of the Brazil-West Germany agreement of 1975, Brazil looked to France as another partner for the development of nuclear cooperation, including new areas such as uranium hexafluoride.(11)

11.3. BRAZIL-WEST GERMANY AGREEMENT

The full programme in which West Germany will provide Brazil with eight nuclear plants over the next 15 years at a total cost of initially US$ 10 billion was signed in June 1975, after years of secret negotiations.(12) The agreement included five basic aspects: uranium exploration, uranium enrichment, reactor and power plants, fuel fabrication and fuel reprocessing. The search for natural uranium deposits will start with the exploration of 73,000 square km's of Brazilian territory in a joint venture between a Brazilian and a West German company. In this joint venture, 80 per cent of the mineral would be a reserve for Brazilian needs and 20 per cent would initially be used by West Germany, whose share would be increased at a later date. Brazil, through its state nuclear energy company, NUCLEBRAS, expects to increase its participation in the programme from its present 30 per cent to 90 per cent by the end of the century.

The project is expected to supply Brazil initially with 10,000 MW, and the total output generated by the end of the century is expected to reach 70,000 MW. Following the agreement, the West German Foreign Minister confirmed in January 1976 that Brazil had agreed to international inspection and supervision of the reactors and all other installations. The inspection does not, however, cover nuclear technology developed by Brazilians on the basis of technology received from the FRG. At the end of 1976, however, the Dutch Government expressed its unwillingness to authorize the URENCO consortium to deliver enriched uranium unless Brazil signed the NPT. Brazil has not signed it, but it was said that Brazil was prepared to consider additional safeguards to obtain URENCO supplies, and negotiations were set up to work out a compromise.(13)

A further tripartite agreement was signed between Brazil, FRG and the IAEA. Although Brazil was not a party to the NPT, the agreement confirmed in Vienna provided effectively for the same inspection and supervision to which signatories to the NPT were subject.

The Board of Governors of the IAEA approved the agreement without restrictions: the Brazilian Government considered this approval an explicit legitimation for the entire fuel cycle programme; moreover, it was viewed as an act of independence both by Brazil and the FRG vis-à-vis the USA.

The contract is being implemented with a multinational consortium which includes joint ventures between NUCLEBRAS and KWU (Kraftwerk Union) and six German consortium banks, plus injection of financial resources by European private banks, under the direction of the Compagnie Luxemburgeoise de Banque. The consortium imports reactors and other heavy equipment.(14)

Initially, four companies were formed to work out the programme, but at present NUCLEBRAS has seven subsidiaries:

NUCLEN, Nuclebrás Engineering, owned by Nuclebrás (75 per cent) and KWU (25 per cent), which will develop components and will provide part of the skilled labour force;

NUCLEP, Nuclebrás heavy equipment, with a participation of 75 per cent of Nuclebrás and a consortium formed by KWU, the German-GHH and Vöst-Alpine from Austria, which will construct reactor components.(15)

NUCLEI, Nuclebrás Enriched Isotopes, with 25 per cent ownership by KWU, which will build the reprocessing plant.

NUCLAN, Nuclebrás Mining Co., which will prospect for uranium. Nuclan will have a participation of 51 per cent from Nuclebrás and 49 per cent from other private companies: URAN G., Natron Consultoria e Projetos associated with French Société du Cycle et d'uranium Pechiney-Ugine Kuhlman

NUCON, Nuclebrás Construction, now responsible for the administration and the management for the new Angra dos Reis nuclear plants.(16)

NUCLEMON, Nuclebrás Monazite and Associated Ltda., responsible for the production of nuclear minerals.

NUSTEP, an enterprise located in West Germany. Nuclebrás owns 50 per cent of it and the German company Steag the remainder. It holds the patent for the centrifugal jet process of isotope enrichment. It will also execute the R&D programme in the area.

Despite the initial euphoria, on both sides, the affair is in many senses far from over. It seems that the further the programme moves towards "application", the more hazardous it becomes. In order to be sure that the contract has been applied, Presidential visits are made, diplomatic and technical contacts are frequent and resentments have arisen on both sides each time the programme is discussed or when it is questioned by businessmen and by the Brazilian scientific community.

Since 1975, three other agreements have been signed to increase technological cooperation; the most important one concerns the construction of a new reactor which will use thorium, the atomic mineral most abundant in Brazil.

The Germans are sceptical about Brazil's ability to fulfil the various aspects of the programme, although everyone is fully aware that this contract could substantially benefit German industry and levels of employment. The Germans fear that Brazil will cut back the number of reactors. Whereas the agreement had established that the plants would be installed by 1981 and 1982, it is believed that Brazil will reach 1990 with only one out of the eight plants foreseen by the agreement. The equipment for Angra II will not be installed until 1984/1985. Brazil does not view this delay as a problem, as the Chairman of Furnas Centrais Elétricas has let it be known that the remaining plants are not essential for the supply of electricity to the southern regions of the country.

In the initial nuclear agreement planning stages, it was thought that Brazil's economically useful hydroelectric potential was less than 100,000 MW. But at the end of 1978, Nuclebrás announced that the potential exceeded 200,000 MW, in other words more than double the 1975 estimate. In reality, Brazil's present hydroelectric capacity exceeds 213,000 MW. Of this total, only 12 per cent is being used. More than half of this potential is to be found in the southern and central regions, and whatever remaining potential there is in the Amazon region is less than 2,000 km's from the consuming centres of the southern region. This distance poses no transmission problems if continuous current is supplied and provided the technical and economic conditions are favourable.(17) It has been suggested that the remaining nuclear reactors, which were planned to be in operation by 1990 or later, are superfluous, and the diminishing enthusiasm is the result, among other reasons, of a rapid increase in their price.(18)

The Germans have assumed that the programme delays would be an 'issue' between the two countries, and they have started to take precautions against the Brazilian authorities' unreliability. The fact is that follow-up of the timetable drawn up by KWU for the construction of the nuclear power plants has shown that this construction has become highly uneconomical for Brazil. To continue with the nuclear programme, as has been advocated by the authorities from the energy sector, in reality means that the country is giving up a relative advantage it could have in exploiting the so-called energy crisis; for, while the highly developed countries, such as West Germany, have had to turn to very expensive nuclear energy because they have already exhausted their conventional hydroelectric and thermic potentials, Brazil would only have to do this in 30 or 40 years, when technology would certainly be more developed.(19)

Many critics have demonstrated the unsound technical and economic assumptions upon which the contract was based. Personal and corporate profits, bribery, etc., appear to have been involved on both sides of the agreement.(20)

11.4. THE US REACTIONS

As mentioned above, the US Government has consistently opposed any autonomous Brazilian nuclear programme. With the conclusion of the Brazil-FRG agreement, the first reaction came from the Vice-President of the US Atomic Energy Commission during Ford's administration, who regretted that the two countries had not consulted the US before they concluded the negotiations. When Carter came to the White House he stated that "the United States is deeply concerned about the consequences of the uncontrolled spread of nuclear weapon capability. We have no authority over the other countries, but we believe that these risks would be vastly increased by further spread of reprocessing capabilities of the present nuclear fuel from which explosives can be derived. So, a review of the US nuclear power programme was expected to occur".(21)

The USA postponed the commercial reprocessing of spent nuclear fuel and the recycling of plutonium produced in US nuclear power plants. Also, they deferred the development of fast breeder reactor programmes and facilitated the supply of enriched uranium to other countries complying with the US non-proliferation objectives, while at the same time they continued to embargo the export of either equipment or technology which would permit uranium enrichment and chemical processing by other countries.(22)

There were other political reasons underlying Carter's opposition to any future development between Brazil and West Germany on nuclear energy; the US long-term strategic goals and the balance of power on a global scale and in the Latin America region; the medium and short-term interest of the multinationals; the fear of having an 'atomic' neighbour in its backyard; and the fear of German rearmament. It is worth noting that the creation of this new industrial sector in Brazil would certainly damage US economic interests. The special relationship between Brazil and West Germany should be seen in terms of the former's wish to diversify its foreign policy interests and the latter's need to strengthen its penetration in the USA's traditional market. For West Germany, the US reaction is no more than a natural retaliation by the loser, who cries loudly for compensation and creates difficulties for the largest export contract ever signed with an old US ally. For

Brazil, the growth of a nuclear sector is a sign of its strengthening international power status.

The acquisition of sophisticated equipment outside of the US market could represent an important loss for the US industrial interests. Finally, it would be unthinkable that, in a matter of such strategic importance, Brazil would ignore American supervision or partnership.(23)

In terms of the extension of the Brazilian programme and of American interests, Reagan's administration views the nuclear question slightly differently. There has been a 'softening' on the part of the Reagan administration, apparent in the declared attitude of the present Assistant Secretary of State for Interamerican Affairs. According to him, "it is the aim of Reagan's Government to work in close collaboration with Brazil, because it is time to revitalize this relationship, improving coordination and cooperation in an ever increasing number of questions".(24) The Brazilian nuclear programme is one such question, and the Assistant Secretary of State has stated that the US hopes it will be able to supply nuclear materials in good faith. The US aim is to refrain from nuclear proliferation, but this goal will be better achieved if the US provides nuclear material in accordance with all security standards. Since American companies already have a contract for the building of a nuclear plant in Brazil, an understanding between the two countries would be an obvious benefit. According to Thomas Enders, Brazil and the US have common preoccupations concerning the maintenance of control over the movement of nuclear materials.

The Brazilian Government's reaction, although conciliatory, does not share this view. According to the Brazilian Foreign Minister, the US wishes to extend the specific safeguards that exist in relation to the nuclear plant of Angra I to all nuclear plants to be installed in Brazil. In the Minister's view, "some countries accept full-scope safeguards for all their relevant activities. Other countries do not. Brazil has always accepted the safeguards of the IAEA, even the most rigorous ones, at the international cooperation level. But as a matter of principle, it maintains that it should not necessarily subject itself, indirectly, to the Non-Proliferation Treaty".(25)

The problem is again under discussion now that the first nuclear plant, bought in 1972 from Westinghouse, has started partial production of the first 10 per cent of its 620,000 kw. The negotiations between Brazil and the US on the reprocessing of fuel for Angra I ended in an impasse. According to a Nuclear Regulatory Commission official, the US refuses to grant a licence for export of enriched uranium for Angra I until Brazil accepts a formal compromise to submit all its nuclear reactors, including the ones to be built in the future with its own resources, to the IAEA safeguards clauses. Brazil agrees to comply with IAEA safeguards for the Angra I reactor. Germany and France, unlike the US, only require that the purchaser submit the reactor to the international safeguards. Furnas Centrais Elétricas, which is responsible for the management of Angra I, should send the uranium to the US to be enriched. Brazil, however, is not prepared to risk sending natural uranium to the State Department only to have it returned unprocessed. On the other hand, Brazil is not dependent on American uranium to operate Angra I. The enrichment processing guaranteed by the US can, through a bilateral agreement, be undertaken by URENCO.

NUCLEBRAS has consulted URENCO about the possibility of supplying the first enriched uranium consignments to be used for the production of fuel. The consortium has approved, and the reloading of Angra I (not supplied by the US) will be manufactured in Germany by Reaktoren Brennelement Union (BRU), a subsidiary of KWU, with Brazilian uranium enriched in Almelo (Holland). According to sources representing the Reagan Government, pressure on Brazil to accept a tripartite agreement for the application of full-scope safeguards by the IAEA are due not to the present Reagan nuclear policy, but are a result of the law of non-proliferation passed in 1977 by the US Congress. In Brazil, government officials believe that the uranium for Angra I will come from the US, due to the nuclear "détente" between Brazil and Argentina; this would remove US fears that both countries have an interest in manufacturing atomic bombs in order to establish regional equilibrium. Furthermore, it would not be in Brazil's best interests to denounce the agreement with the US, because this would mean one important country less in the nuclear scenario for future negotiations. To Westinghouse particularly, the idea of breaking a contract in which Brazil absorbs only 8 per cent of the know-how is not appealing.

11.5. BRAZIL'S DILEMMAS

The military have claimed that full Brazilian control of nuclear technology would be vital for the country's independence. In addition to a megalomania which incorrectly assumes that nuclear energy will miraculously solve all of Brazil's future problems, the present nuclear programme is based on many false assumptions on the strategic, economic and technical problems involved and a misunderstanding of the possibility of achieving national self-sufficiency in nuclear minerals.(26)

The country still awaits a full public explanation of the entire programme and the nature of the agreement signed with West Germany - an agreement which was based on secret negotiations conducted by an authoritarian military regime. Brazil's hydroelectric energy potential was grossly miscalculated, and no other alternative programme was considered. Instead of touching off an open discussion on the "nuclear package", the Government wanted to exploit nationalist sentiment, systematically repelling any serious discussion with scientists, Congress and public opinion. The scientific community was marginalized before, during and after the negotiations with the FRG, and any attempt by individuals or institutions to "disclose the whole nuclear package" was seen by the establishment as a threat to national security.

According to the agreement, Brazil was to provide territory and raw materials, while all the active components will come "fully-packaged" from elsewhere, allowing very little absorption of technology by local scientists and enterprises. As an example, Table 11.1. gives the percentage of participation by Brazilian private enterprise in the supplying of equipment for the nuclear programme, as presented by different sources:

Table 11.1. The Share of National Participation in the Equipment of Brazilian Nuclear Plants

Plants	National participation in the equipment %	Difference %
ANGRA I	8	
		27
ANGRA II ANGRA III	35	
		30
IV V	65	
		15
VI VII	80	
		5
VIII IX	85	

Angra I (Westinghouse contract), Angra II, III and the following plants under Brazil-West Germany agreement.

No guarantee was offered for the entire fuel cycle, and the "jet nozzle system" was inadequately tested: Brazil, in words, is to serve as a "research laboratory" for the transferred equipment. Even the security of the FRG's nuclear projects is questionable.

But Brazilian policy makers tend to justify the programme with power political considerations: "more than territorial size, population, security and economic development, nuclear capacity is the indispensable condition to attain the status of big power. The goal is to increase Brazil's bargaining power in international relations".(27)

11.6. CRITICAL VIEWS

For those who may be the best qualified to judge the nuclear programme, the Brazilian government's policy is not only unsafe but also unsatisfactory.

How will Brazil's socio-economic development be affected, for example? The nuclear programme will certainly accentuate industrial concentration in the southern region, with adverse consequences for the population and for the less-developed regions within the country.

From another viewpoint, what direction is the nuclear policy taking? Let us take the examples of India and Argentina in order to examine Brazil and its nuclear capacity. India has adopted a three-stage nuclear programme: natural uranium and heavy-water reactors (first stage), originated plutonium reactors (second stage) and reproducing reactors (third stage), including the use of thorium as fissionable material.

In the case of Argentina, its nuclear policy has been unaffected during the quarter of a century of its existence by institutional crises or by the socio-economic instability of the country. Since the creation of the Comisión Nacional de Energia Atómica (National Commission of Atomic Energy) in 1950, the country has developed a technical, scientific and industrial infrastructure so that the correct steps towards atomic construction may be taken autonomously. Argentina has a most skilful professional workforce (approximately 1800 highly qualified academic personnel and hundreds of others with scholarships abroad), and its industry achieved 40 per cent participation in the first power plant of Atucha and 55 per cent in the second one. By the 1950s, Argentina had decided to build its own research reactors instead of importing them, and to produce the fuel element itself.

In Brazil the formulation of a nuclear policy has been characterized by a total lack of foresight, together with insufficient preparation of the technical personnel, management irresponsibility and a so-called pragmatic political approach which, in reality, has transformed itself into an irrationality in nuclear options.

Brazilian scientists argue that the programme and the agreement with the FRG should have been considered in connection with other energy sources, principally hydroelectric.(28) The so-called "hydroelectric energy deficit" - officially announced as justification for the nuclear agreement with the FRG - projected for the 1990s is misleading, if not untrue. Moreover, nuclear energy is not the only option. The country has many small waterfalls and there is no evidence that it would be uneconomical, for example, to transmit energy from the Amazon Basin, particularly if the high costs of nuclear energy are taken as the basis for comparison. And what about Brazil's year-round solar energy? One energy expert has already remarked on the paradox that Brazil, which can only supply an eighth of its own oil needs, does virtually nothing to develop its ample solar energy potential, whereas Saudi Arabia, one of the world's largest oil producers, is investing heavily in the solar energy sector.

The scientists also underline the fact that they were left completely out of the negotiations. They point out that the universities, institutes and other research centres do not have enough funds to carry out even the most fundamental research programmes. How can the government expect them to assume responsibility for planning additional high-cost programmes or controlling and operating future nuclear projects?(29) The participation of Brazilian scientists and technicians in the formulation of the methods and systems to be utilized and in the global political debate on the energy options is indispensable for the technological, scientific and cultural development of the country. In order to educate the specialized personnel in quantity and quality, the participation of the Brazilian universities is essential, as is the integration of the nuclear research institutes with the university sector.

Scientists fear that it will not be possible to transfer nuclear and fuel-cycle technology to Brazil. Although government sources have announced the intention of binding specific agreements for the gradual transference of technology to general agreements with partners abroad, there is still doubt about the viability of this scheme. According to the experts, the industrial technology of nuclear reactors is extremely complex and the operations control of a reactor does not permit mistakes. The risk one is taking is that the country will end up by receiving a turn-key reactor from KWU, and the Brazilian operators will merely be "reactor-conductors". There is an additional problem: the very real difficulties involved in establishing a viable Brazilian fuel cycle industry for uranium enrichment. In reality, it is like shooting in the dark.

Another question now being raised by scientists and ecologists is the huge concentration of nuclear plants between the two megalopolis - Sao Paulo and Rio de Janeiro with some 20 million people. It will represent a serious danger for the population and for the environment. The connection between the military's will to possess atomic weapons and the growth of Brazilian arms production is another aspect that has been stressed.(30)

A further problem is the ability of the Brazilian economy to bear the growing economic burden of the nuclear programme. Current estimates of the cost of the German-Brazilian nuclear deal lie around $ 30 billion, compared to an initial projection of about $ 10 billion. Taking into consideration that Brazil has a foreign debt of $ 60 billion the heavy cost of the nuclear programme would seem impossible to bear.(31)

What the society is claiming is that to promote nuclear energy development - if feasible, safe and economically necessary - the country needs to adopt a democratic form of government, where fundamental decisions may be freely discussed and possibly changed.

NOTES AND REFERENCES

My acknowledgements to Diana Valadores for her editorial work on this article.

1. The reactor was a high-powered one of the "swimming-pool" type, producing isotopes for medical and industrial purposes and for the training of atomic scientists. It had a potential force of 5,000 watts. See Keesing's Contemporary Archives, London, February 22, 1958, p. 16 032.

2. Lately, a 'conglomerate' has been formed in the R&D structure which guarantees certain advantages vis-à-vis technological research, technical skills, industrial development and penetration into the international peripheral market.

3. In 1965, Brazil and Switzerland signed an agreement for cooperation in the peaceful uses of atomic energy. Keesing's Contemporary Archives, London, July 10-17, 1965.

4. Brazil signed the Tlatelolco Treaty, banning nuclear weapons in Latin America, but the issue was complex for Brazilian diplomacy. Those who had signed the Treaty - including Brazil - wanted to keep their territories free forever from nuclear weapons, but the Brazilian Foreign Ministry introduced in the text the right to realize nuclear explosions for peaceful uses, including explosions similar to those of nuclear weapons.

5. See Documentation Francaise, Notes et Etudes Documentaires, Problèmes D'Amérique Latine, nos 3558/9, 1968, p. 83.

6. See Nuclear Policy, Visao, Sao Paulo, September 9, 1974, p. 32.

7. Col. Luiz de Alencar Araripe, member of the Brazilian delegation to the Conference of Disarmament in Geneva, in Visao, ibid, p. 32.

8. Cf. Gerhard Meyer-Wöbse, Nuclear Cooperation in the Third World, Aussenpolitik (German Foreign Affairs Review), Vol. 29, No. 1, 1978, p. 71.

9. As reported by the Latin America Political Report (17 March, 1978, Vol. XII, 11), an internal document of the Brazilian Information Service (SNI) said sabotage was delaying the completion of Angra I and was causing damage worth US$ 10 million. But a serious problem involves soil formation around the foundations: technical difficulties with the generators and with one thousand 40 m concrete pillars - at the cost of US$ 250 thousand each - are causing doubts about the efficiency of the plant.

10. During the Venezuelan President's visit to Brazil in 1977, cooperation on nuclear energy was discussed. Venezuela favours the creation of the Latin America Nuclear Enterprise, with OLADE (Latin American Energy Organization) providing the technical framework and SELA (Latin American Economic System) the infrastructure for the building of the new organ. Venezuela emphasized that the small countries should not be able to participate in this high cost energy programme. Jornal do Brasil, November 18, 1977.

11. Brazil has other agreements and contracts with foreign countries. The Soviet Union is supposed to sell enriched uranium at more favourable prices than those of the URENCO consortium. Portugal provides uranium, South Africa has sold uranium and exchanges technical information.

12. If fully applied, the entire cost will naturally be inflated over the years. Just to give a comparative example, the construction of the world's largest hydroelectric ITAIPU - in the Paraná River - was expected to cost US$ 2 billion, but has already reached US$ 18 billion. After delays and disagreements on the priority of the nuclear programme, the present cost of the Brazil-West Germany agreement is evaluated at 30 to 40 billion dollars, by 1980 prices.

13. Latin America Economic Report, Vol. VI, No. 7, 1978, reported that "following strict safeguards worked out with Holland on the supervision of enriched uranium, Brazil is to become the main buyer from the Dutch plant at Almelo, where output is planned to reach 1000 tons by 1985". In 1974, by a Presidential decision, Brazil became a member of the Association for Uranium Enrichment by Ultracentrifugal process, organized by URENCO.

14. The West German Kraftwerk Union was an asociation of two giant companies, Siemens and the AEG (which operates under licence of Westinghouse International) but has from 1977 on been totally owned by Siemens.

15. Representing an initial investment of 230 million dollars, of which 75 per cent has already been spent and the rest of which will have been spent by 1982, NUCLEP has only two orders at the moment, and it will only become profitable from 1984 onwards when, it is hoped, it will be building four reactors simultaneously for the Angra dos Reis's plants. Until then, costs will be paid by Nuclebrás with funds from the Federal Government, that is to say from the Brazilian taxpayer. A study undertaken by the Associacao Brasileira Para o Desenvolvimento da Indústria de Base (ABDIB) shows that NUCLEP has not contributed anything to the country's manufacturing goods except for the orders placed by other Brazilian industries that signed a protocol with Nuclebrás in 1976 and which are, until today, waiting for the start of the programme. According to business critics NUCLEP, with its

enormous idle capacity was established by KWU demands. Cf. Jornal do Brasil, March 8 and 15, 1981.

16. Some large Brazilian manufacturers of heavy equipment are involved in the Brazilian nuclear programme. The major ones are Confab Industrial (Sao Paulo), Bardella, Grupo Villares (associated with Brown Boveri, Switzerland), Jaguaré, Romi and Dedini (all from Sao Paulo). The Associacáo Brasileira de Indústrias de Máquinas (Abimaq) made a study foreseeing the participation of these Brazilian companies up to 70 per cent in the nuclear programme, with cession of numerous components. Jornal do Brasil, March 8, 1981. One of the companies that has profited most from the Brazilian nuclear programme has been the Construtora Norberto Odebrecht. It initially signed a contract for the first two reactors, and now it will also build the third plant, having acquired know-how with the first two. Odebrecht won control over the construction of Angras II and III without public competition and became one of the most profitable construction companies of the country. Due to problems of inefficiency during the first years, Odebrecht had to sign a contract of technical assistance with the German engineering firm Hochtief, so that 50 Hochtief technicians occupied key positions in the direction of the construction. Cf. Norman Gall, O Impasse Nuclear, Jornal do Brasil (Caderno Especial), December 3, 1978, p. 2.

17. Cf. Joaquim Francisco de Carvalho, Aspectos Economicos do Acordo Nuclear Brasil-Alemanha, Jornal do Brasil, March 4, 1981.

18. Even the Brazilian authorities do not know how much the prices of the reactors will increase. The President of Nuclebrás presented two different estimates. First, in his speech at the Brazilian Escola Superior de Guerra, he said that the cost of each plant would be US$ 800 per kw. The second version was given in a leaflet published by Nuclebrás, saying the cost of each kilowatt to be installed is estimated by international prices and not by Brazilian price; a subtle change showing how the costs can be miscalculated. According to other sources, the real cost of each kilowatt is already around US$ 3 000, one of the world's highest outlays for this kind of reactor. According to the director of IBRE (Brazilian Institute of Economy, Fundacao Getúlio Vargas), the cost of a kilowatt is "five time more expensive than the installed kw in the hydroelectric plants", so the nuclear programme is in conflict with the government policy to slow down the inflation, Jornal do Brasil, September 9, 1981.

19. See Joaquim F. de Carvalho, ibid., p. 2.

20. For example, many of the accounts of companies associated with the contract between Nuclebrás and KWU have not been approved by Tribunal de Contas da Uniáo (which is responsible in Brazil for the evaluation and approval of state-owned companies' expenses),

and since 1978 problems have been observed in real estate rents, services and so on.

21. In Keesing's Contemporary Archives, July 29, 1977, pp. 28478/9. A note on that policy and its ambiguity: although the US is the main advocate of "world interdependence", the US energy policy has, in contrast, an independentist approach. Even Carter himself stated that "our Nation's independence of economic and political action is becoming increasingly constrained" (emphasis by the author), ibid., p. 28478.

22. The Director of the IAEA is reported to have warned the US Government of several negative effects of the Carter policy, among them the possible acceleration of programmes for their own uranium enrichment plants by states dependent on imports for their energy needs. He said that the Carter ban on the reprocessing of nuclear fuel and the production of plutonium was a violation of art. 4 of the 1968 NPT, ibid., p. 28481.

23. Earlier in 1977, the Brazilian Foreign Minister realized that a change in Brazil's attitude towards the US was pragmatic and then prepared a new round of talks seeking a clear understanding with Washington. On July 17, 1977, the London Financial Times said the US Department of State had approved nuclear fuel sales to Brazil. The US recommended the export of low-enriched uranium to Angra I, after deciding that it "would not be inimical to the interests of the US, including the common defense and security" (emphasis by the author). A final decision was made by the Nuclear Regulatory Commission. On November 25, 1977, the White House had authorized the delivery of enriched uranium for Brazil's first nuclear reactor. The uranium was purchased from South Africa, enriched in Britain, converted into fuel in the US and can later explode in Brazil... See Latin America Economic Report, Vol. V, No. 46, 1977.

24. Jornal do Brasil, August 20, 1981.

25. Jornal do Brasil, September 9, 1981.

26. A leading Sao Paulo newspaper, Folha de Sao Paulo (February 24, 1978), commented that the programme does not have a real estimate on Brazil's uranium production. The newspaper said that the country's reserves of 70,000 tons, officially shown by the Government, are not reliable and unless new reserves are found, the entire programme is likely to be halted.

27. Cf. Col. Luiz de Alencar Araripe, in Visao, ibid., p. 31.

28. The country's potential is now estimated at 213,000 MW and in this sector Brazilian technology has achieved such a matrix that dependence on foreign sources is negligible.

29. It has been estimated that such a programme will have to employ some 70 to 80,000 people until 1985 at the engineering and technical levels. As a consequence, manpower preparation, training and qualification will involve many economic, scientific and technological considerations. Taking this into account, the education and research systems will have to be able to graduate -in the very elitist Brazilian educational system - more than 500 additional highly skilled scientists and engineers per year during the next 10 years. See R. Nazare Alves, R. Araújo, etc. Requirements for and Development of Trained Manpower Resources, International Atomic Energy Agency, Vienna, 1977.

30. In less than ten years, from an antiquated military system, with seven factories producing guns, gunpowder and ammunition, Brazil's military industry now ranks fifth on the list of export manufacturers. With expansion projects developed with the association between state enterprises and private capital, Brazil has made important advances in its defence economy. In 1975, the Brazilian War Material was created; it was designed to link the country's military sector with private military material and to enter into international arms sales, which are now worth US$ 2 billion in export. See Clóvis Brigagao, The Case of Brazil: Fortress or Paper Curtain?, Impact of Science on Society, Vol 31, No. 1, 1981, pp. 17-31.

31. Cf. Hartmut Krugmann, The German-Brazilian Nuclear Deal, Bulletin of the Atomic Scientists, February 1981, pp. 32-36 and Business Week, July 20, 1981, pp. 58-59.

IV

ALTERNATIVE PERSPECTIVES

Chapter Twelve

THE ECONOMIC EFFECTS OF CONVERSION: A CASE STUDY OF NORWAY*

Nils Petter Gleditsch, Olav Bjerkholt, Ådne Cappelen, and Knut Moum

12.1. DISARMAMENT AND DEVELOPMENT

The charter of the United Nations defines as two of its main purposes the maintenance of international peace and security and the promotion of social and economic development. A series of studies have linked the twin objectives of disarmament and development, mainly from the perspective that the enormous amount of resources vested in the arms race might be utilized to facilitate development. The UN study "Economic and social consequences of disarmament" from 1962, for example, states that "(a) much larger volume of resources could be allocated to investment for productive development in (the developing) countries even if only a fraction of the resources currently devoted to military purposes were used in this way. Disarmament could thus bring about a marked increase of real income in the poorer parts of the world."[1] The 1972 report, "Disarmament and Development", concludes that "most of the resources released by disarmament, total and partial, would be readily transferable to other uses..." and that "disarmament would contribute to economic and social development through the promotion of peace and the relaxation of international tension, as well as through the release of resources for peaceful uses" (p. 23).

The Tenth Special Session of the General Assembly of the United Nations decided to initiate an expert study on the relationship between disarmament and development. The terms of reference for this study were set out in the report of the Ad Hoc Group on the relationship between disarmament and development, in accordance with General Assembly resolution 32/88A of December 12, 1977.[2]

The Final Document of the Special Session instructed the Secretary General to appoint a Group of Governmental Experts, to undertake the study. This group was established in the summer of 1978. It commissioned 41 research projects within its original mandate, and four studies of various aspects of a French proposal to establish an international disarmament fund for development.[3]

The work of the present authors is a result of one of these 41 projects. Our aim is to study the economic effects of conversion; i.e. of decreasing Norwegian arms expenditure and increasing transfers to developing countries.(4)

An earlier study of the economics of disarmament in Norway by one of the present authors investigated the economic importance of military demand in Norway and estimated the economic adjustments necessary to accomodate a hypothetical process of complete disarmament. Using a Norwegian input-output model Bjerkholt found that complete disarmament without any countermeasures would result in a 3.8 % decline in GDP, a 7.0 % decline in employment, and a 2.5 % decline in imports.(5)

Bjerkholt's study also included calculations of the economic effects of a set of counter-measures chosen to consist mainly of increased government expenditure for education, health, and social welfare, and increased investments in machinery, roads, and dwellings. The results showed that the resources released by disarmament could easily be absorbed by other types of demand, at least over a period of a few years. Bjerkholt also argued that disarmament would make possible a higher growth rate in Norway through the release of real resources of labour power and investment. It rejected the idea that disarmament would lead to economic problems.

A later study by Andreassen (1972) replicated Bjerkholt's work using data from 1969. The results were similar to those obtained by Bjerkholt. Andreassen's study indicated that a cut in military spending might have adverse regional effects, due to the concentration of military forces in the sparsely populated northern part of Norway. As a result of the weak data-base, however, this conclusion must be considered with caution.(6)

Neither of the two previous studies dealt with a situation in which a strong constraint is placed on the use of the resources released - such as increased transfers to developing countries. The object of the present study is precisely to study the impact of this kind of restraint.

12.2. THE NORWEGIAN MILITARY SECTOR

Between independence in 1905 and the German invasion in April 1940 Norway pursued a policy of neutrality. During the German occupation in World War II the Norwegian government in exile in London became politically and militarily allied with the Western powers. In 1949 Norway became a founding member of NATO. Military spending rose sharply, particularly after the outbreak of the Korean war. The duration of military service was successively lengthened from 1948 through 1952.

Norway has maintained universal male conscription throughout the post-war period. In 1978 a total of 49,700 person-years were budgeted within the military, or 3.1 % of the total labour force.(7) Of these 21,725 were contributed by conscripts, 988 by enlisted personnel, 12,493 by officers; and 10,703 by civilians.

Along with other industrial nations, Norway has in recent years acquired a number of technologically advanced weapons systems. This might have been expected to lead to a less labour-intensive military sector. The continued use of conscripts as a source of labour should work in the opposite direction, to maintain labour intensiveness. But conscripts are cheap labour, so each of these two factors should theoretically make for low expenditure on labour power. Nevertheless, salaries still represent about two fifths of military expenditure and slightly over half of military consumption. However, unlike the case for civilian government spending, the share of wages and salaries in total military spending has not increased over the past 25 years. Table 12.1. gives a breakdown for 1978.

Most military spending in Norway comes from Norwegian funds. However, from 1951 to 1970 Norway received very substantial military assistance in kind from the United States. The exact value of this aid is hard to calculate, but it is said to have amounted to about 20 % of domestic military spending from 1951 to 1970 and as much as 2/3 in the period 1951-55.(8) Even after the military assistance programme was terminated, a part of the military establishment continues to be funded by external sources, either from NATO or bilaterally from the US or one of the other NATO allies. In 1978 the published figure for such transfers was N.kr. 118.3 mill., i.e. less than 2 % of the defence budget.

Figure 12.1 presents two series of absolute figures for military consumption and for military employment. Figure 12.2. presents a set of relative measures: size of the armed forces relative to total employment, and military spending relative to population, to GDP and to central government expenditure. Both figures show clearly the period of immediate post-war disarmament, followed by a short period of stability - at a higher level than the pre-war military establishment - and then strong rearmament in the early 1950s.

Following the first experience of "detente" in the mid-1950s, military consumption decreased, in both absolute and relative terms. From the late 1950s until today, military consumption has continued to increase, although less steeply than in the early 1950s and with some minor ups and downs. Of the relative measures, military consumption per capita has continued to rise, while consumption in per cent of GDP has stabilized. It is still substantially lower than in the early 1950s, but higher than in the brief period of low tension in the 1940s. Military expenditure in per cent of central government expenditure peaked about 1960 and declined particularly sharply from the late 1960s. This is only marginally related to any international development or policy decision with regard to defence. Rather, it reflects domestic priorities

Table 12.1.   Composition of the Military Budget, 1978 absolute and relative figures

	Absolute figures N.kr. mill.		Relative figures %
Wages and salaries	2,899		42
Materials	2,873		42
Operating expenditure		1,300	19
Investments		1,573	23
Buildings and facilities	577		8
Operating expenditure		262	4
Nationally financed investment	205		3
Jointly financed investment		110	2
Other expenditure	463		7
Transfers to other organizations	37		0.5
Total military expenditure	6,848		100
Total operating expenditures	4,960		72
Total investments	1,887		28

Source:
Defence budget, 1979, p. 11. All figures are final budget figures for 1978. For a discussion of the differences between budget figures and account figures and between military expenditure and military consumption, see Appendix A of Bjerkholt et al., Disarmament and Development: A Study of Conversion in Norway. PRIO, Oslo 1980. Note that military spending is used as a general term, while expenditure and consumption are used as technical terms, with precise definitions.

Figure 12.1. Absolute Size of the Norwegian Military Establishment, 1945-79

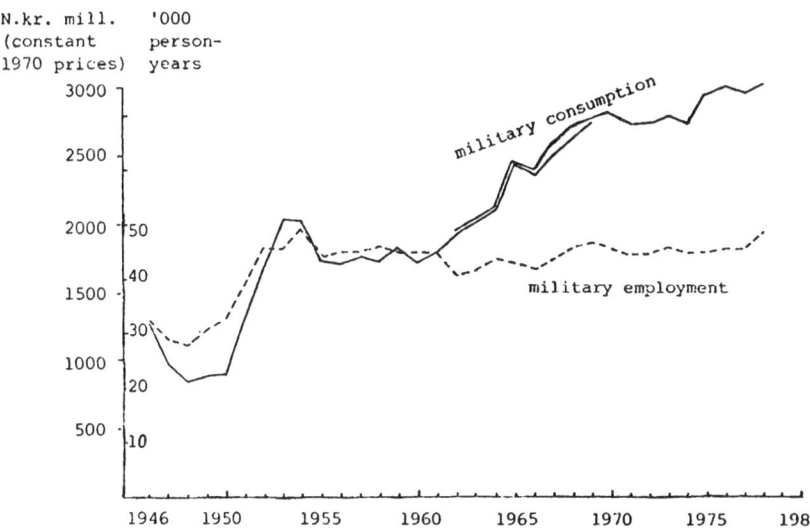

Sources:
Data from Tables A.1, and A.3 in Appendix A of Bjerkholt et al. (1980). The discontinuity in the curve for military consumption is due to changed definitions in the national accounts.

such as the decision in the late 1960s to start a National Pensions Scheme. Education and health expenditures have contributed heavily to a rapid expansion of central government expenditure and the military sector has not expanded equally rapidly. The curves for military employment, absolute as well as relative, show the most stable pattern of all. However, the effect of rearmament around 1950 can also be seen clearly in these curves.

Figure 12.2. Relative Size of the Norwegian Military Establishment, 1945-79

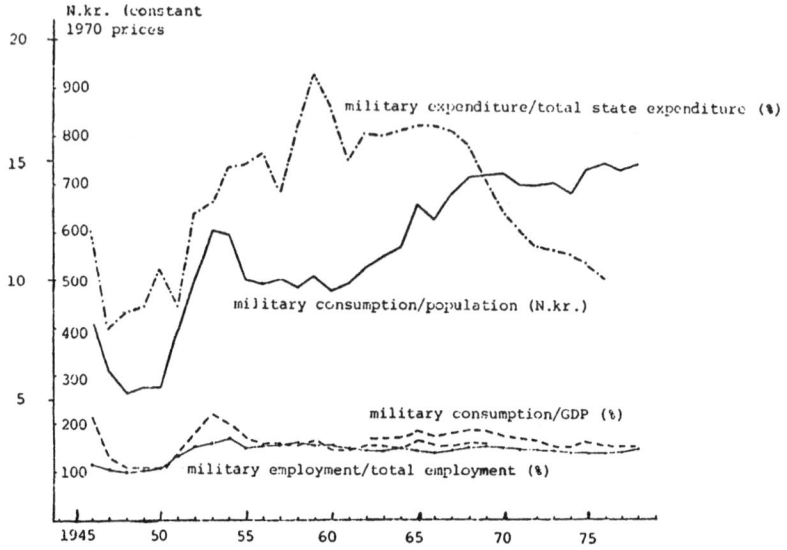

Sources:
Data from Tables A.1, A.2, and A.3 in Appendix A of Bjerkholt et al. (1980). The overlap in the curve for military consumption in per cent of GDP is due to changed definitions in the national accounts.

Disarmament Scenarios

To study conversion, we first need one or more scenarios for the disarmament of Norway. Such scenarios can be based on global or regional disarmament plans, Norwegian political alternatives, more or less arbitrary percentage cuts in defence expenditure, or comparisons with other countries. Of these per-centage cuts are by far the simplest and most flexible. The main disadvantage of this approach is that the scenarios are not linked to politically meaningful alternative policies, whether at the national or international level. However, we have found little help in developing such scenarios in current global or regional disarmament plans, or in current negotiations for arms control. Norwegian defence discussions do not have much to offer either. While there is widespread support for disarmament, little thought has been given to how Norway's defence might be organized if the process of disarmament starts. Therefore, we use fairly arbitrary percentage cuts for our disarmament scenarios, and we assume the cuts to be equal for all resource inputs to the military sector.

We have selected one moderate alternative (reduction of military spending to about 85 % of its current (1978) level by 1990), one radical alternative (reduction to the average military spending levels of Austria and Finland, called two neutrals for easy identification), and finally complete disarmament. The first alternative was suggested by the Norwegian member of the UN Group of Governmental Experts and will be referred to, in short, as the expert group alternative. As a baseline for the other alternatives, we have included in all calculations one alternative which is not a disarmament model, but precisely the opposite. This corresponds to the decision of the NATO Council of Ministers in 1978 to increase real military spending by 3 % per year.(9) Since an overall growth rate of 3 % in the economy will be assumed throughout, the baseline implies that military spending retains a fixed share of the national product.

Table 12.2. gives a precise description of the three scenarios and the baseline. In each scenario, the disarmament goals are assumed to be fulfilled by 1990. Of course they may be modified in the radical or moderate direction simply by shortening or prolonging the time perspective.

In order to handle the conversion problem analytically, we have mostly reasoned as if conversion had taken place in 1978. We have then used hypothetical levels of military expenditure for 1978 as given by Table 12.3.

Table 12.2. Disarmament Scenarios for Norway 1978-90
(absolute figures in N.kr. mill., 1978 prices)

No. Alternative	Hypothetical military expenditure 1990	Difference between 1990 level and 1978 level	Annual change in mil. expend.	
			Absolute[1]	% Change first year
(0) NATO Council decision	9,763	+2,915	+224.2	3.0
(1) Expert group alternative	5,821	-1,027	-79.0	-1.2
(2) Two neutrals	2,050	-4,798	-369.1	-5.4
(3) Complete	0	-6,848	-526.8	-7.7

Budgeted military expenditure was N.kr. 6,848 mill. in 1978. The disarmament models are defined in terms of budgeted military expenditure. To calculate the effects of disarmament on the economy, however, we have looked at a reduction in military consumption of the same magnitude. Military expenditure and consumption differ somewhat, as explained in Appendix A of Bjerkholt et al. (1980), but the consequences for the disarmament models are negligible.

1. These figures are calculated as 1/13 of total difference between hypothetical military expenditure in 1990 and actual military expenditure in 1978. In the baseline alternative the actual annual increase grows from N.kr 205 mill. in 1978-79 to N.kr 285 mill. in 1989-90 (1978 prices).

Before going on to measure the effects of the various disarmament scenarios in combination with increased development aid we note that 1978 data and the 1978 version of the national accounts model (MODIS IV)(10) yields the following results for complete disarmament: reduction in employment 5.6 %, in GDP 3.8 %, and in imports 3.1 %. The results are very close to those found in the two previous studies by Bjerkholt and Andreassen.

Table 12.3. Disarmament Scenarios for Norway 1978
(absolute figures N.kr. mill., 1978 prices)

No. Scenario	Hypothetical military expenditure in 1978	Difference between hypothetical military expenditure in 1978 and budgeted military expenditure in 1978	Hypothetical military expenditure in 1978 in % of budgeted military expenditure in 1978
(0) NATO Council decision	6,848	0	100
(1) Expert Group alternative	5,821	-1,027	85
(2) Two neutrals	2,050	-4,797	30
(3) Complete disarmament	0	-6,848	0

12.3. NORWEGIAN OFFICIAL DEVELOPMENT ASSISTANCE

Norway has no recent history of colonial expansion and thus her development aid has no historical basis in colonial ties and practices.

The most important principles governing Norwegian development aid have been formulated in two government white papers in 1971 and 1972. The main purpose of Norwegian development assistance is to render such assistance unnecessary: "... in the long run, the intention is to develop a form of cooperation which does not include direct assistance, but is based on a mutual exchange of commodities and services between the countries, and which aims at a closer interaction culturally, politically, and otherwise."(11)

More specifically, it has been government policy - with very wide political acceptance
- to raise public development assistance to one per cent of the national product
- to provide the assistance as gifts, not as loans
- to allocate half of the assistance multilaterally through the UN and other international organizations, and the other half bilaterally
- to concentrate the assistance geographically to a small number

of countries where its effect can be greater than if spread over a larger group of recipients
- to adjust the assistance to local development programmes
- to make the ordinary man and woman the main beneficiaries of the assistance.

An important criterion in the selection of recipient countries is whether or not their governments conduct a development-oriented and socially just policy.

By 1978 total official assistance had reached .9 % of GNP. (More recently, the goal of one per cent having been accomplished, the political parties have parted ways with regard to the pace of the increase in the volume of aid.) Multilateral activities represented 46 %, as close as is practicable to an even split. (Loans are not counted as part of the aid.) The aid has been geographically concentrated, with East Africa and South Asia as particularly important target areas. There has been a deliberate effort to channel aid to countries with "development-oriented regimes." But determining which countries qualify for this category remains politically very controversial in Norway. Finally, there have been some attempts to reach "ordinary people", but such efforts meet with obvious bureaucratic obstacles along the way and their effectiveness is hard to evaluate.

Figure 12.3 illustrates the expansion of total aid in constant prices. The strong rise in public development assistance has been accompanied by a reduction in the share of aid through multilateral channels, from about 2/3 in the mid- 1960s to the official goal of about 1/2 from the mid 1970s. There has been a modest tendency in the direction of less emphasis on capital project financing and more on programme assistance and contributions in kind. This has probably resulted in a more extensive use of Norwegian resources (labour and commodities). However, the major share of the bilateral assistance still consists of capital project financing and programme assistance, which also has a strong component of financial transfers.

Figure 12.3.   Norwegian Official Programme for Development Assistance 1956-78 in Constant 1958 prices

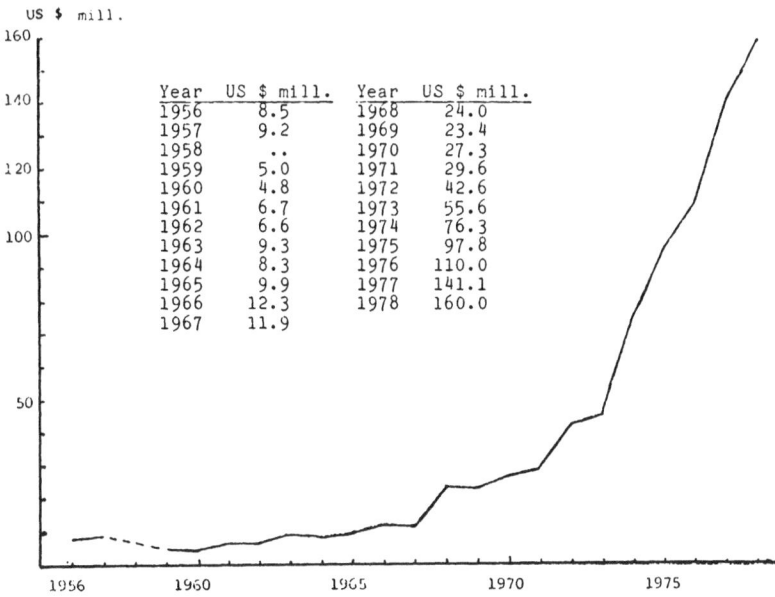

Year	US $ mill.	Year	US $ mill.
1956	8.5	1968	24.0
1957	9.2	1969	23.4
1958	..	1970	27.3
1959	5.0	1971	29.6
1960	4.8	1972	42.6
1961	6.7	1973	55.6
1962	6.6	1974	76.3
1963	9.3	1975	97.8
1964	8.3	1976	110.0
1965	9.9	1977	141.1
1966	12.3	1978	160.0
1967	11.9		

The figures are for net official development aid for all years, except 1956 and 1957. Here total official transfers are given. Note that the US $ was depreciated relative to Norwegian currency by 6 % in 1971 and by 13 % in 1972-73, and declined a further 7 % in the period 1973-77.

Source:
Figures for Norwegian official development aid in US $ are given in Development Cooperation 1968, 1975 and 1978, OECD, Paris, respective years. They are deflated by the official US GNP deflators.

Data for the OECD countries indicate that Norway has moved over the last twenty years from a modest position to the front rank with regard to development aid as a share of GNP (only the figures for the Netherlands, Norway, and Sweden exceed .8 %).(12) Relative to most countries outside Scandinavia, Norway gives aid that is less tied and more multilateral. This is now linked to strong Norwegian support for the demands of developing countries for a New International Economic Order, but the same approach could be detected before the goal of NIEO was formulated.

Increased Aid Scenarios

In order to analyze the quantitative economic consequences of conversion, we require some specific assumptions concerning the kind of development aid that will be given. Instead of trying to predict the most probable composition of development aid in the next decade, we have decided to study the eocnomic consequences of several "transfer scenarios". Unlike the disarmament scenarios defined in the previous sections, these scenarios are not simply percentage variations in the quantity of aid. Rather, our five transfer scenarious (A-E) span some of the most important political alternatives for aid policies in the years to come. The greatest weakness is the lack of any scenario for structural change in the world economy. Actual policies may, of course, be a mix of our scenarios, but the effect of such mixes can easily be judged on the basis of the results from the pure scenarios. The five transfer scenarios are:

(A) Financial transfers

By financial transfers we mean gifts given, either bilaterally or through the UN. We assume that gifts have no effect on domestic production or on employment.(13)

(B) Exports/gifts of commodities that Norway would like to be relieved of

Gifts of commodities have not played any important role in Norwegian aid. In recent years, however, there have been increasing demands from various industries to promote new export markets by using subsidies or cheap credit financed over the development aid budget. In this way, it is argued, one can prevent unemployment in stagnating Norwegian industries while providing developing countries with commodities which may be useful to them. The goods that have been subsidized so far, are products of industries which experienced a considerable slackening in demand in the 1970s. For the purposes of this study it is more important to pinpoint industries that will have difficulties during the 1980s. For various reasons we have discarded such obvious candidates as products from the fishing industry and from the Norwegian textile industry,(14) and have chosen ships instead. Some ships have already been supplied through Norwegian public development programmes, either as gifts or heavily subsidized. The crisis in the shipbuilding industry that affects many developed countries is likely to last, even though many countries plan to reduce their building capacity. In Norway the crisis in the fisheries exacerbates the problem for the ship-building industry. Scenario (B) then consists of exports or gifts of new ships.

(C) Exports/gifts of commodities the developing countries think they need

This scenario is meant to mirror the subjective view of the needs as seen by the developing countries themselves or by their decision-making elites, rather than "real needs". The development aid is used to finance imports of goods and services from Norway, but with no restriction on the goods and services the developing countries can buy. We further assume that the commodity mix of exports resulting from increased aid is equal to the existing export pattern between Norway and the developing countries in 1977. This gives a high proportion of ships due to the subsidized exports of ships.

(D) Export/gifts of commodities that Norway thinks the developing countries need

What Norway thinks is needed in the developing countries cannot be adequately reflected in any existing pattern of exports or gifts. Therefore, we have to look to policy statements. One important principle is "aid for self-reliance". Traditionally this has been interpreted as aid to build infrastructure, hospitals, schools, etc. in addition to increasing capital formation especially in agriculture and fishery. For the purposes of this study, we have specified this to mean aid in the form of fishing technology, machinery for agriculture, machinery for mining, manufacturing, and construction, machinery for hydro-electric power plants, and equipment and personnel for education and health services.

(E) Increased aid with unchanged aid composition

Scenario E assumes that the additional aid has the same composition as that given in 1978. The financial part of the aid (83 %) can be analyzed by scenario A. The rest consists of wages paid to Norwegians (at home or abroad), and expenditure on goods and services (in Norway or abroad). Closer examination of the aid budget shows that some of the transfers in fact are used for domestic purchases of goods and services. We have therefore based our further calculations on the following composition of the aid: financial transfers 63 %, goods and services 26 %, and wages 11 %.(15) In using this transfer scenario for calculations we have made a further rough disaggregation of the goods and services down to the level of specification of the national accounts model.

Economic Effects of Transfer Increases

We are not aware of any previous detailed empirical analysis of the effects on the Norwegian economy of development aid. The only relevant study is Strand (1980), but his model is highly aggregated.(16) Using the national budget model we have calculated the impact on the economy of an increase in transfers of N.kr. 1,000 mill.(17) We shall not give the detailed figures here, but limit ourselves to a few main results: Increased financial transfers have no impact on employment, on GDP, or on imports, because the increased importing capacity of the developing countries is not supposed to have any effect on Norwegian exports. The only effect is a deficit (.48 % of GDP) on the balance of payments. The results for transfer scenarios B, C, and D are very similar at the macro-economic level. In a more disaggregate analysis we find some obvious differences in industry composition. Finally, the results of scenario E are very similar to those of A - which is not too surprising in view of the high proportion of financial transfers in the present aid programme.

12.4. CONVERSION: FROM ARMS TO AID

In the previous two sections we have analyzed separately the economic effects of decreased defence spending and increased transfers. We shall now combine the two, and look at the possibilities for converting armament resources into development aid. Our analysis is not meant to be a blueprint for actual conversion, but rather a preliminary assessment of possibilities and constraints.

As indicators of the possible economic dislocations resulting from conversion we use <u>employment</u>, <u>GDP</u>, <u>imports</u>, and <u>balance of payments</u>. In the first set of calculations - which we call <u>pure conversion</u> - we look at the effect on the indicators for all 15 combinations of disarmament and transfer scenarios. In all combinations the transfers are scaled to match the fiscal implications of the corresponding level of disarmament. This concept of conversion - disarming and using the money saved for development aid - may have an intuitive appeal, but it is superficial from a more basic economic viewpoint. Disarmament will release <u>resources</u>, and these resources may be used for other purposes. The extent and time-phasing of conversion will have to depend upon the amount, composition, and mobility of resources released. The fiscal consequences are of second-order importance only, serving as a possible constraint on measures taken to put conversion into effect. In this connection, <u>labour</u> is the most important resource to bear in mind: both because of the emphasis on full employment in Norway and because of the constraints on labour-supply even in a medium- to long-term setting. Low regional mobility of labour can be a severe constraint on this type of conversion. Such low regional mobility reflects a stable regional pattern of production, which has in itself been a goal of economic policy in Norway.

Pure Conversion

In Tables 12.4 - 12.6. the disarmament scenarios are listed vertically in increasing degree of disarmament. The transfer scenarios are listed horizontally in the order discussed in section 12.3 The results are calculated as if full conversion had taken place in 1978. All the tables give relative effects (percentage changes).(18)

Table 12.4. Effects on Employment of Pure Conversion in 1978 (%)

Disarmament scenario	Transfer scenario				
	Financial transfers (A)	Commodity transfers			Current aid composition (E)
		(B)	(C)	(D)	
(1) Expert group	-0.8	-0.3	-0.3	-0.3	-0.6
(2) Two neutrals	-3.9	-1.5	-1.6	-1.3	-2.9
(3) Complete disarmament	-5.6	-2.1	-2.3	-1.8	-4.2

Total employment excluding self-employed in 1978 was 1,442,000 person-years according to the preliminary estimates in the national accounts.

Transfer scenario A (financial transfers) has no employment effect on the domestic economy. The results in the first column in Tables 12.4, 12.5 and 12.6 thus reflect purely the effect of reduced military consumption. The employment effects vary from a decline in employment of 5.6 % for the case of complete disarmament and transfer scenario A, to a decline of .3 % for the case of disarmament scenario 1 and transfer scenario D. The results also confirm that the three alternative commodity transfer compositions yield results of the same level of magnitude, while current aid composition has employment effects between those of financial transfers and the three commodity transfer alternatives.

Table 12.5. Effects on GDP of Pure Conversion in 1978 (%)

Disarmament scenario	Transfer scenario				
	Financial transfers (A)	Commodity transfers			Current aid composition (E)
		(B)	(C)	(D)	
(1) Expert group	-0.6	-0.1	-0.1	-0.1	-0.4
(2) Two neutrals	-2.6	-0.7	-0.7	-0.6	-1.9
(3) Complete disarmament	-3.8	-1.0	-0.8	-0.8	-2.7

Gross domestic product was N.kr. 209,579 mill. in 1978.

Table 12.6. Effects on Imports of Pure Conversion in 1978 (%)

Disarmament scenario	Transfer scenario				
	Financial transfers (A)	Commodity transfers			Current aid composition (E)
		(B)	(C)	(D)	
(1) Expert group	-0.5	0.2	0.2	0.2	-0.3
(2) Two neutrals	-2.2	0.7	0.7	0.8	-1.7
(3) Complete disarmament	-3.1	1.0	1.0	1.2	-1.8

Imports were N.kr. 89,187 mill. in 1978.

Table 12.7. Effects on the Balance of Payments of Pure Conversion in 1978 (% of GDP)

Disarmament scenario	Transfer scenario				
	Financial transfers (A)	Commodity transfers			Current aid composition (E)
		(B)	(C)	(D)	
(1) Expert group	-0.3	-0.1	-0.1	-0.1	-0.2
(2) Two neutrals	-1.4	-0.3	-0.3	-0.3	-0.9
(3) Complete disarmament	-2.0	-0.4	-0.4	-0.5	-1.3

A negative figure means an increased deficit or a reduced surplus.

It may not be intuitively obvious that a shift in expenditure from armaments to commodities for development transfers implies a net result of <u>less</u> employment and <u>more</u> imports. An important part of the explanation is the labour-intensiveness of military expenditure and the fact that a considerable part of military demand, such as construction, is <u>less</u> import-intensive than production of industrial goods in general. The total effect on GDP is very small in each case. Transfer scenario D (exports/gifts of products Norway thinks the developing countries need) is the most favourable alternative in terms of <u>employment</u> and <u>production</u>. However, the effects on <u>imports</u> and the <u>balance of payments</u> are not so favourable as for scenarios B and C. From a macro-economic point of view, transfer scenario D seems to be one to select for the Norwegian government. This is somewhat surprising, since scenario B is the one that was formulated with Norwegian interests directly in mind. However, these interests were not mainly of a macro-economic nature, but to secure continued employment in the ship-yards.

Both transfer scenarios A and E include financial transfers (in fact, scenario A is nothing else). The import requirements of these scenarios are correspondingly lower, as revealed by Table 12.6. On the other hand, financial transfers have a direct and negative effect on the balance of payments. The last column in all the tables shows the effect on the macro-economic variables of conversion and increased aid, with unchanged aid composition. The results are a combination of those in the four preceding columns and the effects are near the average of such a combination.

In Bjerkholt et al. (1980) we have reported results for an extended form of conversion, in which the disarmament takes effect gradually over a 12 year period until 1990.(19) The effects of conversion on the four indicators of economic dislocation turn out - somewhat surprisingly - to be larger than in the case of conversion during a single year. The main reason for this is that the base scenario (no disarmament) involves a 50 % real increase in military spending. Thus, each of the disarmament scenarios involves a much larger reduction in military spending in the long term than in one year. The gradual adaptation of the economy to the small decrease in military expenditure per year is not well taken care of by the national accounts model.

Conversion with Counter-Measures

Although the economic dislocation of the pure conversion alternatives is not very large, it is sufficiently large to present a political problem - particularly with regard to employment. Various domestic counter-measures may be suggested to compensate for the employment-reducing effects of pure conversion. In general, a suitable countermeasure should
- be highly labour-intensive

- give a good geographical spread of employment
- tap a labour reserve (previously unused or liberated by disarmament)
- fill an unmet social demand
- be popular and visible
- be publicly financed already (or a natural candidate for public financing)
- be relatively independent of other scarce or slowly developing resources (such as city land or trained manpower)
- have no other major adverse effects (e.g., a negative effect on female employment).

We have looked into four domestic programmes: social home-help services for the old and the sick, day-care institutions for children, relief and stand-in arrangements in agriculture, and support for small grocery stores and other service facilities in small or isolated communities. All four programmes fulfil some of the eight criteria above, but three of them fail on several of the eight.

However, social home-help services is a programme that does well on all criteria. Essentially, this programme functions as an alternative to the institutionalization of the old and the sick in hospitals, nursing-homes, or retirement homes. The programme is highly labour-intensive (about 83 % of all costs in 1972-78 were labour costs); it gives a good geographical spread (since 1974 all Norwegian municipalities have been administering such programmes); to some extent it taps an unused labour reserve (experienced housewives, although others may be trained for the job without any extensive educational programme); potential demand is enormous (as evidenced by the current rapid expansion of the programme); the programme can affect every family and therefore is quite visible and popular (and would probably contribute to public acceptance of the conversion package as a whole). Furthermore, adverse public opinion is not likely to be a problem; the programme is already largely publicly financed (93 % in 1977); there are no other major bottlenecks except financing; and finally the programme has a favourable rather than negative effect on employment for women and no other important known adverse effects. Since 1977 the public financing has been shared by state and local council budgets, approximately on a 50/50 basis. However, in order to offset possible negative effects on local council finances, the percentage of state financing can be easily adjusted. It can also, if necessary, be adjusted differentially on a regional basis if one wants to compensate for military employment in Northern Norway.

One possible counter-argument is that such a compensatory programme may lean _too_ heavily towards female employment, and that conversion at the level of military expenditure might also require a social conversion at the family level. However, as home-help programmes expand, more emphasis can be put on extending janitorial services, etc., repairing domestic equipment in the home, etc., and this would create a demand for employment with technical skills. In the short term, such skills seem more likely be found among men.(20)

Table 12.8 presents the economic effects, as calculated by the national budget model, of a number of compensatory measures, including social home-help programmes, reductions in personal income taxes, increases in government investment, increases in private investment, and increases in general central government expenditure.

We have also included the effects of increased spending for military expenditure and development aid (transfer scenario D). The point of the table is to compare the effects of various forms of public spending - the absolute level of the increase in spending (N.kr. 1,000 mill.) is a purely arbitrary example. The table shows that although central government expenditure in general is a good counter-measure from the point of view of our four economic indicators, social home-help services is the only programme which does better than or as well as military expenditure on all four.

Table 12.8. Economic Effects of Various Counter-Measures (%), 1978

Increase spending by N.kr. 1,000 mill. for	Effects on			
	Employment	GDP	Imports	Balance of payments
Tax reduction[1]	0.3	0.3	0.5	-0.2
Government investment[2]	0.5	0.5	0.5	-0.2
Private investment[3]	0.4	0.4	0.6	-0.2
Central government expenditure[4]	0.7	0.6	0.4	-0.2
Social home-help services	1.1	0.6	0.4	-0.2
Military expenditure	0.8	0.6	0.5	-0.2
Development aid (transfer scenario D)	0.6	0.4	0.6	-0.3

1. Central government taxes, local government taxes and employees contribution to social security have almost identical effects.
2. Both central and local government investment.
3. Excluding ocean transport, crude petroleum and natural gas production, pipeline transport of oil and gas, and oil well drilling.
4. Central government consumption excluding military consumption.

Table 12.9. Effects on GDP of Conversion with Counter-Measures 1978 (%)

Disarmament scenario	Transfer scenario				
	Financial transfers (A)	Commodity transfers			Current aid composition (E)
		(B)	(C)	(D)	
(1) Expert group	-0.02	-0.01	-0.01	-0.01	-0.02
(2) Two neutrals	-0.04	-0.01	-0.01	-0.01	-0.04
(3) Complete disarmament	-0.05	-0.02	-0.01	-0.02	-0.05
Conversion index:	23 %	45 %	42 %	48 %	28 %

The conversion index is the proportion of the financial value of the resources released through disarmament which is allocated to development aid.

Table 12.10. Effects on Imports of Conversion with Counter-Measures 1978 (%)

Disarmament scenario	Transfer scenario				
	Financial transfers (A)	Commodity transfers			Current aid composition (E)
		(B)	(C)	(D)	
(1) Expert group	-0.06	0.01	0.00	0.01	-0.05
(2) Two neutrals	-0.11	0.01	0.01	0.02	-0.09
(3) Complete disarmament	-0.14	0.01	0.01	0.03	-0.11
Conversion index:	23 %	45 %	42 %	48 %	28 %

Table 12.11. Effects on the Balance of Payments of Conversion with Counter-Measures, 1978 (%)

	Transfer scenario				
Disarmament scenario	Financial transfers (A)	Commodity transfers			Current aid composition (E)
		(B)	(C)	(D)	
(1) Expert group	-0.01	-0.00	-0.00	-0.00	-0.01
(2) Two neutrals	-0.02	-0.00	-0.00	-0.01	-0.02
(3) Complete disarmament	-0.03	-0.01	-0.00	-0.01	-0.02
Conversion index:	23 %	45 %	42 %	48 %	28 %

A negative figure means an increased deficit or a reduced surplus.

Conversion with Social Home-Help Services

In the next three tables we have combined our three disarmament scenarios with a mix of a transfer scenario and social home-help services which keeps overall employment exactly constant.(21) This means that the proportion of released resources allocated to development will vary between the transfer models. For each transfer model the percentage allocated to development will be reported as the conversion index. These results should be read as an illustrative example of a possible conversion, rather than as a politically viable alternative.

Column 1 in each table shows the joint effect of disarmament, development transfers (only 23 % of the reduction in military consumption), and increase in home-help services. Because the purely financial transfers in scenario A have no effect on employment, a large part of the resources released by dis-armament is used domestically to keep employment unchanged. Effects on the national product are now scarcely noticeable, and effects on the balance of payments are also very moderate. There is, of course, no table for the effects on employment, since these have been pre-set at zero for all scenarios.

The three commodity transfer scenarios (B, C, D) yield very similar results in this case as in the case of pure conversion. About 55 % of the reduction in military consumption is used domestically in these three transfer scenarios. The effects on the economy are now so small that it is not possible to show clearly the difference between the disarmament scenarios.

In the case of transfers with the present composition (scenario E) only 28 % of the reduction in military consumption is transferred abroad. The results are very similar to transfer scenario A, because spending on home-help services dominates the effects.

Conversion in a Global Context

So far we have dealt with disarmament and conversion of military resources in a purely national context. The results of the various conversion models analyzed could be interpreted as the results of unilateral Norwegian political decisions to reduce military expenditures and reallocate economic resources so that development aid could be correspondingly increased. The results could, alternatively, be interpreted as the result for Norway of a multinational or even worldwide agreement on conversion of military expenditures. The frame-work provided by the UN Group of Governmental Experts, which was instrumental in the initiation of this and several other research projects, is obviously that of a global effort towards disarmament and development.

If conversion takes place within a regional or global setting the policy changes in other countries will obviously have some effects for Norway. Decreased demands for military products and increased transfers to development aid may have negative and positive implications for the exports of Norwegian products and thus for employment and other key economic variables. It is not obvious without detailed empirical study whether the negative will outweigh the positive effects or vice versa.

It seems very likely that effects of conversion in other countries will be much smaller than the effects of domestic conversion. However, Norway's exports and imports in 1978 made up 44 % and 42 %, respectively, of the national product. Therefore, changes in the world demand for products in which Norway trades heavily may have a far from negligible impact on the domestic economy.

In principle such external effects can be modelled in the same way as the effects of domestic policy changes. However, until recently there has been no economic model to permit us to do this with even approximately the same kind of forecasting accuracy as the national budget model for the domestic economy.

Recently, however, Leontief and associates have developed a world input-output model which can be used to simulate the crossnational effects of conversion.(22) The model does not have individual states as units, with the exception of the Soviet Union. The world economy is divided into 15 regions (including the Soviet Union as a separate region). Norway is one of 17 countries in the region called "Western Europe (High income)". Thus, the effects for Norway can be assessed from a solution of the world model and the trade pattern of the Norwegian economy. Each region is described in terms of 45 sectors of economic activity. This is considerably less than in the Norwegian model, which divides domestic production into about 150 industries. (23) Nevertheless, the Leontief model is undoubtedly the most successful attempt at extending the flexible and comprehensive input-output approach to the world economy.

The World Model of Leontief et al. was originally developed to study international development policies in connection with the Second United Nations Development Decade. More recently it has been extended to include specifications of military expenditure categories. (24) This version of the model has been used in reports to the UN Group of Governmental Experts and the US Arms Control and Disarmament Agency to study some global scenarios for conversion.(25)

The detailed results of applying the World Model to calculate the effects for Norway will be given in separate publications by the present authors. It may be indicated at this point that although our scenarios involve more disarmament than those of Leontief and Duchin, they have very limited economic effects in the developed countries. The effects in some of the receiving countries are, however, quite substantial. For Norway the net effects are fairly limited. This is due to the fact that the export of military goods is only a small part of Norwegian exports and reductions of international military demand for other goods important in Norwegian exports, e.g. aluminium, is to a considerable degree compensated by increased demand for development purposes.

Local Effects of Conversion

So far we have only reported national effects of conversion. These effects can be disaggregated in several different ways. One may look at the effects by region or by industry. Or one may look at the situation for particular factories or military bases. Military employment varies by region from 1.6 % in the South and Southwest to 9.1 % in Northern Norway.(26) If the proportion between direct and indirect military employment was the same at the regional level as at the national level, complete disarmament without countermeasures would lead to a reduction in employment of 17 % in this region. However, this figure represents an upper limit, since "import leakage" is much higher in Northern Norway than in the rest of the country. Therefore a larger part of the indirect effects of military employment occurs outside the region. 17 % is an unacceptably high figure. For some municipalities, the figures are even higher. For instance, Andreassen, although he does give figures for the total military employment, reports that in 1969 18 % of the local taxes in Porsanger municipality in Finnmark (population 3,861 in 1970) were paid by personnel of the armed forces. He also estimates that in the two municipalities of Bardu and Målselv in Troms (population 3,896 and 7,937) close to 40 % of the retail trade is due to demand from military personnel.(27) Even municipalities in Southern Norway may experience considerable conversion problems. The percentage of military production in two large publicly owned munition factories, Kongsberg Våpenfabrikk and Raufoss Ammunisjonsfabrikker, hovers around 50 % and their production plants are concentrated in a small number of locations.(28) In Raufoss, for instance, the total employment of RA in 1970 was 2,483 and the military share can be estimated to 1,018. This is 19 % of total employment in that municipality.(29)

A more detailed investigation of such local effects of conversion will be undertaken later by the present writers.

12.5. CONCLUSIONS AND RECOMMENDATIONS

The aim of this study is to analyze the effects of converting national economic resources from armaments to development aid. The general background to such an analysis may vary, from a purely unilateral study of conversion of resources within the national economy to a world-wide programme of dis-armament and development.

For a rich country with 3 % of its resources devoted to military purposes, a shift in the composition of demand away from armaments may be analyzed as a marginal change in the economy which does not upset the economic structure or the functioning of the economy at large. The impact for particular industries and smaller regional areas may be considerable; but the overall extent of the problem strongly suggests that from a macro-economic viewpoint a smooth transition is perfectly possible, if appropriate measures are taken to maintain external and internal balance in the economy. The adjustment required is, of course, of a different order of magnitude than that involved in conversion from a war economy to a peace economy or vice versa. For example, Britain spent about 60 % of its GNP on the war effort during World War II and in the US the percentage reached 40.(30)

The suggestion that relatively minor adjustment involved in conversion can be undertaken without major problems has been supported by several empirical studies in the 1960s and 1970s, including the earlier studies of Norway by Bjerkholt and Andreassen. This study confirms the earlier findings for Norway. Norwegian experience in the immediate postwar period after 1945 also supports this condusion. In response to a large and abrupt increase in the labour supply the level of employment increased sharply and the unemployment rate in 1947-1950 was lower than ever before or after. It was widely belived at the time that large-scale unemployment due to shortages and the need for reallocations was inevitable.(31)

Our preliminary work on the World Model also indicates that the conclusion will remain the same if the effects for Norway of global disarmament are taken into account. But the earlier studies did not couple disarmament with increased transfers to developing countries. In Bjerkholt's study, which in many ways has been a model for ours, the author was free to devise a set of countermeasures which would reduce the problems of transition to complete disarmament. In this study we have imposed the additional restraint that at least a significant portion of the released resources should be made available for increased transfers. From a domestic economic point of view this is clearly a less advantageous starting-point. Our analysis of the Norwegian development aid programme in section 12.3 shows that 63 % of the aid in 1978 consisted of financial transfers. Since Norway is a small part of the world economy, increased financial transfers from Norway alone are unlikely to have any significant feed-back effect in the Norwegian economy. Therefore, expansion of Norway's aid programme with the current profile is strictly a burden from a domestic economic point of view: it adds little to the national product, provides practically no employment, and makes a negative contribution to the balance of payments.

In an economy with moderately high growth, scarcity of labour, and a surplus in the balance of payments an increase in development aid is a small sacrifice. Norway is expected to be in this situation in the 1980s due to the large North Sea petroleum reserves. The balance of payment effects, which in many countries would be a serious obstacle to conversion from armaments to financial transfers, therefore provide less cause for worry in Norway. The main obstacle in Norway to quick and comprehensive conversion is the problem of reallocation of capital and labour over industries and regions in an economy with high capacity utilization rates and a tight labour market.

From this study four strategies emerge for dealing with any negative effects of the extreme case of pure conversion to financial transfers within one year:

1. Disarm less (change of disarmament scenario)

2. Disarm more slowly (extended conversion)

3. Select a type of development aid which in itself counteracts some of the transition problems (change of transfer scenario)

4. Use some of the resources for domestic programmes which counter-act some of the negative effects of conversion, particularly unemployment (conversion with countermeasures).

Our study provides data which can shed some light on all of these four strategies. Table 12.12 takes as a baseline the "extreme case" of complete disarmament and pure conversion to financial transfers. This is the worst case from the point of view of the domestic economic

Table 12.12   Strategies to Decrease the Negative Effects of Conversion

Strategy	Effect in 1978 on				Conversion ratio (%)	Type of transfer
	Employment (%)	GDP (%)	Imports (%)	Balance of payments (% of GDP)		
0 Extreme case (Complete disarmament, pure conversion, financial transfers) (Scenario A 3 in one year)	-5.6	-3.8	-3.1	-2.0	100	Financial
1 Less disarmament (Scenario A 3 in one year)	-0.8	-0.6	-0.5	-0.3	15	Financial
2 Extended conversion first year (Scenario A 3 in 12 years)	-0.4	-0.3	-0.2	-0.2	8	Financial
3 "Best" transfer model (Scenario D 3 in one year)	-1.8	-0.8	+1.2	-0.4	100	Commodity
4 Countermeasures (Scenario A 3 in one year with countermeasures)	0	-0.1	-0.1	-0.0	23	Financial

Source: Tables 4.2 - 4.5, 4.12 - 4.14 and Tables B.1 - B.9 in Bjerkholt et al. (1980).

Note that a negative figure means a negative impact in columns 1, 2 and 4, but a positive impact in column 3.

The conversion ratio is the proportion of military consumption converted to transfers to developing countries in 1978, i.e it si not identical to the "conversion index" reported in Tables 12.9 - 12.11.

transition problems. Table 12.12 further contains examples of results for the four strategies to counteract the transition problems. Strategy 1 is illustrated by the most modest disarmament model - the Expert group alternative. For Strategy 2 we have selected the effects for the first year of extended conversion (complete disarmament in 1990). To illustrate Strategy 3 we have selected the commodity transfer scenario which gives the most advantageous effect on the four indicators. And finally Strategy 4 is exemplified by the case of conversion with counter-measures, i.e. social home-help services. The table shows some effects of the extreme case that are probably politically unacceptable - at least the 5.6 % reduction in employment. At the same time, any one of the four strategies 1 - 4 will significantly reduce the problems. As the two final columns of the Table indicate, this can happen either at the cost of reducing the conversion ratio, thereby making less available for increased transfers (strategies 1, 2, and 4) or by changing the form of transfers to a variety of tied aid (a commodity transfer).

Both of these have disadvantages, and the relative weight of the disadvantages will be evaluated differently by different people. Our own preference would be to retain the principle that most if not all of the aid should be given on an untied basis, i.e. as financial transfers.(32) But Table 12.12 should give the reader a better basis on which to form his or her own choice.

How significant is the conclusion that the economic problems involved in conversion can be mastered? Is it not obvious, even trivial? So it may seem, particularly since it reiterates the conclusion of a number of previous studies.

There are two answers to this objection. One is that this study differs from the previous studies in Norway in emphasizing conversion rather than merely disarmament plus an arbitrary set of counter-measures. In fact, Bjerkholt (1965) took pains to point out that disarmament did not simply release a sum of money which one was free to spend on e.g. increased development aid, or a tax reduction: the crucial point was to channel the released resources into other activities.(33) This study shows, however, that it is possible to release a large increased financial transfer to developing countries, provided some appropriate counter-measures are put into effect at the same time.

Another reason why the results are not trivial is that one frequently finds expression of the idea that the military sector contributes in important ways to overall employment, regional balance, etc. Bjerkholt (op.cit.) pointed out that this notion had little relevance to Norwegian conditions, particularly since Norway did not have a large specialized production capacity for sophisticated weapons systems.(34) However, since his study, Norwegian official policy has placed increased emphasis on securing employment from major weapons purchases. The high-point in this endeavour is the decision in 1975 to purchase 72 F-16 aircraft. An important consideration in the selection of F-16 over its two most serious contenders was the nature of the compensation agreement offered to Norway by the US. In return for the purchase of the aircraft, Norway was offered a share of the production of the F-16 planes which was calculated to amount to 4 - 5,000 person-years of employment. If the main point of the F-16 purchase had been to generate employment in Norway, it would have been an expensive strategy: each budgeted person-year of employment cost Norway N.kr. 750,000 (1975 prices). More realistically one can take as the cost of generating this employment the Defence Ministry's own estimate of the price <u>increase</u> due to the co-production arrangement, i.e as a result of a loss of economies of scale. This figure is N.kr. mill 403.(35) An increase in public spending generally corresponding to this price increase would have generated about 5,600 person-years of employment, exceeding the Ministry's estimate of the employment effect of the F-16 co-production arrangement by 12-40 %. In actual effect, the estimated employment effect of the compensation agreement was probably optimistic. This is not to say that co-production arrangements cannot be justified in other terms, such as gaining experience in high-technology programmes. In the long run such spin-offs can have positive effects on employment. But the F-16 case can hardly be justified on the basis of the estimated direct employment effects alone.

<u>Wallensteen</u> and <u>Frensborg</u> (1980) in a study of the Swedish arms industry have argued that there have been <u>two</u> conversion processes from their starting point in the early 1930s: first a process of tooling up for the production of war material and then a process of retooling for civilian production.(36) Similarly we may say that there are two parallel forms of conversion planning: disarmament planners plan conversion from war production, while defence planners plan how a country can get the maximum out of its defence purchases in terms of domestic production and employment. These two forms of planning are not in direct contradiction, since the disarmers plan for a contingency which is not yet here (and may never arrive), while the defence planners plan for the present situation. Yet, the two forms of conversion planning are in opposition to each other: success in the latter makes contingency planning for the first more difficult.

In our view, even if disarmament is unlikely, planning for it is not unimportant. First, the consequences of a run-away arms race are grim. In this sense conversion is like war or occupation a low-probability event with important consequences. Conversion planning, then, has one vital similarity with defence planning: although the contingency one plans for may never occur, the consequences of low preparedness may be serious. The major difference between conversion planning and planning for war is as obvious as this similarity: conversion, unlike war, is a <u>desirable</u> contingency.

Secondly, an opportunity for conversion may not arrive slowly or gradually. It may present itself as a historic opportunity to take advantage of a favourable international climate. As Norway's former

Foreign Minister Knut Frydenlund has argued in connection with conversion: "...the basic problem is political in nature. We should see to it, however, that we possess the means to follow up any political breakthrough in this field".(37) Thus - to continue the military metaphor - countries should keep their powder dry for conversion. This should include further study of the problem, particularly at the industry and local level. Such study is necessary in order to allay possible fears that conversion may be disastrous to certain local communities. We say "allay fears" because our working hypothesis is that such regional problems can be overcome, given adequate planning and sufficient ingenuity. We have indicated that there may be serious problems in Northern Norway following conversion, even though we have been unable at this stage to determine the exact size of the problem. And if conversion planning has not been adequate, or the results have not been communicated to those who fear for their livelihood, conversion many be resisted. To may of those personally affected by conversion, the losses from conversion are more obvious and visible than the gains. A job actually generated by military demand is here now; the job that may be generated by increased commodity transfers to developing countries, by increased social home-help services, or by some other counter-measures, is in the future and therefore not perceived in the same concrete terms. Besides, those who stand to lose from conversion are likely to be contiguous, geographically or by industry, while those who gain are apart and unorganized. Hence a negative pressure-group has a starting lead on a positive one.

In addition to sponsoring further research the authorities might give higher priority to conversion planning. This could be done in a number of ways: One would be to draw up limits for each industry or each region as to its "defence dependency", i.e. the fraction of its production (or exports) which derives from war material. In the case of Norway, imposing such limits might be particularly relevant in certain communities in Northern Norway and in a few major government-owned factories with a concentration on defence production. Another would be to strengthen the disarmament planning function within the national bureaucracy. A small organizational nucleus exists in the Foreign Ministry, in the form of the secretariat of the Norwegian Government's Advisory Committee for Arms Control and Disarmament, the Division for policy planning and research, and the position of Special Adviser for Disarmament (currently merged with the position as Director-General of the Planning Division). But this represents only a very modest beginning. Strengthening the bureaucracy for disarmament and conversion planning would enable it to undertake or commission studies of the conversion potential of various arms procurement decisions and contracts for arms exports, somewhat along the lines of the US Arms Control and Disarmament Agency's Arms control impact statements. The introduction of such impact statements is currently under discussion in Norway. If introduced, they should definitely include consideration of the impact on conversion.

In developing alternative defence models, the conversion potential of these models should be taken into account. It is characteristic of the low status currently accorded to conversion planning that in the report of the Defence Commission of 1974 (majority as well as minority position), as well as the Report to the Storting from the Ministry of Defence based on the defence commission report, no consideration is given to conversion. This is not to say that the commission would have been opposed to conversion, not to mention the mere study of it. But the very fact that the issue is not mentioned at all in the report indicates that the idea does not have great priority. In the future conversion planning should be included in the process of defence planning.

NOTES AND REFERENCES

* This article is in large part a summary of a longer report prepared for the Norwegian Government's Advisory Committee on Arms Control and Disarmament (Utvalget for Rustningskontroll og Nedrustning) as part of the reserch programme on disarmament and development initiated by the United Nations (Olav Bjerkholt, Ådne Cappelen, Nils Petter Gleditsch and Knut Moum, Disarmament and Development: A Study of Conversion in Norway. PRIO, Oslo 1980, PRIO publication S-7/80). However, it also includes some material from later phases of the project, which will be reported in later reports by the same authors. The project expenses have been covered by a grant from the Committee, and the work has been carried out as a project of the International Peace Research Institute, Oslo (PRIO). The authors are employees of the Norwegian Central Bureau of Statistics (Bjerkholt, Cappelen), PRIO (Gleditsch) and the Institute of Economics at the University of Oslo (Moum). For detailed credits to the numerous assistants and colleagues who have contributed in various ways, the reader is referred to the preface of the first report. In addition, Magne Barth provided research assistance for this article, which can be identified as PRIO publication S-21/81.

1. Economic and Social Consequences of Disarmament. United Nations, New York 1962. Sales No. 62.IX, p. 51. Relevant UN reports are also Economic and Social Consequences of the Arms Race and of Military Expenditures. United Nations, New York 1972, Sales No. E. 72.IX.16, Disarmament and Development. United Nations, New York 1972, Sales No. E.73.IX.1., Report of the Ad Hoc Group on the Relationship between Disarmament and Development. United Nations, New York 1977, UN Document A/S-10/9 and Economic and Social Consequences of the Armament Race and Its Extremely Harmful Effects on World Peace and Security. Report of the Secretary General. United Nations, New York 1977. UN General Assembly, report No. A/32/88Add, September 12, 1977. For reviews of other literature, see Review of Research Trends and an Annotated Bibliography: Social and Economic Consequences of the Arms Race and Disarmament, Reports and papers in the social sciences, No. 39, UNESCO, Paris 1978 and

Manne Wängborg, Disarmament and Development: A Guide to Literature Relevant to the Nordic Proposal, Stockholm 1979, no publ., (also distributed as Swedish Working Paper on Available Literature Relevant to the UN Study on Disarmament and Development, with a 567 pp "draft bibliography" as an Appendix) and Manne Wängborg, The Use of Resources for Military Purposes: a Bibliographical Starting-Point, Bulletin of Peace Proposals, Vol. 10, No. 3, 1979, pp. 319-331.

2. For details, see Report of the Ad Hoc..., United Nations, op. cit. 1977, pp. 5-10.

3. For an overview of the projects and a list of the final reports, see Bo Hovstadius and Manne Wängborg, The United Nations Study of Disarmament and Development: an Overview, Journal of Peace Research, Vol. 18, No. 2, 1981, pp. 209-217. For the conclusions of the Expert Group, see Study on the Relationship between Disarmament and Development. Report of the Secretary-General. United Nations, General Assembly A/36/356, 5 October 1981, New York.

4. The term conversion is frequently used to describe the process whereby a person, a firm, or an industry retools from swords to plowshares. Our own analysis is confined to examining economic effects at the macro-level, rather than at the micro-level. In our usage conversion means retooling the economic structure of the country as a whole. But we have no objection to readers mentally replacing conversion by reallocation.

5. Olav Bjerkholt, Økonomiske konsekvenser av nedrustning i Norge (Economic consequences of disarmament in Norway), Tidsskrift for samfunnsforskning, Vol. 6, No. 4, 1965, pp. 249-67 (PRIO publication 12-2) and Olav Bjerkholt, An Analysis of the Economic Consequences of Disarmament in Norway, in Disarmament and World Economic Interdependence, ed. by Emile Benoit, Oslo 1967 (PRIO publication 12-1).

6. Tormod Andreassen, Forsvarets virkninger på norsk økonomi (The impact of the defence on the Norwegian economy), Samfunnsøkonomiske studier, No. 22, Central Bureau of Statistics, Oslo 1972.

7. Defence Budget, 1978, p. 9. This figure differs a little from that used elsewhere in Bjerkholt et al., op. cit. 1980. For an explanation see Appendix A to that report.

8. Johan Jørgen Holst, Vår forsvarspolitikk. Vunderinger og utsyn (Our defence policy. Evaluation and Overview), Oslo 1978, p. 95.

9. This was also the policy of the Labour government which left office in October 1981. The new Conservative government is

committed to a 4 % real increase over the next few years.

10. MOdel of a DISaggregated type. Bjerkholt's and Andreassen's studies used earlier versions of MODIS.

11. Report to the Storting, No. 94 (1974/75), p. 20. A good secondary source of policy statements is Olav Stokke, Norsk Utviklingsbistand (Norwegian development assistance). Nordiska Afrikainstitutet, Oslo/Uppsala 1975.

12. Cf. Table 3.1 in Bjerkholt et al., op. cit. 1980.

13. A justification for this assumption is given in Bjerkholt et al., op. cit. 1980, p. 49.

14. The reasons for discarding them are given in Bjerkholt et al., op. cit. 1980, p. 50.

15. Based on personal communication from Jon Strand of the Institute of Economics, University of Oslo. Cf. also Jon Strand, Virkninger av utviklingshjelpen på norsk økonomi (Effects of development aid on the Norwegian economy), Sosialøkonomen, Vol. 34, No. 1, 1980, pp. 13-19.

16. Ibid.

17. Bjerkholt et al., op. cit. 1980, p. 57.

18. Corresponding tables for absolute effects can be found in Appendix B of Bjerkholt et al., op. cit. 1980.

19. Ibid.

20. Details of the costs and labour intensiveness of this programme are reported in Bjerkholt et al., op. cit. 1980, p. 80, but are omitted here.

21. We could have performed these computations instead under the restraint that GDP, balance of payments, or imports were to remain unchanged under conversion. Our choice of employment reflects our view that a potential negative effect on employment is the politically most sensitive issue in conversion.

22. Wassily Leontief et al., The Future of the World Economy. A United Nations Study. New York 1977.

23. Olav Bjerkholt and Svein Longva, MODIS IV - A Model for Economic Analysis and National Planning, Samfunnsøkonomiske studier, No. 43, 1980, Central Bureau of Statistics, Oslo.

24. Wassily Leontief et al., Preliminary Study of World-Wide Eco-

nomic and Social Implications of a Limitation on Military Spending (An Input-Output Approach). New York University, Department of Economics, Center for Applied Economics 1978.

25. Wassily Leontief and Faye Duchin, Worldwide Economic Implication of a Limitation on Military Spending. Institute for Economic Analysis, New York University for Center for Disarmament, United Nations 1980 and Wassily Leontief and Faye Duchin, Worldwide Implications of Hypothetical Changes in Military Spending (an Input-Output Approach). Institute for Economic Analysis, New York University for US Arms Control and Disarmament Agency, 1980.

26. Bjerkholt et al., op.cit. 1980, p. 22.

27. Andreassen, op. cit. 1972, p. 124 and 110.

28. For more detailed figures, see Magne Barth, Military Integration between Norway and the Federal Republic of Germany 1955-1981. Oslo, PRIO 1981 (PRIO publication S-18/81).

29. Employment at RA from Report to the Storting no 16 (1970-71). The estimate for the military share assumes equal productivity in civilian and military production. Population figures from the 1970 census (Folke- och boligtelling I. November 1970, 0529, Vestre Toten).

30. Laurence Martin, The Management of Defense. New York 1976, p. 72.

31. Central Bureau of Statistics, Norges Økonomi etter krigen (The Norwegian post-war economy), SØS, No. 12, Oslo 1963, pp. 91-94.

32. That aid be given as financial transfers is a necessary, but not sufficient condition for its being untied. In fact, all Norwegian bilateral aid is politically tied in the sense that countries with development-oriented policies are given priority. Nevertheless, the high proportion of multilateral aid ensures that Norwegian aid remains largely untied.

33. Bjerkholt, op. cit. 1965.

34. Ibid.

35. Report to the Storting, No. 18 (1976-77, p. 9.

36. Peter Wallensteen and Olof Frensborg, New Wine and Old Bottles. Product versus Organization: Swedish Experiences in Changing From Military to Civilian Production. Report prepared for the UN Group of Governmental Experts. Department for Peace and Conflict Research, Uppsala University 1980.

37. Opening address by Mr. Knut Frydenlund, Norwegian Minister of Foreign Affairs, at the International Conference on Disarmament and Development, Sandefjord, Norway, May 6, 1980. <u>The Sandefjord Report on Disarmament and Development</u>. The Norwegian Ministry of Foreign Affairs and The Norwegian Committee for Arms Control and Disarmament, Flekkefjord 1980, p. 28.

Chapter Thirteen

CONVENTIONAL DISARMAMENT - A LEGAL FRAMEWORK AND SOME PERSPECTIVES

Allan Rosas

13.1. INTRODUCTION

Originally this paper was envisaged to deal exclusively with the legal aspects of the international transfer of conventional weapons. In view of the scarcity of international legal norms in force regulating arms transfers, a certain broadening of the subject was thought desirable. We purport to set out a legal framework for conventional disarmament and arms control (hereafter referred to as conventional disarmament) in general, also taking into account questions relating to the production, possession, stationing and use of conventional weapons. This approach seems all the more pertinent as there is a particular link between these different aspects of conventional disarmament. There is a certain emphasis in the paper on limitations with respect to weapons, but some attention is also paid to the question of the reduction and regulation of armed forces.

The framework we are presenting is termed a legal one as we approach the subject as it were with a lawyer's mind, paying attention to the distinction between the binding and the non-binding and to such traditional branches of international law as the law of neutrality and the law on methods and means of warfare. This does not mean, on the other hand, that we limit ourselves to a description of international law in force. Non-binding arrangements, proposals made in disarmament negotiations, etc. are also considered to a certain extent. As the paper is preoccupied with international legal norms and arrangements, national legislation, e.g. on arms transfers, will only be considered in passing. The paper has no theoretical ambitions. This delimitation, coupled with the broad sphere of subjects considered, implies that the paper, at best, can provide a general survey rather than an analysis proper of specific problems. In conclusion, however, some sketchy notes and reflections will be offered on the present political perspectives for conventional disarmament.

13.2. A GENERAL CLASSIFICATION

Without attempting to give a clear-cut definition of the concepts of conventional weapons and conventional armament it should be noted that the paper is based on the traditional dichotomy between weapons of mass destruction (mainly ABC-weapons) and conventional weapons. The concept of "new weapons of mass destruction" illustrates the difficulties in making sharp distinctions.

Like nuclear disarmament, conventional disarmament consists of several components, which may be treated independently in disarmament negotiations but which are bound to affect each other. Looking at the matter from the viewpoint of a given state faced with conventional armament/disarmament, and assuming that weapons rather than troops are involved, one can distinguish between at least the following phases:

- Planning, research and development. Here we have in mind activities preceding the actual production (or import) of weapons.
- Production. A state manufactures weapons for its own use or for export.
- International transfer. Weapons and weapons technology are passed into the possession of another state. This question may, of course, be approached from the viewpoint of either the supplier or the recipient.
- Possession and stockpiling. Weapons are in the immediate control of a state whether it has manufactured them itself or has acquired them from another state.
- Stationing. Here one can distinguish between the case of weapons being stationed by one state on the territory of another and the case of weapons being stationed by a state on some particular area of its own territory.
- Employment. Here we have in mind both testing and other uses of weapons in peacetime and the use of weapons in armed conflicts. The question of testing may, of course, also be approached in the context of planning, research and development.

These components may, of course, intertwine and be present in one and the same disarmament treaty. Yet the following survey will on the whole be structured in accordance with the above classification.

As far as armed forces are concerned, a corresponding classification is imaginable. From a disarmament angle, however, the question seems to reduce to the following aspects:

- Formation and possession of armed forces (their size and composition).
- Stationing of armed forces either on the territory of another state (e.g. military bases) or on a particular area of a state's own territory.
- Employment of armed forces either in peacetime (e.g.

military manoeuvres) or in armed conflicts.

As is demonstrated by the Vienna talks on the mutual reduction of forces and armaments and associated measures in Central Europe, a given negotiation process may cover not only these components but also arrangements related to specific weapons. In the example given, even nuclear weapons have been touched upon in the talks.

An example par excellence of a disarmament measure which may affect both weapons and troops, and both conventional and nuclear weapons, is offered by the reduction of military budgets. This question will be ignored in the following survey, despite its obvious relevance.

13.3. PLANNING, RESEARCH AND DEVELOPMENT

While there is no general convention prohibiting planning and research as such with respect to some specific weapon, the development of a weapon would presumably be prohibited on the basis of a prohibition on its production. The 1972 Convention on biological weapons expressly prohibits the development of such weapons (art. 1). There is no comparable convention concerning a conventional weapon.

There is now, however, a little known rule of international law imposing certain restraints on states in the study and development of new weapons or other means or methods of warfare. In the 1977 Protocol Additional to the Geneva Convention of 12 August 1949, and Relating to the Protection of Victims of International Armed Conflicts (hereafter referred to as Protocol I of 1977) the following provision has been included:

> Article 36 - New weapons
> In the study, development, acquisition or adoption of a new weapon, means or method of warfare, a High Contracting Party is under an obligation to determine whether its employment would, in some or all circumstances, be prohibited by this Protocol or by any other rule of international law applicable to the High Contracting Party.

This provision is a novelty in international humanitarian law applicable in armed conflicts.(1) It highlights the link which exists between the use of weapons in war on the one hand and their development and acquisition on the other.

The provision, as such, does not hinder a state from studying and developing weapons whose use is prohibited or restricted. The obligation "to determine" whether their employment would be illegal is perhaps not a very strong one. However, the provision might provide some restraint on the development, production and acquisition of certain dubious types of weapons in that it reminds national decision-makers and arms producers of possible legal limitations on the use of a weapon in the situations it has been designed for. This would seem to presuppose that some national body, including experts on disarmament and international humanitarian law, be entrusted with the task of assessing new weapons and methods of warfare in accordance with the article.(2)

13.4. PRODUCTION

While the production of nuclear weapons (in regard to non-nuclear states) and biological weapons is prohibited under the Non-Proliferation Treaty and the 1972 Convention on biological weapons respectively, there is no similar convention in force banning the production of a particular conventional weapon. Nor is there any global convention providing for quantitative ceilings on the production of conventional weapon systems.

The history of disarmament contains several serious efforts to curb the arms race with regard to weapons which today are termed conventional. The Covenant of the League of Nations contained rather far-reaching provisions (as compared to the UN Charter) on disarmament, stating, inter alia, that the members of the League "recognise that the maintenance of peace requires the reduction of national armaments to the lowest point consistent with national safety and with the enforcement by common action of international obligations" (article 8, paragraph 1).

The most notable achievements of this period were the Washington and London Naval Treaties of 1922 and 1930, respectively, which were in force until 1936. The treaties contained, inter alia, ceilings on the tonnage of war-ships. These limitations also affected the construction of ships by the five naval powers which were party to the treaties.(3) Proposals made at these and other conferences to outlaw certain specific weapons such as the submarine did not materialize.(4) The fate of the General Disarmament Conference convening in 1932 is well known.

Nor did the work of the UN Commission on Conventional Armaments (established in 1947) or the Disarmament Commission (1952) produce any concrete results with respect to the reduction of armaments. During the ensuing period of nuclear arms control even proposals for the outlawing of some conventional weapon-types have been rare. One example is provided by resolutions 2932 A (XXVII), 3076 (XXVIII) and 3255 (XXIX), adopted by the UN General Assembly in 1972-74, where reference is made not only to the prohibition of the use of certain cruel or indiscriminate weapons, in particular incendiary weapons, but also to the possibility of prohibiting their production and stockpiling. In resolution 3255 (XXIX) the General Assembly urged all states "to refrain from the production, stockpiling, proliferation and use" of napalm and other incendiary weapons. Since then, the emphasis has been merely on the question of the use of cruel or indiscriminate weapons in war (see below, 8.3.).

The above considerations have concerned limitations of a global character, not restraints imposed upon a particular state, e.g., in connection with peace settlements. The partial demilitarization of Germany after the First and Second World Wars is here a case in point.(5) Another example is provided by the 1947 Peace Treaty with Finland, which imposes certain limitations on the military strength of Finland. The Treaty, inter alia, prohibits the production, possession and testing of atomic weapons, offensive missiles, certain anti-ship mines and torpedos, submarines and torpedo-boats (article 17). The Treaty prohibits Finland from manufacturing war material and from maintaining capacity to manufacture war material in excess of what is required for internal purposes and for the defence of borders (article 18).

13.5. INTERNATIONAL TRANSFER

While the transfer of nuclear and biological weapons has been prohibited since 1968 and 1972 respectively, there again exists no general convention prohibiting the transfer of particular conventional weapons or regulating arms transfers in peacetime. Such conventions have existed in the past, however. Moreover, international law in force contains certain provisions which cannot be disregarded in a discussion on the legal aspects of arms transfers.

Historical Considerations

First of all the international transfer of weapons has been restricted by the law of neutrality, applicable in time of war. During the nineteenth century the principle became established that neutral states were exempted from providing direct military assistance to the belligerents. On the other hand a neutral power was not required to prevent individuals from exporting arms. Possible restrictions in this regard imposed by the neutral power were to be applied impartially to both belligerents. These principles were codified, above all, in the Hague Conventions of 1907, which are still formally in force (see further below).

The first multilateral convention to deal with the international transfer of weapons in peacetime was the Brussels Act of 1890, restricting the arms trade to Africa. The Brussels Conference of 1889-1890 was attended by 17 states. The Act adopted by the Conference, inter alia, prohibited (with certain exceptions) the import of arms and ammunitions to a zone comprising the central parts of Africa. The purpose of the convention was to combat the slave trade, to reduce bloodshed in African conflicts and last, but not least, to further the colonization of Africa.(6) The Act clearly had some moderating impact on the import of arms to Africa around 1890-1910.(7)

The question of the international trade in arms received attention at a more general level in the Covenant of the League of Nations. According to article 23 (d), the members of the League entrusted the organization with "the general supervision of the trade in arms and ammunition with the countries in which the control of this traffic is necessary in the common interest". The ideological affinity with the Brussels Act was more openly expressed in article 22, paragraph 5 on so-called B-mandate territories ("other peoples, especially those of Central Africa"), which should be administered subject, e.g., to the prohibition of abuses "such as the slave trade, the arms traffic and the liquor traffic..."

An effort to supplement and broaden the Brussels Act of 1890 and to give concrete substance to the principles of the Covenant was made by the Convention of Saint-Germain of 1919, signed by 23 states. The geographical zone affected by a prohibition on the export of arms was extended to include most parts of Africa and the Middle East and even what afterwards became the Georgian, Azerbaijan and Armenian Soviet Socialist Republics. Mainly due to the refusal by the United States to ratify the convention it was not ratified by the main suppliers and thus did not materialize.(8)

In order to revise the abortive convention of Saint-Germain, a conference for the supervision of the international trade in arms, munitions and implements of war was convened in Geneva in 1925 and attended by 44 states. The convention adopted by the conference contained not only a prohibition (with exceptions) on the export of arms to a specific zone (which was smaller in scope than the zone adopted at the Saint-Germain convention), but also an obligation to publish statistics on the arms trade. Certain categories of weapons could only be exported and imported by governments or under government licence. This convention, however, also failed to attract a sufficient number of ratifications,(9) although the Geneva Protocol outlawing chemical and bacteriological warfare, adopted by the same conference, entered into force, and is still valid today. An American proposal to prohibit the transfer of such weapons was not accepted.(10)

Even before the Geneva Conference of 1925 the League of Nations Secretariat, in 1924, started the publication of a statistical yearbook on the trade in arms, munitions and implements of war. The last volume appeared in 1938.(11)

Following the unratified treaties of Saint-Germain and Geneva, no concrete results were obtained. The question of the trade in arms was increasingly viewed as an integral part of disarmament in general. Proposals for curbing the arms trade were presented to the General Disarmament Conference, convening in 1932. The failure of the Conference as a whole determined their fate..(12)

Different Types of Restraints

One basic dimension in controlling arms transfers relates to the dichotomy between war and peace. The following discussion concerns arrangements which are primarily designed for peacetime purposes, whereas the question of neutrality in time of armed conflict is treated separately (5.7.). The arrangements applicable in peacetime may, of course, be so designed that they retain their validity in time of armed conflict as well.

One set of variables relates to the question of the number of <u>actors</u> involved, i.e. whether arrangements are initiated on a global, regional, bilateral or unilateral level.(13) This question does not necessarily coincide with the <u>territorial scope</u> of restraints agreed upon. For instance, an agreement between a considerable number of states may apply only to the transfer of weapons to one particular state.

If the arrangements are initiated on a global level (e.g., in a UN context) they presumably involve both suppliers and recipients. If not, one can envisage arrangements initiated by <u>suppliers</u> and those initiated by <u>recipients</u>, as well as arrangements involving both type of actors. Moreover, arrangements can affect either the <u>export</u> or the <u>import</u> of weapons, or both types of activities.

As regards the more precise content of arrangements, there is a large scale ranging from a total prohibition of arms transfers to modest regulations involving, e.g., measures of registration and publicity. A rough distinction can here be made between <u>reductions</u>, <u>restraints</u> and <u>regulations</u>.(14) Other variables to be taken into account are, e.g., the types and quantities of <u>weapons</u> affected by an arrangement. And finally, the arrangements may be <u>binding</u> under international law or they may be <u>nonbinding</u> recommendations or agreements.

Considering this variety of variables it seems preferable to proceed on the basis of the territorial scope of limitations, starting with arrangements which are global or near-global in application.

Arrangements of Global Application

One example of a global arrangement is provided by the above-mentioned unratified Geneva Convention of 1925. The references to the arms trade in the Covenant of the League of Nations may also be mentioned in this context. The UN Charter contains no comparable provision. No treaty or other formal agreement of global application has, of course, been concluded since 1945.

Suggestions for studying the possibilities of such agreements have been put forward from time to time in the UN and elsewhere. In 1965 and 1968 the question of registration of arms transfers was approached in draft resolutions put forward in the General Assembly by Malta and

Denmark, respectively. In 1976 and 1977 Japan attempted to take up the question of arms transfers in the General Assembly. These initiatives did not even lead to the adoption of non-binding resolutions.(15) But in 1978 the following passage on arms transfers was included in the Final Document of the special session devoted to disarmament:(16)

> 85. Consultation should be carried out among major arms supplier and recipient countries on the limitation of all types of international transfer of conventional weapons, based in particular on the principle of undiminished security of the parties with a view to promoting or enhancing stability at a lower military level, taking into account the need of all states to protect their security as well as the inalienable right to self-determination and independence of peoples under colonial or foreign domination and the obligations of States to respect that right, in accordance with the Charter of the United Nations and the Declaration on Principles of International Law concerning Friendly Relations and Co-operation among States.

This passage is followed by a reference to the 1979-1980 UN Conference on certain inhumane and indiscriminate weapons (see Chapter 13.8.) and a request that the results of this Conference (dealing with the question of use of weapons in war) "should be considered by all States, especially producer States, in regard to the question of the transfer of such weapons to other States" (paragraph 88).

In 1977 the United States and the Soviet Union initiated a series of preliminary bilateral talks on conventional arms transfers. One possibility considered was to set up certain guidelines (a "code of conduct") for transfers to Third World countries in general and/or specific regions or countries in particular. A source of inspiration was provided by the unilateral restraints proclaimed by the Carter administration in 1977 (repealed by the Reagan administration in July 1981), involving, *inter alia*, a proclamation that the United States would not be the first supplier to introduce into a region newly-developed advanced weapons which would create a new or significantly higher combat capability, that the United States would not permit the development of advanced weapons solely for export and that the United States would not allow U.S. weapons or equipment to be transferred to third countries without U.S. consent.(17) The so-called CAT talks between the United States and the Soviet Union have not been resumed since December 1978, however.(18)

On the other hand it would seem that certain informal understandings involving particular restraints on arms transfers have existed from time to time between these two major suppliers or between them and other suppliers.(19) From a theoretical viewpoint one cannot rule out the possibility of such agreements, too, being binding under international law.(20)

As to unilateral restraints, all major suppliers, of course, have some national legislation and policy guidelines affecting the export of arms.(21) Apart from the fact that the border line between unilateral restraints and informal agreements may be fuzzy, unilateral restraints do not normally enter the realm of international law and are not further considered in this report. It should be pointed out, however, that unilateral declarations may also in some circumstances be binding under international law.(22) This presupposes some articulation of a rule as a norm intended for international application.

Taking into account the role played by the transnational corporations in the transfer of weapons and weapons technology, there would be some point in including certain rules on arms transfers in the codes of conduct being developed for these corporations. Such ideas appear to have existed but they are not reflected in the drafts which have been considered.(23)

Arrangements of Regional Application

Some of the above arrangements and proposed arrangements have both global and regional implications. Some agreements and declarations, however, have been specifically designed for certain regions or other groups of states.

One example is provided by the Tripartite Declaration on the Middle East signed in 1950 by Great Britain, France and the United States. In the declaration these supplier states pledged to send to Israel and the Arab states only such arms as they needed for their internal security, legitimate self-defence and "the defence of the area as a whole". The recipients were not to commit aggression against other states of the region. The suppliers held regular consultations about arms deliveries to the region. The declaration was not scrupulously honoured by the signatories and suffered a major setback in 1955 when the Soviet Union, which was not a signatory, became a major supplier to the region. The declaration ceased to have any validity during autumn 1956, in connection with the Suez conflict.(24)

Whereas the Middle East declaration was initiated by suppliers, the by now famous Declaration of Ayacucho, signed by eight Latin American countries in December 1974, provides an example of recipient-initiated restraints of a regional character. In this statement the representatives (including some Heads of State and Government) of Peru (the host country), Argentina, Bolivia, Chile, Colombia, Ecuador, Panama and Venezuela declared their commitment to a number of policy principles of relevance for Latin America. One passage reads:(25)

> We undertake to promote and support the building of a lasting order of international peace and co-operation and to create the conditions which will make possible the effective limitation of

armaments and an end to their acquisition for offensive purposes, so that all possible resources may be devoted to the economic and social development of every country in Latin America.

The wording is not limited to the question of arms transfers. On the other hand the passage quoted, even if it had been intended to have binding force (which seems unclear), does not contain any unequivocal commitment to specific disarmament measures ("... and to create the conditions which will make possible ..."). As far as arms transfers are concerned a reference is made to the acquisition of "offensive" weapons only.

The declaration of Ayacucho does not seem to have led to any reduction in the acquisition of arms by the eight signatories.(26) But the relevance of the Declaration, as suggested by the wording itself, lies in the fact that it constitutes an authoritative policy statement which forms a certain basis for further negotiations. Thus, at the time of the UN special session devoted to disarmament, the Ministers for Foreign Affairs of the eight signatories to the Declaration met in Washington, on 22 June 1978, to reaffirm the principles of the Declaration. According to the joint communiqué they also "expressed their willingness to explore, together with the other Latin American countries, possibilities for reaching an agreement on limiting conventional weapons in Latin America".(27)

Hosted by Mexico, which is not a signatory to the Declaration, an informal meeting of Latin American and Caribbean countries was held in Tlatelolco, Mexico, on 21-24 August 1978. Twenty governments were represented, including seven of the signatories to the Ayacucho Declaration. The meeting considered, above all, the establishment of a "flexible consultative mechanism" to study and to make recommendations on the possible limitation of the transfer of certain types of conventional weapons to Latin America as well as among countries of the region, and of the use of certain types of conventional weapons considered excessively harmful or indiscriminate.(28) No follow-up meeting seems to have been held to this date, however.

A further reference to the Ayacucho Declaration was made in the Riobamba Charter of Conduct, signed on 11 September 1980 by the Presidents of Ecuador (the host country), Colombia and Venezuela and the Personal Representative of the President of Peru. Here these four signatories to the Ayacucho Declaration pledge, inter alia, "to promote a process of subregional and regional disarmament based on the postulates of the Declaration of Ayacucho ..."(29)

At the Tlatelolco meeting of 1978 mentioned above discussions also dealt with the question of prohibiting or restricting the use of certain conventional weapons, in view of the Preparatory Conference for the UN Weapons Conference which was to be held in August-September 1978 (see below 8.3.). And at that Conference a Mexican proposal for a convention on restricting the use of certain conventional weapons included a reference to regional and subregional arrangements concerning limitations on both the transfer and use of such weapons.(30) This reference, however, was not included in the Convention adopted in 1980.

Arrangements Affecting One State

Multilaterally initiated limitations on the transfer of weapons to one particular state usually occur in connection with peace settlements. One example is again provided by the Paris Treaty of Peace with Finland, which, as noted above, prohibits the possession and production of certain weapons and of excessive war material. Furthermore, the Treaty contains an explicit prohibition on the acquisition of war material of German origin or model and on the employment of German personnel (article 19).

Regulations for one particular state are frequently included in bilateral agreements between the supplier and the recipient. Such agreements may include a prohibition on re-transfer or on the use of the weapons delivered for aggressive purposes. A clause of the latter kind seems to appear in an agreement of 1952 between Israel and the United States, a fact which assumed a certain topicality in connection with the Israeli raid on the Bagdad nuclear reactor in June 1981.(31)

UN Sanctions

Whereas the UN Charter contains no reference to the question of arms transfers as such, it provides for a centralized sanctions system, conferring upon the Security Council the power to take action in the case of threats to the peace, breaches of the peace and acts of aggression. The sanctions can be either non-military (article 41) or imply the use of armed force (article 42). Although arms embargos are not explicitly mentioned in the list of examples of non-military sanctions in article 41, it is clear that such measures are possible.

Article 41 has been applied in two cases, namely (Southern) Rhodesia in 1966 and 1968 and South Africa in 1977. In the case of Rhodesia, the Security Council in resolution 232 (1966) decided on a partial prohibition on imports from and exports to Rhodesia. One point in the resolution specifically mentioned the sale or shipment to Southern Rhodesia of arms, ammunition, military aircraft, military vehicles and equipment and materials for the manufacture and maintenance of arms and ammunitions. In resolution 253 (1968) the sanctions were broadened so as to encompass the import and export of all commodites and products to Rhodesia as well as investments, flight connections, etc.(32) These sanctions have been lifted with the political solution involving the independence of the state of Zimbabwe. As to South Africa the Security Council imposed an arms embargo by resolution

418 (1977), the relevant part of which reads as follows:

> 2. Decides that all states shall cease forthwith any provision to South Africa of arms and related matériel of all types including the sale or transfer of weapons and ammunition, military vehicles and equipment, paramilitary police equipment, and spare parts for the aforementioned, and shall cease as well the provision of all types of equipment and suppliers and grants of licencing arrangements for the manufacture or maintenance of the aforementioned.

The fact that these sanctions are legally binding on member states has not eliminated arms transfers to South Africa altogether.(33) The political and moral weight of such binding sanctions is not to be discounted, however.

Apart from the binding decisions of the Security Council under Chapter VII of the Charter, both the Council and the General Assembly may adopt resolutions recommending abstention from or restraints on arms transfers to a particular state or region. Such resolutions have been adopted from time to time in relation to specific conflicts.(34)

The Law of Neutrality

As was noted above, the law of neutrality which had evolved during the nineteenth century was to a large extent codified at the Second Hague Peace Conference of 1907, which adopted a Convention (V) respecting the Rights and Duties of Neutral Powers and Persons in Case of War on Land and another Convention (XIII) concerning the Rights and Duties of Neutral Powers in Naval War. Certain basic principles concerning neutral property at sea had already been included in the Paris Declaration respecting Maritime Law of 1856. These principles were specified in a declaration concerning the Laws of Naval Warfare of 1909 which, however, was not ratified by any of the ten signatories.(35)

The main principle concerning arms transfers is expressed in article 6 of Hague Convention XIII: "The supply, in any manner, directly or indirectly, by a neutral Power to a belligerent Power, of war-ships, ammunition, or war material of any kind whatever, is forbidden". The same Convention also obliges a neutral Power to employ the means at its disposal to prevent the fitting out or arming of any vessel within its jurisdiction which it has reason to believe is intended to engage in hostile operations against a Power with which it is at peace (article 8). Belligerents are forbidden to use neutral ports and waters as a base of naval operations (article 5), to carry out repairs of war-ships in neutral ports which add to their fighting force (article 17) and to make use of neutral ports or territorial waters for increasing the supplies of war material or the armament of war-ships (article 18). Similar principles are inherent in Convention V on neutrality in land warfare,(36) although it is stricter on the presence of belligerent personnel on neutral territory.(37)

Despite the prohibition incumbent on the neutral government to export arms to belligerents, the Hague Conventions do not require that government to prevent the export or transit by private individuals and firms, for the use of either belligerent, of arms and ammunitions (with the above-mentioned exception concerning vessels intended to engage in hostile operations). Nor is the responsibility of a neutral Power engaged "by the fact of persons crossing the frontier separately to offer their services to one of the belligerents" (Convention V, article 6). If the neutral Power prohibits or restricts these activities, the measures must be impartially applied by it to both belligerents. The private individuals exporting weapons are in any case dependent on the vicissitudes of war in that the other belligerent may capture and condemn neutral goods defined as contraband of war (weapons, etc.) and under certain circumstances even the vessel carrying contraband.

The above principles would, of course, imply serious restrictions on the transfer of weapons in wartime. Moreover, it is arguable that the distinction between government and private exports is today devoid of relevance, as arms production and export always entail strong government involvement, and that the Hague Conventions should be interpreted as prohibiting such private transfers as well.(38) The crux of the matter, however, relates to the very status of the traditional law of neutrality. The practice of states during the two World Wars, including the concepts of non-belligerency short of neutrality, has made that status unclear. And a further blow to the traditional law of neutrality has been struck by the Kellogg-Briand Pact of 1928 and the UN Charter, which are based on the distinction between just (self-defence) and unjust (aggression) wars. In the period since 1945 third-party states have often delivered arms to a belligerent, despite the Hague Conventions. As is noted in a UN document of 1971:(39)

> The doctrinal position, as to the extent of the rights and duties of third States with respect to instances of armed conflict (which may of course vary greatly in intensity) is uncertain, but in general would appear to support the view that, subject to observance of the fundamental principles of international law and the relevant provisions of the Charter, third States have a considerable liberty in determining their policies in this regard.

Elsewhere(40) we have argued that the development from an obligation to strict neutrality to liberty of action and even to a certain obligation of partiality (UN imposed sanctions, etc.) can be illustrated in the following way, taking the Covenant of the League of Nations (1919), the Kellogg-Briand Pact (1928) and the UN Charter (1945) as points of departure:

	1919	1928	1945
duty of discrimination			///
liberty of action		///	///
duty of strict neutrality	///	///	

One possible interpretation would be that the column to the right (1945) only concerns armed conflicts which are not "wars" in the formal sense. In the latter type of conflict, the traditional law of neutrality would still be incumbent on the states not being parties to the conflict. It is to be noted that most armed conflicts occurring after 1945 have been viewed as armed conflicts short of war.(41) However, although the distinction between war in the formal sense and other armed conflicts does continue to play a certain role in international law and diplomacy it seems to us that this distinction no longer offers a clear-cut basis for defining obligations with respect to the application of the law of neutrality.

If this is so, supplier states (usually the major powers) are not committing a clear breach of international law in furnishing parties to armed conflicts with weapons and weapons technology, even if these conflicts are defined as war proper. The situation may be deplorable but it is certainly in accordance with "reality". There is also a matter of principle involved, however. The traditional law of neutrality stems from an age when war itself was regarded as a legitimate instrument of national policy. A return to that law in its strict sense even for the sake of restraining arms transfers would seem to imply a return to the philosophy underlying that law as well.

This does not mean that the principles embodied in the law of neutrality offer no guidance in the present-day situation. First of all, if a third state adopts a position of strict neutrality (which in most cases it is entitled to do), while receiving certain benefits from such a position, it is simultaneously bound by the prohibition on arms transfers referred to above. Secondly, the law of neutrality could be used as a source of guidance in efforts to work out multilateral guidelines for present-day arms transfers. One such guideline could contain at least restrictions on the transfer of arms to areas of conflict and crises.(42) Unilaterally, such restraints are followed, e.g., by the Federal Republic of Germany, Finland, Sweden and Switzerland (in the latter case it follows already from Switzerland's status of permanent neutrality).(43) Such restraints should also apply to internal conflicts. At present, international law in force is highly unclear on this point. Probably the traditional rule still applies at least as a starting point, allowing arms transfers to the "lawful" government but prohibiting transfers to "rebels".(44)

13.6. POSSESSION AND STOCKPILING

As the question of possession and stockpiling as far as weapons are concerned usually goes hand in hand with the question of production, there is not much to add to what has already been said.(45) The provisions on disarmament contained in the Covenant of the League of Nations, the naval treaties of 1922 and 1930, etc., by and large covered both aspects. Furthermore, limitations on one particular state, such as the provisions of the 1947 Peace Treaty with Finland, normally cover both the production and possession of certain weapons. Theoretically speaking it is, of course, imaginable that a state is prohibited from producing a weapon although it is allowed to acquire, possess and stockpile it.

With respect to <u>armed forces</u> the emphasis in disarmament efforts is on maintenance rather than "production". No global or regional convention exists which would put ceilings on the quantity and/or quality of armed forces. The Vienna talks on the mutual reduction of forces and armaments and associated measures in Central Europe deal with this aspect.(46)

An example of limitations on armed forces affecting one state only is again provided by the 1947 Peace Treaty with Finland. Here ground forces are limited to 34400 men, naval forces to 4000 men and air forces to 3000 men (these limitations are interpreted as concerning personnel on active military service only, not reserve forces).

13.7. STATIONING

As witnessed by the Non-Proliferation Treaty, a prohibition on the production and acquisition of a certain weapon does not necessarily imply a prohibition on stationing it on the territory of one state by another state allowed to produce and possess that weapon. The Treaty of Tlatelolco and the concept of nuclear-weapon-free zones in general on the other hand point to the possibility of encompassing the question of stationing in disarmament arrangements.

With respect to conventional weapons there are no agreements comparable to the Tlatelolco Treaty. The concept of <u>zones of peace</u>, which has been a popular frame of reference for certain arms control endeavours of a regional character (the Indian Ocean, South-East Asia, the Mediterranean), seems to entail the idea of repatriation of foreign forces as well as the dismantling of foreign military bases and installations.(47) And the Vienna talks, of course, are to a large extent concerned with the stationing of troops in Central Europe.

Certain agreements have already been concluded for uninhabited areas, however. Without going into details, mention can be made here of the 1959 Antarctic Treaty, which provides that Antarctica shall be used for peaceful purposes only and prohibits, inter alia, measures of a military nature such as the establishment of military bases and fortifications. The 1967 Outer Space Treaty may also be mentioned in this context. Here the complete prohibition on military measures applies to the moon and other celestial bodies only.

Under this heading, reference can also be made to the possibility of limitations on a state's right to station weapons and troops on a particular area of its own territory. History knows of a number of demilitarized zones. In a Nordic context mention should be made of the demilitarization of the Åland Islands (since 1856), a portion of the Swedish-Norwegian border (1905) and Svalbard (1920).(48) A provision regulating the establishment and status of demilitarized zones on a general level has been included in Additional Protocol I of 1977, relating to the protection of victims of international armed conflicts (article 60).

13.8. EMPLOYMENT

Employment in Peacetime
With regard to weapons, the question of the testing of weapons may be mentioned in this context (this, of course, also relates to the question of the study and development of weapons discussed earlier in this paper). No agreement of a global character prohibiting or limiting the testing of some particular conventional weapons exists. Agreements on demilitarized zones, however, often include a prohibition on the testing of weapons. The above-mentioned Antarctica and Outer Space treaties are examples. The prohibition of certain weapons contained in the 1947 Peace Treaty with Finland includes a prohibition on their testing as well (article 17).

In this connection reference should also be made to the 1977 Convention on the prohibition of military or any other hostile use of environmental modification techniques. The prohibition of the use of certain environmental modification techniques contained in this Convention (see below) is also applicable in peacetime.

Demilitarized zones often contain a prohibition on military manoeuvres. In a European context, certain regulations concerning such manoeuvres have also been included in the Final Act of the Conference on Security and Co-operation in Europe, in which reference is made to prior notification of military manoeuvres and major military movements and to the exchange of observers at military manoeuvres. The Final Act is not a treaty although it may contain legally binding commitments.(49) In the Document on confidence-building measures forming part of the Final Act, these measures are in one way or another stated to be voluntary in character but the formulation, especially on the notification of "major" military manoeuvres (more than 25,000 men), suggests a certain commitment not entirely devoid of legal relevance.(50)

Use in War

A basic principle relating to the use of weapons in war is, of course, the prohibition of the threat or use of force contained in the UN Charter (2:4). Under this provision the use of all weapons is prohibited, if not for self-defence or as a sanction initiated by the Security Council. In the following discussion, however, attention is paid to the law regulating warfare (ius in bello) and particularly to rules prohibiting or restricting the use of specific weapons.

The laws and customs of war, of course, contain a number of restrictions on the use of weapons and troops (methods and means of combat). It is not possible here to give a full description of these restrictions and their relevance today. It should be noted, however, that a considerable part of the law regulating warfare has been reaffirmed and developed by the Geneva Diplomatic Conference on the Reaffirmation and Development of International Humanitarian Law Applicable in Armed Conflicts (1974-77), which in June 1977 adopted two Protocols additional to the 1949 Geneva Conventions for the protection of war victims.(51)

What interests us here are those parts of the laws and customs of war - or, to take the more modern expression, international humanitarian law applicable in armed conflicts - which are specifically addressed to the use of certain conventional weapons. Some basic principles are to be found, e.g., in Additional Protocol I of 1977. According to article 35, it is prohibited to "employ weapons, projectiles and material and methods of warfare of a nature to cause superfluous injury or unnecessary suffering" and to "employ methods or means of warfare which are intended, or may be expected, to cause widespread, long-term and severe damage to the natural environment". Moreover, the traditional obligation to distinguish between the civilian population and combatants and between civilian objects and military objectives is stated in article 48.

During the preparatory phases of the Conference (1971-72) it had been proposed, particularly by Sweden and some other non-aligned countries, that the sweeping formulations on methods and means of warfare should be supplemented by specific prohibitions or restrictions on the use of certain conventional weapons deemed to cause unnecessary suffering or to be indiscriminate in nature. One of the Committees of the 1974-77 Diplomatic Conference dealt with this question. It was not possible at this Conference, however, to obtain other rules relating to weapons than those mentioned above, including the provision on the study, development, acquisition or adoption of new weapons mentioned earlier.(52)

Instead the weapons question was referred to the UN, which in 1979-80 convened a Conference on Prohibitions or Restrictions of Use of Certain Conventional Weapons Which May Be Deemed to Be Excessively Injurious or to Have Indiscriminate Effects. In the earlier discussions reference had been made above all to napalm and other incendiary weapons, small-calibre weapon systems, mines and booby-traps, non-detectable fragments, and certain new and highly lethal blast and fragmentation weapons such as cluster bombs and fuel-air explosives ("concussion bombs"). The Convention with annexed Protocols adopted by the Conference in October 1980 prohibits only the use of non-detectable fragments and certain booby-traps and restricts the use of mines and booby-traps and of incendiary weapons. The Convention was opened for signature on 10 April 1981, when it was signed by 35 states.

Taking the results of this Conference into account, the use of the following weapons is prohibited or restricted under international law (apart from the general principles prohibiting weapons causing superfluous injury or having indiscriminate effects referred to above):

The St. Petersburg Declaration of 1868 prohibits the employment "of any projectile of a weight below 400 grammes, which is either explosive or charged with fulminating or inflammable substance". The continued validity of this Declaration is open to doubt, however, especially with regard to aircraft and anti-aircraft ammunition.(53)

The Hague Declaration (IV, 3) of 1899, adopted by the First Hague Peace Conference, prohibits the so-called dum-dum bullet, defined as "bullets which expand or flatten easily in the human body, such as bullets with a hard envelope which does not entirely cover the core or is pierced with incisions". The Declaration is certainly valid today, but its relevance is diminished by the introduction of new small-calibre ammunition (5,56 mm. and below) which, although having similar effects, is not regarded as falling under the prohibition on dum-dum bullets. Although no provision on such ammunition was included in the 1980 Convention, the Conference adopted a resolution which, inter alia, "appeals to all Governments to exercise the utmost care in the development of small-calibre weapon systems, so as to avoid an unnecessary escalation of the injurious effects of such systems".

According to the 1977 Convention on the Prohibition of Military or Any Other Hostile Use of Environmental Modification Techniques, the parties undertake not to engage in such use of environmental modification techniques "having widespread, long-lasting or severe effects as the means of destruction, damage or injury to any other State Party" (article 1). It may be asked, of course, whether environmental modification techniques are "conventional" methods or means of warfare. The provision of Additional Protocol I of 1977 referred to above, however, prohibits the employment of <u>any</u> method or means of warfare which is intended, or may be expected, to cause "widespread, long-term and severe damage to the natural environment".

The Protocol on Non-detectable Fragments (Protocol I) annexed to the 1980 UN Convention prohibits the use of "any weapon the primary effect of which is to injure by fragments which in the human body escape detection by X-rays".

Protocol II annexed to the 1980 Convention prohibits the use of "any booby-trap in the form of an apparently harmless portable object which is specifically designed and constructed to contain explosive material and to detonate when it is disturbed or approached" (e.g., toys, pencils) as well as the use of booby-traps attached to certain specified objects such as internationally recognized protective signs, sick, wounded or dead persons, children's toys and food or drink. The Protocol furthermore contains a number of restrictions on the use of mines and booby-traps and provisions on the recording and publication of the location of minefields, mines and booby-traps.

Protocol III contains restrictions on the use of incendiary weapons such as napalm. Attacks against civilians and civilian objects by incendiary weapons are prohibited (such attacks, however, would be prohibited even without the Protocol), as well as attacks against "any military objective located within a concentration of civilians ... by air-delivered incendiary weapons". The Protocol also restricts the right to make such military objectives the object of attack by other than air-delivered incendiaries and to make forests or other kinds of plant cover the object of attack by incendiaries.

The results of the 1980 UN Conference are, of course, rather modest.(54) But the Conference and the discussions related to it are an interesting sign of a growing concern for conventional armaments and the use of cruel and highly lethal conventional weaponry in recent armed conflicts. It is to be hoped that efforts to prohibit or restrict the use of such weapons have not come to an end. The 1980 Convention provides for a review and follow-up machinery, including the right of any High Contracting Party to demand, after the period of ten years following the entry into force of the Convention, the convening of a conference to review the scope and operation of the Convention and to consider possible proposals for amendments or for additional protocols (article 8).

Finally, some words may be said about the employment of armed forces in war. Apart from the prohibition of the very use of force referred to above (including the prohibition of military interventions) the law of war contains a number of provisions restricting the employment of troops. Suffice it to note here that some rules exist even on the structure and composition of armed forces. Thus, Additional Protocol I of 1977 requires that armed forces are subject to an internal disciplinary system which, <u>inter alia</u>, shall enforce compliance with the rules of international law applicable in armed conflicts. Only members of organized armed forces, groups and units which are under a command responsible to a party to the conflict for the conduct of its subordinates may claim combatant status (article 43). Mercenaries are excluded from combatant status under the Protocol (article 47).(55)

13.9. RECENT TRENDS AND PERSPECTIVES

As has been indicated above, conventional disarmament has recently been discussed in a UN context particularly with respect to the questions of transfer and use. These questions have been broached at a regional level, too, that is to say among some Latin American countries, while arms transfers have also been the subject of bilateral talks between the Soviet Union and the United States in 1977-78. In a European context the possibility of mutual reductions of forces and armaments has been discussed in Vienna since 1973 and so-called confidence-building measures at the ECSC-Conference and its follow-up meetings. The only concrete results are the CBM-measures mentioned in the Helsinki Final Act of 1975 and the conventions on environmental modification techniques (1977), international humanitarian law applicable in armed conflicts (1977) and the prohibition or restriction of the use of certain conventional weapons (1980).

In a UN context in particular, conventional disarmament has not been much discussed in the sixties and seventies. The efforts to take up the question of arms transfers in the General Assembly in 1965, 1968 and 1976-77 did not succeed mainly due to opposition from Third World countries. The Final Document of the 1978 special session may perhaps be seen as a modest revival of interest in conventional disarmament, referring as it does to the limitation and reduction of armed forces and conventional weapons in general, to regional and bilateral arrangements, to the limitation of arms transfers, to the prohibition or restriction of use of certain weapons, to the reduction of military budgets, to confidence-building measures and to the carrying out of studies on certain topics (paras. 81-98).

That these clauses in the Final Document have not generated a consensus on how to tackle the question of conventional disarmament in the UN may be seen from the recent discussions on a Danish proposal to conduct a UN study on conventional disarmament.

At the second substantive session of the UN Disarmament Commission (May-June 1980), Spain submitted a working paper on limitation and control of the production and transfer of conventional weapons(56) and Denmark a paper on approaches to conventional disarmament within the framework of the UN.(57) On the Danish proposal, the General Assembly in resolution 35/156 A has approved "in principle" the carrying out of a study on all aspects of the conventional arms race and on disarmament relating to conventional weapons and armed forces, to be undertaken by the Secretary-General with the assistance of qualified experts.

The Disarmament Commission was entrusted with the task of working out, at its 1981 session, "the general approach to the study, its structure and scope". The Secretary-General was requested to submit a progress report on the study to the second special session devoted to disarmament (1982) and a final report to the 38th session (1983) of the General Assembly. In the First Committee the socialist states and Brazil and India voted against the resolution while 24 non-aligned states abstained.(58) At the recent session of the Disarmament Commission (18 May - 5 June 1981), Denmark submitted a new paper on the general approach, structure and scope of the study on conventional disarmament.(59) The Commission did not succeed in working out a general framework for the study at this session, however.(60) Some other studies of relevance for conventional disarmament have been completed (e.g., the study on all the aspects of regional disarmament completed in 1980) or are under way (e.g., the study on confidence-building measures).(61)

As to the prospects for conventional disarmament in the near future, it is obvious that no dramatic results will be obtained. To a certain extent it even seems advisable to play down efforts to increase deliberations on conventional disarmament in a UN context, in so far as possibilities for concrete results are slight, while such discussions may divert attention and resources from the primary subject of weapons of mass destruction. This is not to say, of course, that conventional disarmament should be discarded by the UN, nor that the proposal for a UN study on conventional disarmament is a bad one. As to the appropriate forum, it would seem that the Disarmament Commission is the body which should put a certain emphasis on conventional disarmament in its work, while the Committee on Disarmament for the moment should concentrate on present and unsolved topics on its agenda.

Speaking on substance it is clear that no global prohibition of the development, production or possession of some particular conventional weapon-type will be achieved in the near future. Nor is it likely (or indeed desirable) that there will be serious efforts to update the traditional law of war or law of neutrality (excluding the question of prohibitions on the use of specific weapons).

It might be possible, however, to establish certain guidelines for international arms transfers. Even if the major suppliers could reach some concrete results (which seems unlikely at the moment) such agreements would suffer from a certain great power bias (cf. the clearly imperialistic conventions of 1890 and 1919). We are inclined to believe that there is a slight possibility that such guidelines could be worked out in a UN framework, with all major suppliers and recipients participating in the process. The possibility of linking the question of transfer to the question of use, and of obtaining some kind of formal or informal "package deals", should also be borne in mind. Possibly some tangible results on the question of negative security guarantees to non-nuclear states could increase the willingness of Third World countries to agree to restraints on their right to acquire conventional weapons.(62)

In view of the modest results of the 1979-1980 UN Conference, a more far-reaching instrument could also be worked out, say, among Latin American countries. The question of the prohibition or restriction of the use of conventional weapons seems to be a topic where the strict adherence to the principle of universal consensus should be seriously questioned. Why not follow the example of 1925 (chemical and bacteriological weapons) and make a convention prohibiting altogether the use of, e.g., incendiary weapons, cluster and concussion bombs and "tumbling" bullets (only applying, of course, in the relations between those states that adhere to such an agreement)? In any case history teaches us that it is easier to achieve prohibitions on use than prohibitions on production or on transfer.

As has been frequently stressed during the last few years, the regional approach is particularly suited for conventional disarmament. Here again one can envisage some linkage between the question of transfer (acquisition) and the question of use, as demonstrated by the discussions among Latin American countries. Be that as it may, regionally and, why not, unilaterally initiated recipient controls should be strongly encouraged. As far as Europe is concerned, the development of confidence-building measures is within reach. And if détente survives and even makes progress, the reductions contemplated in the Vienna talks might suddenly become reality.

Generally speaking, the present situation requires imaginative and unorthodox policies from states genuinely interested in disarmament. The importance of unilateral gestures and measures should be stressed, taking into account their bearing upon public opinion. For instance, if a Nordic Nuclear-Weapon-Free Zone were about to materialize, the same countries could follow the example set by some Latin American states and initiate discussions on Nordic conventional disarmament, involving, e.g., restraints or prohibitions on arms exports(63) coupled with commitments not to produce or acquire certain weapon-types and to reduce military budgets. Apart from the Ayacucho Declaration and its follow-up, the limitations on armaments in the 1947 Peace Treaty with Finland as well as the existing and proposed demilitarized zones in Northern Europe could here serve as sources of inspiration.

NOTES AND REFERENCES

1. See, e.g., International Committee of the Red Cross, <u>Draft Additonal Protocols to the Geneva Conventions of August 12</u>, 1949, Commentary, Geneva 1973, p. 42.

2. Particularly in Sweden such bodies have been used for some time, see, e.g. <u>Conventional Weapons, Their Deployment and Effects</u>

from a Humanitarian Aspect, A Swedish Working Group Study, Stockholm 1973, pp. 7-10.

3. See, e.g., John Eugene Harley, Selected Documents and Material for the Study of International Law and Relations with Introductory Chapters, Los Angeles 1923, pp. 42-83; John W. Wheeler-Bennett, Disarmament and Security since Locarno, 1925-1931, London 1932, pp. 103-215.

4. See, e.g. Wheeler-Bennett, pp. 178-179.

5. See, e.g. Romain Yakemtchouk, Les transferts internationaux d'armes de guerre, Paris 1980, pp. 82-89, 162-167.

6. The imperialistic nature of the convention is illustrated by the following statement in a report by a British consul-general to London in 1888: "Unless some steps are taken to check this immense import of arms into East Africa, the development and pacification of this great continent will have to be carried out in the face of an enormous population, the majority of whom will probably be armed with first-class breech-loading rifles", cited from Yakemtchouk, p. 48.

7. Yakemtchouk, pp. 56-64.

8. Naoum Sloutzky, La Société des Nations et le contrôle du commerce international des armes de guerre (1919-1938), Genève 1969, pp. 13-16; Yakemtchouk, pp. 89-95.

9. Sloutzky, pp. 31-74; Yakemtchouk, pp. 97-113.

10. Sloutzky, pp. 43-51; R.R. Baxter and Thomas Buergenthal, Legal Aspects of the Geneva Protocol of 1925, American Journal of International Law 1970, pp. 860-861.

11. See, e.g. Yakemtchouk, pp. 116-118.

12. Sloutzky, pp. 83-114; Yakemtchouk, pp. 120-123.

13. For different typologies of controls see, e.g., Raimo Väyrynen, Tavanomaisten asetoimitusten kansainväliset rajoittamismahdollisuudet, Aseidenriisunnan avainkysymyksiä, Ulkoasiainministeriö, Aseidenriisunnan neuvottelukunta, Helsinki 1980, pp. 374-380; Trevor Taylor, The Evaluation of Arms Transfer Control Proposals, The Gun Merchants, Politics and Policies of the Major Arms Suppliers, ed. by Cindy Cannizzo, New York 1980, pp. 169-176.

14. Cindy Cannizzo, Prospects for the Control of Conventional Arms Transfers, The Gun Merchants (see note 13), p. 187.

15. See The United Nations Disarmament Yearbook, Vol. 1:1976, pp.

227-232; Ibid. Vol. 2:1977, pp. 263-271.

16. UN doc. S-10/2. Final Document of the Tenth Special Session of the General Assembly.

17. On the arms sales policy of the Carter administration see, e.g., Lucy Wilson Benson, Turning the Supertanker: Arms Transfer Restraint, International Security, Vol. 3, No. 4, 1979, pp. 3-13; Nicole Ball and Milton Leitenberg, The Foreign Arms Sales Policy of the Carter Administration, Alternatives Vol. 4, No. 4, 1979, pp. 534-542; James E. Strunck, Curbing the International Trade in Conventional Arms, Work Paper, Madrid Conference on the Law of the World (September 16-20, 1979), pp. 1-5; Jo L. Husbands, The Arms Connection: Jimmy Carter and the Politics of Military Exports, The Gun Merchants (see note 13), pp. 25-40.

18. On these talks see, e.g., Jo L. Husbands, The Conventional Arms Transfers Talks: Negotiation as Proselytization, paper prepared for delivery to the Annual Convention of the American Political Science Association, Washington 1-3 September 1979; SIPRI Yearbook 1980, pp. 121-124; Väyrynen, pp. 396-400.

19. Strunck, p. 6.

20. On informal agreements see, e.g., Ian Brownlie, Principles of Public International Law, Third Edition, Oxford 1979, p. 633.

21. The policies of the US, the USSR, Great Britain, Federal Republic of Germany and France are analyzed in The Gun Merchants (see note 13). See also Yakemtchouk, pp. 231-250.

22. See, e.g., Brownlie, pp. 634-636.

23. Lars Backström, Transnationella företag, med speciella hänsyn till deras roll vid överföringen av militärteknologi till tredje världen, avhandling pro gradu, Abo Akademi 1980, p. 56. On the role of transnational corporations in arms transfers see Raimo Väyrynen, Transnational Corporations and Arms Transfers, Instant Research on Peace and Violence, Vol. 7, No. 3-4, 1977, pp. 145-166; Helena Tuomi and Raimo Väyrynen, Transnational Corporations, Armaments and Development, Aldershot (GB), 1982.

24. Taylor, pp. 170-171; Yakemtchouk, pp. 173-190.

25. The text of the Declaration has been published as an official document of the UN General Assembly, A/10044 (28 January 1975). On the Declaration of Ayacucho see also Manoutchehr Fartash, Curbing the International Trade in Conventional Arms, Work Paper, Madrid Conference on the Law of the World (September 16-20, 1979), p. 31; Jacques Huntzinger, Regional Recipient Restraints, in Controlling Future Arms Trade, ed. by Anne

Hessing Cahn and Joseph J. Kruzel, New York 1980, pp. 186-187; Väyrynen, Aseidenriisunnan avainkysysmyksiä (note 13), pp. 413-417.

26. Väyrynen, pp. 415-416. See also Augusto Varas, Carlos Portales and Felipe Aguero, The National and International Dynamics of South American Armamentism, Current Research on Peace and Violence, Vol. 3, No. 1, 1980, pp. 1-23.

27. UN doc. A/S-10/AC. 1/34 (23 June 1978).

28. See Document presented by the Chairman of the Meeting of Latin America and Caribbean countries on conventional weapons, ARCON/I/1, August 24, 1978.

29. UN doc. A/C.3/35/4 (annex).

30. A/CONF.95/PREP.CONF./L. 8 (11 September 1978).

31. See Newsweek, June 22, 1981, p. 8. Concerning similar restrictions in internal American law see Karen M. Hayworth, The Arms Export Control Act: Proposals to Improve Observance of American Arms Law, New York University Journal of International Law and Politics 1979, pp. 135-158.

32. See, e.g., Ralph Zacklin, The United Nations and Rhodesia, New York 1974, pp. 45-58.

33. See Tuomi and Väyrynen, p. 159.

34. Such resolutions are mentioned by Yakemtchouk, pp. 418-425.

35. For the text of this Declaration (as well as other instruments on the law of war) see Dietrich Schindler and Jiri Toman, The Laws of Armed Conflicts, second revised and completed edition, Geneva 1981.

36. According to article 7 of Convention V a neutral Power is not called upon to prevent the export or transport, on behalf of one or other of the belligerents, of arms, munitions of war, or, in general, of anything which can be of use to an army or a fleet. This article, however, allows private export only. See also Ingo F. Wallas, Die völkerrechtliche Zulässigkeit der Ausfuhr kriegswichtiger Güter aus neutralen Staaten, Hamburg 1970, pp. 28-33.

37. According to Convention XIII belligerent war-ships may pass through the territorial waters and temporarily visit the ports of neutral Powers, whereas belligerent troops received on neutral territory shall be interned (unless they are sick and wounded in authorized transit).

38. The effects of the growth of the public sector on the law of neutrality are commented upon, e.g., by Georg Schwarzenberger, International Law as Applied by International Courts and Tribunals, Vol. II, London 1968, pp. 654-656.

39. UN doc. A/CN. 4/245, pp. 212-213.

40. Allan Rosas, Sodanaikainen puolueettomuus ja puolueettomuuspolitiikka, Turku 1978, p. 84.

41. On the concepts of war and armed conflict see, e.g., Allan Rosas, The Legal Status of Prisoners of War, Helsinki 1976, pp. 224-239.

42. The question of restraints on arms resupply during conflict is discussed from a politological angle by Robert E. Harkavy, Arms Resupply during Conflict and the Carter Administrations Arms Control Policies, paper delivered at the annual meeting of the International Studies Association, Los Angeles, March 19-22, 1980.

43. In the case of Finland the policy is not expressly stated in internal law.

44. See, e.g., Allan Rosas, Kansainvälinen oikeus ja rauhan edistäminen, Rauhaan tutkien 3/1977, p. 11.

45. For a short discussion on the question of possession see Bert Röling, International Law and the Right to Possess Arms, The Unesco Courier, September 1980, pp. 20-24.

46. Finnish contributions to the extensive literature on the Vienna talks are: Jorma K. Miettinen, Euroopan asevoimien supistaminen, Aseidenriisuntavihkot 6, Turku 1978; Pertti Joenniemi, Asevoimien supistamisneuvottelut (AVS): nykytilanne ja tulevaisuus, Aseidenriisunnan avainkysymyksiä (see note 13).

47. The concept of zones of peace is commented upon in the recent UN study on all the aspects of regional disarmament, A/35/416 (8 October 1980), pp. 20-24, 55.

48. See, e.g., J.O. Söderhjelm, Démilitarisation et neutralisation des Iles d'Aland en 1856 et 1921, Helsingfors 1928; Stig Jägerskiöld and Torgil Wulff, Handbok i folkrätt under neutralitet och krig, Uddevalla 1971, pp. 32-35, 182-183; Bengt Broms, The Demilitarization of Svalbard (Spitsbergen), Essays in Honour of Erik Castrén, Helsinki 1979, pp. 6-18.

49. See Rosas, Sodanaikainen puolueettomuus ..., p. 95.

50. See the UN report mentioned in note 47 above, p. 14.

51. See, e.g., Allan Rosas, Sodan oikeussäännöt, Aseidenriisuntavihkot 5, Turku 1978.

52. On the background of the question of the use of certain conventional weapons at the 1974-77 Conference see, e.g., Pertti Joenniemi and Allan Rosas, International Law and the Use of Conventional Weapons, Tampere Peace Research Institute, Research Reports, No. 9, 1975.

53. Joenniemi and Rosas, pp. 29-30.

54. The results are discussed, e.g., by Yves Sandoz, A New Step Forward in International Law - Prohibitions and Restrictions on the Use of Certain Conventional Weapons, International Review of the Red Cross 1981, pp. 3-18; SIPRI Yearbook 1981, pp. 445-455.

55. For details see Rosas, The Legal Status ..., pp. 293-419.

56. UN doc. A/CN.10/12 (6 May 1980).

57. UN doc. A/CN. 10/13 (9 May 1980).

58. A/C.1/35/PV.47 (29 November 1980).

59. A/CN.10/25 (15 May 1981). At this session also India (A/CN.10/27) and the German Democratic Republic (A/CN.10/31) submitted working papers concerning a study on conventional weapons.

60. See the report of the Disarmament Commission, A/36/42, pp. 13-14. According to the report "the intensive discussions and consultations revealed a significant divergence of views on the matters before the Commission on this item". Two working papers by the Chairman on this issue appear as annexes II and III of the report.

61. SIPRI Yearbook 1981, pp. 480-482, contains a list of studies completed, in progress or requested by the General Assembly.

62. On the question of negative security guarantees see, e.g., Allan Rosas, Ydinaseiden käytön kieltäminen ja negatiiviset turvallisuustakuut, Aseidenriisunnan avainkysymyksiä (see note 13), pp. 240-331.

63. There is in Finland (as well as in Sweden) a vivid discussion on arms sales. The Social Democratic Party of Finland has at its congress in June 1981 demanded that all exports of weapons of war should cease.

V

DISCUSSION

Chapter Fourteen

IS THE CONVERSION IDEA TO BE CONVERTED? SOME SPECIAL COMMENTS FROM A NON-CONVERT

Jan Øberg

14.1. INTRODUCTION

Entering the 1980s, world military expenditures amount to US dollars 1.5 billion per day. In fixed prices this is more than 4 times the level of 1945, and it represents an annual sum 25 times larger than OECD official development aid. The rate of military expenditure increase is also growing rapidly -especially in the United States under the Reagan administration.

This is the price of what is most often termed "national security". Such allocations worldwide should, if theories came true and means lead to ends, make all of us more secure - decreasing the human fear of war in the nuclear age. If arms lead to security and peace - and if the balance of power were the predominant means to achieve this - there should be more peace on earth. However, the 20th century is probably the most war-ridden of all in the history of Mankind - at least 100 million people have lost their lives in war since 1900, and since 1945 alone the world has witnessed some 130 wars with combined casualties of roughly 30 million.

Much of this is common knowledge to some - but it is far from being common knowledge to everyone. Human, natural and economic resources are consumed for military purposes (not security, that is) at a staggering rate, in a world than desperately needs those resources for constructive socio-economic development. Presently, studies indicate that structural underdevelopment for the majority -largely in consequence of overdevelopment for a minority, i.e. maldevelopment of the entire system - causes the death of some 50,000 human beings every day, 18 million per year.

It can therefore safely be concluded that never before have so many people been so potentially _insecure_ and facing the threat of so much violence - structural as well as direct - as is the case today. "National security", its theoretical grounding as well as the defence and security policies pursued by the world's some 160 independent states, leads to a profoundly insecure world and insecure human beings. National security is something very different from global security and human security - that has still to be achieved.

Maldevelopment as well as insecurity of the world system are basically structural phenomena. True human and social development as well as security - what would add up to some kind of peace - cannot be expected to emerge through stockpiling of either development aid/capital/"economic growth" or more weapons. They demand, they are in themselves and they lead to: structural transformation.

In other words, the two essential problems facing mankind are those of development and security both of which are here understood primarily as clusters of human needs which can only be realized through macro-systems that are fundamentally different from those existing now. If the two are combined in a "negative", destructive fashion, social systems as well as the world order as such are heading for militarism - here understood as the combined result of maldevelopment and insecurity. This is, of course, basically the existing trend.

If, on the other hand, development and security are combined in a "positive", constructive manner, systems and the world at large have a chance of realizing peace - here understood as the combined result of structural transformation and a set of defence strategies including alternative defensive arms and non-military efforts. (Figure 14.1 below).

Figure 14.1   A Generalized Model

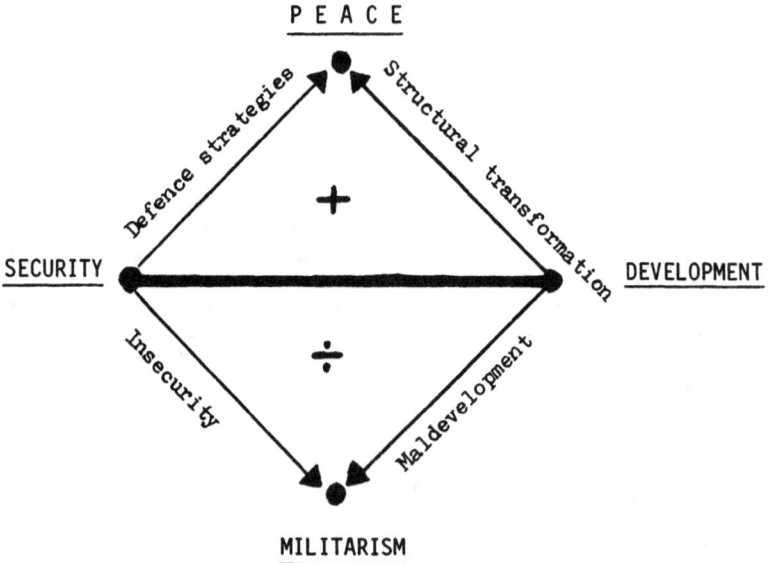

This model serves as an intellectual point of reference for the following discussion - it is not discussed any further here. Peace is a process as well as a structure - not a state of affairs reached once and for all. The same applies to theories of peace - and, in principle, to peace research. Peace is more than the absence of direct and structural violence - a cherished idea within peace research itself. The tricky question immediately following suit is this: What is it the presence of? To answer in a very preliminary way: Peace is the process of developing security and secure development (as understood above), taking the individual as the point of departure and the world order as frame of reference.

Likewise, militarism is more than the absence of security and the presence of "overarmament" or absence of civilian control functions. It has to do with basic human and global insecurity and civilian maldevelopment - deep structural similarities between civilian and military spheres of social formations where the explanatory value of the concept of isomorphism suggests itself.

In a recent analysis of major peace research contributions, it has been shown that there is extremely little focus on peace concepts and peaceful societies.(1) One wonders who should occupy themselves with these subjects if not peace researchers?

14.2. CONVERSION

Arms control, or what is often called "disarmament" negotiations, have proved a failure. The reasons are many and shall not be discussed here. The arms control approach is directed towards already existing weapons (or symptoms of problems) in a politico-military and strategic framework. Or it is aimed at managing future armaments, in a primarily quantitative way, to the satisfaction of involved parties' "national security".

Conversion measures are mainly directed towards the production of weapons, i.e. precluding future production and deployment and changing facilities like e.g. bases into socially useful purposes. The focus is on the individual firm level, the defence industrial sector or national conversion of parts of the military establishment. As is well known, this takes place mostly within an economic framework.

The idea of transformation and alternative defence adds a sociological/cultural dimension to the above politico-military and economic dimensions of the armament problem. It is directed towards the deep social, structural features of society and the world system which contribute to the "need" - real or imagined - for armament. It maintains that societies must change radically to get rid of the armament syndrome and that there must be some "realistic Utopia" to switch to intellectually before decision-makers can be convinced not only about the counterproductivity of present trends but also about the viability of some constructive alternatives.

Where arms control and conversion measures represent the thinking that: "We know there is something very wrong - so let's reduce this 'wrong' somewhat" -the transformation idea suggests the following: "Yes, this may be better than increasing the madness - but why not try to visualize what would be '<u>good</u>' and work out strategies for it?"

A very comprehensive reader in the problems of conversion of military industries and bases rightly points out that conversion is a 'reformist' concept and that studies of it have a clearly liberal, econometric, and technical orientation leaving social and political issues - 'the most formidable problem' -largely untouched. At the same time, efforts to penetrate the interrelationships between armament, disarmament, real security and development (the latter understood not merely as pure economic growth) are still few and far between.

This is well reflected in e.g. the so-called Nordic proposal to the United Nations, which is barely more than a list of 18 issues without much inner coherence.(2)

14.3. THE WHY, WHO, HOW, WHAT ETC. OF CONVERSION

<u>Why conversion?</u> The purpose of conversion studies and conversion activities is to make possible the transfer of resources from the armament sector to the development sector. The crucial catchwords are "possible", "disarmament", "resources", "transfer" and "development".

As to the first, it seems that conversion studies are undertaken in order to show to decision-makers that disarmament is economically - and sometimes technologically - feasible, that a well-planned conversion effort is possible in most cases, either at local (firm), regional, national or even global levels. If this is so, the following question arises: Are conversion studies carried out under the assumptions that a) the armament and security problems are basically economic by nature, i.e. it is economic factors that impede progress in disarmament talks, b) that decision-makers, if properly convinced by analyses about the feasibility of conversion, will start conversion planning and actions in the real world, i.e. that good economic arguments will persuade military, industrial, bureaucratic and research elites, and c) that the nations and the world <u>can</u> disarm - more or less - without further and supplementary social and political changes, i.e. that the 'most formidable problem' is not really the most formidable.

In other words, it remains to be clarified what conversion studies actually make possible, what they are supposed to lead to and for whom they are undertaken.

Secondly, there is the term "disarmament". <u>Hovstadius</u> and <u>Wängborg</u>

in a recent article in the Journal of Peace Research correctly state that economic criteria have long since been a recurrent theme in disarmament discussions and are often linked to the possibility of an increase in development assistance. Disarmament is taken to mean simply a reduction in military expenditures without further military, technical or political elaboration. The word 'reduction' does not mean, necessarily, that present levels of military expenditures are decreased, but rather implies a slow-down <u>in the rate of growth</u>.(3)

It goes without saying that this is a very poor conceptualization of the disarmament problem - formed more in order to fit econometric modelling and input-output analyses than real-world complexities, and suiting military-industrial and bureaucratic elite interests within ministries of defence and the United Nations general thinking and vocabulary more than alternative security and peace pursued by people's interests and popular movements, because it allows further increases in what is also called the "armament madness". Disarmament as a term ought not be equated with increased military expenditures in real terms!

Take the <u>Leontief/Duchin</u> global input/output model: Hovstadius and Wängborg emphasize that it is based on assumptions that "turn out to produce a considerable increase in economic assistance <u>while allowing for continued growth of world military expenditure in real terms</u>".(4) It is not self-evident that such modelling - obviously mistreating the idea of disarmament -should pass a Journal of Peace Research uncritically.

This is not only problematic from a theoretical-methodological-value point of view. It is politically highly dubious. It shows clearly that you can have both! All kinds of Brandt Commission report-like proposals of arms trade tax or military expenditure tax converted into development aid funds will be made possible through <u>increasing</u> the armament levels, and in principle development aid would be made dependent upon a certain rate of growth of military expenditures in the future. Or - as in the case of arms trade taxes - it would boost clandestine operations and 'moonlighting' to avoid the 'income tax form'.

Thirdly, there is the issue of resources. Little needs to be said here. The basic link between "disarmament" and "development" is that of money - a rather Western, mechanical conceptualization again, deeply rooted in economism. Fourthly, transfer is something that takes place through a state-centric, governmental control and via state institutions, existing international organisations or new international fund arrangements. In this way, substantial political problems are reduced to organisational issues and made a management problem - within the established philosophy of development aid bureaucracies. More money flowing through this system is supposed - tacitly, at least - to lead to more development.

The last but very central issue, therefore, is that of development. Again we find a narrowing-down to economistic reasoning -

development implying pure economic growth - or more capital and resources pumped through the existing (maldeveloped) world order - distributed as development aid without any consideration for basic human needs, development and change actors (at local level in the periphery as well as within centre countries), social restructuring, self-reliance or non-material dimensions. This is the worn-out Western quantitative development idea - brushed up in times of overall world crisis where Centre decision-makers desperately need new slogans and the Occident as such needs a new 'mission' (like e.g. the Marshall aid-like suggestions of the Brandt Commission report).

These problems of conceptualization pertaining to the 'why' of conversion and conversion studies are substantial. Take econometric methods and UN-like vocabulary - and the concepts, implications, orientation, value-commitments are changed. It is doubtful (to the present author) whether the gains and benefits from participating in governmental and United Nations analyses of the above character justify the neglect of some of the most cherished peace research conceptualizations and value commitments. Likewise, it is a research priority question whether as peace researchers we should try to "beat" liberal, quantitative economic expertise on its own terms - or spend some time defining other and perhaps more relevant fields for the pursuit of real security and true human and social development.

What is converted? Most often it is arms manufacturing units and military bases. In principle, however, the United Nations study also encompasses research development, service facilities, land use, raw materials and and overall markets. By and large, what should be converted is all those production factors which arms production demands, which can be measured by available statistics and which are considered relevant for the narrow idea of economic growth.

But - the focus is still on the arms themselves, the symptoms of much deeper problems. The important difference - and advantage -compared with the arms control approach is that the armament problem is addressed in an early stage -i.e. before the actual weapons system is deployed and integrated in overall military doctrines.

However, it is pertinent to ask: What is not considered important to convert? It does not seem important to study the conversion of general security thinking among present decision-makers. Conversion of decision variables and processes vis-à-vis democratically elected parliaments and the general populace - in order to open up for people's participation in security affairs - is not considered either.

There is no attention to the problems of converting from war to peace of the present world order, no studies of how to convert those social and structural features that make for ever increasing armament.

Literally, the term 'conversion' means to turn around, to transform, to change faith or values. It is a deep change. This is what conversion studies should be about - as has also been pointed out by Mary Kaldor:

> "It seems to me that our first task is to try to think of disarmament not simply as an act of will, but as something which reverses the process of armament; in other words, a process which transforms the set of social relationships which currently serve to promote armaments...If we are to do that, we must try to understand the relationship of armaments and society, and then think about how we can change this relationship."(5)

In other words, we would hold it highly unlikely that conversion will lead to real disarmament unless it is part of a <u>larger strategy</u> which encompasses (a) a converted attitude among decision-makers as to what <u>security</u> is about, (b) a fundamental democratic control of the <u>social driving forces behind armament</u> and (c) a concern for true human and social development brought about through <u>the structural transformation and dissolution of those conflict formations that lead to war.</u>

Surely this is to ask for a great deal - so much that it would not be attractive to the armament elites, state bureaucracies - or to the United Nations "disarmament/development" philosophy.

As long as weapons are considered as the predominant means of achieving security in the state-centric world system - and as long as this is also a commonly held view among large proportions of citizens at large, it has to be asked: What should motivate these decision-makers to go for conversion of existing arms if they do not have an alternative idea of defence and security? What they can be expected to convert are production facilities no longer competitive, bases no longer needed and weapons no longer sophisticated enough - i.e. conversion will be seen as an improved management technique, another word for "phasing out" smoothly. <u>Therefore</u>, it will not bring about disarmament in the true meaning, it will not threaten the built-in militarism. And for this reason one may expect it to be a slogan in the disarmament negotiations during the 1990s. <u>Then</u> will appear the articles titled "The Crisis of Conversion"! - and another decade will have been lost for true disarmament and a new security.

<u>Who is to convert and be converted</u>? The simplest answer would be that Centres carry out the conversion planning pertaining to the Peripheries. It can hardly have skipped anybody's attention that it is first and foremost labour in weapons factories that will be converted - through measures of national planning. The problems faced by the Lucas workers when attempting to carry out conversion by and through themselves and challenge the privileges of management are well known by now. Their initiative was based on an alternative social vision and re-distribution of power - locally and in the longterm also globally.

Conversion studies seem to be carried out on the basis of the assumption that changes will take place through the "push" effect of enough hard data presented to central decision-makers about the present maldevelopment. They are not based on the idea of "pulling" decision-makers by means of popular, alternative visions of peace and constructively defended societies. Researchers, in other words, support elites in managing the "trickling down" of freed resources as aid - more than they support an international mass movement for radical changes and a struggle for survival and peace "4 minutes to midnight", to quote the Bulletin of the Atomic Scientists.

It is only indicative that conversion studies have done more to refine economistic methods and analyses - including the processing of sometimes thousands of items of data - than to create theoretical and conceptual/intellectual innovations, bureaucratic rejuvenation or to further hopes for real changes among those millions of people whose security is at stake.

This is, of course, the outcome of a deliberately selected research policy, a value-commitment putting emphasis on senior, top-level management of changes towards disarmament rather than on popular pressures and general opinion formation.

Or, to put it differently, conversion implies support for an outdated "national security" paradigm instead of supporting a "human and global security" paradigm that must gain momentum if the catastrophes are to be avoided.

This may serve as a sceptical answer to the question of how to convert? However, state officials are of course already developing strategies of how not to convert, should the conversion idea suddenly gain momentum.

One such example can be taken from the Danish Ministry of Foreign Affairs. In its 1980 report, the Danish Disarmament Committee has reprinted the ministry's response to the UN Secretary General's request of February 28, 1979 to supply information to the United Nations study on the relationship between disarmament and development. The report concerns military expenditure figures, arms exports and imports, military aid, military energy consumption measured in kroner, and land used by the defence.(6) However, the very last issue deals with arms production, and here the Ministry states:

> "Military equipment and arms are normally procured abroad. However, many Danish industrial firms participate in sub-contracting in the production of matériel for the armed forces. In these cases, the production normally covers such commodities (spare parts, components, parts built together etc.) that can be used for civilian as well as military purposes. Therefore, no Danish firm and no part of Danish industry can be

labelled 'defence industry'."(7)

In the only existing, publicly available survey of Danish defence industries -based exclusively on available sources and questionnaires to individual companies -it is shown that Denmark has more than 70 companies producing weapon systems or parts thereof. The most well known is of course the co-production of the F 16 fighter aircraft. In total, Danish defence industry is estimated to amount to at least 500 million Danish kroner and there are plans to expand it considerably.(8)

The Ministry of Defence employs a definition of "defence production" that labels military products civilian if they also have a civilian function (i.e. somewhere else) and a definition of "defence industry" that implies that if a company is not 100 % engaged in weapons production - which companies seldom are - it is not to be labelled "defence industry". In a response to a critique of this procedure raised by the present author, the Minister of Foreign Affairs, Mr. Kjeld Olesen emphasizes that the information delivered by the ministry is "drawn by a broad brush" but that it is covering what is needed by the United Nations study, that the few and small companies (more than 70 and some quite big! - JØ) cannot be conceptualized as "defence industry" - which is more of a conjuration than an explanation, to say the least - that the Ministry has limited resources, and that Norway has also responded that it does not have any "defence industry"(9).

Thus, new loopholes are being developed to define away defence industries. Should the idea of conversion gain political momentum in the real world, the Ministers of Foreign Affairs of Denmark and Norway will be able to cable the United Nations, when asked to deliver plans for actual defence industry conversion: "Sorry, we would love to take part in this important step towards disarmament, but fortunately - as we have already informed you - we do not have any defence industry at all!"

14.4. FINAL REMARKS

I will not repeat the arguments discussed in this chapter.(10) It is first and foremost an effort to provoke a discussion about the merits and demerits of the idea of conversion, and secondly a sceptical questioning of the relationship of peace researchers to such endeavours and their role in furthering peace one way or another.

It has been general in the sense of not doing justice to each and every single conversion study of which some are clearly much more critical and aware of the problem raised here than others.

However, I deem it important - to say the least - that peace researchers constantly and self-critically evaluate what they do, how they do it, whom they serve and what values they further. The seminar of which this book is an outcome was, I think, less than succesful in terms of taking seriously those questions that were first raised 18 years ago by the Journal of Peace Research - in a slight reformulation: What is the peace relevance of what we do? What is the peace research relevance? Who is the target group? And what can others gain by listening to peace researchers?

There is a risk, all the time, of being absorbed by the empirical analysis of the existing, maldeveloped and insecure world (and we already know quite a lot about it and what is 'wrong' with it) and neglecting the needs of the future world (where we all lack the ability to visualize 'attractive futures' of a more just, peaceful world or to advise strategies to achieve it). When asked by government bodies or the United Nations to work on a specific task there is also the risk of compromising theories, concepts and values otherwise adhered to. In the field of armament/disarmament studies, the preoccupation with present armament data - without attention to the above, more fundamental questions - will inevitably lead to a kind of "self-militarization" and rather dull 'reporting', instead of examining the entire research process covering empirical analysis, criticism and constructive alternative thinking.

There is a need to be sensitive all the time to the use and misuse of such central concepts as development, security, peace, human rights etc. - no matter what kind of influence peace research is seeking.

Conversion may be another gimmick - for the reasons I have spelled out above. I think it will be if it is not placed within a larger framework of transformation from the war system to the peace system, from destructive, offensive defence to constructive, defensive defence, from maldevelopment to development through transformation. Conversion will hardly change the world if we do not know what we are converting to. Conversion is not an independent goal of its own, it is a sub-strategy that can be employed when we know, and when the rulers of the world know, why and how the world can do with less armoury.

Up till then, there is a risk that conversion studies will be a "dream that came false" but contributed to converting some of the most dearly held value-commitments of, for instance, peace researchers.

NOTES AND REFERENCES

1. See Håkan Wiberg, JPR 1964-1980 - What Have We Learnt about Peace, in Journal of Peace Research Vol. 18, No. 2. 1981, p. 113 and 142 and 143.

2. Experiences in Disarmament. On Conversion of Military Industry and Closing of Military Bases, ed. by Peter

Wallensteen, <u>Department of Peace and Conflict Research, Uppsala University, Report nr. 19</u> - see especially Ulrich Albrecht's excellent introduction based on no less than 3000 titles dealing with conversion.

3. See Bo Hovstadius and Manne Wängborg, The United Nations Study of Disarmament and Development: An Overview, in <u>Journal of Peace Research</u> Vol. 18, N0. 2.,1981, p. 209-219 (my italics).

4. <u>Ibid</u>. p. 213.

5. <u>The Sandefjord Report on Disarmament and Development</u>; the Norwegian Ministry of Foreign Affairs, The Norwegian Committee for Arms Control and Disarmament. Mary Kaldor's address p. 45-52.

6. Udenrigsministeriet, <u>Beretning til Udenrigsministeren</u>, Copenhagen 1981, p. 161-163.

7. <u>Ibid</u>. p. 163.

8. Jan Øberg, <u>Myter om vor sikkerhed. En kritik af dansk forsvarspolitik i et udviklingsperspektiv</u>, Mellemfolkeligt Samvirke, Copenhagen 1981, chapter 9 and by the same author Fører ministeriet FN bag lyset? in Politiken, September 7, 1981 (Copenhagen).

9. Kjeld Olesen, FN er ikke ført bag lyset, in <u>Politiken</u>, September 10, 1981 (Copenhagen).

10. More arguments can be found in the author's Disarmament, Conversion and Transformation. Some Elements of a Strategy Towards Constructive Defence and Peaceful Development, in <u>Bulletin of Peace Proposals</u> Vol. 10, No. 3., 1979.

ANNEXES 1-6: THE LARGEST ARMS PRODUCERS IN WESTERN EUROPE

Source: Archiv Arbeitsgruppe Rüstung und Unterentwicklung. Insitut für Friedensforschung und Sicherheitspolitik, Universität Hamburg 8/79.
Figures on arms production are estimates; + means the real figure is probably higher, - means the real figure is probably lower.

Annex 1. The Largest Arms Production Companies in France, Turnover in 1977 above 100 Million DM

Name	Capital owner***	Total turnover in mio FF	Total turnover in mio DM	Total employment	Per cent of arms production in turnover	Turnover in arms production in mio DM
1. Thomson-Brandt	(Paribas)	19,683	9,066	10,000	33	- 3,000
2. SNI Aerospatiale	French State	8,551	3,940	33,855	75	2,955
3. Avions M. Dassault Brequet	M. Dassault, French State	5,697	2,624	14,819	91	2,390
4. Direction Technique de Construction Navale	French State	ca. 5,000	2,300	ca. 35,000	- 100	- 2,300
5. Groupement Industrielle Armament de Terra	French State	3,238	1,490	16,843	- 100	- 1,490
6. SNECMA	French State	3,559	1,547	18,426	65	1,000
7. Matra		2,103	969	5,141	+ 49	+ 475
8. SNPE	French State	982	452	6,208	+ 100	- 452
9. Turbomeca	J. Szydlowski	932	429	4,480	+ 75	+ 322
10. GBS (CSEE, SAT, Sagem)	(Paribas)	2,950	1,359	19,000	+ 22	+ 300
11. Creusot Loire	Schneider, F. Empain, B. Marine Wendel, F.	10,564	4,896	50,516	- 6	- 294
12. Panhard	PSA, Peugeot	568	262	597	- 100	- 262
13. Renault	French State	49,230	22,675	243,456	1	225
14. CIT-Alcatel	CGE	5,124	2,373	23,369	- 9	- 210
15. SEP	French State	850*	392	2,500	- 50	- 196
16. Manurhin	(Matra)**	817	376	4,142	- 50	- 188
17. TRT	Philips, NL	905	417	4,547	- 40	- 167
18. Crouzet	J. Jullien (Banque Vernes)	713	328	5,994	33	108

* 1978
** August 1978
*** The data refer to the situation before the Presidential Elections in 1981. The purpose of the Mitterand government is to nationalize the largest French arms producers.

Annex 2. The Largest Arms Production Companies in the United Kingdom, Turnover in 1977 above 100 Million DM

Name	Capital owner	Total turnover in mio £	Total turnover in mio DM	Total employment	Per cent of arms production in turnover	Turnover in arms production in mio DM
1. British Aerospace	UK State	860	3,322	68,800	80	- 2,500
2. Rolls Royce Ltd. (State-owned)	UK State	704	2,721	61,786	70	1,900
3. General Electric Co.	spread	2,343	9,055	192,000	15	- 1,360
4. Vickers Ltd.	spread	409	1,582	27,095	- 40	- 615
5. Royal Ordnance Factories	UK State	+150	+580	23,800	- 100	+ 580
6. British Leyland	UK State	2,602	10,057	194,610	+ 5	+ 500
7. Plessey	spread	611	2,359	63,890	22	+ 500
8. Westland	spread	139	537	12,894	87	467
9. Racal	family	182	703	5,824	60	422
10. Vosper	D. Brown	98	379	8,500	100	379
11. EMI	spread	851	3,289	51,300	11	362
12. Ferranti	UK State	125	483	16,786	55	266
13. Decca	spread	181	700	12,064	- 38	- 266
14. Swan Hunter	Hunter	156	603	25,000	+ 33	+ 200
15. Dowty	spread	136	526	13,886	37	195
16. Hunting	spread	88	340	6,946	53	180
17. Lucas Industries	spread	886	3,424	68,778	+ 5	171
18. Cable Wireless	UK State	156	603	9,488	+ 26	157
19. Imperial Metal Industries	ICI, GB	467	1,805	26,664	- 9	- 155
20 Sperry Rand	Sperry Rand, USA	88*	340	6,946*	41	140
21. Smiths Industries	spread	224	866	20,400	+ 15	130
22. Yarrow	D. Brown	32**	124	5,400**	100	124
23 Philips (UK) (MEL, Pye Mullard, Graseby)	Philips NL	630	2,435	45,698	+ 5	+ 120
24. Dunlop Holdings	spread	+ 361	5,260	102,000	2	104
25. British Manufacture and Research Co.		+ 25	+ 100	1,000	100	+ 100

*   1975
** 1976

Annex 3. The Largest Arms Production Companies in Italy. Turnover in 1977 above 100 Million DM

Name	Capital owner	Total turnover in mio L	in mio DM	Total employment	Per cent of arms production in turnover	Turnover in arms production in mio DM
1. Fincantier	Italian State	ca. 700	1,700	22,000	+ 33	+ 560
2. Oerlikon/Contraves Italia	Oerlikon-Bührle, Switzerland	200	500		85	- 425
3. Agusta-Gruppe	Italian State Agusta family	255	620	8,250	- 80	- 500
4. Snia Viscosa	Italian State	1,144	2,779	41,000	- 17	- 470
5. Fiat-Gruppe	Agnelli family spread	11,449	27,821	341,700	+ 1	+ 365
6. Oto-Melara	Italian State	118	287	2,340	100	287
7. Aeritalia	Italian State	134	326	9,300	68	221
8. Selenia	Italian State	100	243	5,600	- 75	- 182
9. Aermacchi	family	52	126	2,000	- 100	- 126
10. Alfa Romeo	Italian State	1,056	2,566	44,700	+ 4	+ 100

Annex 4. Largest Arms Producers in Smaller NATO Member States in Western Europe

Name	Capital owner	Total turnover in mio national currency	in mio DM	Total employment	Per cent of arms production in turnover	Turnover in arms production in mio DM
VFW-Fokker*	Krupp, State of Bremen		1,705	17,500	- 60	- 1,020
Philips, NL	spread	31,164 hfl	28,979	384,000	- 3	- 1,000
Fabrique Nationale, Belgium	Belgian State	10,469 bf	665	9,800	80	530
Rijn/Schelde Verolme, NL	spread	2,603 hfl	2,421	29,300	- 20	- 500
SABCA, Belgium	Fokker, NL Dassault, F	2,515 bf	160	1,840	- 95	- 152
PRB, Belgium	Belgian State	16,658 bf	1,057	8,890	+ 15	+ 150
DAF-van Doorne	Durc State, Int. Harvester, Cdn	1,204 hfl	1,120	8,650	+ 10	+ 110
Kongsberg Våpenfabrikk, N	Norwegian	656 nKr	251	3,380	+ 40	+ 100

* Dissolved in 1980.

Annex 5. Largest Arms Producers in the Neutral Countries in Western Europe

Name	Capital owner	Total turnover		Total employment	Per cent of arms production in turnover	Turnover in arms production in mio DM
		in mio national currency	in mio DM			
Oerlikon-Bührle, Switzerland	D. Bührle, Switzerland	2,722 sFr	2,477	21,350	60	1,617
Bofors, Sweden	spread	2,325 sKr	1,055	14,000	55	580
Saab-Scania, Sweden	spread	10,796 sKr	4,899	42,000	+ 10	+ 500
FFV, Sweden	Swedish State	1,000 sKr	454	8,500	+ 66	+ 300
Steyr-Daimler Puch, Austria	spread, Austrian State	10,541 ÖS	1,463	17,000	- 20	- 300
Eidgenössische Militärwerkstätten, Switzerland	Swiss State	n.a.		5,200	- 100	ca. 250
Volvo, Sweden	spread	16,168 sKr	7,337	60,000	3	- 200
LM Ericsson, Sweden	spread	7,832 sKr	3,554	66,000	+ 4	+ 150
Philips, Svenska	Philips NL	1,420 sKr	645	1,500	+ 7	+ 100

Annex 6. The Largest Arms Producing Companies in the FRG, Turnover above 100 Million DM in 1977

Name	Capital owner	Total employ-ment	Total turnover in mio DM	Rank Among the largest companies	Per cent of arms produc-tion in turnover	Turnover in arms produc-tion in mio DM
1. Siemens AG, München	State	319,000	25,198	2	8	2,000
2. AEG-Telefunken, Frankfurt	State	158,400	14,286	9	- 10	- 1,400
3. Messerschmitt-Bölkow-Blohm GmbH, München	Siemens, Thyssen, State of Bayern, state of Hamburg	20,700	1,801	87	60	1,080
4. Vereinigte Flugtechnische Werke-Fokker GmbH, Bremen*	Krupp, State of Bremen	17,500	1,705	91	- 60	- 1,020
5. Krauss-Maffei AG, München	Flick	4,600	1,005	155	70	705
6. Motoren- und Turbinen- Union GmbH, München/ Friedrichshafen	Daimler-Benz, MAN	11,000	1,063	150	52	550
7. Rheinmetall GmbH, Düsseldorf	Röchling	7,500	779	204	67	520
8. Maschinen-fabrik Augs-burg-Nürn-berg AG	Haniel	62,000	6,329	30	+ 8	+ 500
9. F. Werner Indu-strieanlagen	DIAG (State)	1,702	441		- 100	- 441
10. Karl Diehl GmbH & Co KG, Nürnberg	Diehl	13,200	1,220	126	35	430

Name	Capital owner	Total employment	Total turnover in mio DM	Rank Among the largest companies	Per cent of arms production in turnover	Turnover in arms production in mio DM
11. Dornier GmbH Friedrichshafen	Dornier	6,700	723	212	- 51	370
12. Thyssen-Industrie AG, Düsseldorf	Thyssen	42,500	4,291	38	+ 8	+ 330
13. Howaldtswerke-Deutsche Werft AG, Hamburg/Kiel	Salzgitter, state, state Schleswig-Holstein	13,800	1,215	129	20	+ 250
14. Blohm & Voss AG, Hamburg	Thyssen Siemens	6,500	633	238	40	250
15. Dynamit Nobel AG, Troisdorf/Köln	Flick	14,900	1,956	75	+ 12	+ 235
16. Industriewerke Karlsruhe AG	Quandt	8,100	623	244	33	235
17. Klöckner-Humboldt-Deutz AG, Köln	Henle	31,200	4,015	43	5	200
18. Standard Elektrik Lorenz AG, Stuttgart	ITT, USA	32,800	2,735	59	6	165
19. Wegmann & Co., Kassel	Wegmann	2,400	250-300		- 55	- 165
20. Zahnradfabrik Friedrichshafen	city Friedrichshafen	19,800	1,903	78	+ 7.5	150
21. Bodensee Gerätetechnik GmbH und Bodenseewerk Perkin Elmer & Co., Überlingen	Perkin Elmer, USA	1,600	160		95	150

Name	Capital owner	Total employment	Total turnover in mio DM	Rank Among the largest companies	Per cent of arms production in turnover	Turnover in arms production in mio DM
22. MaK Maschinenbau GmbH, Kiel	Krupp	3,600	500		30	150
23. Luther Werke** Braunschweig Mainz		2,600	170		85	145
24. Industrieanlagenbetriebsgesellschaft, München	state	1,600	160		80	130
25. Deutsche Philips, Hamburg	Philips, Netherlands	31,000	4,026	12	+ 3	120
26. Rohde & Schwarz, München	Rohde, Schwarz	3,733	360		33	120
27. Fr. Lürssen-Werft, Bremen	Lürssen	1,100	+ 100		100	+ 100
28. Daimler-Benz AG, Stuttgart	spread	169,200	24,723	3	0.4	100
29. Elektronik-System Gesellschaft, FEG-Gesellschaft für Logistik, München	AEG, Rohde & Schwarz, Siemens, SEL, Eltro, Honeywell, USA, Litef, Teldix	900	100		100	100
30. Heckler & Koch GmbH, Oberndorf	Heckler & Koch	2,000				

* partnership with Fokker was terminated in 1980
** bankruptcy of the Braunschweig branch in June 1979

Annex 7. Rank Order of the 25 Largest Third World Arms Importers, 1977-80

Figures are SIPRI trend indicator values, as expressed in constant US $ million, at constant 1975 prices.

	Importing country	Total value	Percentage of Third World total	Largest exporter per importer
1.	Iran	3446	8,7	USA
2.	Saudi Arabia	3133	8,0	USA
3.	Jordan	2558	6,5	USA
4.	Syria	2311	5,9	USSR
5.	Iraq	2172	5,5	USSR
6.	Libya	2107	5,5	USSR
7.	Korea South	1987	5,0	USA
8.	India	1931	4,9	USSR
9.	Israel	1778	4,5	USA
10.	Vietnam	1220	3,1	USSR
11.	Morocco	1121	2,9	France
12.	Ethiopia	1086	2,7	USSR
13.	Peru	995	2,5	USSR
14.	Yemen South	964	2,4	USSR
15.	South Africa	950	2,4	Italy
16.	Algeria	882	2,2	USSR
17.	Taiwan	737	1,9	USA
18.	Kuwait	664	1,7	USSR
19.	Argentina	642	1,6	FR Germany
20.	Brazil	641	1,6	United Kingdom
21.	Egypt	594	1,5	USA
22.	Indonesia	522	1,3	USA
23.	Pakistan	512	1,3	France
24.	Chile	482	1,2	France
25.	Thailand	412	1,0	USA
	Others	5657	14,3	
	Total	39 504	100,0	

Source: SIPRI Yearbook 1981.

Annex 8. Rank Order of 12 Largest Third World Major-Weapon Exporters, 1977-80

Figures are SIPRI trend indicator values, as expresses in US $ million, at constant 1975 prices.

	Exporting country	Total value	Percentage of total Third World	Largest importer per exporter
1.	Brazil	421	33,1	Chile
2.	Israel	367	28,9	South Africa
3.	South Africa	116	9,1	Zimbabwe
4.	Libya	98	7,7	Syria
5.	Egypt	72	5,7	Somalia
6.	Korea South	38	3,0	Indonesia
7.	Argentina	35	2,8	Chile
8.	Saudi Arabia	31	2,4	Somalia
9.	Singapore	17	1,3	Thailand
10.	Indonesia	16	1,3	Benin
11.	Cuba	15	1,2	Peru
12.	India	12	0,9	South Africa*
	Others	33	2,6	
	Total	1271	100,0	

Source: SIPRI Yearbook 1981.

Nicole Ball is a visiting research associate at the Swedish Institute of International Affairs, Lilla Nygatan 23, S-111 28 Stockholm, Sweden.

Olav Bjerkholt is the director of research of the Central Bureau of Statistics of Norway, Dronningensgt. 16, P.B. 8131 Dep., N-Oslo 1, Norway.

Clóvis Brigagao is professor of the Centro de Estudos Afro-Asiaticos (CEAA), Universidade Canadido Mendes Rua Joana Angélica 63, CEP 22420 Rio de Janeiro RJ, Brazil.

Michael Brzoska is a research fellow of the Arbeitsgruppe Rüstung und Unterentwicklung of the Institut für Friedensforschung und Sicherheitspolitik (IFSH), University of Hamburg, Von-Melle-Park 15, 2000 Hamburg 13, FRG.

Ådne Cappelen is a researcher of the Central Bureau of Statistics of Norway, Dronningensgt. 16, P.B. 8131 Dep., N-Oslo 1, Norway.

Klaus Engelhardt is professor of international relations of the Institut für International Politik und Wirtschaft (IPW), Breite Strasse 11, 102 Berlin, DDR.

Nils Petter Gleditsch is a research fellow of the International Peace Research Institute (PRIO), Rådhusgt. 4, Oslo 1, Norway.

Bo Hovstadius is a research fellow of the Institute for Economic Studies, National Defence Research Institute, S-104 50 Stockholm, Sweden.

Ron Huisken is with the Department of Defence, Canberra, A.C.T. Australia 2600.

Michael T. Klare is a research fellow of the Institute for Policy Studies, 1901 Que Street, Northwest, Washington, D.C. 20009, USA.

Signe Landgren-Bäckström is a research fellow of the Stockholm International Peace Research Institute (SIPRI), Bergshamra, S-171 73 Solna, Sweden.

Milton Leitenberg is a visiting research associate at the Swedish Institute of International Affairs, Lilla Nygatan 23, S-111 28 Stockholm, Sweden.

Knut Moum is a research assistant of the Institute of Economics, University of Oslo, Norway.

Allan Rosas is the professor of state law and international law of the Department of Law, Åbo Akademi, SF-20500 Turku 50, Finland.

Inga Thorsson is the Under-Secretary of State of the Ministry of Foreign Affairs, Stockholm, Sweden, and was the Chairman of the United Nations Group of Governmental Experts on the Relationship between Disarmament and Development.

Helena Tuomi is a research fellow of Tampere Peace Research Institute (TAPRI), P.O. Box 447, SF-33101 Tampere 10, Finland.

Manne Wängborg is a research fellow of the Institute for Economic Studies, National Defence Research Institute, S-104 50 Stockholm, Sweden.

Raimo Väyrynen is the professor of international relations of the Department of Political Science, University of Helsinki, Aleksanterink. 7, SF-00100 HELSINKI 10, Finland.

Jan Øberg is the acting director of the Department of Peace and Conflict Research, Magle stora Kyrkogata 12 B, S-223 50 Lund, Sweden.

For Product Safety Concerns and Information please contact our EU
representative GPSR@taylorandfrancis.com
Taylor & Francis Verlag GmbH, Kaufingerstraße 24, 80331 München, Germany

www.ingramcontent.com/pod-product-compliance
Lightning Source LLC
Chambersburg PA
CBHW071343290426
44108CB00014B/1425